Frontier Military Series
XXVI

Fort Laramie

MILITARY BASTION
OF THE
HIGH PLAINS

by
Douglas C. McChristian
Foreword by Paul L. Hedren

THE ARTHUR H. CLARK COMPANY

An imprint of the University of Oklahoma Press

Norman, Oklahoma

2008

ALSO BY DOUGLAS C. MCCHRISTIAN

An Army of Marksmen: The Development of United States Army Marksmanship during the Nineteenth Century (Fort Collins, Colo., 1981)

Garrison Tangles in the Friendless Tenth: The Journal of Lieutenant John Bigelow, Jr., Fort Davis, Texas (New York, 1985)

The U.S. Army in the West, 1870–1880: Uniforms, Arms, and Equipment (Norman, 1995)

Fort Bowie, Arizona: Combat Post of the Southwest, 1858–1894 (Norman, 2005)

Uniforms, Arms, and Equipment: The U.S. Army on the Western Frontier, 1880–1892, 2 vols. (Norman, 2007)

Library of Congress Cataloging-in-Publication Data

McChristian, Douglas C.

   Fort Laramie : military bastion of the High Plains / by Douglas C. McChristian ; foreword by Paul L. Hedren.

       p. cm. — (Frontier military series ; 26)

   Includes bibliographical references and index.

   ISBN 978-0-87062-360-8 (hardcover (cloth) : alk. paper) — ISBN 978-0-87062-361-5 (hardcover (ltd. ed. leather) : alk. paper)

   1. Fort Laramie (Wyo. : Fort)—History. 2. Frontier and pioneer life—Wyoming. 3. Frontier and pioneer life—High Plains (U.S.) 4. Frontier and pioneer life—West (U.S.) 5. Indians of North America—Wars—1866–1895. 6. West (U.S.)—History—1848–1860. 7. West (U.S.)—History—1860–1890. 8. West (U.S.)—History, Military—19th century. 9. High Plains (U.S.)—History—19th century. 10. High Plains (U.S.)—History, Military—19th century. I. Title.

   F769.F6M39 2009

   978.7'18—dc22

2008028287

Fort Laramie: Military Bastion of the High Plains
is Volume 26 in the Frontier Military Series.

The paper in this book meets the guidelines for permanence and durability of the Committee on Production Guidelines for Book Longevity of the Council on Library Resources, Inc. ∞

Copyright © 2009 by the University of Oklahoma Press, Norman, Publishing Division of the University. Manufactured in the U.S.A.

1 2 3 4 5 6 7 8 9 10

To Sergeant Tom Lindmier

"we were 'bunkies,' him and me"

TABLE OF CONTENTS

Maps and Illustrations

FOREWORD

Doug McChristian has it right when he calls Fort Laramie, Wyoming, a quintessential frontier army post. For nearly forty-one years the garrison of this storied military outpost figured in the lives and consequences of Lakotas and Cheyennes, overlanders, expressmen, Argonauts, surveyors, campaigners, and cattlemen. Its soldiers fought and died in a score of Indian fights large and small, some occurring within the immediacy of the post or at nearby trading houses, others at more distant ranches in the Laramie or Platte valleys or at the fort's pinery near Laramie Peak. And from its environs, Indian commissioners and military generals attempted repeatedly to resolve the irreconcilable differences between Plains Indian tribes and the westward-sweeping tide of American settlement.

The geography of the Great Plains helped drive Fort Laramie to prominence. Envision the great heartland of the United States, marked by well-known rivers in the east and the Rocky Mountains in the west, and Canada and Mexico to the distant north and south. And then imagine the very center of this grassed-over empire, and there lay Fort Laramie. Founded as a fur-trading establishment called Fort William in 1834, Fort Laramie through the years functioned as a figurative and literal commercial and social hub, with spokes connecting from Independence, Fort Leavenworth, Nebraska City, and Omaha, and radiating to western destinations in Utah, Oregon, California, Colorado, New Mexico, and Montana, and regional termini like Cheyenne, Fort Fetterman, Red Cloud and Spotted Tail agencies, Camp Robinson, and Custer City and Deadwood.

Fort Laramie, nay Fort John then, was a weather-beaten adobe trading post when the U.S. Army arrived in 1849 and quickly raised an
American flag atop a towering new staff. Picturesquely situated along
the banks of the quiet but reliable Laramie River several miles above
its confluence with the seemingly ever turbulent North Platte, the post
was never palisaded or bricked, the complex as constructed and recon-
structed in the ensuing decades being a strange mish-mash of slabbed
and clapboarded frame buildings, stuccoed adobes, gingerbreaded cottages, and eventually sturdy grout or concrete edifices. The sum always
more nearly resembled a small, unplanned community than an imagined orderly army post, but that too was a factor of local geography,
dictated by the bounds of the river and its lowlands and higher bench,
all consumed over time as Fort Laramie expanded through the years.
Despite its palpable architectural dishevelment, always did that American flag flutter above, usually stiffly in a determined Wyoming wind,
denoting Fort Laramie as an outpost of the nation.

Remarkable episodes in Fort Laramie's long history scored its
legacy. Indian tribes still point to the Fort Laramie or Horse Creek
Treaty of 1851, and especially the Fort Laramie Treaty of 1868, as mile-
stones in their own tumultuous intercourse with whites in the mid-
nineteenth century. The Grattan Massacre in August 1854, exceptionally vividly told here, was a milestone of another sort, as were events
through the dark, strife-torn years along the overland trail during the
Civil War, as well as warfare locally and across the northern plains
associated with the Black Hills gold rush in the mid-1870s. Interspersed among its inordinate peaks of importance, the army repeatedly
envisioned abandoning Fort Laramie whenever the post's usefulness
ebbed, or when engines of enterprise like the transcontinental railroad
literally bypassed from afar, and yet always another event or calamity
renewed its need, even into the 1880s.

Geography served Fort Laramie well, even at its end. The very conditions applied by the army in the late-nineteenth century to define its
strategy for maintaining active posts—nearness to railroads, especially,
and to Indian reservations particularly—never factored into Fort
Laramie's history. But this persistent isolation deterred Laramie's
complete destruction when troops finally marched away in March

1890. And while the immediate locale was never zealously coveted by homesteaders, it did beckon a newer generation in the 1920s and '30s seeking out and revering the true places of American Western history. By then, considerable portions of Fort Laramie had been dismantled or weathered away, and yet enough, a substantial sum, in fact, survived. The showcase included such noteworthy buildings as "Bedlam," the first structure constructed when the army arrived in 1849 and ever after heralded for its ribald days as a bachelor officers' quarters; the imposing two-company, two-story barracks built of grout in 1874; and the sturdy iron bridge dating from 1875 spanning the North Platte River, these among several dozen buildings and prominent ruins marking the site then as now.

Fort Laramie's exceptionally diverse role in American history, coupled with the fact that so much of its physical complex survived abandonment, led to the site's addition to the National Park System in 1938. Even today, the fort's conspicuous isolation allows visitors to immerse themselves in the days of Lieutenant John Grattan, Colonel Thomas Moonlight, Chiefs Red Cloud and Spotted Tail, and Brigadier General George Crook amidst meticulously restored officers' quarters, storehouses, bakeries, and guardhouses, all evoking the days of infantry and cavalry on the frontier, in a setting largely unmarred by the contrivances of modern America.

Surprisingly, despite Fort Laramie's considerable attributes, it has lacked a comprehensive military history, drawn particularly from the rich array of surviving primary documents in the National Archives and at Fort Laramie National Historic Site itself. But this is precisely what Doug McChristian delivers with flourish in Fort Laramie: Military Bastion of the High Plains. Certainly, historians have circled and chipped away on this military legacy through the years, reporting in focused fashion on such matters as the Grattan affair, army medicine at Fort Laramie, the fact and fancy of the "Portugee" Philips ride, grizzled old Leodegar Schnyder, and the fort's prominent role in the Great Sioux War, and readers have long benefited from a number of very well written general histories as well.

In his book, McChristian meticulously recounts virtually every critical stage in the forty-one-year military span of this lustrous site, for the first time providing essential contexts for episodes like the Grattan fight, treaty making, the protection of emigrant and commercial trails, and the bureaucratic wrangling and social whirl of army life at this bustling Wyoming outpost. He delivers keen insight as well, into resolute Fort Laramie characters like Hugh B. Fleming, a junior officer himself but uniquely Grattan's commander in 1854; Richard B. Garnett, better remembered today as the most prominent fatality in Pickett's Charge in the Battle of Gettysburg; William O. Collins, intractable commander of the Eleventh Ohio Volunteer Cavalry who lost his son, Caspar, in a fight with Indians in 1865; and First Lieutenant Levi H. Robinson, killed by Sioux in 1874 and subsequently the namesake of one of Fort Laramie's eventual successors, Fort Robinson, Nebraska. And McChristian adds measurably to our understandings of better-known Fort Laramie officers like Wesley Merritt, John Gibbon, and Henry C. Merriam, and venerable Ordnance Sergeant and postmaster Leodegar Schnyder, who served continuously at the post from 1849 to October 1886.

As this writer can attest, Fort Laramie is a place that gets in one's blood. It captivated soldiers and civilians like Schnyder, James Regan, John Hunton, and Cynthia Capron in its original day, and has captivated historians like McChristian in the present. McChristian's career tours with the National Park Service took him to Fort Laramie twice, once as the park's supervisory historian in the mid-1970s (when most of its rangers were historians), and again as a staff historian for the park service's Intermountain Region. These occasions provided ample opportunity for him to explore the park's archival collections and library, both incredibly rich—if largely unknown beyond park service circles.

In the writing, McChristian was challenged by his editors at the Arthur H. Clark Company and University of Oklahoma Press to particularly expand his story to include details on the affairs and travails of Fort Laramie in the years between the army's departure and the National Park Service's arrival, since its caretakers in those early years were nearly all Fort Laramie veterans and were, in fact, a literal continuation of the site's remarkable military legacy. So we should be grateful for John Hunton, Joe and Mary Wilde, and Hattie Sandercock, each of whom owned and preserved large segments of the old fort and property, and for Doug McChristian, who brought his considerable talent as a military historian and his personal verve as a Fort Laramie veteran of another sort, to deliver this thoughtful, long overdue military history of one of the American West's most venerable historic places.

PAUL L. HEDREN
Omaha, Nebraska
November 12, 2007

PREFACE

F ort Laramie is a special place. The dozen or so remaining buildings, interspersed among numerous ruins, are nestled along the Laramie River in a pastoral setting that is little changed from the nineteenth century. I first saw the place at the age of nine, as one stop during a family vacation. The experience made such a lasting impression on me that I still hold a dim memory of touring the buildings under the guidance of a park ranger. I visited the site a second time during the summer of 1964, just prior to my senior year of high school. Having already developed an interest in frontier military history, and considering a direction for my life, it occurred to me that working at a place like Fort Laramie—on the very ground where history happened—could be ideal. Inspired, I mustered up the courage to inquire of an indulgent ranger about how one might get such a job. He patiently explained the requirements—advice I took seriously—yet I could not have imagined that little more than a decade later I would be a member of the staff at Fort Laramie National Historic Site. It was a dream come true.

Reflecting on my thirty-five-year career with the National Park Service, I consider my time at Fort Laramie to be one of the highlights—a thoroughly enjoyable, challenging, and rewarding assignment. Over the years, I had numerous official opportunities to return for special events, as a living history trainer and a historical furnishings consultant. Near the end of my career, I was fortunate to be assigned there as a research historian for the regional office in Denver and thus spent another hitch at that one-time haunt of American Indians, mountain men, emigrants, soldiers, plainsmen, Pony Express riders, miners, coachmen, and ranchers. It is truly an extraordinary place with an undeniable aura that one must experience to appreciate.

The marvelously complex story of Fort Laramie has been treated previously in LeRoy R. Hafen and Frances M. Young, Fort Laramie and the Pageant of the West (1938), a classic general history of the post, and Remie Nadeau's more focused Fort Laramie and the Sioux Indians (1967). Both, however, have become rather dated with the passage of time. A more recent publication is Paul L. Hedren's Fort Laramie in 1876: Chronicle of a Frontier Post at War (1988), an excellent telling of the post's role in the pivotal Great Sioux War. As the title of this book implies, Fort Laramie: Military Bastion of the High Plains provides a comprehensive operational history of Fort Laramie in its glory days, utilizing the larger body of information that has become available during recent decades. Fort Laramie, unlike many abandoned frontier military posts, refused to die after the army left and carried on as a viable element in the civilian community, a period historians have previously given only passing notice. This volume, therefore, transcends the military period through the dark days when Fort Laramie fell on hard times, yet survived to eventually become a unit of the National Park System.

This volume originated as two historical studies prepared for the National Park Service. After Charles E. Rankin, editor-in-chief of the University of Oklahoma Press, read the original studies, he suggested that I revise them for a general readership and consolidate them into a single volume tracing the fort's history up to the eve of its acquisition by the National Park Service. Considering my long personal and professional association with Fort Laramie, I feel privileged to have the opportunity to try my hand at relating its marvelous story. It is indeed unique, occupying an unrivaled place in the history of the American West. Weighed against the more than two hundred forts active in the western United States during the second half of the nineteenth century, Fort Laramie represents the quintessential frontier army post, ranking as the most historically significant of them all.

Many people contributed their time and talents to this project. Librarian Sandra Lowry and Park Ranger Steve Fulmer, both on the staff at Fort Laramie National Historic Site, lent invaluable assistance throughout the project. Sandy's intimate knowledge of the library and archival collections, as well as her willingness to copy or lend me much material, greatly aided my research at the park. She and Steve invariably responded with patience and thoroughness to my many telephonic and e-mail requests for follow-up bits and pieces of information. Steve was also kind enough to provide a careful review of the draft manuscript and to offer many insightful comments based on his intimate knowledge of all that is Fort Laramie. Thanks also to James Mack, former superintendent of Fort Laramie National Historic Site, for facilitating my work at the park during his tenure.

I wish to thank Michael Pilgrim and Deanne Blanton at the National Archives, Washington, D.C., for the valuable assistance they lent in accessing materials during my visit. Jean Brainerd, reference historian at the Wyoming State Archives in Cheyenne, accommodated me by providing thorough and always cordial assistance. Equally responsive to my requests was friend Venice Beskey at the Wyoming State Library. On numerous occasions, Venice demonstrated her uncanny ability to locate the exact source to fill my needs. I also appreciate the help of Brent Wagner, librarian in the Western History Department, Denver Public Library, in accessing the Collins, Ward, Ellison, and other manuscript collections held there. Staff members at other repositories who hosted my visits or filled long-distance requests were: Historian John A. Doerner at Little Bighorn Battlefield National Monument, Crow Agency, Montana; David Hays, Norlin Library, University of Colorado, Boulder; Carl Hallberg at the American Heritage Center, University of Wyoming, Laramie; Lilly Library at the University of Indiana, Bloomington; Russ Taylor and Helen Hoopes, Harold B. Lee Library, Brigham Young University, Provo, Utah; Jim Potter, Nebraska Historical Society, Chadron; Lisa F. Leibfacher of the Ohio Historical Society, Columbus; the library and archives staff at the Kansas State Historical Society, Topeka; my longtime friend and Fort Laramie alum, Thomas A. Lindmier, now of the Wyoming State Parks and Historical Commission, Laramie; the staff at the Goshen County Clerk's Office, the Goshen County Library staff, and the staff of the Homesteaders Museum, all in Torrington,

Wyoming. I am most grateful to all for their generous assistance, so willingly rendered.

I owe special thanks to R. Eli Paul, museum director of the Liberty Memorial Museum in Kansas City, for sharing with me the previously undiscovered Oscar F. Winship inspection report and maps relating to Fort Laramie. Finally, I wish to recognize historians Paul L. Hedren (with whom I served during Fort Laramie's golden years), Gordon Chappell, and William A. Dobak, all former park rangers at Fort Laramie and dedicated students of its history, for reading and commenting on the initial manuscript. Their encouragement and many thoughtful suggestions for improving the final product are greatly appreciated.

Territorial Designations
of Fort Laramie

The nineteenth century represented a period of rapid growth and change in the trans-Mississippi West. As the United States acquired new lands, the geography of the region was modified accordingly. Fort Laramie was one of the first military posts to be established on the far frontier and happened to be situated in an area that, over time, was claimed by several developing territories. To avoid confusion for the reader, the author has intentionally not attached territorial labels to Fort Laramie throughout the text. The following table is provided as a reference to its official location at any particular time.

June 16, 1849   Unorganized U.S. territory acquired by the Louisiana Purchase in 1803. (Military correspondence was addressed, "Fort Laramie, Oregon Route.")

May 30, 1854   Nebraska Territory (encompassing much of the Louisiana Purchase)

July 10, 1863   Idaho Territory (embracing most of the present states of Idaho, Montana, and Wyoming)

May 26, 1864   Dakota Territory (present states of North and South Dakota and Wyoming)

July 25, 1868   Wyoming Territory (same boundaries as the present state)

July 10, 1890   State of Wyoming

INTRODUCTION

Fort Laramie was destined to achieve unrivaled historical importance because of its strategic location deep in the heart of the Plains Indian country. The confluence of the Laramie and the North Platte rivers in southeastern Wyoming defines an area of geographical transition, where the once buffalo-laden northern Great Plains join the Rocky Mountains. The headwaters of the North Platte originate in the high country, what is now northern Colorado, whence the river traces a northerly course into central Wyoming, before arcing southeastward to its juncture with the South Platte in western Nebraska. Combined, they form the trunk of the Platte River, a natural line of demarcation segregating the central from the northern plains.

Beaver abounded along the meandering, swift-flowing Laramie, a major tributary among numerous crystal streams debouching from snow-crowned peaks near the present Colorado-Wyoming border.[1] The north fork of that stream, however, forms farther north in the watershed of Laramie Peak, a prominent natural landmark visible to the human eye for nearly a hundred miles out on the plains. The two branches merge near modern Wheatland, Wyoming, and flow to the confluence with the North Platte a few miles downstream.

By the early part of the nineteenth century, that area marked the convergence of hunting territories claimed by several American Indian

---

[1]The Laramie River allegedly owes its name to a Canadian trapper of French descent named LaRamee, who, according to oral tradition, was killed by Indians on that stream in 1821. His first name may have been Jacques, though it was more likely Joseph, the third son of Joseph (Sr.) and Jeanne LaRamee, a farming family that lived at Yamaska, Quebec. McDermott, "The Search for Jacques Laramee: A Study in Frustration," in *Visions of a Grand Old Post*, 14–19.

tribes. The dynamics of that volatile environment developed as the result of migrations and intertribal warfare spanning more than a century, with each tribe striving to survive by preserving, or expanding, its hunting range. Among those tribes were the Crows, a powerful group that for centuries had occupied the region of the Big Horn Mountains eastward to the Black Hills and from the Musselshell as far south as the North Platte River. The Crows warred with most of their neighbors, notably the British-supplied tribes on their northern flank, as well as the Sioux and Cheyennes, comparative newcomers who had migrated from the headlands of the Mississippi to the Black Hills and, by the late 1700s, had penetrated as far west as the Powder River country.

The seven subtribes of the Teton (also called Western or Lakota) Sioux, sharing a common dialect of the Sioux language, included the Oglala, Brule, Miniconjou, Two Kettles, Hunkpapa, Blackfeet (not to be confused with the Blackfoot Tribe in northern Montana), and Sans Arc. The Oglalas, first capturing or bartering for horses from the sedentary tribes living along the Upper Missouri, moved onto the plains during subsequent decades. In the vicinity of the Black Hills, they encountered the equally warlike Cheyennes, who had the advantage of being supplied with horses through intertribal trade avenues extending to the Spanish Southwest. The Cheyennes, in fact, had migrated to the plains somewhat earlier, displacing the weaker Kiowas then inhabiting the Black Hills. Following a brief conflict during the 1790s, the Cheyennes and Sioux arrived at an accommodation that gradually formed into lasting alliance. The Lakotas, formerly woodland hunters and gatherers, quickly adapted to buffalo hunting and became a true horse-and-buffalo society, a development that radically altered and defined their way of life for the next century.

By the early decades of the nineteenth century, the Pawnees were occupying the Loup Fork region of the Platte, with some bands operating along the principal valley as far west as the junction of its tributaries, the North and South Platte Rivers. The Pawnees were a numerous and aggressive people who resisted incursions into their territory by both the Sioux and Cheyennes. In fact, they clashed with almost all of the surrounding tribes in the region, even going so far as to launch extended raids far to the south against the Kiowas,

Comanches, Southern Arapahos, and Southern Cheyennes. When successful, those conflicts rewarded the Pawnees with the arms, munitions, and horses required to maintain their supremacy in the region.

The Shoshones (also called Snakes), once the dominant force in the Yellowstone River country, had been compelled by their better-armed foes, the Blackfeet, Crees, and Assiniboins, to withdraw southward into the Wind River Range. The Shoshones nevertheless continued to launch hunting and raiding expeditions onto the plains drained by the North Platte, an area frequented by another hunter-warrior tribe, the Arapahos, whose range extended southeastward to the South Platte and eastern Colorado.

Following the Louisiana Purchase in 1803, American traders penetrated the plains and the Rockies in search of beaver, thus extending in that region white influence initiated earlier by the Spanish, French, and British. The financial success of those trading companies depended on positive relationships with independent and company-employed trappers, as well as with the Native inhabitants. As the traders fostered amicable relations with the Indians by supplying their acquired appetite for manufactured goods, along with liquor, they also became a factor in tribal rivalries and conflicts.

By the 1820s, John Jacob Astor's American Fur Company (AFC), counterpart to the famed Hudson's Bay firm in Canada, dominated trade on the Upper Missouri. Even though other companies attempted to infringe on the business, Astor's grip on the region was so firm that he could afford to manipulate prices to drive his competitors out of business. After the failure of one such attempt, the fledgling Rocky Mountain Fur Company (RMFC), a partnership formed by veteran plainsmen James Bridger, Thomas Fitzpatrick, Milton Sublette, Jean Baptiste Gervais, and Henry Fraeb, began fielding large brigades of white trappers in the Rockies and as far north as Powder River. Rather than establishing fixed trading posts after Astor's model, however, the RMFC relied on an annual summer rendezvous, often held on Green River or one of its tributaries, an event that became the hallmark of the mountain fur trade. St. Louis traders transported eastern goods to the rendezvous, where they would barter with the assembled white trappers and Indians for the past year's catch of furs. The system worked successfully for several years, but by the mid-1830s it faced a two-fold threat—the declining beaver population resulting from over-trapping, combined with a dwindling market for beaver felt hats. Beaver fell out of style when silk top hats became fashionable for gentlemen in the "States," and in Europe.

The fur companies quickly turned to the Indian trade in bison (buffalo) hides to supplant the diminishing beaver trade. White trappers gradually faded from the economic scene as trade increased with the Indians, who possessed combined skills as superb horsemen and adept buffalo hunters. However, the market in robes created fundamental and important differences that changed the nature of the business. While beaver skins were relatively easy to press, bundle, and transport to St. Louis, large buffalo hides were quite another matter. Heavy and bulky, the bison hides required permanent storage facilities on the plains where they could be amassed and protected until spring, when the winter run-off would make streams deep enough to accommodate boats by which the robes could be transported to St. Louis. Trading establishments, usually incorporating log or adobe stockades, proliferated across the northern plains. Such posts provided the owners means to secure robes and trade goods, and to protect their vulnerable horse herds within the walled corrals. Rather than the companies transporting goods to the rendezvous sites, a characteristic of the beaver trade, Indian hunters now brought scraped hides to the trading posts.

William L. Sublette and Robert Campbell, both seasoned trappers, formed a three-year partnership in 1832 with the intention of challenging Astor's monopoly on the Upper Missouri. They subsequently drew a license, in compliance with newly legislated federal trade and intercourse acts, to conduct business at numerous points on the Missouri and to establish as many as a dozen trading posts, some of them practically next door to existing AFC stations. Prior to the fur magnate's retirement and sale of his "Western Department" to the firm of Bernard Pratte & Company, the powerful AFC had habitually dismissed minor threats such as that posed by Sublette and Campbell.[2]

---

[2]Bernard Pratte and Pierre Chouteau, Jr., first competitors, then affiliates of John Jacob Astor, joined forces to acquire the American Fur Company's former western district, which was part of Chouteau's grand scheme to monopolize the fur and Indian trade all the way from Three Forks of the Missouri, in southcentral Montana, to the Arkansas River. Barbour, "Fur Trade at Fort Laramie," 16.

However, the new controllers, Pratte and his partner, Pierre Chouteau, Jr., decided to make an exception when the upstarts actually carried out their plan to build a post adjacent to Fort Union, situated at the confluence of the Yellowstone and the Missouri. Although Astor's successors were initially inclined to gamble that another of the vicious trade wars between companies might well defeat the determined newcomers, they also recognized that the trade situation, not to mention profits, would be disrupted, perhaps with far-reaching effects. In a move that pleased, but probably surprised, Sublette and Campbell, Pratte & Company agreed to a compromise whereby they would buy Sublette and Campbell's new fort and much of the merchandise on hand. In addition, Pratte and Chouteau consented to allow the partners free reign for one year to trade in the territory south and west of a line commencing on the Arkansas River (twenty-four degrees west longitude) and extending north to the Platte, thence along the watershed of the Missouri to the Rocky Mountains all the way to the Three Forks of the Missouri. Chouteau and Pratte would retain their monopoly over the area north and east of that line.

In accordance with that agreement, Sublette and Campbell quickly abandoned their Missouri River interests and moved into the Sioux and Cheyenne country to establish a new post at "a point of timber on the south side of the Grand river Platte, called Laremais' point, about ten miles below the Black Hills . . . [indicating the hills near modern Guernsey, Wyoming]."[3] The party made camp near the mouth of the Laramie, an already familiar spot to the trappers, and quickly began constructing a small log fort. The stockaded post was christened "Fort William," probably honoring Sublette, although one account suggests the surname name was chosen in recognition of both the partner and William Marshall Anderson, a company employee present at the time.[4]

---

[3]Much of this discussion relies on ibid., 19–25. The quotation is found on p. 20. See also Sunder, *Fur Trade on the Upper Missouri*, 7–12. Barbour's more recent research contradicts the interpretation that Sublette and Campbell raced competitor N. J. Wyeth up the Platte to the 1834 rendezvous, Campbell stopping en route to construct Fort William, while Sublette pushed ahead. Hafen and Young, *Fort Laramie*, 25–27; Campbell himself wrote that he sent a party of men, with furs from their post on the Upper Missouri, southward from the Yellowstone River to the Laramie; Barbour, "Fur Trade at Fort Laramie," 26. An even more far-fetched and unfounded tale contends that Sublette and Campbell followed the Santa Fe Trail to Colorado before turning north to the North Platte and by so doing, arrived at the rendezvous too late. Hyde, *Red Cloud's Folk*, 44.

[4]Barbour, "Fur Trade at Fort Laramie," 26–27; Hafen and Young, *Fort Laramie*," 30n32.

To their credit, Sublette and Campbell had already anticipated the changes to the plains economy and had foreseen the advantages of having a trading post at the confluence of the North Platte and the Laramie. With their chief competitor effectively barred from the region, they were in a position to redirect their commercial efforts to a burgeoning demand in the States for buffalo robes. Fort William would provide an ideal location to take advantage of the Indian trade, as well as to secure whatever business might still be had in beaver pelts. The district was well known as a place where tribal territories merged because of the abundance of buffalo, and it lay in the heart of the territory now dominated by the Northern Cheyennes, Oglalas, and Brulés. Moreover, the confluence afforded the requisite sources of good water and timber, as well as grazing lands for the post's domestic animals. Vital, too, was an overland route for transporting goods in from St. Louis and packing out the fort's return shipment of heavy hides. Even though the depth of the North Platte varied along its course, it usually afforded shallow-draft boats a direct avenue to the Missouri.

Fort William, commonly referred to as "Fort Laramie" within a short time after its construction, lay in the midst of a neutral zone where not only whites and Indians met in a generally harmonious environment, but where members of rival tribes also tolerated one another, at least briefly. It was a situation that thrived on mutual dependency. Traders relied on the Indians for the furs and hides they harvested, and the Indians coveted American goods, not the least of which was whiskey, offered by the traders. It was a coexistence that might have thrived for some time, had it not been for developing influences beyond the Indian trade.

The Platte Valley, portions of which had been used for many years by Indians in their nomadic travels and the seasonal pursuit of bison, also presented a natural and watered passage from the Missouri to the mountains. Although Lewis and Clark had no reason to explore the Platte during their epic expedition, the French had included its general course on maps prepared in the late seventeenth century. Americans discovered the advantages of the North Platte route at least as early as the summer of 1812, when a party of Astor's men, led by Robert Stuart, traveled from the northwest coast, via St. Louis, en route to New York. Afterward, trapping and trading parties moving between St. Louis and the mountains followed this easily traveled avenue from "the States" to the Rockies and back. It first came to the official attention of U.S. authorities when Lieutenant Zebulon M. Pike, during his circuitous expedition to New Mexico in 1804, examined a portion of the valley in Nebraska, as did Major Stephen H. Long in 1820. Even though the trail witnessed limited use by small parties of civilian travelers during the mid-1830s, no one, particularly the Indians, could have envisioned the torrent of humanity it would bring within a few years, much less the impact it would have on the dynamics of civilization on the plains.

By 1841, through a complex series of mergers and sales, Fort Laramie fell into the hands of Pierre Chouteau & Company, a successor to the American Fur Company.[5] Probably because it had been constructed in haste of green timber, the earlier Fort William had deteriorated rapidly. Chouteau, valuing its ideal situation for the robe trade, decided to build a more substantial structure of adobe bricks. Two years later, Second Lieutenant John C. Frémont, Topographical Engineers, arrived at the fort in command of a party of U.S. troops conducting

---

[5]Robert Campbell, tired of the hard frontier life, elected to give up the trading business in favor of managing his financial affairs in the more comfortable environment of St. Louis. Sublette suffered from tuberculosis and he, too, favored selling Fort William within a year after it was built. In 1834, Sublette's brother, Milton, and his partners Thomas Fitzpatrick and James Bridger (Fitzpatrick, Sublette, & Bridger) formed a new company that included former members of the Rocky Mountain Fur Company. Within a few months, however, they merged with Fontenelle, Drips, & Company to form Fontenelle, Fitzpatrick, & Company, named for the two principal shareholders. (Complicating matters, the company subsequently worked in concert with Pierre Chouteau, Astor's successor, to lead some of his "Rocky Mountain Outfits.") The resulting partnership brought together enough capital for Fontenelle, Fitzpatrick, & Co. (i.e., the Rocky Mountain Fur Company) to buy out Sublette and Campbell's interests at Fort William in 1835. That concern lasted only a year.

An agent acting on behalf of Chouteau negotiated to buy out Fontenelle, Fitzpatrick, & Co., including Fort William, during the 1836 rendezvous, thus consolidating Pratte, Chouteau & Company's (i.e., the American Fur Company) control of the fur and Indian trade west of the Missouri River to the central Rockies. Of particular benefit to the American Fur Company was the consolidation of its supply system, which Barbour explains "made it possible to move goods upriver [the Missouri] to Bellevue at the mouth of the Platte, from whence wagons could easily carry merchandise overland to Fort William. Upon arrival at the timber fort on Laramie Creek, good could be assorted into smaller outfits and transported to the annual mountain rendezvous until the supply system was ended in 1840" (p. 41). The succession of Fort Laramie's ownership during the 1830s is detailed in Barbour, "Fur Trade at Fort Laramie," 31–41.

the first military reconnaissance of the North Platte route. Frémont described the post, subsequently renamed Fort John, as

> a quadrangular structure, built of clay, after the fashion of the Mexicans, who are generally employed in building them. The walls are about fifteen feet high, surmounted with a wooden palisade, and form a portion of ranges of houses, which entirely surround a yard of about one hundred and thirty feet square. Every apartment has its door and window, all, of course, opening on the inside. There are two entrances opposite each other and midway the wall, one of which is a large and public entrance, the other small and more private: a sort of postern gate. Over the great entrance is a square tower, with loopholes; and, like the rest of the work, built of earth. At two of the angles, and diagonally opposite each other, are large square bastions, so arranged as to sweep the four faces of the walls.

Frémont added, prophetically as it turned out, his observation that the North Platte and Laramie confluence "was the most suitable place, on the line of the Platte, for the establishment of a military post. It is connected with the mouth of the Platte and the Upper Missouri by excellent roads, which are in frequent use, and would not in any way interfere with the range of the buffalo, on which the neighboring Indians mainly depend for support." In addition to its importance on the Oregon Route via South Pass, Fort Laramie also sat astride a trail used for decades by both trappers and Indians leading from Fort Pierre to Taos, New Mexico. That Fort Laramie was strategically situated to facilitate movement along a north-south axis, as well as from east to west, would make it militarily valuable for many years to come.

Because the United States had few commercial or strategic interests worth protecting in the trans-Mississippi region during the first three decades of the nineteenth century, the army devoted only scant attention to what Major Long dubbed the Great American Desert. Trappers and traders took care of themselves, and congressional apprehension of a standing military force kept the Regular Army too small to be of much consequence in such a vast domain. The army, consequently, had no defined mission in the West for years, other than conducting an occasional exploration and manning a longitudinal line of forts intended as a buffer delineating a permanent Indian frontier. Only in the mid-1830s did a few small parties of missionaries, bent on carrying

Christianity to the Indians, and emigrant farmers, begin risking the arduous and, at times, dangerous trek to Oregon. At the beginning of the following decade, Mormons wishing to establish an exclusive society in the western wilderness, far from the religious persecution they had experienced in the States, also made their way along the Platte westward to settle eventually in the valley of the Great Salt Lake.

The conquest of the Southwest by the United States as an outcome of the Mexican War, the discovery of gold in California, and resolution of the Oregon boundary dispute with Great Britain combined in rapid succession to create a surge of emigration across this "desert" that would become known as the Great Plains. Americans became imbued with the notion that it was their manifest destiny to occupy the continent from ocean to ocean, regardless of the Native inhabitants already residing west of the Mississippi. The Lakota bands of Sioux, who by that time firmly controlled most of the region from the North Platte to the great bend of the Missouri, observed with mounting uneasiness the proliferation of whites passing through the country. Accelerating the depletion of the great buffalo herds by the Indians themselves, who hunted the beasts for both sustenance and the hide trade, whites shot large numbers of the animals simply for sport, leaving the carcasses to rot. Over time, herds and other game avoided coming near the Platte road altogether. Although the trickle of whites passing through their territory initially caused no great alarm among the Indians, the steadily increasing traffic in wagons, animals, and people crossing the plains by the end of the 1840s began to sorely test the patience of the Sioux.

The gold rush to California and the lure of lush farming lands in the Pacific Northwest, added to the Mormon pilgrimage, created compelling matters Congress could hardly ignore. With American citizens crossing the plains by the tens of thousands, the federal government faced obligations to provide protection for the people from potentially hostile Indians, if not to protect tribesmen from reciprocally hostile whites. Moreover, there was the duty to establish the basics of government and mail service for the distant new settlements along the Pacific Coast and in Utah. And, in a strategic sense, the United States now had a vulnerable west coast that had to be defended against potential foreign invasion. The United States Army, a mere ten thousand men strong at the time, was ill-prepared to meet those challenges. Nevertheless, in 1846 Congress enacted legislation to establish several military garrisons along the route to Oregon to assist and protect the emigrants. The first of those, Fort Kearny, would be situated on the Platte River where the various emigrant trails from Missouri and Iowa converged to form the main artery of the Oregon Route. Fort Hall, already a familiar Hudson's Bay Company establishment on the Snake River, would protect the far western segment of the road. The third would lie in between, at or near the mouth of the Laramie River. Thus, Fort Laramie was destined to make the transition from trading post to an instrument of the government in the conquest of the trans-Mississippi West.

Throughout the 1850s and 1860s, Fort Laramie remained the principal station on the trunk line of overland routes branching farther west to Utah, California, and Oregon. It was not surprising that many emigrants recorded their arrival at that milestone, most of them likening Fort Laramie to an oasis in the desert where they could rest and refit, trade for fresh animals, catch up on news from the States, and, if they were lucky, find mail awaiting them from back home. Many travelers, so far from home, remarked that the stars and stripes floating over the little post served to reassure them that they were still in U.S. territory. Fort Laramie also marked the point of no return in their journey. If one had "seen the elephant" and lost heart, this was the place to turn back because it marked the end of the "easy" part of the trip. Emigrants electing to continue on faced only more acute hardships in the form of mountains, torturous rivers, vast deserts, and, at times, violent weather. Many emigrants felt, rightfully so, that upon departing from Fort Laramie, they had left behind the last vestige of civilization as they knew it.

Although the federal government never intended Fort Laramie to be a permanent establishment, the needs of the garrison quickly outgrew the walls of Fort John, and the army began constructing quarters, storehouses, and other buildings on the adjacent plateau. Like most of its contemporaries, Fort Laramie was never again surrounded by any sort of protective stockade. From time to time over subsequent years, the army proposed abandoning Fort Laramie, yet somehow a justification always arose causing the government to retain it a while longer, and the longer it stayed, the larger the post grew. By the late 1860s, Fort Laramie had become a post of considerable size, by frontier standards, frequently housing a garrison of several hundred officers and soldiers in addition to scores of dependents and civilian employees. The facilities continued to expand until, by the end of the following decade, the plateau and the lowlands immediately to the north were literally covered with buildings, ranging from officers' quarters and barracks to huge storehouses, mechanics' shops, a hospital, guard houses, an arsenal, bakeries, stables, corrals, and literally dozens of privies. Oddly enough, in the 1880s, after the mission to subdue the Indians had subsided, even more new buildings were erected, aside from such amenities as street lamps, bird baths, and picket fences. More than ever, the fort began to resemble the very frontier settlements made possible by the army's presence. Indeed, in its later years Fort Laramie became the economic and social center for local ranchers and settlers, a role it continued to play even after the army left in 1890.

Fort Laramie, more than any other military post during the frontier era, witnessed the salient events that shaped the western United States—the great westward migrations, the gold rushes, the Pony Express, the transcontinental telegraph, landmark peace-treaty councils, and the overland mail to California. It served as the base for several major army campaigns against the Teton Sioux and Northern Cheyenne tribes. This, then, is the saga of the quintessential frontier army post that for forty-one years served the nation in peace and in war as a virtual hub of the West.

CHAPTER ONE

"The Chain of Posts to Oregon"

W hen United States soldiers first raised the stars and stripes over a decaying Fort John on June 26, 1849, no one could have imagined that four decades of army occupation would follow. Four years earlier, Colonel Stephen Watts Kearny made his epic trek up the Oregon route as far as South Pass. Along the way he took every opportunity to awe the Indians with the might of the federal government by showing off two bronze mountain howitzers, as well as his soldiers' sabers and carbines. Arriving at Fort John in mid-June 1845, Kearny camped on grassy bottomland along the Laramie River a short distance above the trading post. There, during an unseasonable snowstorm, he met with Sioux leaders in an effort to induce them to avoid the evils of liquor offered by the traders and, more importantly, to stage no opposition to the white man's road that had gradually been opened through their country.

Convinced that seasonal patrols over the emigrant route to Oregon would suffice to control the peacefully inclined Indians, Kearny argued to his superiors that permanent posts would be expensive and largely unnecessary for most of the year, considering the short migration season. His opinion stemmed not only from his own observations, but also relied on Colonel Henry Dodge's earlier expedition to the Rocky Mountains in 1835 and a subsequent one led by Major Clifton Wharton to visit the Pawnee villages on the Platte. Kearny later boasted that mounted expeditions "would serve to keep the Indians perfectly quiet, reminding them of (as this one proved) the facility and rapidity with which our dragoons can march through any part of their country, and that there is no place where they can go but the dragoons can follow and, as we are better mounted than they are, overtake them."[1]

Kearny's views contradicted those expressed some years earlier by Secretary of War Joel R. Poinsett, as well as his successor, John C. Spencer, both of whom advocated the establishment of a chain of permanent garrisons along the Oregon Route, the army's official term for the route often today still called a "trail." To oversee the safety of emigrants, Poinsett suggested three military stations: one where the various tributary trails converged with the trunk line on the Platte, in what is today central Nebraska; another at or near Fort Hall, a Hudson's Bay post on the Snake River; and a third, considered by Poinsett as particularly important, between them, "on the north fork of the river Platte, near the confluence of the Laramie's fork."[2] No less a figure than Thomas Fitzpatrick, a former partner in the Rocky Mountain Fur Company and co-owner of "Fort" Laramie, also weighed in on the strategic significance of the place in his assessment of the changing tribal dynamics in the region. "A post at or in the vicinity of Laramie is much needed," Fitzpatrick wrote in an uncannily accurate prophecy. "It would be in the vicinity of the buffalo range, where all the most formidable Indian tribes are fast approaching, and near where there will eventually (as game decreases) be a great struggle for the ascendancy."[3] Presidents John Tyler and James K. Polk concurred with Fitzpatrick's views and petitioned Congress in subsequent annual messages to provide funds to build the forts, and to provide for an "adequate force of mounted riflemen . . . to guard and protect them [emigrants] on their journey."[4] The statement was particularly far-

---

[1]Kearny, "Report of a Summer Campaign to the Rocky Mountains, &c, in 1845," *Senate Executive Documents*, no. 2 (480): 212 (hereinafter abbreviated as *Sen. Ex. Docs* with U.S. Serial Set number). Kearny's column departed from Fort Leavenworth on May 18, 1845. The expedition proceeded to South Pass, stopping en route at Fort Laramie for a few days. The column again passed by Fort Laramie in July en route to Bent's Fort on the Arkansas River. By the time Kearny returned to Fort Leavenworth, he had covered more than two thousand miles in ninety-nine days. Lt. H. S. Turner to Col. A. E. Mackay, October 22, 1849, Letters Sent, Fort Laramie, Record Group 393, National Archives, Washington, D.C. (hereinafter cited as ls, fl); Hunt, *Major General James Henry Carleton*, 91–94; Frémont, "Report of the Exploring Expedition to the Rocky Mountains in the Year 1842 and to Oregon and North California in the Years 1843-'44," *Sen. Ex. Docs*, 28th Cong. 2nd Sess. (461): 41, 47–48.
[2]*Sen. Ex. Docs.*, 26th Cong., 1st Sess. no. 31 (231): 2.
[3]Hafen and Ghent, *Broken Hand*, 139.
[4]Unruh, *The Plains Across*, 202.

reaching in its effect as a formal commitment by the government to facilitate emigration to the Pacific Northwest territories.

After years of debate, Congress eventually adopted the concept of fixed stations on the Oregon Route, and in May 1846 allocated funds to acquire Fort Laramie. Even though the secretary of war directed the army to proceed with establishing the two easternmost forts along on the emigrant road, the onset of war with Mexico precluded the military from carrying out the order at that time. Two years later, however, a battalion of Missouri Volunteers was dispatched to establish the first station, subsequently named Fort Kearny. Prior to that time, Fort Leavenworth, situated on the Missouri near the origin of the Santa Fe Trail, had been the only military garrison in proximity to the more recently established Oregon Route.

Also included in the appropriation was the sum of $76,500 for organizing a special unit, designated as the Regiment of Mounted Riflemen, to garrison the posts and patrol the Oregon Route. The regiment was recruited and organized during summer and fall 1846, and by November was ready to take the field. The enabling legislation notwithstanding, the demands of war took precedence over the unit's intended frontier mission. The regiment was soon en route to Mexico where it participated in numerous engagements during the next two years. When the war ended, the regiment performed several months of provost duty in Mexico City before being sent back to Jefferson Barracks, Missouri, to reorganize and prepare to carry out its original mission along the emigrant road.[5]

Spring 1849 found five companies of Mounted Riflemen at Fort Leavenworth, ready to make what would be recorded as an epic two-thousand-mile march all the way to Vancouver, Washington. The cavalcade, including a supply train numbering 436 wagons and carry-

---

[5]The record of engagements for the Regiment of Mounted Riflemen included: Vera Cruz, Plan de Oro, National Bridge, Molino de Ray, Churabusco, and it was present at the capture of Mexico City. The unit was reorganized as the Third U.S. Cavalry in 1861. Rodenbough, *The Army of the United States*, 193–98; Settle, ed., *Mounted Riflemen*, 13–15. The riflemen represented a combination of infantry and dragoons. In addition to a distinctive uniform, they were specially armed with the Model 1841 "Mississippi" rifle, a .54-caliber percussion-primed weapon having considerably longer range and better accuracy than the smoothbore muskets used by the infantry. The riflemen were expected to travel by horseback, then dismount and engage the Indians more effectively on foot using light infantry tactics. Garavaglia and Worman, *Firearms of the American West, 1803–1865*, 122.

ing over a half-million pounds of supplies, would be the first military body to travel over the full length of the trail to the Pacific Northwest. In recognition of the momentous occasion, department commander Brigadier General David E. Twiggs traveled from his headquarters at St. Louis to review the riflemen on their departure. On May 10, with the companies formed on the parade ground, highly polished arms and buttons glinting in the morning sunlight, Twiggs himself bellowed the order setting the battalion in motion for its long trek across the continent.

Rather than tracing the usual emigrant route, the column marched almost directly north into Nebraska Territory, arriving nine days later at Fort Kearny, described by Major Osborn Cross as "not very pleasing . . . having nothing to recommend it in the way of beauty."[6] Along the way, the troops passed numerous trains of emigrants stricken with cholera that had been contracted through exposure to contaminated water prior to the journey. Nevertheless, even those who recognized the symptoms were eager to be on their way west, mistakenly concluding that the healthy climate of the prairie would prove to be a panacea for the disease. Cross regretted that "the number who had died with it was sufficient evidence that the emigrants were suffering greatly from its effects. They are truly to be pitied, as no aid in any way could be afforded them."[7] While the troops fared better than the civilians, probably because the officers exercised great care in selecting clean campsites and good water, they failed to escape the scourge completely. Eleven enlisted men died from the disease during the first three weeks of the march.

The first contingent of Mounted Riflemen, led by Major Winslow F. Sanderson, sighted Fort Laramie on the morning of June 16, having traveled some 639 miles during the six weeks since leaving Fort Leavenworth. An emigrant camped nearby witnessed the moment the troops rode into view: "then came the sound of the cannon that was fired to greet the arrival of Major Sanderson came booming from the fort. The hills around echoed the report one from another and it dwelt

---

[6]Settle, *Mounted Riflemen*, 57.

[7]When the column passed through Pawnee country, Cross noted that smallpox had taken such a heavy toll on their population that their war-making powers had been reduced to the point that neighboring tribes no longer feared them. The Sioux, in particular, took advantage of the situation to encroach into Pawnee hunting grounds. Ibid., 56.

long among them before it died away. It was soul stirring their successive reports in this expansive wild."[8]

The other battalions, retarded by the slower-moving supply trains, arrived during the next few days and bivouacked a short distance above the post. Sanderson was accompanied by First Lieutenant Daniel P. Woodbury, Corps of Engineers, who was charged with finding a suitable location for the military post and was vested with the authority to purchase the fur-company post should it prove to be situated on the best site. The two officers lost no time conducting a reconnaissance for approximately sixty miles farther up the Oregon road, following the "ridge" or "mountain" branch as far as Boise (Big Timber) Creek, and returning via the so-called river road.

Sanderson and Woodbury concluded that the mountaineers had chosen well; there was no better site than the one already occupied by Fort Laramie. They found abundant grass suitable for making hay within six miles, as well as limestone and pine timber for building purposes within fifteen miles. Sanderson described the Laramie River as "a beautiful and rapid stream, and will furnish an abundance of good water for the command."[9] Of more immediate importance, the fur traders' adobe trading post afforded ready-made shelter for the supplies that were already arriving, even though Adjutant General Don Carlos Buell had previously cautioned Sanderson not to be unduly swayed by that "momentary advantage."[10] All things considered, however, the site was a good one, and Woodbury acted quickly in opening negotiations with Bruce Husband, the resident factor (or manager) for the American Fur Company. Although Congress had authorized only three thousand dollars for the purchase, Husband insisted that the owners had instructed him to accept no less than four thousand. Woodbury considered the price too high, but signed the contract nevertheless, justifying his decision on the savings that would be realized by not losing supplies through exposure to the elements. The deal

---

[8]Farnham Diary, transcribed notation for June 16, 1849, McDermott File, library, Fort Laramie National Historic Site (FLNHS).

[9]Maj. W. F. Sanderson to Maj. Don Carlos Buell, Assistant Adjutant General, (hereinafter AAG), Military Department No. 7, June 27, 1849, LS, FL. In the foregoing letter, Sanderson stated that he arrived at the post on June 17, but the Post Returns record the date as June 16. Post Returns, June 1848, Fort Laramie, RG 94, NA (hereinafter cited as PR, FL).

[10]Buell to Sanderson, April 19, 1849, Letters Received, Fort Laramie, RG 393, NA (hereinafter cited as LR, FL).

concluded, the traders immediately relinquished the property and Fort Laramie officially became a United States Army post.[11]

On the morning of June 25, the battalion of riflemen destined for Oregon broke camp and forded the Laramie River to begin the remainder of the journey. Following behind were the wagon trains, now considerably lighter after the freighters deposited several months of supplies at the post.

Meantime, the men of Company E, the unit assigned to garrison the post, were busy settling into their new home. Within days after their arrival, Sanderson had the men preparing hay, cutting and hauling timber, and burning lime to produce mortar and plaster for repairing the old fort, as well as constructing new buildings. Some of the soldiers were detailed to assemble a saw mill that had been transported up the trail by wagon, while others dug sawpits for laborious hand sawing to augment lumber production. Sanderson announced to his superiors at St. Louis that "everything is being pushed forward as rapidly as circumstances will admit."[12]

The little garrison had taken possession of the fort just in time to play host to a party of Topographical Engineers, commanded by Captain Howard Stansbury, en route to survey a site for the new Fort Hall, after which they were to proceed to Utah to map the Great Salt Lake Valley. Arriving on the Laramie in early July, the little expedition laid over for six days to rest the animals and repair wagons before continuing the trek. First Lieutenant John W. Gunnison, Stansbury's assistant, described their visit in a letter to his wife:

> There are two army ladies here—one made a present to her husband of an infant the day we arrived and the other we understand is about to do equal service to his family & the country . . . We are better situated here being close at the Fort and open doors at the Mess table have been offered to all of us. It is a Rifle company here and pretty green on military etiquette, at which Capt S. had taken offense & won't come to the Fort—the com-

---

[11]The American Fur Company, having no legal title to the land upon which Fort John stood, conveyed only the buildings and an exclusive trading right with the Indians within a ten-mile area surrounding the post. To make certain it was acquiring sole domain over the property, the government stipulated that the company surrender any claims it may have made to building materials and land. Copy of Deed of Sale by Pierre Choteau, Jr. and Company, June 26, 1849, quoted in McDermott File.

[12]Sanderson to Buell, June 27, 1849, LS, FL.

mander not having been over to his camp. But it is understood among us that we are at home, and technical courtesies not required or even practical on the plains, particularly as those who are journeying to the posts are acquaintances & meet & stay at quarters when & as long as they choose.[13]

Shortly after Stansbury's party left on July 18, the garrison was augmented by the timely arrival of Captain Benjamin S. Roberts and his Company C of the Mounted Riflemen. Those sixty-two men provided Sanderson the additional manpower needed to prepare for the coming winter. Accompanying Roberts were Department Quartermaster Aeneas Mackay and First Lieutenant Stewart Van Vliet, an assistant quartermaster assigned to oversee construction of the new post. Quartermaster General Thomas S. Jesup had directed Mackay to supervise operations along both the New Mexico and Oregon routes, with special attention to making arrangements for the establishment of the new posts on the latter.

In his report, Mackay described the government's recent purchase: "Enclosed in a square of about 40 yards of Adobe wall of 12 ft. height. On the east side are quarters of two stories with a piazza. On the opposite side, the Main Gate, Lookout, Flag Staff, &c with shops, storehouses &c to the height of the wall on their right & left, and each of the other two sides ranges of Quarters on one story—all opening on a small Parade in the Centre. It is in a good deal of decay & needs repairs."[14]

Although the old fort was adequate for storing supplies and corralling animals, it was only marginally fit for human habitation. With

---

[13]First Lieutenant John W. Gunnison to his wife, July 13, 1849, Gunnison Papers, Hunting Library; Goetzmann, *Army Exploration*, 219–20. For Stansbury's own observations of Fort Laramie and the surrounding area, see Stansbury, *Exploration and Survey*, 52–54.

[14]Major Aeneas Mackay to Quartermaster General Thomas S. Jesup, November 1, 1849, LS, FL; Mackay to Jesup, August 14, 1849; ibid. Lieutenant D. P. Woodbury provided more specific details in a later report: "The old fort consists in the main of 19 rooms, varying in size from 12 feet square to 12 by 29 feet, and running round an open space 80 feet by 72 feet. Two of the 19 rooms belong to a two story building having two rooms in the second story, making 21 rooms in all. The outside walls are 3 feet thick at bottom, and diminish, by two off-sets on the inside to less than 2 feet at the top. The partition walls are generally two feet thick. Adjacent to the open space above mentioned, and connected with it by a passage 8 feet wide, is another open space about 80 feet by 45 feet, surrounded on one side by buildings already described, on another by a barn 25 feet square and a stable 12 feet by 18 feet, on the third by a 3 foot wall about 15 feet high and on the fourth by a similar wall. The rooms will average 8 feet high. The roofs are covered with earth sloping about 1 foot in four. There are towers 6 feet square at two of the angles and another over the principal entrance." Woodbury to Totten, November 15, 1849, LS, FL.

two companies of the Mounted Riflemen already present, and another of the Sixth Infantry due to arrive in August, the construction of additional quarters became a high priority. Confirming that the army had no intention of occupying the old trading post over the long term, Van Vliet wrote upon his arrival, "The new post is to be erected in the immediate vicinity."[15] Mackay also noted that the troops even then were engaged in constructing new quarters on the low plateau outside the walls, and with some crowding, the garrison could be sheltered by winter.

When Lieutenant Woodbury rendered his annual report in September, he could boast that the construction program was proceeding smoothly. Several civilian carpenters, probably hired in the vicinity of Leavenworth, Kansas, had almost completed framing a large, two-story frame officers' quarters, later dubbed Old Bedlam for the reputation it gained as the raucous home of bachelor officers. The interior of the plantation-style house was temporarily partitioned into sixteen rooms to accommodate all the officers and a few dependents through the winter. Nearing completion at the north end of the parade ground stood a new frame barracks, which was also a two-story edifice. Although the building was designed to house only one company, circumstances dictated that double the number of men be crowded into it that first winter. Near the river, along the east perimeter of the parade ground, were two frame stables for sheltering the riflemen's horses. Of particular necessity to the garrison was a bakery, which Woodbury constructed a short distance north of the parade ground. Woodbury added that he had a remaining balance of only ten thousand dollars for construction, an amount that would provide for another block of officers' quarters and a hospital, but would be insufficient to build quarters for the recently arrived Sixth Infantrymen. The lieutenant predicted that most of the work on the first group of buildings would be finished before winter, even though detachments had to travel to the Black Hills (north of present-day Guernsey, Wyoming) to find suitable timber. Bolstering his justification for additional funds to complete the post, Woodbury recorded that nearly eight thousand

---

[15]Captain Stewart Van Vliet to Jesup, July 27, 1849, Consolidated Correspondence File, RG 92, NA (hereinafter cited as CCF).

wagons and approximately thirty thousand people, most of them bound for California, had passed by the fort that summer.[16]

Meanwhile, St. Louis businessman John S. Tutt was preparing to profit from that traffic, in addition to having a monopoly on trade with the Fort Laramie garrison. Tutt maintained a shadowy financial arrangement with Robert Campbell, one of the original owners of the fort, and John Daugherty, with whom Campbell was partnered in a freighting business. Another man, identified only as Wilson, also joined in the venture. While Campbell and Daugherty were manipulating influential contacts with the government to secure the contract for hauling army freight, Tutt and Wilson cornered the lucrative post sutler position at Fort Laramie. Tutt erected an adobe store, situated approximately a hundred yards north of the officers' quarters, and was conducting business by late summer. [17]

Despite rapid progress toward establishing the three military forts on the heavily traveled overland road to the Pacific Coast, some officers unfamiliar with the region continued to argue that maintaining the garrisons year-round would be both expensive and unnecessary. Brigadier General David E. Twiggs, for example, pointed to the difficulty of providing enough grain and hay for the animals as one of the most critical and costly logistical problems, forewarning it would cost at least $45,000 a year to supply forage, much less purchase supplies for the troops. Others went so far as to propose that the livestock be returned to Fort Leavenworth during the winter months to avoid the expense of maintaining it during a season when the animals would seldom be used. Mackay,

---

[16]Woodbury to Totten, September 7, 1849, LS, FL; *Annual Report of the Secretary of War*, 1849, 225–26 (reports hereinafter cited as *ARSW* with year); Mattes, "Surviving Structures." The army's estimates were probably low, since many trains had passed Fort Laramie prior to the arrival of the troops in mid-June. A more accurate tabulation of the 1849 emigration is 39,697 bound for the Pacific Coast, plus 1,500 more traveling to Utah; Unruh, *Plains Across*, 120. Lieutenant Woodbury of the Engineers had been sent to determine the best site for Fort Laramie, but the construction of buildings was properly the province of the Quartermaster Department. Consequently, responsibility for construction at Fort Laramie was transferred from the Engineer Department to the Quartermaster Department effective August 16, 1850. *Special Orders No. 57*, Adjutant General's Office, August 16, 1850; Captain F. H. Masten to Jesup, November 22, 1850, CCF.

[17]Daugherty to Campbell, April 27, 1849, Daugherty Papers, copy in McDermott File; Barbour, "Fur Trade at Fort Laramie National Historic Site," 148–49; Tutt and Wilson apparently were the licensed sutlers at Fort Kearny as well as Fort Laramie. Mattes, "The Sutler's Store at Fort Laramie," *Visions of a Grand Old Post*, 23–24 (hereinafter cited as "Sutler's Store"); Barbour, "Fur Trade at Fort Laramie," 150.

however, saw things in a more positive light. "At Laramie, in the Valleys," he reported to Jesup, "the grass grows very high and in the latter part of the season, dries and becomes hay upon which they subsist."[18]

Indeed, in only six weeks, the Mounted Riflemen had already cut and stacked sixty tons of native hay to feed their horses during the coming winter. Many of the preconceptions about the inadequacies of Fort Laramie, in Mackay's view, were entirely unfounded. On the contrary, the place had many advantages that may have been minimized by the American Fur Company in an effort to discourage potential competitors from establishing their own posts in that area. At the end of July Mackay informed the quartermaster general, "Since my arrival here, I have been much more favorably impressed with the advantages of this station than I ever expected to be. Indeed, the prejudices which appear to have existed in the minds of everybody in regard to it, have unjustly deprived it of the credit of many recommendations to which it is entitled."[19] Fort Laramie, Mackay predicted, would "soon make Herself as desirable a spot as perhaps could be found any where so remote from those parts which we are in the habit of thinking only capable of furnishing with comfort and happiness."[20]

To reduce the anticipated high cost of supplying the distant Fort Laramie, the Quartermaster Department considered alternative routes from the main depot at Fort Leavenworth. Twiggs suggested to Adjutant General Roger Jones that establishing a new supply depot farther up the Missouri would significantly reduce expenses for maintaining both Forts Laramie and Hall. An improved road roughly following the northern segment of the old trapper trail from Fort Pierre to Taos, via Fort Laramie, Twiggs argued, would reduce the distance to only 250 miles. Goods could be transported more economically by steamer to Fort Pierre than by freighting them over the longer Oregon Route. Mackay himself, along with an escort of Mounted Rifles, returned to Fort Leavenworth via Fort Pierre, measuring the distance to verify the claim. Another potential route lay along the Republican River. To test the practicality of that course, Mackay directed Captain Langdon C.

---

[18]Mackay to Jesup, May 27, 1849, LS, FL.

[19]Mackay to Jesup, July 31, 1849, LS, FL.

[20]Jones to Scott, June 22, 1849, CCF; Twiggs to Jones, April 23, 1849, McDermott File. The quotations are from Mackay to Jesup, November 1, 1849, LS, FL.

Easton, an assistant quartermaster who had conducted a train of supplies to Fort Laramie, to return to Fort Leavenworth following this
southerly route. Easton left the post on August 2, following various
stream courses until he eventually reached the Republican in what is
now extreme eastern Colorado. Arriving at Fort Leavenworth in mid-
September, Easton admitted that the route he took offered no advantages over the Platte road and that it was two hundred miles longer.
"With regard to the road," he reported, "I doubt if as good a one could
be obtained, as the one leading up the Platte, that road being almost
unexceptional."[21]

Although the overland route to Fort Pierre was considerably shorter,
long winters in that latitude made travel on both land and water imprac-
tical. Consequently, for the next two decades, the principal avenue to
Fort Laramie would be the road leading to Oregon and California.

The Oregon Route, as the army called it, actually originated from
three termini, and depending on the traveler's destination, it could be
known by any of three names, or a combination of them: Oregon,
California, or Utah (Mormon). The route from Missouri and Fort
Leavenworth generally coursed along the south side of the Platte
River, while Mormon emigrants starting their journey from Council
Bluffs usually stayed on the north side of the stream until they reached
Fort Laramie. If they had not crossed the river before arriving there,
the "Saints" forded the North Platte to continue their trek along the
south bank. Meantime, many emigrants leaving Missouri followed the
road along the south side of the Platte until they were compelled to
cross the Laramie River at one of several fords between the confluence
of the two streams and the fort. Some also crossed the North Platte to
avoid less desirable conditions farther upstream.

Although wagons usually forded the Laramie River with little difficulty, the Platte was wider, deeper, and more treacherous in spring, the
result of snow melt in the Rocky Mountains, just when most emigrant
trains reached Fort Laramie. An unidentified entrepreneur took advantage of the increasing emigrant traffic, as well as the obvious potential

---

[21]Mackay to Jesup, November 1, 1849, ibid. Mackay recorded the average time for a freight train
to travel the distance between Fort Leavenworth and Fort Laramie as thirty-three days. Mackay
to Jesup, October 30, 1849 ibid.; Easton to Mackay, October 12, 1849, CCF; Mattes, ed., *Capt. L.
C. Easton's Report.*

of business with government supply trains, by establishing a ferry at that critical point during 1849. He was charging two dollars for each wagon when Stansbury's survey party arrived early that summer.[22]

That first winter was not an agreeable one for the garrison newly settled on the Laramie. Both officers and men endured cramped, unfinished quarters, and bathing was out of the question. By every standard, Fort Laramie was isolated, and more than a year passed before regular mail service became available. Communications to and from the post were carried intermittently by government supply trains, and occasionally by "expresses" consisting of small detachments of mounted soldiers.[23]

When supply wagons were being loaded the previous spring, one officer had predicted that because of the fort's remoteness it would be impossible to provide it with fresh vegetables for at least two years. Although he stressed that anti-scorbutic foods were necessary to prevent an outbreak of scurvy among the troops, not even dried fruits were included in the wagons bound for Fort Laramie. Despite the lack of vegetables, however, only two cases of scurvy appeared, and those late in summer. And yet the disease reappeared during the winter, afflicting thirteen men, one of whom died. "The habitual use of salt and unwholesome food, conjoined with fatiguing labor, were the exciting causes of the disease," one report concluded. Dr. John Moore treated the victims with "fresh animal food . . . in conjunction with vegetable acid drinks." No cases of scurvy were reported among the officers, perhaps because of the wider variety of canned fruits and vegetables regularly available to them. The surgeon requested and received a large supply of more healthful food for the garrison, after which the disease disappeared.[24]

Emigrants and Indians fared even worse. Van Vliet told the quartermaster general that seven hundred new graves dotted the roadside

---

[22]Mattes, "Potholes in the Great Platte River Road," 7. It is interesting to note that two experienced plainsmen stated they never heard the term "Oregon Trail" used during the historical era, rather the road was always known to them as either the California or Overland Trail. William Garnett interview, transcribed Walter Camp Field Notes, Brigham Young University, 651; Luther North to Walter Camp, January 27, 1928, Letter no. C23, Ellison Papers. The ferry was allegedly sunk by drunken Californians having a spree on June 9; however, it must have been repaired by the time Stansbury arrived in July; Hafen and Young, Fort Laramie,159.

[23]White, "A Postal History of Fort Laramie," typescript in vert. files, library, FLNHS (hereinafter cited as "Postal History").

[24]Coolidge, Statistical Report, 82; McCarty to Daugherty, April 5, 1850, Daugherty Papers, copy in vert. files, FLNHS.

between the Missouri and Fort Laramie. He urged that supplies be rushed forward to prevent further unnecessary losses. However, one emigrant thought the casualties had been exaggerated; he attributed the majority of deaths not to cholera, but to bad water, which his party avoided by boiling and skimming it. Despite his claim, Indians coming in contact with whites along the way suffered terribly from the disease.[25]

The army recognized from the beginning the potential for farming the North Platte Valley, thereby creating a local source of fresh vegetables, but the troops were too busy trying to shelter themselves to make any attempts at agriculture that first season. Although the soldiers planted a garden the spring of 1850, the results must not have been encouraging because the post quartermaster sent a request to Taos for a dozen New Mexican farmers, laborers, and herdsmen. He noted that the garden required proper irrigation, a skill mastered by the Hispanics of that region. Further, in an official attempt to improve hygiene, the secretary of war issued a directive the following year for all posts to plant vegetable gardens. No record of the results has been located, but his annual report admitted the general failure of gardening at most of the frontier posts.[26]

Regular mails still were not running by early April 1850, yet the residents at Fort Laramie anticipated service would begin at any time. Even though sutler Tutt had been appointed postmaster a month earlier, it would be summer before a mail contract was secured with the Independence, Missouri, firm of Samuel H. Woodson for $19,500 a year.[27] The irregular service notwithstanding, emigrants often found mail from home awaiting them at the store, and took advantage of this last opportunity to send letters to relatives and friends back in the "States."

By May, the seasonal migration began to appear at Fort Laramie, with Van Vliet recording the passing of one thousand people by the

---

[25] Coolidge, *Statistical Report*, 79–80; Van Vliet to Jesup, July 7, 1850, LS, FL; O. F. Davenport Letters; Coolidge, *Statistical Report*, 79–80.

[26] Van Vliet to Jesup, July 23, 1850, CCF. When scurvy broke out again at Fort Laramie during the winter of 1855–56, the commanding officer sent six wagons to Fort Kearny in March to bring back a supply of potatoes. Of the one thousand bushels shipped, only two hundred finally reached the post, and those were beginning to spoil. The garrison successfully grew a crop of potatoes in 1856, but the yield was small due to poor seed. Forty-two cases of scurvy were reported at the post in 1857–58. McDermott, "No Small Potatoes," 165–67.

[27] McCarty to Daugherty, April 4, 1850, Daugherty Papers, copy in vert. files, library, FLNHS. Woodson retained the first mail contract from 1850–1854. Gray, "Salt Lake Hockaday Mail," 12.

fourteenth. "They require considerable assistance in the way of repairs, which I render as far as it is in my power to do so . . . I burnt during the winter a large amount of [char]coal. Collected a large quantity of old iron which had been thrown away by the last emigration and prepared temporary shops for their use . . . Loads are generally lightened and rearranged at this place and such things as are not absolutely necessary are either sold or thrown away."[28]

Twenty-nine-year-old Lucena Parsons, an Illinois emigrant who visited the post early in August, wrote, "This morn went to the Fort to get some blacksmithing done but could not they have so much work. This is a pretty place to look at, it is so clean. There are 250 soldiers & some 12 families. They have a saw mill, one public house, one store . . . They are now building several fine frame buildings. They say they have 75 thousand pass here this season & some days there were 1500 here. There was some sickness among them & some deaths. There are hundreds of wagons left here which can be bought for a few dollars each from the soldiers."[29]

The post also afforded the only source of professional medical assistance between Fort Kearny and Fort Hall. During the second half of 1849, the surgeon treated four or five victims of accidental gunshot wounds, the result of their own carelessness, while four civilians died from various causes at the post during the following season. Because many emigrants took up the long journey ill-prepared, the army began stocking extra quantities of certain staples, such as flour, hams, bacon, and dried fruit, intended for sale to destitute travelers. The post was overrun with emigrants during the summer of 1850. Tutt's clerk, William A. McCarty, noted that some four hundred men came to the post during a single day. The crest of the wave passed quickly, however, and by July most of the travelers had moved beyond Fort Laramie. By summer's end, approximately fifty-two thousand people had trekked west, most of them seeking their fortunes in the gold fields of California.[30]

---

[28]Van Vliet to Jesup, May 14, 1850, CCF; Unruh, *Plains Across*, 120.

[29]Lucena Parsons, 1850, quoted in "Contemporary Descriptions of Fort Laramie," 4, typescript in vert. files, FLNHS.

[30]McDermott, "No Small Potatoes," 165; Unruh, *Plains Across*, 229. A contemporary account indicated that over nine thousand wagons and forty-two thousand people had passed Fort Laramie by July 1, 1850, and that by that time the emigration was "pretty well over" for that season. Van Vliet to Jesup, July 1, 1850, CCF.

The troops, meantime, were occupied with patrolling the road to Fort Kearny and with construction duties. Despite Major Sanderson's intention to finish the quarters before snowfall, his successor, Captain William Scott Ketchum, wrote just before Christmas that when Sanderson left in September, "not a single set of quarters was completed and that the soldiers were in canvas. Since that time, 'G' Co. 6th Infty has been comfortably quartered in one end of one of the large stables, & the two Rifle Cos, in a new building intended for one Company. The Infantry moved into quarters, one block, so as to accommodate four officers. This block still requires pillars to the porches, which are now being sawed, also a ceiling to the upper porches, and yards, the post for which are on hand, and the slabs being sawed."[31]

Ketchum's redoubled efforts also resulted in the completion of three canvas storehouses to protect supplies, a guardhouse at the northeast corner of the parade, and a kiln for firing bricks. Details of soldiers laid the foundation for another set of officers' quarters as well. With the arrival of Post Chaplain William Vaux in May, the need for housing had become critical. At that, progress was slow and the garrison was compelled to spend another winter in temporary and unfinished buildings.[32] Nevertheless, Fort Laramie was a permanent military installation and it would play an increasingly important role in shaping events on the northern plains.

---

[31]Ketchum to AAG, Mil. Dept. No. 7, December 23, 1850, v. 1, Orders, FL, RG 393.
[32]Masten to Jesup, February 5, 1851, LS, FL.

CHAPTER TWO

"The First to Make the Ground Bloody"

A lthough the overland route to California and Oregon may have represented the path of empire for Euro-Americans, it was the harbinger of a less promising future for Plains Indians. Observing with mounting anxiety the burgeoning cavalcade of emigrants and U.S. troops passing through the Platte River country during the late 1840s, the various tribes resisted any predisposition they may have had to challenge the interlopers.[1] By 1851, however, some of the tribesmen could no longer condone the ever-increasing depletion of game and other resources along the road. Alarmed, the once-friendly Northern Cheyennes were the first to openly resist the invasion through minor confrontations with the travelers, initially trading for things they needed, later demanding gifts of food and other goods as tolls for passage through their territory. Meanwhile, the Sioux remained comparatively passive; nevertheless, the government feared that it was only a matter of time until some incident, even intertribal warfare among the Indians, would spark open conflict with the whites.

Former trapper and trader Thomas Fitzpatrick, known to the Indians as Broken Hand after the explosion of a rifle left him crippled, had been appointed as Indian agent on the plains in 1846. Wintering at

---

[1]During the first two years of military occupation at Fort Laramie, only one isolated incident near Scott's Bluff resulted in the death of a white man at the hands of an Indian, and that murder was attributed to blind reprisal for the loss of the warrior's father to cholera. Major Sanderson, heading a detachment of Mounted Riflemen, proceeded to the village to investigate, but took no action when he learned that the Indians had exacted their own justice. Mackay to Jesup, August 14, 1849, LS, FL.

Bent's Fort on the Arkansas two years later, Fitzpatrick met with leaders of some of the southern tribes to discuss the potential for an accord intended to curtail intertribal conflicts throughout the Great Plains by defining tribal boundaries. He also thought the government should compensate the Indians for their loss of game. The agent suggested that the tribes gather for a grand council at some convenient point as soon as he could secure permission from the newly created Interior Department.[2] In March 1849 Fitzpatrick journeyed to St. Louis to propose his plan to Colonel David D. Mitchell, an ex–fur trader on the Upper Missouri and veteran of the Mexican War, who had been appointed as superintendent over the western Indians in 1841. Although Mitchell concurred with Fitzpatrick's idea, he lacked the necessary authority to approve it, and therefore urged Fitzpatrick to proceed to Washington to personally promote it at higher levels. Both the commissioner of Indian Affairs and the secretary of war enthusiastically embraced the proposal for a grand council, at the same time pointing out that such a conference required congressional sanction. In their opinion, there would be little opposition by the legislators. Meanwhile, Fitzpatrick returned to the plains with instructions to lay the groundwork for a conference the following year, taking with him five thousand dollars' worth of government supplies, which, when distributed among the Indians, would ensure their continued good will.

Although the Senate passed the legislation for a council in 1850, the bill stalled unexpectedly and died in the House of Representatives. Still, the Indians' faith in Fitzpatrick served to preserve the peace despite escalating emigration and its negative impacts on the buffalo and other natural resources along the Platte. After Congress eventually passed an appropriations bill that included one hundred thousand dollars to support the council, Fitzpatrick and Mitchell met at St. Louis and decided on Fort Laramie as the logical meeting place, with the conference to begin on September 1. Importantly, they also prevailed on the influential Jesuit missionary Father Pierre-Jean De Smet to induce the northern tribes to participate in the council and contribute to its goal, a treaty between them and the United States.

---

[2]Before the establishment of the Interior Department in 1849, Indian affairs were managed by the War Department. The Central Superintendency at St Louis dealt with all the tribes along the Rocky Mountains and the Oregon Route. Unruh, *Plains Across*, 221.

During subsequent months, Fitzpatrick trekked up the Arkansas spreading word along the way that the great council was to be a gathering like no other previously seen on the plains. Although the Cheyennes and Arapahoes readily agreed to go to Fort Laramie, the Kiowas and Plains Apaches refused to participate. Arriving at Fort Laramie a few weeks later, Fitzpatrick dispatched messengers to all the northern tribes, urging them to come to the council. A serious impediment to the future success of the treaty the government hoped to draft, however, was the omission of the tribes in southeastern Nebraska—the Pawnees, Omahas, Poncas, and other tribes generally friendly with the whites—that were being elbowed out of their traditional range by the more aggressive Sioux, Cheyennes, and Arapahoes. Exclusion of indigenous tribes from the treaty's land agreements not only would give their enemies the upper hand in claiming hunting rights, but would encourage further raiding against them. Mitchell realized the potential effects of such an oversight and at the last minute attempted to convince the Pawnees to accompany him to Fort Laramie. Learning of this move, the Sioux sent word welcoming their bitter enemies to attend but promised they would be attacked and destroyed immediately afterward. The Pawnees, intimidated, declined Mitchell's invitation to participate.[3]

In a show of military might, the secretary of the interior suggested the army assemble a large force of troops at Fort Laramie to impress the Indians, thereby subtly influencing them to agree to a binding peace. Army Headquarters, however, argued that the troops required for such a grandiose display were more urgently needed elsewhere. Adjutant General Roger Jones considered the present force of two companies of soldiers adequate to protect the commissioners, although he ordered an additional company of dragoons to accompany Colonel Mitchell from Fort Leavenworth to augment the Fort Laramie garrison. Mitchell's party, including high-level representatives from the *Missouri Republican* and the *New Orleans Picayune*, along with Robert Campbell, left Fort Leavenworth on July 25 with Company B, First Dragoons as escort.[4]

---

[3]McGinnis, *Counting Coup*, 85–88.

[4]A contemporary account lists the members of the party as George Knapp, owner, and B. Gratz Brown, correspondent, of the *Missouri Republican*. Lowe, *Five Years a Dragoon*, 60–62. Another names Colonel Chambers, editor of the *Republican*, along with H. C. King, of Georgia, and J. H. King of England in addition to Campbell, Kendall, and William. *Publications of the Nebraska State Historical Society*, 234–35 (hereinafter cited as *Nebraska Publications*).

Arriving at Fort Laramie in late August, the dragoons found that the livestock at the garrison as well as that of passing emigrants, had already depleted the vegetation for some distance around the post. To find adequate forage, they moved "four miles above the post, on the opposite side of the river . . . an amphitheater of rugged hills, the pure clear river with its pebbly bottom running gently by, fringed with willows, orchards of box elders in the bottoms, cedars, and pines upon the hills" to reestablish Camp Maclin, a bivouac the dragoons had used earlier that summer.[5]

As the dragoons marched upstream, they met an impressive array of Indians, numbering nearly five hundred lodges, already camped in the fort's vicinity to await the start of the council. Dragoon sergeant Percival G. Lowe remembered, "The plain between our camp and [Fort] Laramie was filled with Indian lodges, mostly Sioux, but here was a large camp of Cheyennes and Arapahoes."[6] With villages stretching along the valley both above and below the fort, the post was soon crowded with Indians whose main interest was visiting the sutler's store, which overflowed with men and women eager to trade for manufactured goods. Wisely, the army prohibited the sale of liquor, fearing it would ignite fights among the Indians and thereby ruin any chance of successful negotiations. Word nevertheless reached the post that James Bordeaux, one of several French traders married to Sioux women who resided in the area, was dispensing liquor at his establishment about eight miles below Fort Laramie. A search party sent to Bordeaux's place allegedly found only one pint of whiskey. Consequently, Fitzpatrick took no punitive action against him. If the agent in fact discovered a larger quantity, as he probably did, he diplomatically chose to turn a blind eye because of the trader's potential value as an ally against any future Indian conflict. Whatever the evidence, the point was made.[7]

---

[5]Lowe misspelled the name as "Macklin." The correct spelling derives from Major Sackfield Maclin, a paymaster whom Lowe's company escorted from Fort Leavenworth to Fort Laramie in June 1851. They used the same ground for their bivouac at that time, hence its christening in tribute to Maclin. Lowe, *Five Years a Dragoon*, 46–47, 62; Heitman, *Historical Register*, 1:676.

[6]Lowe, *Five Years a Dragoon*, 62. Sutler Tutt also reported about five hundred lodges of Cheyennes, Arapahoes, and Sioux in the vicinity. Tutt to Daugherty, August 22, 1851, Daugherty Papers, copy in McDermott File, FLNHS.

[7]Ibid.

Next to arrive were about sixty Shoshones (Snakes), riding down from the mountains of the Wind River country. Arrayed in all their ceremonial finery and led by their head chief and friend of the whites, Washakie, they made a magnificent appearance. Accompanying them was mountain man Jim Bridger, an old and trusted friend who would interpret for them at the council. Because of the intense mutual animosity between the Shoshones and the vastly more numerous plains tribes, they camped above the dragoons, creating a buffer between themselves and their enemies. Indeed, there was fresh resentment on the part of the Shoshones. Even though the various tribes had agreed to come in peace, a party of Cheyennes could not resist attacking the Shoshones en route, killing and scalping two men. As a precaution, half the dragoons were posted on guard to forestall further trouble.

While the Indians continued to congregate, swelling the camps with every passing day, Mitchell anxiously awaited the arrival of the overdue supply train from Fort Leavenworth bearing several tons of food and gifts for the tribesmen. The supplies were critical, for without presents the Indians would refuse to convene the talks, thus threatening the entire treaty process. Word had it that the train had left Kansas more than two and a half weeks earlier, yet there was still no sign of it. Mitchell therefore arranged to have several wagonloads of goods brought from Fort Laramie as an inducement for the Indians to begin the council. With so many Indians already camped near Fort Laramie, the already limited grazing was quickly exhausted for miles around and the odor of accumulated human and animal waste was overwhelming. With more tribes en route, it was obvious to Mitchell and Fitzpatrick that the council would have to be moved to another location, and quickly.

They selected the broad bottomlands of the Platte, near the mouth of Horse Creek, some thirty-five miles downstream. Not only would that area provide sufficient space, grass, and water for the large assemblage, Mitchell shrewdly calculated that it would shorten by two days the distance to be traveled by the tardy supply train. Runners carried word through the camps and on September 4 the great exodus to the new council site began. Two companies of soldiers led the way, followed by the dignitaries and the supply train. Behind them, riding and walking, came the Indians—men, women, children, and thousands of horses, along with packs of barking dogs—in a meandering cavalcade that stretched for miles down the valley. Two companies of Mounted Riflemen brought up the rear, leaving behind only one company to garrison the post.

The column reached the new location the following afternoon and began making camp. The infantry and a company of dragoons established their headquarters on the first terrace south of the Platte, just below the Horse Creek confluence, while the Mounted Riflemen camped above the tributary. The Sioux, Cheyennes, and Arapahoes were told they could erect their lodges above Horse Creek on either side of the river so long as they were not close to the troops. Prudently, the Shonshones were assigned the area below the creek adjacent to the headquarters bivouac and wagon park. Captain Ketchum designated the council site nearby and laid out a generous parade ground on the adjacent prairie.[8]

More Indians—including Gros Ventres, Mandans, Arikaras, Assiniboins, and Blackfeet—continued to swell the camps on the sixth, until there were nearly ten thousand Indians camped along the valley. The next day being Sunday, Mitchell informed the Indians that the council could not begin because it was the white man's "medicine day." Sioux and Cheyenne women proceeded to erect a semicircular pole-and-brush arbor for the council, with the traditional opening to the east. Feasting, visiting, and dancing continued throughout the day and into the night.

Next morning, the sharp report of a howitzer reverberating across the valley signaled the beginning of the treaty talks. From all directions, Indians filed to the great circle where headmen took their places around the arbor with men of lesser stature standing behind. Women and children occupied the ground outside the circle. Colonel David Mitchell opened the proceedings by acknowledging the universal professions of good faith, after which he explained the government's desire to compensate the tribes for the losses caused by the great migration of settlers.

---

[8]Lowe, *Five Years a Dragoon*, 67–68; *Nebraska Publications*, 236. Much of the description of the treaty council provided herein is drawn from Hill, "The Great Indian Treaty Council of 1851," 94–103, and Ghent, *Broken Hand*, 228–45.

He further explained that the "Great Father," as the president was called, wished to ensure the safety of both whites and Indians by establishing military posts along the road. More to the point, the tribes also would agree to adopt defined boundaries for their hunting grounds, thus eliminating the traditional rivalries that fueled unremitting warfare on the plains and threatened to embroil whites as well. Such a proposal challenged the very foundation of a culture in which men proved themselves as warriors and gained stature as tribal leaders. In a further contradiction to Indian mores, Mitchell stipulated that each tribe was to elect one head chief to act on its behalf. In return, each tribe would receive fifty thousand dollars in supplies annually, for a period of fifty years. The Indians, who chose their leaders by consensus, were undoubtedly puzzled by the superintendent's strange demands.

On the tenth of September, the camps were electrified by the news that the Crows, traditionally friendly to whites but staunch enemies of the Sioux, had been sighted coming down the valley after an eight-hundred-mile journey from the upper Yellowstone country. Assigned a place to camp, their leaders were immediately shown to the council circle to join the talks. Most of the discussions centered on the escalating poverty of the tribes and their desire to see the goods already promised, which still had not arrived. Father De Smet and Robert Campbell also arrived late that day, along with a delegation of more Crows, Minnetaris, Assiniboins, and Arikaras. De Smet's powerful influence over all the Indians did much to ameliorate tensions throughout the duration of the council.

The commissioners worked diligently during the following days to mediate discussions over tribal ranges, a difficult task because borders and boundaries were largely foreign concepts to the Indians. Although the respective tribes recognized certain general hunting regions, those boundaries had always been fluid, often changing as one tribe encroached into the territory of another to take game, horses, or captives. The Sioux had been particularly aggressive in this respect for more than half a century as they expanded onto the plains. Undaunted, Campbell, Bridger, and Fitzpatrick used their intimate knowledge of the mountains and rivers, as well as the usual haunts of the various tribes, to argue that game for all would be abundant and

gently guide the leaders to consensus. Day after day the talks continued, until disagreements were eventually resolved and the treaty document was prepared for signatures.

The commissioners and Indian leaders assembled again on the September 17 to conclude the agreement, even though there was as yet no
sign of the supply train from Fort Leavenworth. In its final form, the
treaty contained a number of provisions, chief among them that the
United States had the right to construct roads and military posts within
the respective Indian territories and that the Indians would make restitution for any wrongs committed against the people of the United
States while passing through their country. In addition, the assembled
nations consented to an "effective and lasting peace" through recognition of the boundaries laid out in the accord. In return, the government
would protect the Indians against depredations by Americans.[9]

Of particular significance to Fort Laramie was the territory specified
for the Sioux. Beginning at the mouth of White Clay River on the
Missouri, the line extended southwesterly to the forks of the Platte,
then followed up the North Platte as far as Red Butte, near present-
day Casper, Wyoming. From that point the boundary angled northeast, skirting the Black Hills, to the headwaters of Heart River, tracing that stream to the starting point on the Missouri, at present-day
Bismarck, North Dakota. In short, the Sioux were reserved an area
encompassing all of western Dakota Territory, Nebraska, and northeastern Wyoming, in recognition of their comparatively recent claim
to the Black Hills region.[10] The Cheyennes and Arapahoes would
inhabit the region south of Red Butte to the source of the Platte in the
Rocky Mountains, southward along the range to the headwaters of the
Arkansas, thence down that stream to the Cimarron Crossing of the
Santa Fe Trail. The line then extended back to the forks of the Platte.

With the Horse Creek treaty concluded, Mitchell was more anxious
than ever to know the whereabouts of that long-awaited ox train plod-

---

[9]Kappler, ed., *Indian Affairs: Laws and Treaties* 2: 594–95 (hereinafter cited as *Indian Affairs*).

[10]In the late eighteenth century, the Black Hills region was occupied by the Arapahoes, Crows,
and somewhat later, shared with the Cheyennes after Sioux pressure forced them from an agrarian subsistence east of the Missouri. Only during the 1820s did the Sioux invade that area,
claiming it as their own. McGinnis, *Counting Coup*, 10, 16, 102; Hassrick, *The Sioux*, 66–68;
Nadeau, *Fort Laramie and the Sioux*, 20–21.

ding up the road from Leavenworth. The Indians had cooperated with the whites, and now they demanded the goods that had been promised them. An increasingly nervous Mitchell continued stalling for time by compiling a list of all the Indian chiefs and headmen, attempting to arrange them in their relative order of influence within the respective bands and tribes, a process that consumed several more days. At length, the supply train pulled in on September 20. Distribution of gifts began with each leader being presented an officer's uniform, a saber, a presidential medal, and a certificate of good character. Mitchell rewarded each of the highest-ranking chiefs with the uniform of a major general, while lesser chiefs and headmen were issued uniforms of lower military ranks according to their importance in the respective tribes. Subsequently, the leader of each band was assigned an area where his portion of goods was piled. The members encircled the mounds of foodstuffs, cloth, beads, cooking utensils, clothing, and all types of trinkets to draw their shares. Satisfied that the word of the whites was honorable, tribe members began taking down their lodges and moving off in various directions, now in search of winter camps.

The 1851 Horse Creek treaty was doomed from the outset. Almost every provision was flawed, starting with the selection of chiefs designated to speak for entire tribes. Although in perfect accord with the white concept of political organization and authority, the document meant little to Indians subscribing to a complex system of leadership usually divided along lines of tribal domestic and war needs. Certainly, the seasoned mountaineers in attendance at the council appreciated this aspect of Indian society, yet they apparently neglected to point it out. Men influenced the affairs of the band by earning status through their accomplishments in war, demonstrations of sound judgment, and generosity to other members of the tribe, rather than by any notion of arbitrary rank. Just how the commissioners selected the head chiefs remains a mystery to historians today. Illustrating the government's lack of understanding was its assumption, for example, that a treaty had been concluded with all the Teton Sioux, when only three bands, Brulés, Oglalas, and Two Kettles, were actually represented at the council. Conquering Bear, named by the commissioners as chief of all the Sioux, knew full well that he spoke only for his own Brulés. In fact, three other

signatories also were Brulé chiefs. Another, representing the Yankton-
ais, belonged to the Nakota division of Sioux that resided far to the
northeast and had virtually no influence in the country traversed by the
Oregon Route. Yet, the wording of the fourth article of the treaty stated
that in the event of any depredations against any parties, the signers
agreed to make restitution "for any wrongs committed . . . by any band
or individual of their people," implying that *all* bands of the Teton Sioux
were bound by the agreement. That error alone rendered the treaty
unenforceable, a fact that would become apparent all too soon.[11]

While the agreement may have comforted the whites that emigrants
would not be molested, there was no way to enforce peace among the
disparate tribes. The Sioux, occupying the most critical portion of the
Oregon road as a result of their own expansion into the Platte River
region, posed the greatest threat to emigration—and any comprehensive peace hinged on their cooperation. Their continuing conquest of
additional territory kept them in conflict with neighboring tribes, particularly the Pawnees and Crows. Earlier differences with the
Cheyennes had been settled through an informal alliance and even
intermarriage between the two groups. Because the Sioux had
emereged as the most numerous and most powerful tribe on the
northern plains, and had demonstrated considerable success in domi-
nating a large region west of the Missouri, they had no motive to cease
the expansion they had begun decades earlier. Were that not enough
to derail the treaty, a little-noticed provision in it recognized that "the
aforesaid Indian nations do not hereby abandon or prejudice any right
or claims they may have to other lands; and further, that they do not
surrender the privilege of hunting, fishing, or passing over any of the
tracts of country heretofore described."[12] In short, there was nothing
to prohibit one tribe from trespassing on the lands of another. The
increasing competition for game, especially for the declining numbers
of buffalo, was in fact a central factor promoting intertribal warfare.

In late 1851, the commissioners forwarded the document to the Senate for ratification, a process requiring several months during which
the provisions were carefully reviewed and debated. An amendment

---

[11]Anderson, "The Controversial Sioux Amendment to the Fort Laramie Treaty of 1851," 211–12.
[12]Kappler, *Indian Affairs* 2: 595.

they added to the document unilaterally reduced the period of distributing annuities from fifty to only ten years, but with a presidential option to extend the payments for an additional five years. Although the Horse Creek treaty was ratified on May 24, 1852, the Senate wisely recommended withholding public proclamation until the Indians were given the opportunity to review and concur with the changes. Nearly a year passed before the concerned tribes were contacted, but eventually they too ratified the accord, though it is by no means clear that they fully comprehended the final version's drastic reduction of the government's obligations to them. The Indian Bureau, to its credit, purchased and delivered the annuity goods to the appropriate tribes in the fall of 1852, following Senate approval, rather than waiting until the revised and amended document actually reached the tribes the next spring. Acting under instructions from the commissioner of Indian affairs, agent Fitzpatrick informed the Indians that failure to approve the annuities amendment would result in withholding goods in the future. Although most of the Indians probably did not realize its implications for their cultural survival, the treaty also signaled the beginning of their complete dependency on the federal government.[13]

By the early 1850s, the military presence at Fort Laramie was unmistakable even to the most casual observer. An Oregon-bound traveler, for example, expressed the elation, even surprise, emigrants often experienced upon reaching the post:

When we came in sight of the fort it looked like a settlement of houses. Every one was straining his eyes to catch a glimpse of white settlements. The day we passed, Laramie was a very fine looking place. Though it was Monday we all stopped and went over to see. Our feelings were something like the sailor when [he] gets in port after a long voyage. There was a store, a grocery, several dwellings, and the fort and soldiers' quarters, which was a long shed or stable appearing building, and the magazine house. The fort [old Fort John] is a long hollow square about 30 feet high and walls about 20 inches thick, built of unburnt bricks; three or four cannon mounted on the walls. There are several small rooms on the inside of the square, and a

---

[13]Some historians have doubted the validity of the 1851 treaty because for a century afterward it was believed by many that the Indians had not been contacted to ratify the Senate amendment. Later evidence, however, proved that the various tribes did indeed approve the amendment. The question is conclusively resolved in Anderson, "Controversial Sioux Amendment."

kind of porch on the inside four or five feet of the top, so wide that six men can walk in abreast. Near this is the magazine house. It is under guard day and night. This squad of buildings is situated about two miles from the Platte, on the Laramie fork . . . There was about 60 soldiers stationed here when we passed. The whole squad of buildings seemed under guard when we were there. I presume this was done more for form than necessity. The soldiers are under absolute control by their officers. They are mostly boys and foreigners. They have blue caps, white pants and roundabouts. The outside seams of their pants are trimmed with blue ferriter [*sic*] (tape), blue patches on their shoulders and stripes of blue on the front of their caps.[14]

Reflecting the continuing development of the emigrant road, several enterprising local civilians formed a company in 1851 to construct a toll bridge spanning the Laramie near its mouth, which would accommodate emigrants and thereby avoid the dangers of fording the stream. Since the bridge, described by Post Commander Richard B. Garnett, a young second lieutenant, as "an insufficient structure," lay within the ten-mile-square military reservation, the army consented to its operation in return for free passage for government traffic and a share of the profits derived from civilian trains. The partnership, however, turned contentious when the army demanded that the bridge be repaired and made safe for its heavy freight wagons. "I perceived much animosity and harsh feelings among the contractors (which on one occasion proceeded to blows among some of them), as well as a great want of concert," Garnett wrote.[15] Whether or not the lieutenant was successful in his effort to affect the needed repairs became a moot point the next spring when the annual runoff from mountain snows collapsed the rickety structure and flushed the wreckage down the stream. Later that summer, the new post sutler, Seth E. Ward, and his partner, Henry F. Mayer, contracted with the army to build a replacement bridge over the Laramie just above its mouth. In exchange for the

---

[14]Silas W. Miller to Hugh Miller, November 24, 1852, typescript copy in vert. files, FLNHS. The term "roundabout" referred to a short, tight-fitting uniform jacket often called a shell-jacket. Although the army adopted a new uniform in 1851, Miller's description leaves no doubt that the Fort Laramie garrison was still garbed in the regulation clothing in use since 1839. Todd, *American Military Equipage*, 51; Steffen, *Horse Soldier* 1: 111–21. Unless otherwise noted, original spellings have been preserved in all quoted material.

[15]Garnett to Cooper, AG, USA, July 24, 1853, LS, FL.

exclusive right to maintain a bridge on the reservation, Ward agreed to pay the army 5 percent of the gross receipts.[16]

Bridging the deeper and more forceful North Platte with the material means at hand presented a greater engineering challenge than the Laramie River had been, as it seldom exceeded fifty yards in width. Over the years, trappers had used several fords on the Platte within a mile above the confluence to access Forts William, Platte, and John, and those best suited to wagons had been adopted by the first emigrants. Then, in 1849 or early 1850, the army installed a ferry, soon to be called the Platte Ferry, at the site of a ford frequently used by Mormon wagon trains and began charging a dollar to convey each wagon and team across. The ferry probably consisted of a flatboat connected to an overhead rope-and-pulley guideline, the boat being drawn across the stream by the force of the current and stabilized by fore and aft lines. The runoff of melting snow nevertheless made the crossing turbulent and hazardous in spring, just when the westward migration was heaviest. When the ferry sank on April 25, one man was drowned, and a subsequent swamping two days later almost claimed two more lives.[17]

By June 1853, eighty to one hundred lodges of Miniconjou Sioux (one of the seven Teton sub-tribes), came down from the Black Hills to join their Brulé and Ogalala relatives for the summer hunting season. They were camped on the north bank of the Platte not far from the ferry. Unlike the Oglalas and Brulés, the Miniconjous had not

---

[16]"Article of Agreement Between 1st Lieut. R. B. Garnett, 6th Regt. of Infantry and Seth E. Ward and Henry F. Mayer," July 16, 1853, LR, FL.; Garnett to Col. Samuel Cooper, AG, USA, July 24, 1853, transcript in vertical files, FLNHS; Mayer to commanding officer, Fort Laramie, N.T., March 5, 1860, Hunton Collection, Wyo. State Archives.

[17]"The 1850 Overland Diary of Dr. Warren Hough," 211. Thunder Bear, a Sioux, testified that the ferry was about where the bridge stands today; MSS 57, box 2, Walter M. Camp Collection, Brigham Young University. That the traditional crossing of the Platte, at or near the bridge site, was used for some time prior to the arrival of the army is borne out by Quartermaster Aeneas Mackay. He stated that when he and an escort of Mounted Riflemen, with wagons, departed for Fort Pierre on August 17, 1849, "we crossed the Platte immediately at the Fort and proceeded in a N. Easterly direction." Mackay to Jesup, November 1, 1849, LS, FL, copy in vert. files, FLNHS; a new ferry was established at the crossing of the North Platte under contract with ex-sergeant Enoch Raymond & Co. on May 9, 1854. Raymond was obligated to keep a good flat boat, manned by not less than two men, and not to sell liquor or goods. The army received 5 percent of the gross revenue on tolls collected; Articles of Agreement between Enock W. Raymond & Co. and 1st Lieutenant R. B. Garnett, May 9, 1854, LR, FL.

inhabited that part of the country on a regular basis and therefore had no established relationship with the white traders in the vicinity of Fort Laramie. However, this band, led by Little Brave, had been in the Platte country from time to time during the previous two years. Not long after their appearance at the crossing, Miniconjou warriors began harassing passing emigrants, obstructing their way by riding in front of the wagons, and extorting them for presents in return for their safety. Emboldened by their earlier successes at intimidating the whites, one warrior seized an emigrant, rifled his pockets, and found some letters, which he ground into the dirt with his foot.

Soon thereafter, Sergeant Enoch W. Raymond, in charge of a vegetable garden near the crossing, became involved in an altercation with the unruly Sioux. En route to Fort Laramie on June 15, Raymond discovered upon his arrival at the Platte that several Miniconjous had strong-armed the civilian ferryman and commandeered the boat. Raymond, acting alone, immediately dispersed the warriors, took possession of the barge, and reported the incident to Lieutenant Garnett. As the sergeant was returning to camp later that day, however, he found the Indians once again in control of the ferry. Raymond coerced them into giving it up and, according to a passing emigrant, refused a request by one of the Indians to be taken across in the boat. When Raymond reached midstream, the offended warrior fired his musket, the ball striking the water near the skiff. Whether the Indian intended to hit the soldier or merely register his displeasure will never be known, but the sergeant reported it to Garnett as an act of aggression.[18]

Garnett, who would later wear the stars of a Confederate general and be killed at the Battle of Gettysburg, concluded that continued indulgence of the unruly Indian element would only encourage the young warriors to make further trouble. He therefore ordered Brevet Second Lieutenant Hugh B. Fleming to proceed to the village with a

---

[18]The best account of the incident written by an emigrant is in Maria Parsons Belshaw and George Belshaw, *Crossing the Plains*. Maria Belshaw apparently talked with someone having personal knowledge of the incident, who faithfully related the story to her when the Belshaw Train camped near the crossing of North Platte on June 16. The military reports and Belshaw's account are in close agreement. It is worth noting that both Maria and her father were concerned for the safety of their party during that night and extra guards were posted. Less descriptive accounts of the incident are found in the entry for June 23, *Diary of James Woodworth*; James Galloway journal, vertical files, FLNHS.

detachment of soldiers for the purpose of arresting the culprit and bringing him back to the post. In the event the Indians refused to surrender the man, Garnett authorized Fleming to seize two or three hostages for bargaining purposes.[19]

Young Fleming, only a year out of West Point and eager to prove himself, assembled a twenty-two man detachment from G Company, Sixth Infantry, the only unit garrisoning Fort Laramie at that time.[20] Assistant Surgeon Charles Page accompanied the little column as it marched out of the fort that evening en route to the village. Aware that post interpreter Lucien Auguste was residing with his Sioux wife in the village, Fleming sent Doctor Page ahead with instructions to notify Auguste of his mission. Arriving at the Miniconjou camp a short time later, Fleming directed the interpreter to locate headman Little Brave and inform him that he was to turn over the man who had fired at Raymond, or face arrest himself. Auguste discovered, however, that the chief was not in the camp. Undaunted by that revelation, Fleming then peremptorily demanded that the entire band surrender, a command the villagers refused to obey.

Instructing Sergeant Raymond and four men to remain at his side, the lieutenant immediately dispatched the remaining soldiers to form a cordon around the village. Meantime, Fleming's group moved to the center of the village. As the soldiers advanced, the Indians suddenly bolted toward a nearby ravine, firing at the troops as they ran. Fleming's men promptly returned fire, driving the Indians from their posi-

---

[19]Robert Brooke Garnett, a Virginian, attended the U.S. Military Academy from 1836 to 1841. Upon graduation, he was appointed a second lieutenant in the Sixth Infantry and served with the regiment throughout the Mexican-American War. He received his captaincy in 1855, but resigned his commission to join the Confederate States Army six years later. As a brigadier general, he was killed in action at the Battle of Gettysburg; Heitman, *Historical Register*, 1: 447. Garnett's subordinate, Hugh Brady Fleming, graduated from West Point in June 1852, after which he was appointed a brevet second lieutenant pending a permanent assignment. Congress confirmed his appointment on June 9, 1853, less than a week prior to the Platte Ferry encounter, and in all probability, word of it had not yet reached the post. Fleming continued to serve in the Regular Army until his retirement in 1870; ibid., 424.

[20]Only Company G, Sixth Infantry, garrisoned Fort Laramie at that time. Sergeant Raymond and five privates were camped at the kitchen garden approximately a mile north of the post, while twenty-one men were siphoned off on extra or daily duty. Accordingly, Garnett had only two sergeants, three corporals, two musicians, and twenty-five privates available for duty. Post Returns for August 1853, Sixth Infantry, Returns from U.S. Army Regular Infantry Regiments, RG 94, NA, M665, roll 67 (hereinafter cited as Returns, Sixth Infantry, with month).

tion in only a few minutes. Four or five Indians reportedly fell during the brief nighttime skirmish, while the soldiers suffered no casualties. Although the troops had failed to seize the guilty warrior, they had managed to capture two women who were afterward jailed at the fort.[21]

The next morning, Garnett dispatched Auguste to bring Little Brave to the fort to discuss the incident, but the interpreter discovered that the villagers had made a hasty departure downstream during the night. Word reached Little Brave nevertheless, whereupon he and approximately sixty of his men warily returned to Fort Laramie a few days later to confer with Garnett. The lieutenant, firm in his approach, informed the Miniconjous that although he regretted having to kill any of their people, he supported the actions of his subordinate, emphasizing that "under similar circumstances, I should always act precisely in the same manner."[22] The chief conceded that the army's reaction may have been justified, according to white custom, and he was willing to leave it at that. However, when Little Brave demanded a gift to seal the bargain according to Sioux custom, Garnett refused, reasoning that such a gesture would acknowledge the Sioux as the aggrieved party. He maintained that the Indians had initiated the trouble by harassing the emigrants and subsequently shooting at a member of his command. Garnett insisted that the army's relationship with the Miniconjous depended entirely on their future conduct. Nev-

---

[21]The number of Indian casualties reported varies from one account to another. Fleming, who should have been in the best position to know, stated that he saw two killed near him, and his men reported three or four others killed; Fleming to Garnett, June 16, 1853, LR, FL (hereinafter cited as Fleming report). Both Maria and George Belshaw, writing in separate journals, recorded five killed and two wounded. Maria additionally reported the two prisoners, Belshaw and Belshaw, *Crossing the Plains*, entries June 16. Galloway, writing on June 16, also reported five killed, Galloway journal. An anonymous correspondent to the *St. Louis Republican*, who resided at the fort, asserted that four were killed and two were wounded. This person also provided other details which I have incorporated in this account. Unidentified newspaper article, n.d., in vertical files, FLNHS. Henry Allyn recorded the highest number, six killed, while Benjamin Owen and James Woodworth set the number at three or four, *Allyn Journal*; Owen, *My Trip*; *Diary of James Woodworth*.

[22]The army's version of the incident at the ferry is taken from Garnett to Major F. N. Page, AAG, June 30, 1853, LS, FL, and Fleming's report. A subsequent report concerning the Grattan affair states that "nearly all the warriors were absent" from Little Brave's camp at the time the soldiers arrived. This suggests that only a few warriors were left behind to protect the families, therefore Fleming had the upper hand; Captain Ed. Johnson to Brevet Lieutenant Colonel William Hoffman, October 10, 1855, ARSW, 1856, 22.

ertheless, as a gesture of good will he released the captives. Maria Parsons Belshaw, member of an emigrant train that had passed Little Brave's band going in the opposite direction, asserted that "the Indians no more look smiling, but have a stern solumn [*sic*] look."[23]

In reality, had the Miniconjous desired, they could have easily exacted vengeance for the attack by ambushing any of several outlying parties of soldiers, such as the detachment working at the post garden, as well as hay cutters and herd guards in the vicinity of Fort Laramie. Also in the immediate area were numerous emigrant trains. All were vulnerable, and Garnett's small garrison of infantry would have been hard-pressed to prevent such attacks or to retaliate. Taking no chances, the Belshaw train, an emigrant party camped about two miles from the fort, posted sixteen guards on each of two shifts that night. That the Sioux refrained from making a counterattack suggests they had no desire to further escalate hostilities and were willing to maintain the peace. In fact, when Garnett met with Conquering Bear the day after the fight, the Brulé chief dismissed the affair, characterizing the visiting Miniconjous as interlopers who were not to be trusted.[24]

Although the Platte Ferry skirmish did not result in further armed confrontations between the army and the Sioux in the near term, it nonetheless conveyed a clear message to the Indians, and it established a precedent in the minds of the officers at Fort Laramie. The troops had not previously exhibited overt hostile intent toward the Sioux, but the incident demonstrated to the local tribes that the army could, and would, react with deadly force to comparatively minor provocation. Despite the deceptively passive behavior of the Sioux in the immedi-

---

[23]Quotation from Belshaw and Belshaw, *Crossing the Plains*, entry June 16.

[24]Thus far unsubstantiated is a statement by Maria Belshaw on June 22 that "a husband, wife, and two children were murdered on Monday the 20th near the Fort on the south side of Platte River. The alarm was given at the Fort, the soldiers came and killed one Indian [and] wounded one. There were four in the company. They took the dead bodies and the team to the Fort." Ibid., entry June 22. No mention of this event is in the post records, and I found only one other emigrant diary that contained anything similar. On June 16, Jotham Newton recorded, "We are now in the Black Hills. A man and his wife and child were killed yesterday." Newton, "Trip to California Overland, 1853," ms., Bancroft Library, copy at FLNHS. If Newton's date is correct, these murders would have occurred *prior* to the skirmish at the Miniconjou village on the evening of June 15. It stretches the imagination to think that Garnett would have failed to add the murder of innocent emigrants to his justification for sending Fleming to the village. In any event, Newton recorded the alleged murders a week before Belshaw made her entry.

ate aftermath of the confrontation, resentment simmered in the camps along the Platte. When agent Fitzpatrick delivered the revised Horse Creek Treaty to the Sioux three months later, the headmen confided to him that the very presence of soldiers at Fort Laramie was objectionable. The role of the troops, according to the chiefs' understanding of the treaty, they declared, was primarily to protect the Indians, but as one indignant leader exclaimed, "now the soldiers of the great father are the first to make the ground bloody."[25] The contradiction in intent so angered the Sioux, in fact, that they initially refused to accede to the modified treaty. Only through Fitzpatrick's diplomatic coaxing, and Garnett's personal reiteration of his motives for sending soldiers to Little Brave's camp, did the headmen grudgingly affix their marks to the document. Although the Lakotas were ostensibly appeased, the relationship had been irreparably damaged and the Sioux would thereafter be wary of the U.S. army.

For the army, Fleming's skirmish established a false impression that a comparatively small force of soldiers, putting up a bold front, could intimidate a superior number of Sioux. That mindset would have disastrous consequences at Fort Laramie just fourteen months later when the post would be commanded, ironically, by none other than Second Lieutenant Hugh B. Fleming.

Despite the seemingly amicable settlement of the affair, Fleming's attack marked the first breech in the formerly harmonious relationship between the army and the Teton Sioux. The spilled blood created an atmosphere of mutual distrust and heightened tension at Fort Laramie, warning signs that should have been heeded by higher military authority, but were ignored. If the example set at Platte Ferry inspired the officers at Fort Laramie with a sense of overconfidence in their arms, then it was equally instructive for the Sioux, who were not inclined to be so tolerant a second time.

---

[25]That the garrison at Fort Laramie did not fully trust the Sioux is revealed in the agent's request to Captain Michael E. Van Buren, temporarily camped nearby during the September council, to remain there with his two companies of Mounted Riflemen "lest any accidental disorder should arise." Fitzpatrick to Alfred Cumming, November 19, 1853, *Annual Report of the Commissioner of Indian Affairs,* 1853, 366–67 (hereinafter cited as *ARCIA* with year).

CHAPTER THREE

"THE UNFORTUNATE AFFAIR"

The early 1850s marked the high tide of westward emigration. In 1852 alone, some seventy thousand people tramped past Fort Laramie, and over half that number arrived the following season. In the six years after counting began, more than a quarter of a million Americans traveled the road seeking their fortunes or new beginnings in Oregon, California, and Utah. The Oregon Route also was marked by the dust clouds raised by the enormous ox-drawn government freight wagons of Brown and Russell and of David Waldo—626 loads during one year from Leavenworth to Forts Kearny and Laramie.[1]

Monthly mail coaches also plied the trail in an initial attempt to link the nation with its new territories. The summer of 1854 witnessed the letting of a new transcontinental mail contract to William M. F. McGraw and John Reeside to replace Woodson's Salt Lake mail runs. McGraw and Reeside were joined in the venture by the Hockaday brothers, John and Isaac, who initiated passenger service in conjunction with carrying the mail by using two vehicles, a light wagon for the mail and a coach for passengers. By July, McGraw had built six relay stations between the Big Blue River in Kansas and Fort Bridger, with one of those situated about a mile below Fort Laramie near Ward and Mayer's bridge. The stations provided changes of teams, along with meals, but on the long stretches in between, the drivers and passengers camped out.[2]

---

[1]Unruh, *Plains Across,* 120; Walker, *Wagonmasters,* 237.
[2]Gray, "The Salt Lake Hockaday Mail," 12.

Despite the great volume of traffic on the road, the various Sioux bands abided by the treaty insofar as not opposing the emigrants or stage drivers. It was well known, however, that the Indians had become beggars of the first order, and would turn surly when travelers were not forthcoming with sugar, coffee, or other goods to assure their safe passage. So prevalent had the practice become that departing emigrants were advised to purchase extra quantities of food for that purpose. The army, meantime, had become so secure in its belief that the treaty would insure the peace that its two companies of Mounted Riflemen were transferred from Fort Laramie immediately thereafter, leaving only one company of infantry at that vital location. Noting this, Commissioner of Indian Affairs John W. Whitfield remarked that "the military posts located in this agency are perfect nuisances. The idea that one company of infantry can furnish aid and protection to emigrants who pass through this agency is worse than nonsense. They can protect themselves no further than their guns can reach; they have no effect upon the Indians so far as fear is concerned; neither respect nor fear them; and as to protecting the traveler on the road, they are of no more use than so many stumps."[3]

The clash at Platte Ferry the year before should have sounded a warning to the army, but if anyone heard it, the signal was not heeded. The combination of under-strength garrisons and young, inexperienced officers was to prove tragic for both the army and the Indians during coming years.

August witnessed the passage of the last trickle of emigrant trains that had jumped off from the Missouri River late that season. The Sioux had gathered near Fort Laramie in July to claim the annuity goods that had been recently deposited at the trading post managed by J. P. B. Gratiot, five miles down the Platte.[4] The little fort was ideally situated on the river's south bank, just where the bluffs forced the trains to pass near the front gate of the place. This post, constructed by the American Fur Company after the sale of Fort John, actually was

---

[3]*ARCIA*, 1855, 95.

[4]The train carrying the annuity goods accompanied a Mormon train, sometimes traveling ahead of the Mormons and at other times with or behind them. Apparently, the government train pulled ahead by a couple of days prior to reaching the American Fur Company post because the supplies had been delivered before the Mormons' arrival. Lydia D. Alder, "The Massacre at Fort Laramie," 636.

owned by the old plains trader Pierre Chouteau, Jr., but was known locally as the Gratiot Houses. That summer J. B. Didiar managed the place for Gratiot, who had returned to the comforts of St. Louis. Charles Gereau, a resident of the Indian country for many years, who would later serve as post interpreter at Fort Laramie, clerked in the store.[5] While Oglalas camped on the riverbottom not far below the Gratiot Houses, the Brulé Sioux, under the leadership of head chief Conquering Bear (also, Bear That Scatters), established their village adjacent to a trading house owned by James Bordeaux, located about three miles downstream from Chouteau's. The village, composed of two hundred to three hundred lodges arrayed in a great circle opening to the east, lay on gently sloping land just north of the road and about three hundred yards from Bordeaux's house. Since the annuity goods could not be issued until agent Whitfield arrived from St. Louis, the hungry Indians waited, but were growing more impatient each day.

As a train of Mormon converts passed by Bordeaux's on August 18, a footsore cow strayed into the nearby Brulé camp. Abandoned animals were a common occurrence along the road, thus a visiting Miniconjou thought nothing of killing and butchering the serendipitous gift. Some contemporary accounts assert that the warrior first shot an arrow at the passing herder, then dispatched the animal in retribution for a relative killed in the Platte Ferry skirmish the previous year. That both Lieutenant Fleming and Lewis Dougherty later corroborated that part of the incident lends credence to that version of the story. In any event, the train proceeded to Fort Laramie where the cow's owner filed a complaint with young Fleming, then commanding the post.[6]

---

[5]By the 1860s, the old post was owned by James Beauvais of St. Louis. It was reportedly located just below the five-mile boundary of the military reservation in the N 1/2 of SE 1/4, Sec. 6, T25N, R63W. In 1918 the site was said to be at the headgate of the Grattan Ditch, and was then eroding into the river, transcribed notes, 263, Walter M. Camp Collection, Harold B. Lee Library; Deposition by J. B. Didiar, August 3, 1855, Choutous Manuscript Collection, copy in vertical files, FLNHS (hereinafter cited as Didiar deposition).

[6]This statement was offered by J. H. Reed, a visiting civilian convalescing in Grattan's quarters. He had the opportunity to speak with Indian witnesses after the affair. Unless otherwise cited, most of the details of the Grattan incident related herein are drawn from a series of official interviews and reports contained in *ARSW*, 1856. That the Miniconjou man was seeking revenge for relatives killed near the Platte Ferry is supported by Lewis B. Dougherty to John B. Dougherty, August 29, 1854, R. H. Miller Papers, Kansas City Public Library, copy in vert. files, FLNHS. Dougherty was a clerk in the sutler's store at the time of the incident, which gave him the opportunity to speak with Indians who had been in the camp.

Later that day, Conquering Bear came to the fort to explain the incident from his perspective and offered to make amends. In his discussion with Fleming, Conquering Bear acknowledged that the Miniconjou band had "bad hearts" towards the whites, resulting from the ferry incident, and had committed depredations in the vicinity of former Missourian John Richard's toll bridge across the North Platte near Red Butte, about 130 miles west of Fort Laramie. Conquering Bear explained that he and his Brulés had no desire to be implicated in the killing of the cow simply because the perpetrator happened to be visiting their village at the time. Conquering Bear pointed out that the Miniconjous had only two or three friends in the Brulé camp and the chief felt certain that if the soldiers would come for the warrior, he would surrender. Fleming declined, however, expressing his desire to defer the matter until Agent Whitfield arrived to adjudicate the matter. The chief seemed content with that and left.[7]

Swayed by the insistence of Brevet Second Lieutenant John L. Grattan to settle the matter by force, Fleming reconsidered his course of action. The next day he ordered Grattan to take twenty men to arrest the warrior and bring him back to the post to await Whitfield. Since Conquering Bear had informed Fleming that the Miniconjous occupied only a few lodges in the camp, the lieutenant assumed the more numerous Brulés would not oppose Grattan's actions. Moreover, his own experience of the previous summer convinced him that the Indians would submit to a strong show of force. Having only a single infantry company at his disposal, Fleming augmented Grattan's detachment with two twelve-pounder howitzers, one a mountain gun and the other a larger field piece, to ensure the intimidation was complete. Fleming purportedly admonished Grattan to use his own discretion in the event the Indians refused to surrender the man, stipu-

---

[7]A Sioux version, although second hand, declared that Bear offered the Mormon his choice of any horse in the chief's personal herd. When Fleming refused to settle the matter that way, Bear supposedly told the officer to come get the man himself, declaring, "That is all I have to say. My band is not going to help you." Frank Salaway, November 3, 1906, Jensen, ed., *Ricker Interviews*, 1: 333 (hereinafter cited as Salaway interview). If the exchange occurred as described, Fleming omitted these details from his official report. *ARSW*, 1856. Man Afraid of His Horses, an Oglala, testified that Conquering Bear offered a mule in payment for the cow, but this did not occur until after Grattan arrived at the camp the next day. Captain Ed. Johnson to Brevet Lt. Col. William Hoffman, October 10, 1855, ibid., 24.

lating that he was not to bring on a fight unless he was certain of success, that is, by confining it to the few Miniconjous present in Conquering Bear's camp.

John Grattan was perhaps the most ill-suited man in the entire army to be assigned such a delicate and potentially volatile task. A twenty-four-year-old native of Vermont, he had been appointed to the U.S. Military Academy in 1848 and graduated five years later. A month after being appointed as a brevet (or extra) second lieutenant, he was assigned to the garrison at far-off Fort Laramie to await his commission. Grattan was full of bravado and his disdain for Indians soon became common knowledge around the post. Even Chaplain William Vaux, who expressed his reluctance to criticize the young officer after his death, felt that Grattan "had an unwarrantable contempt of Indian character, which frequently manifested itself in my presence and at my quarters; and often, at the latter place, have I reproved him for acts which I conceived highly improper, such as thrusting his clenched fist in their faces, and threatening terrible things if ever duty or opportunity threw such a chance his way."[8]

On other occasions, Grattan had told J. H. Reed, a civilian with whom he temporarily shared quarters, that "if it was ever necessary to fight Indians when they were in their village, that he would place his artillery some three or four hundred yards from their village, and run the risk of their driving him from his position." Fleming's experience at the ferry the previous summer served as a strong influence on Grattan's notions of how he might handle a similar situation. A reviewing officer later concluded: "It was after this occurrence that Lieutenant Grattan solicited, and had the promise made him, that, on the occurrence of any other difficulties, he, Lieutenant Grattan, should be sent against the Indians. It is said that he considered that the officer in command on this occasion [Lieutenant Fleming] had distinguished himself, and he was anxious for a like occasion. The occasion presented itself, and he claimed the honor. He earnestly and strongly urged it, and he was sent as above stated."[9]

Rather than assembing the twenty men his superior had authorized,

[8]Chaplain William Vaux to Col. William Hoffman, October 4, 1855, ibid., 26–27.
[9]Johnson to Hoffman, October 10, 1855; ibid., 22–23.

Grattan violated his instructions by calling for volunteers to report for dangerous duty. To Grattan's delight, two noncommissioned officers and twenty-seven men responded. As Grattan's detachment made their preparations, Man Afraid of His Horses, an Oglala warrior, watched with considerable foreboding. Ordnance Sergeant Leodegar Schnyder, a seventeen-year veteran who had arrived at Fort Laramie as a member of the Sixth Infantry in 1849 and was destined to become a fixture at the post for the next three decades, issued munitions from the stone magazine. Aware of the sergeant's experience, Grattan invited Schnyder to accompany his old comrades on the coming adventure—an offer Schnyder wisely declined because, as he later acknowledged, he had no confidence in the inexperienced lieutenant's judgment. While his men readied themselves, Grattan put on a swaggering performance at the sutler's store, bragging to those present that he hoped to have a fight and that with only ten men he could whip any number of Sioux.[10]

With the men crowded aboard the wagon and the two gun limbers, Grattan directed his detachment to start down the road at about three o'clock in the afternoon, assuring the men he would catch up with them. Accompanying the lieutenant was Lucian Auguste, the post interpreter known to the Sioux as Wayus or Yuse. Two others also went along unofficially—Man Afraid of His Horses and Obridge Allen, a veteran emigrant guide who had arrived at Fort Laramie only the previous day. Auguste, having no mount of his own, borrowed a horse from sutler Ward and while it was being saddled for him, the Frenchman went to the store to bolster his nerve with whiskey. There he encountered Grattan, who continued his antics by chiding Auguste to get moving, while playfully prodding him with his sword. Eventually the four men rode out with a highly excited Grattan proclaiming in mock heroics that he would "conquer them or die."[11]

The little expedition rumbled across the new bridge over the Laramie

---

[10]Ibid., 22; Lloyd McCann, "The Grattan Massacre," 9–10; for a complete biography of Sergeant Schnyder, see McDermott, "Fort Laramie's Silent Soldier: Leodegar Schnyder," *Visions of a Grand Old Post*, 120–32.

[11]The interpreter's identity has often been corrupted as "Lucien," however the name used herein was provided by his daughter. Julia Clifford interview with Walter M. Camp, January 12, 1920, Ellison Papers, DPL; Johnson to Hoffman, *ARSW*, 1856, 23; McCann, *Grattan Massacre*, 11n21.

and proceeded down the emigrant road toward the villages. Lucian Auguste soon produced a bottle of liquor and began indulging freely. As Grattan's men ascended the bluffs overlooking the Platte, they were met with an impressive sight, one that should have given Grattan pause to reconsider. Before them lay the Oglala camp, stretching along the river about three-quarters of a mile to the left of the road. A mile and a half farther down, surrounding Bordeaux's trading post, was the great Brulé circle—some six hundred lodges (approximately 4,200 people) in all. An astonished Allen gasped, "Lieutenant, do you see how many lodges there are?" "Yes," Grattan replied, "but I don't care how many there are; with thirty men I can whip *all* the Indians this side of the Missouri." Thereupon, Man Afraid also implored Grattan to reconsider, but the lieutenant turned a deaf ear to the warrior's entreaty.

By the time the troops reached the Gratiot Houses, Auguste was becoming intoxicated, and with good reason. When Grattan made a rest stop at the trading post, the interpreter took the opportunity to procure more whiskey, as did some of the soldiers. Before long, the Frenchman found his courage, brandishing his pistol and loudly "threatening to give the Indians a new set of ears." Some of the American Fur Company employees tried to reason with him, to no avail. A French-speaking soldier in the detachment told a half-blood Oglala working at the post that he thought the whole affair was foolishness and feared Auguste would get them all killed.[12]

Before leaving the Gratiot Houses, Lieutenant Grattan ordered the soldiers to load their muskets and fix their bayonets, and a short distance below the store he paused to give the men a pep talk, outlining his expectations of them in the event of a skirmish. He instructed them to listen only to his commands and those of the sergeant, and "When I give the order, you may fire as much as you damned please." Grattan concluded by saying, "Men, I don't believe we shall have a fight; but *I hope to God we may have one.*"[13] Meantime, Auguste began running his horse back and forth to wind the animal, at the same time slurring threats at the Indians. Allen suggested that the interpreter might need all of his horse's speed before the day was out, to which

---

[12]Salaway interview; statement by Man Afraid of His Horses, Ricker Tablets.
[13]Johnson to Hoffman, October 10, 1855, *ARSW*, 1856, 23; Statement by Obridge Allen, ibid., 8.

the inebriated Frenchman paid no heed. Grattan and his men proceeded down the road. Behind them, at a distance, a stream of Oglalas
followed and began filing off to the north, toward the river. Beyond
the camp circle, the men could be seen driving in the horses, an ominous sign of coming combat.

Oblivious to the Indians' behavior, Grattan led his men directly to
Bordeaux's house, situated a short distance north of the road. As they
approached, unsuspecting though inquisitive villagers began walking
up from the nearby lodges. Auguste rode out to meet them, shouting,
"We have come to fight, not to talk. Last summer we killed some of
you, but now we have come to wipe you out; you are women. If you
want to fight, come on; we have come to drink your blood and eat
your *liver raw!*" While Auguste ranted, Bordeaux came out of his
house and immediately told Lieutenant Grattan to silence him, or
there would be trouble. Bordeaux felt certain that if the interpreter
could be squelched, the matter could be settled amicably, but at this
Grattan was unsuccessful. Most of the Oglala villagers, meanwhile,
had positioned themselves near the south bank of the Platte, where
they could better observe what was happening. Another half-dozen
people mounted a low, but commanding, eminence about a quarter of
a mile west of the trading post.[14]

Bordeaux sent word requesting Conquering Bear to meet with
them, and in a few minutes the chief appeared, somewhat puzzled to
see the troops at his camp. Speaking through Bordeaux, Grattan
informed the chief that he had come to take the man who had killed
the cow and that he was there to take the offender back to the fort,
where he would be held until the agent came to resolve the dispute.
Conquering Bear procrastinated by telling Grattan that before he
could give an answer, he had to return to his lodge to get appropriately
attired in the general's uniform presented to him at the treaty council.
Somewhat later, Conquering Bear returned, along with three other

---

[14]This group included Charles Gereau, from the American Fur Company post, and Frank Salaway, a half-blood Oglala. These men, who had provided themselves with a telescope, had a
ringside seat above the village. Salaway interview, 334. The hill on which they stood is about four
hundred yards south of the Grattan burial monument and is approximately fifty feet higher than
the surrounding land. When I visited the site, it lay within a cornfield. The Oregon Trail passed
between this eminence and the village. Author's note based on personal examination of the site
and a sketch map drawn from memory by Salaway in 1906.

headmen—Big Partisan, Little Thunder, and Man Afraid, who had already exerted his influence to try to resolve the situation peacefully. They had no sooner arrived when a messenger from the camp ran up to say that High Forehead, the accused Miniconjou, refused to be handed over to the soldiers, and was waiting in his lodge, armed and prepared to resist to the death. Conquering Bear, consequently, told Grattan that he had no authority over a guest in his camp, therefore he could not force High Forehead to surrender.

The lieutenant swore angrily to Bordeaux, "You tell the Bear that I have come down here for that man, and I'll have him or die."[15] Grattan then told the chief to point out the lodge occupied by High Forehead, and ordered his men to load the two howitzers. As the troops advanced toward the circle of lodges, the assembled Brulés withdrew to the village. Conquering Bear went along, mounted double behind Auguste. Just inside the circle of lodges, a second Indian messenger confronted Grattan, informing him that High Forehead would not be taken alive. The lieutenant turned to his men to repeat his intentions, at the same time cautioning them to remain cool and to fire only on his order.

Bordeaux, who had warily accompanied the lieutenant into the camp, warned the chiefs that they had better present the man, but the leaders objected on grounds that it was customary to make such a demand four times before taking any action. Grattan steadfastly refused, as tensions mounted on both sides. Thoroughly familiar with Indian psyche, Bordeaux advised the young officer that he was dealing with a very dangerous situation and that if he advanced any farther, he had better be ready to fight. Grattan displayed more cockiness than good sense by confidently replying that he had two revolvers with twelve shots. With that, Bordeaux turned back toward his store, remarking that the lieutenant had better un-holster his pistols. All the while, Auguste continued to taunt and harangue the Indians who remained deeper in the village.

Back at the trading post, Bordeaux climbed atop a robe press (a large machine used for compressing and bundling cured buffalo robes) to get a better view of the rapidly unfolding events. From that vantage point, he watched Grattan lead his men to the far side of the circle and there deploy them in a single rank spaced about sixty yards from the Indian

---

[15]Statement by Obridge Allen, *ARSW*, 1856, 8–9.

lodges. Grattan positioned the two artillery pieces and their crews in the center, with a squad of infantrymen flanking them on either side. Directly in front of the troops were three lodges—Conquering Bear's tepee somewhat to the right, the Miniconjouses' to the left. Grattan was unaware that warriors already lay concealed in a dry slough immediately beyond the camp. And more were readying themselves nearer the river.

About fifty villagers gathered about as Grattan and the interpreter, both still mounted, confronted Conquering Bear in the space between his lodge and the adjacent one. Lucien Auguste, not surprisingly, failed to accurately interpret the conversation, and without Grattan's knowledge continued to goad the Brulés to fight. Oddly enough, also unaware of the impending danger, the soldiers lounged on the ground during the protracted exchange, which suggests that Grattan and his sergeant were exercising little authority over the situation.

Grattan reiterated his demand for Conquering Bear to turn over the Miniconjou warrior, yet the chief attempted to placate him by offering a mule in exchange for the Mormon's cow simply to keep the peace until Indian Agent Whitfield arrived. Grattan repeatedly rebuffed the chief's proposals, maintaining that his orders did not permit him to accept restitution; only the culprit would do.

Obridge Allen, meanwhile, had paused to visit a friend employed by Bordeaux. Just as Allen mounted to rejoin Grattan, Man Afraid returned from the village to implore the trader to intervene. "My friend," he pleaded to Bordeaux, "come on, the interpreter is going to get us into a fight, and they are going to fight if you don't come."[16] A reluctant Bordeaux asked to borrow Allen's horse, which he mounted and rode toward the village. Allen, meanwhile, climbed atop Bordeaux's house to gain a better view of the village. Although Bordeaux would later claim that he was compelled to turn back because the stirrups were too short, it was obvious he wanted no further involvement in the volatile situation. He had no sooner returned to his store when Man Afraid once more implored him to use his influence to prevent a confrontation. Bordeaux again consented to try, but the two men had gone only about 150 yards when sudden commotion in the village signaled that it was already too late. Woman and children were fleeing

---

[16]Johnson to Hoffman, October 10, 1855, ibid., 24.

the village, while warriors beyond were mounting and winding their horses, sure indications that a clash was imminent.

Having reached an impasse, Grattan drew his watch from his pocket and announced, "It is getting late and I can't wait any longer."[17] Conquering Bear responded that he could do nothing more; if the soldiers wanted High Forehead, they would have to take him by force. Instantly, all was pandemonium. At Grattan's command, the soldiers sprang to their feet. Bordeaux saw one man on the right of the line fire his musket into the Indians grouped near Conquering Bear's lodge. In the momentary lull that followed, an Indian, probably Conquering Bear himself, shouted to his kinsmen not to fire, saying that the soldiers had killed one man and might be content to let it go at that. Hardly had he uttered those words when soldiers on the left flank loosed a volley and a split second later one of the howitzers cracked, sending a load of canister ripping through the tepees. The warriors immediately loosed a fusillade of arrows and a few gunshots as they rushed forward, killing two bluecoats in the initial onslaught. Three others were wounded and were quickly helped into the wagon by their comrades. Grattan himself dismounted and leaped to the other gun, yanked the lanyard, and was instantly overwhelmed. The shots from both cannons, aimed too high, miraculously missed the Indians, still the muzzle blasts alone made them reel momentarily.[18]

Three or four soldiers fell on the skirmish line, while the others began withdrawing, loading and firing as they fell back toward the road. Allen remembered them making a fairly disciplined retreat, suggesting that

---

[17]Hoffman to Brevet Major J. N. Page, AAG, Dept. of the West, November 19, 1854, ibid., 2. An Indian who allegedly overheard the conversation related that Grattan ordered Conquering Bear to seize the Miniconjou, which he consented to do, but first had to arm himself. Just as the chief turned to enter his lodge, Grattan ordered his men to fire. Salaway interview, 334.

[18]Presumably, Grattan had the guns loaded with canister, an antipersonnel round consisting of a cylindrical tin container of bore diameter. Those for mountain howitzers contained approximately 148 .69-caliber lead musket balls; those for field guns, one-inch diameter cast iron balls. *Ordnance Manual*, 36, 275. It is difficult to imagine how both shots could have missed at point blank range. A plausible explanation may be that the inexperienced infantrymen manning the guns had the muzzles elevated too high. Indians who later showed up at Fort Pierre apparently told the agent that was what had happened. Alfred J. Vaughan to Colonel Alfred Cumming, October 19, 1854, *ARCIA*, 1854, 88. Another theory is that the Indians simply dove to the ground when they saw the soldiers were about to fire. The pause noted between the first musket shot and the cannon fire might have permitted just enough time for the Indians to drop down. This scenario, purportedly based on an Indian account, is found in Rodenbough, *The Army of the United States*, 489.

one, or both, of the noncommissioned officers survived the initial skirmish to take command after Grattan fell. However, the driver aboard
one of the limbers panicked, turned about, and whipped the mules
toward the road without waiting for anyone. The army wagon followed
closely, with one soldier struggling desperately to maintain a grip on the
tailgate as he ran along behind. The pursuing warriors shot him down
within just a few yards. Other mounted warriors quickly overtook the
limber within a quarter of a mile, killing the driver.

The rest of the soldiers kept up their fire as they retreated south
toward the road. Other warriors, some afoot, some mounted on ponies,
moved around their flanks, launching arrows into the now tightly
bunched soldiers. The troops managed to reach the first terrace approximately one-half mile south of the village, probably hoping to attain a
more defensible position on higher ground. Just at that moment, however, Oglalas coming down the road from the upper camp intercepted
the wagon, killing the teamster. The surviving soldiers, about eighteen
according to one witness, were quickly surrounded and cut down.

In the confusion of the first shots, Auguste, still astride his borrowed
horse, broke out of the circle and made for the river east of Bordeaux's.
Alongside rode a soldier who had caught and mounted Grattan's horse.
But a group of tribesmen coming from the north compelled the two
men to veer to the right, circling back around Bordeaux's house. The
mounted warriors gave chase. Auguste and the soldier probably sought
safety at the store, but may have been waived off by the traders, who
had no desire to risk their lives by trying to harbor the two whites. Gal-
loping at full speed, the panicked men crossed the road and appeared
to be making good their escape when a hunter returning to the village
appeared on the benchlands bordering the valley. A pursuing Lakota
signaled to the hunter, who fired, bringing down both horses. The others were on them in a moment, quickly dispatching the loud-mouthed
Frenchman who had done so much to incur the wrath of the Indians.

It was all over within ten minutes. The bodies of the dead soldiers
lay scattered along their line of retreat from the abandoned cannons all
the way to the bench, where the last of them had made a brief stand.
The villagers immediately vented their wrath on the bodies, stripping,
scalping, and mutilating them, according to Sioux custom, to deprive
the spirits of an afterlife. They slashed the throats of some, others had

hands, feet, or even arms and legs severed. The warriors, and probably some of the women, used clubs and hatchets to disfigure most of
the heads beyond recognition.[19]

Immediately after the fight, the women of both villages, fearing that
the troops at Fort Laramie would retaliate, dismantled the lodges and
began moving toward Rawhide Creek, eight miles north of the river.
Only one lodge was left at the old Brule camp. Conquering Bear, who
had been wounded in three places, was in no condition to be moved
and thus remained in his tepee, where a number of warriors stood
guard over him that night.

Some of the Indians, whose blood was now hot to kill all the whites
they could, immediately descended on Bordeaux's post, threatening to
wipe out the traders for good measure. However, Bordeaux's wife,
Marie, was the daughter of Swift Bear, a respected Brule war chief.
She had numerous kin in the band, and Bordeaux himself had established many close relationships during his years of trading among the
Sioux. Fortunately for the whites, some of those allies stepped forward
to protect the trader and pacify the hotheads.

Still not content, both Brulés and Oglalas threatened to go to Fort
Laramie, kill all the whites there, and burn the fort to the ground.
Regardless of the threats made on his life, Bordeaux was generally
respected among the Sioux and he used that influence to calm the warriors and eventually dissuade them from attacking the post. Instead,
they helped themselves to the goods in his store and appropriated his
cattle and horses. Thunder Bear, an influential leader of Conquering
Bear's ilk, explained that the people were hungry, but he knew too that
some of the warriors were simply trying to pick a fight as an excuse to
loot the store. He moved among the warriors that night calmly urging
restraint. The traders, along with Allen, who had taken sanctuary in
the store after the skirmish, stayed awake all night to guard against a
surprise attack in the event the Indians changed their minds.[20]

During the night, some friendly Brulés discovered and brought in a
seriously wounded soldier. Private John Cuddy, like his comrades, had

---

[19]L. B. Dougherty to J. B. Dougherty, August 29, 1854, Miller Papers.
[20]Virginia Cole Trenholm, "The Bordeaux Story," 121–22; statement by James Bordeaux, August
   29, 1854; statement by James Bordeaux in *ARCIA*, 1855, 93–94; statement by James Bordeaux, *ARSW*,
   1856, 6.

sprinted toward the high ground that afternoon, but had diverged to the left to take refuge in bushes growing near a spring behind Bordeaux's house. The Indians had not seen him in the confusion and had later overlooked him during the subsequent mutilations. Shortly after Cuddy was brought in, Swift Bear appeared and expressed his concern that the soldier would be discovered by the more hostile factions, who would use his presence at the house as an excuse to kill Bordeaux and his family. Cuddy, still conscious, expressed his desire to return to Fort Laramie if someone would assist him. Bordeaux therefore sent one of his white employees and two reliable Indians to escort the wounded man to the post under cover of darkness. The three returned a short time later, saying they had gone only about a mile when Cuddy told them he could make the rest of the way on his own.

At about one o'clock on the morning of Sunday the twentieth, Bordeaux sent a runner to Lieutenant Fleming with the news of the fight and the fate of Grattan's detachment. Meanwhile, Private Cuddy turned back, either because of weakness or his reluctance to try to slip past the intervening Oglala village. Whatever the reason, Bordeaux was astonished the see the soldier staggering back to his post shortly after daylight. How Cuddy managed to traverse the open prairie between the two Indian villages without being caught remains a mystery. Nevertheless, Bordeaux secreted the soldier in his blacksmith shop until Monday, when Obridge Allen took him safely to the fort. By that time, however, Cuddy had been without medical attention for almost two days and was in critical condition. His wounds, apparently not too serious initially, had become infected by that time. He died at the post hospital the following day without being able to give an account of the fight.[21]

On Sunday morning, Conquering Bear had been carefully moved to the temporary camp across the Platte, while approximately five hundred

---

[21]A cogent description of the site of the place where Cuddy concealed himself is given in McCann, "Grattan Massacre," 16n29 and 20n38. McCann concluded that the spring may have been west of the trading post. However, Antoine Bordeaux, who was eight years old at the time, recalled that the slough was behind the house, that is, to the north, and the spring was on the hillside beside the slough. The store faced south, toward the road. Antoine Bordeaux interview, Camp Papers, Lilly Library; William Garnett interview, 654, Camp Collection, BYU; James Bordeaux statement, ARSW, 1856, 6–7; Colonel William P. Carlin (formerly 6th Inf. during the 1850s) to Bancroft, November 14, 1884, typescript in vert. files, FLNHS. Swift Bear was later credited with protecting Cuddy and trying to save his life. Colonel William Hoffman, Sixth Infantry, presented him with a letter of recommendation, sometimes called a 'begging paper,' for the purpose of securing favorable treatment by whites. Letter No. 60, Collins Family Papers, DPL.

warriors rode to the Gratiot Houses to claim their treaty goods. Didiar informed them that the supplies were locked up in storerooms that he had no authority to open until the agent arrived. The Indians became belligerent, telling Didiar they had waited long enough and now demanded the food because they had nothing to eat. The traders resisted, though probably not very strenuously, as the warriors forced their way into the fort and broke open the warehouses. After sacking the rooms containing the annuity goods, the Indians loaded the supplies on their ponies and re-crossed the Platte. They returned to the fort shortly after daybreak on the twenty-first, boldly threatening to kill the residents if they did not turn over all of Chouteau's goods as well. Didiar steadfastly refused. Then, despite the intervention of a few influential men among the Sioux, the warriors used tomahawks and axes to break through the gate to the fort and overwhelm the occupants.

Didiar, Gereau, and most of the others fled to Fort Laramie, daring not return until the following day. When they did, they found the shelves of the store empty and the place thoroughly ransacked. Flour, sugar, and coffee were strewn about; bolts of cloth had been unrolled, while all sorts of other goods were destroyed and scattered throughout the post. Fortunately, they had overlooked the whiskey because Didiar had carefully concealed it.[22]

Nor did the depredations stop there. A party of warriors came to within a mile of Fort Laramie to raid the new McGraw & Reeside mail station. Although no one was killed in the attack, the tribesmen pillaged the station and made off with ten company mules, along with twenty-six head of horses and mules owned by sutler Lewis Dougherty that happened to be in the same corral. As panic spread throughout the valleys of the North Platte and the Laramie, some white traders moved "lock, stock, and barrel" to the perceived safety of the fort, while others took refuge with the still friendly Cheyennes.[23]

With more than a thousand warriors bent on death and destruction suddenly rampaging in the area, Fort Laramie itself was in grave peril.

---

[22]Didiar deposition; Frank Salaway, one of the employees, recalled that Charles Gereau, the interpreter, fled all the way to Green River in Utah, while his wife and child joined her band at Fort Laramie. Gereau did not return for a month; Salaway interview, 335.

[23]This raid apparently occurred later the same night, after the Grattan fight. L. B. Dougherty to J. B. Dougherty, August 29, 1854; affidavit by Jesse A. Jones, Samuel Rider, and N. A. Mitchel, November 1, 1854, Records of the Upper Platte Agency, copy in McDermott File, FLNHS.

Besides himself, Lieutenant Fleming had only Assistant Surgeon Page, Ordnance Sergeant Schnyder, and forty-five soldiers left to defend the post. Fleming wisely made use of old Fort John by concentrating most of the garrison and civilians inside its walls and fixing "it up for the last resort," according to Dougherty. He undoubtedly had his men move the ammunition from the magazine to the adobe fort as well. How many pieces of artillery remained after the loss of Grattan's two is not known, but there was almost certainly another twelve-pounder field howitzer on hand, with a large supply of ammunition.

Dougherty also recorded on August 29 that "a small blockhouse is being erected which, held by ten men, will add greatly to the strength of the post and protect the frame building from being fired."[24] The blockhouse Dougherty mentioned was situated a few yards off the east corner of the magazine and was situated to command the floodplain between the two rivers. It was, in fact, one of two identical structures (Dougherty failed to mention the second), the other located between old Fort John and the Laramie River to defend the diagonally opposing corner of the post.[25] Nevertheless, thanks to the efforts of James Bordeaux, who dissuaded the Indians from attacking the fort, a last-ditch defense never became necessary. Had they carried out their plans, the Sioux almost certainly would have succeeded.[26]

With those preparations underway, Fleming dispatched a courier to Fort Kearny with news of the incident and an urgent request for reinforcements. At the same time, he responded to Bordeaux's message: "Sir: Your letter of the 19th has been received by me, and in reply I say that I am unable to take further notice at present of this unfortunate transaction; and I wish you to speak to the Bear and other Chiefs with reference to the matter. Make the best terms with them you can for the present, for your own safety, and the safety of others likewise unprotected in the country. I wish you to use all means in your power

---

[24]Ibid.

[25]These blockhouses, not previously recorded, each measured twenty-two-feet square, but other architectural details are lacking. They appear on a plat of the fort, prepared by Major Oscar F. Winship a few days after the Grattan incident and are contained in "Report of An Inspection of Forts Ripley, Ridgely, Snelling, Laramie Kearney, Riley, Leavenworth, and Atkinson," LR, AGO (Main Series), NA, microfilm publication 567, roll 508.

[26]In Bordeaux's opinion, only the lateness of the day discouraged the warriors from sacking Fort Laramie. "If the sun had been two hours higher," he stated, "they couldn't have stopped it." Statement by James Bordeaux, ARSW, 1856, 6.

to procure the restoration of the bodies of those who have been killed."[27]

The next day, Monday, August 20, Bordeaux and his men went to the deserted campsite to bury the soldiers. However, before they had accomplished their task another train of Mormon emigrants passed through the battlefield, which one of the travelers described as "the sickening sight of forty [*sic*] dead faces upraised to the blazing sun, murdered and scalped, but still unburied beside the wreckage of a train that had been looted by the Indians."[28] The emigrant failed to realize that the mostly nude bodies and the wrecked vehicles actually belonged to Grattan's command. The lieutenant's body, along with two others, still lay where they had fallen near the artillery pieces, the carriages of which the villagers had chopped to pieces with axes. Grattan's corpse, pierced with twenty-four arrows—one of them through the head—was identified only by a watch that the Indians had overlooked in the pocket of his trousers. No one was present who might have identified any of the enlisted men, even if that had been possible after the disfigured and swollen corpses had baked in the sun for two days. Bordeaux scraped out a shallow pit on the terrace near where most of the bodies lay and deposited the remains therein. The only exception was the body of one soldier, probably the man who had nearly escaped on the lieutenant's horse, who was buried where he fell some distance south of Bordeaux's place. Grattan was also buried on the field, though his remains were later removed to the national cemetery at Fort Leavenworth.[29]

---

[27]Quoted in *Nebraska Publications* 20: 261; Assistant Quartermaster E. A. Ogden to Major General Thomas Jessup, September 5, 1854, CCF, typescript in bound correspondence, FLNHS.

[28]Statement by James Bordeaux, ARSW, 1856, 7; Alder, "Massacre at Fort Laramie," 637.

[29]Bordeaux to Samuel Smith, August 21, 1854, in *Nebraska Publications* 20: 259–60. The statement regarding one soldier being buried separately was made by Antoine Bordeaux, Camp Papers, Lilly Library; Grattan's remains were exhumed and moved to Fort Leavenworth sometime prior to August 1857. His grave may be seen today in the National Cemetery at that post; Gove, *The Utah Expedition*, 49. Initially, the mass grave was simply mounded with earth, but prior to 1864, someone, probably Sixth Infantry troops from Fort Laramie, erected a stone cairn "two feet high and ten feet square." Ware, *Indian War of 1864*, 218. Gove noted the mound, ibid. John Hunton, the last post trader, was familiar with the grave and, in fact, guided the later exhumation party to it after the post cemetery had been abandoned. He was also instrumental in marking the location of the grave with its present monument. Hunton noted at the time that the grave was "at the center of and nearly against the east side of the quarters of Mr. Quick. Battle was about 300 feet west and 100 feet north of this. Bordeaux's Store was at center of S ½ of Sec. 14, a little more than ½ mile east, almost due east of battlefield." Hunton interview, envelope E-8, typescript 261, Camp Collection, BYU; McChristian, "Fort Laramie: The Private Property Era 1890–1937," 127–28.

There can be no doubt that John Grattan's impetuosity, arrogance, and lack of judgment were the immediate causes of "the unfortunate affair," as agent Whitfield afterward termed it, though to most it became the Grattan Massacre. Not only was Grattan unreasonably contemptuous of the Sioux, he seems to have been obsessed with demonstrating to the Indians the government's military might and his own prowess in combat. Lieutenant Fleming's brief skirmish at the ferry the year before served to motivate Grattan, who sought a similar opportunity for distinction. However, both he and Fleming underestimated the effect of the Platte Ferry fight on the Sioux mindset. After the skirmish of June 15, 1853, the Indians were no longer naïve enough to believe the soldiers would not fire on them. Although the Lakotas did not invite armed conflict a year later, they were prepared to react with force when Grattan's blustering made it obvious he was spoiling for a fight.

But the blame did not rest on Grattan alone. The Indian Bureau also bore a share of the responsibility for the tragic event. The underlying purpose of the 1851 treaty was to prevent the Indians from interfering with traffic on the Oregon-California Road. Yet, by locating the Upper Platte Agency at Fort Laramie, the Indians were in fact drawn to the road, where they camped for weeks awaiting the issue of their goods. Accordingly, the Indians and the emigrants were placed in a situation where contact, if not collision, was inevitable. Forethought should have suggested establishing the agency at some other convenient point farther removed from the trail, perhaps at the forks of the Laramie River, or on Chugwater Creek to the south.

Similarly, Lieutenant Grattan's superiors committed mistakes in judgment that had a direct bearing on the events of August 19. Indeed, after speaking with Conquering Bear at Fort Laramie, Fleming initially made the proper decision to defer the matter to agent Whitfield, since the army had no clear authority to act on such a complaint. Lieutenant Fleming was well aware that his youthful subordinate was "rash and impulsive almost beyond belief," yet he allowed himself to be coerced into reversing his decision to await the agent's arrival. Compounding his error, Fleming consented to allow Grattan to command the detachment sent to arrest High Forehead. The post surgeon subsequently opined that the entire matter of the cow might have been overlooked had it not been for Grattan's insistence that an expedition be sent to arrest the accused warrior. Interestingly, there is nothing to suggest that the Mormon who lost the ox ever demanded compensation from the Indians, or that he remained at the fort long enough to witness the outcome of his complaint. That the key witness quickly disappeared from the official record indicates that he moved on with his train and that the plan to take the offending Indian into custody was hatched afterward by Fleming and Grattan simply to flex their military muscles. At the least, more mature judgment should have suggested that the commanding officer personally handle such a sensitive assignment, while leaving his junior in charge of the post. Fleming's acquiescence to Grattan's demands had serious consequences for which he must bear a large share of the responsibility.[30]

A question also arises as to why the department commander, Major General David E. Twiggs, allowed command of an important post like Fort Laramie to devolve on an inexperienced second lieutenant only two years out of West Point. Why were all senior officers allowed to be away from that isolated frontier command? And, why had the garrison at Fort Laramie dwindled to but a single company of infantry during a time of mounting tensions with the Sioux? It should have been obvious to department headquarters that a single company of foot soldiers would be hard pressed to perform the necessary garrison duties, much less police the road. No less a figure than David D. Mitchell penned an editorial castigating the army for its lack of preparedness:

> The miserably mistaken policy which the Government has pursued in establishing petty little Forts, along the Arkansas and Platte, for the purpose of protecting traders and travelers, and at the same time overawing the Indians, has been worse than a useless waste of the public money.

---

[30]Another of Grattan's motives probably stemmed from his making fun of some local civilians who had recently pursued a party of Cheyennes guilty of killing an ox belonging to Lucian Auguste. When the whites caught up to the Indians, they lost their courage and turned back. Lieutenant Grattan made much of this incident, therefore he felt he could not fail when the opportunity arose for him to deal with the Indians, lest he suffer similar ridicule. Statement by Assistant Surgeon Charles Page, *ARSW*, 1856, 12. The army's final report on the Grattan affair alluded to Fleming's inexperience, but stopped short of formally censuring him, probably out of deference to a young officer just beginning his career. Consequently, most of the blame was heaped on the deceased Lieutenant Grattan. Johnson to Hoffman, October 10, 1855, *ARSW*, 1856, 25–26.

These little Forts were generally garrisoned by the fragments of a company of *infantry*, a force that could be of no more use in protecting travelers, or chastising Indians, than so many head of sheep. The Indians being well mounted, could at any time come within sight of a fort and commit any murders or outrages that chance might throw in their way, and laugh with scorn at any impotent attempts that might be made to punish them.[31]

If the army had lulled itself into a state of complacency, with the self-assurance that the 1851 treaty would prevent problems along the emigrant road, the incident at the ferry should have awakened commanders to the very real potential for further trouble. Yet, it did not. Although the two junior officers at Fort Laramie foresaw, in fact hoped for, another confrontation after the skirmish at Platte Ferry, higher authority apparently dismissed it as an isolated event. The Sioux, however, did not take it so lightly, and when similar circumstances arose again the following year, they were not so forgiving.[32]

---

[31]*Nebraska Publications*, 20: 260–61.

[32]Fort Laramie had been commanded by First Lieutenant Richard B. Garnett, a thirteen-year veteran, including his service in the Mexican-American War from July 1852 until May 1854. At the time of the Grattan affair he, like G Company commander Captain William S. Ketchum, was assigned to general recruiting duty, a detail that amounted to a furlough in the East. That left Second Lieutenant Fleming in command of both the company and the post during the summer of 1854. PR, FL.

CHAPTER FOUR

"A Thunder Clap"

In the aftermath of the clash at Bordeaux's Trading Post, the Sioux fragmented into small bands, each going its own way in search of game. The Cheyennes and Arapahoes, however, who had avoided involvement in the trouble, remained peaceably disposed in the Fort Laramie area. Conquering Bear died of his wounds several days after the fight, and the Sioux, having forcibly obtained their annuity goods, only invited further trouble by staying in the area. Nevertheless, after their women, children, and elders were removed a safe distance to the north, war parties began frequenting the Oregon Route, prompting Indian Agent Alfred J. Vaughan at Fort Pierre to predict that "any white man found on the road will certainly be killed by them. They state openly that next spring they will keep parties constantly on the emigrant route, and kill all they find."[1]

The reality of the threat was evidenced on November 13, 1854, when a small party of Brulé Sioux warriors, among them Red Leaf, Spotted Tail, Young Conquering Bear, and Long Chin, returned to the Platte to kill white men in retaliation for their chief's death. The raiders encountered and pounced on a mail coach at Cold Spring, twenty-four miles below Fort Laramie, killing the driver and the conductor riding alongside. The only passenger, Salt Lake businessman Charles A. Kinkaid, was wounded in the leg but escaped. The Indians destroyed the mail and took the mules, along with over ten thousand dollars in gold coin, leading the Sioux to record the winter count of 1854 as the year of "Much Money." The attack caused John Reeside to

---

[1]*ARCIA*, 1855, 88.

forfeit the mail contract, thus forcing Isaac Hockaday to dissolve his partnership in their passenger service. Despite those losses, the increased trouble along the Upper Platte prompted the army to send two additional companies of the Sixth Infantry to reinforce the garrison at Fort Laramie.[2]

Writing to his superiors, Indian Agent Whitfield was convinced that the time had come for punitive action against the plains tribes. "It is evident to every man who has travelled over the plains recently, that the time is not very far distant when the buffalo will cease to furnish a support for the immense number of Indians that now rely entirely on them for subsistence; and as soon as this is the case, starvation is inevitable, unless they can be induced to change their mode of life, which never can be done until the government gets the control over this people, and that can only be done by giving every band of Indians from Texas to Oregon a genteel drubbing."[3]

Agent Vaughan at Fort Pierre echoed Whitfield's views, recounting that in a recent meeting with some of the Sioux at his agency, Red Leaf had flaunted his disdain for the whites by overtly destroying the provisions Vaughan had presented to the tribesmen. According to Vaughan, even the traders on the plains felt threatened by the sudden belligerency of the Indians—yet no other deaths resulted.

Depredations continued early the following year when the Sioux struck near Fort Laramie, driving off sixty-five head of horses and mules from the Ward and Guerrier trading post at Register Cliff. Thomas S. Williams reported that raiders also stole livestock from his party near Devil's Gate, as well as all the animals belonging to the mail company and to two other ranchers at the same point. Miniconjou warriors subsequently scooped up four army mules just west of Fort Laramie early in May. Then in June at Deer Creek Crossing, Sioux

---

[2]Frank Salaway interview; Gray, "Salt Lake Hockaday Mail," 13; Antoine Bordeaux interview, 442, Camp Papers, BYU. A Tenth Infantry officer marching over the trail in 1857 recorded that he "passed near or rather through the gap where the mail party was killed the same year [1854]"; Gove, *The Utah Expedition*, 49. An attack on Fort Laramie was registered on August 28, 1854, yet no mention of it is found in the post records; Heitman, *Historical Register* 2: 401; This may allude to approximately two hundred Cheyennes who made a symbolic raid on the post at about ten o'clock at night and fired three shots. Although no date was recorded, other evidence shows that Whitfield arrived soon after the Grattan fight; John W. Whitfield to Colonel Cumming, September 27, 1854, ARCIA, 1854, 94.
[3]Ibid., 95.

warriors shot down Robert Gibson, the leader of a wagon train from Missouri, as he was in the act of shaking hands with them. The same party attacked another group of emigrants near the same place a few days later, lancing a man and a woman and running off some stock.[4]

Even before most of these incidents occurred, Secretary of War Jefferson Davis had decided that Grattan's death could not go unavenged. The previous October, he and General of the Army Winfield Scott had hatched a plan to strike a blow at the Sioux to teach them that whites could not be killed without consequences. Scott named Colonel William S. Harney, a blustering, hard-bitten old dragoon officer then on leave in Paris, to head the expedition. Harney, who had recently been promoted to the rank of brevet brigadier general, arrived at St. Louis on April 1, 1855, to begin making preparations for the coming Sioux Campaign. By July, he was bound for Fort Kearny where the troops would assemble prior to making the thrust into Sioux country. The expedition numbered about six hundred men in all, including elements of the Second Dragoons, the Sixth and Tenth Infantry, and part of the Fourth Artillery. Leading the mounted force was Lieutenant Colonel Philip St. George Cooke, an experienced officer who had authored the army's recently adopted manual of cavalry tactics. Major Albemarle Cady, a veteran infantryman who had distinguished himself at Molino del Rey during the Mexican War, commanded the foot troops.

As Brevet Brigadier General Harney was about to launch his campaign, the Indian Bureau subdivided the large unwieldy agency that had encompassed most of the plains, to form a smaller one headed by Whitfield especially to serve the tribes along the Arkansas River. Thomas S. Twiss, an 1826 graduate of the U.S. Military Academy, was appointed to head the new Upper Platte Agency. Following graduation, Twiss had accepted an appointment as assistant professor of philosophy at West Point, while serving concurrently in the Army Corps of Engineers. He resigned his commission just two years later when he was hired as a professor at South Carolina College, a position he retained for the next eighteen years. He subsequently worked as an engineer for an iron works and a railroad. It was probably during his

---

[4]Hafen and Young, *Fort Laramie and the Pageant of the West*, 237–39; Antoine Bordeaux interview, Camp Papers, Indiana University; Thunder Bear interview, MSS 57, Box 2, Camp Papers, BYU.

time with the railroad that he made the political contacts that led to
his selection as an Indian agent. Upon his arrival at Fort Laramie on
August 10, Twiss established a temporary office at the nearby Ward
and Guerrier trading house.

Although Little Thunder professed to be friendly, the young warriors who had been raiding along the Platte road resided in his village,
then situated on Blue Water Creek, a tributary that flowed into the
Platte near Ash Hollow. The chief failed to heed Twiss's warning to
move south of the river for protection, lest the army consider his people as hostile. Little Thunder's decision to continue hunting north of
the Platte would prove a fatal error.

In early September, General Harney's scouts discovered the Brulés
still camped on the Blue Water. Directing Cooke and four companies
of mounted men to maneuver undetected into a blocking position
above the village, Harney moved up the creek with the infantry. At
dawn on September third, the Sioux sighted the advancing foot soldiers and began withdrawing northward, directly into Cooke's hands.
Waiving aside Little Thunder, who made a last minute plea for peace,
Harney ordered his infantrymen forward and to open fire as soon as
they came within musket range of the Brulé camp. The Indians were
stampeded in a headlong panic directly into the path of the onrushing
cavalry. Surrounding the rim of the canyon, troops on all sides fired
into the Sioux cowering below, shooting down men, women, and children alike. Cooke's troopers then thundered down the ravine, scattering the Indians and cutting down survivors as they ran. Finally,
eighty-six Brulés lay dead, with seventy women and children captured.
Harney lost only four men. Soldiers plundering the abandoned lodges
in the aftermath found uniforms stripped from the bodies of Grattan's
men, as well as items taken in the raid on the Salt Lake mail, thus
Harney felt vindicated that he had punished the guilty band.[5]

Following the Blue Water fight, Harney established a temporary
cantonment, appropriately christened Fort Grattan, at the mouth of
nearby Ash Hollow. Leaving a small garrison behind to man the new
station, the Sioux Expedition marched upstream to Fort Laramie,

---

[5]Brevet Brigadier General William S. Harney to Lieutenant Colonel Lorenzo Thomas, September 5, 1855, Selected Letters—Sioux Expedition, (hereinafter cited as Sioux Expedition Letters).
For a comprehensive account of the battle and surrounding events, see Paul, *Blue Water Creek*.

arriving there on the fifteenth. Agent Twiss, at Harney's request, had sent runners to summon the other bands to meet with him, the Oglalas at Ward and Guerrier's, the Brulés at Bordeaux's post. Confiding that he thought the reports of attacks by the Sioux had been falsely magnified, Twiss informed the army that he had assembled the peaceful Indians under his protection on the Laramie River to prevent their being mistaken for free-roamers, who resisted the whites. He had taken the further precaution of warning other Indians to move south of the Platte for their own protection. The Indian leaders present assured Twiss that the Cheyennes, Arapahoes, and Oglala Sioux had remained firm friends of the whites during the recent troubles and that the government had been right in whipping Little Thunder because "he had no ears." Likewise, most of the Brulés, now headed by the more moderate Thunder Bear, had no further desire to confront the army. Twiss had correctly determined that the Wasagahas, a sub-band of the Brulés to which Conquering Bear had belonged, were the culprits responsible for the murders of the mail party and other depredations.

General Harney found some four thousand Lakotas, representing several bands, gathered in a great camp thirty-five miles above Fort Laramie. Mustering all of his considerable pomposity for the occasion, the general admonished the headmen to cease plundering and to return all stolen stock they might have in their possession. He further warned that if any of the perpetrators of the mail coach attack were among them, they should be surrendered to authorities. In an effort to deprive the tribesmen of guns, powder, and lead, Harney issued an edict prohibiting all trade with the Sioux, except in the immediate vicinity of military posts. Post commanders were authorized to exert stronger control over the traders by ordering them to relocate their activities nearer the forts, at places designated by the army.[6]

An unexpected benefit accrued from Harney's Indian-camp visit when he later outlined to the secretary of war the strategic importance of Fort Laramie: "The habit of the Indians of concentrating about it, has long existed & doubtless will be kept up. It is also an important point on the great route of Emigration to Utah, Oregon, & Washing-

---

[6]Circular, Headquarters, Sioux Expedition, September 18, 1855, Sioux Expedition Letters. As a result of this directive, Ward and Guerrier moved their operation to a site on the Laramie River opposite Fort Laramie.

ton Territories & California. The large trains of wagons which pass on this route in summer, offer tempting inducements for Indian depredations which are often invited & provoked by the insolence & violence of the whites themselves."[7] He backed his words by detaching five companies of infantry, a company of the Fourth Artillery then serving as cavalry, and portions of three companies of dragoons to bolster the garrison. Then, in a grand display of force, the general marched the remainder of his column through the heart of Sioux country to Fort Pierre, located on the Missouri River approximately three hundred miles northeast of Fort Laramie, where he planned to convene a general council with all the Sioux bands.

Writing from Bordeaux's house in October, Twiss sent a letter to the commissioner of Indian Affairs recommending that a separate agency be established for the Arapahoes and Cheyennes on the South Platte, perhaps at St. Vrain's fort. This, Twiss implied, would remove them from the potentially evil influences of being too closely associated with the Sioux. "In a very short period of time," he predicted, "the Araphoes and Cheyennes would become fixed and settled, and a part of each tribe . . . would become agriculturists, rude it is true, yet sufficiently skillful to raise corn, potatoes, and beans, and dwell in cabins or fixed habitations." The Sioux, on the other hand, would be consolidated at an agency in the vicinity of Fort Laramie. Trouble was, the Teton Sioux were scattered from the Powder River region in the north, westward to Utah, as far south as the Arkansas River, and eastward to the Pawnee villages. "Their habits are roving, and, consequently, predatory; and the sooner the government shall take steps to break these habits the better will it be for the Indians." He concluded his remarks by noting that Harney's attack had been a "thunder clap" to the Sioux that had impressed upon them the power of the government.[8]

Thunder Bear subsequently sent word to Twiss that he desired peace, and to prove his good intentions, he would see that those guilty of the mail coach murders were surrendered to the army. The agent placed little confidence in the promise, but to his surprise, Spotted Tail, Long Chin, and Red Leaf showed up at the agency on October 17, expressing their earnest desire to surrender themselves to prevent any further

---

[7]Harney to Secretary of War, November 10, 1855, Sioux Expedition Letters.
[8]All quotations are from *ARCIA*, 1855, 402–403.

war being made on the Brulés. They were told they would be imprisoned at Fort Leavenworth, to which they acceded, but they were not
then prepared to make such a long a journey. The men promised to
return in ten days, after they had seen to the welfare of their families
and gathered necessary belongings. The other two perpetrators, they
informed Major Hoffman, were mere boys. One had joined a Sioux
band residing near the Missouri River, and the other was seriously ill
and could not travel. Nevertheless, Hoffman insisted they be brought
in. A delegation composed of Little Thunder, Man Afraid, and other
chiefs assured Hoffman a few days later that they would comply with
his demand as an added gesture of good faith. With winter approaching, the major determined to send the first three captives to Fort Leavenworth, accompanied by a guard detachment and a small party of relatives, for confinement as soon as they returned. When the others
surrendered, they would either be jailed at Fort Laramie for the winter,
or sent to Leavenworth with one of the mail escorts.[9]

A month later, Red Leaf's nephew appeared at the fort to present
himself as a surrogate prisoner in lieu of the man who had gone with
the Missouri River Sioux. The fifth member of the raiding party,
probably Young Conquering Bear, still lay ill with consumption in the
Brulé village. The nephew was shackled to a ball and chain and placed
in a lodge adjacent to the guardhouse until he could be transferred to
Leavenworth when the road cleared in spring. Meantime, the youth
had second thoughts and took advantage of a chance to escape while
the guards were eating supper. Eventually, the real offenders were
brought in to join their tribesmen in prison.

The Sioux having been thoroughly chastised and in a submissive
mood, Secretary of War Davis authorized General Harney to negotiate another treaty with them to secure peace on the plains. To that
end, the general sent word for the tribal leaders to meet with him at
Fort Pierre on March 1. By claiming to be the sole agent of the government in the proposed council, Harney usurped the authority of the
Indian Bureau, a transgression that clearly galled Twiss. The general
took further steps to isolate the Sioux, thus making them more
dependent on the army, when he ordered Twiss to instruct the traders

---

[9]Hoffman to Assistant Adjutant General, Sioux Expedition, November 4, 1855, Sioux Expedition
Letters.

to have no communication with the Indians, nor could the traders dispatch messengers inviting the Indians to their camps. Harney also insisted that traders not be permitted to visit the agency unless they had business with Twiss; even then they could not speak with any Indians without the government interpreter present.[10]

The antagonism brewing between agent Twiss and General Harney erupted into open conflict the following month when the general returned from an absence to learn that Twiss had told the Oglala and Brulé headmen not to attend the Fort Pierre council. Harney was livid. "This is not the first occasion which Mr. Twiss has embraced to meddle in the affairs of the Sioux," he thundered in a letter to Major Hoffman at Fort Laramie, "but his conduct at this time, has so seriously impeded the General's plans and arrangements, as to call for decisive action on his part, to prevent any further bad consequences."[11] Harney instructed Major Hoffman to make office space available for Twiss at the fort and to order the agent to move there immediately, the better to keep an eye on him. By that time, Twiss had relocated his operation back at the old American Fur Company post, which had been acquired more recently by James Beauvais. Harney also restricted Twiss from having any dealings whatsoever with the Sioux; thereafter he was to confine his activities exclusively to the Cheyennes and Arapahoes. Harney alone would deal with the Sioux. Nevertheless, Twiss's ploy had delayed the two Lakota bands so long that it was now impossible for them to reach Fort Pierre in time for the conference. Harney, still simmering over the agent's shenanigans, had no choice but to meet with them at a later time. At that, Twiss thumbed his nose at Harney by ignoring the general's directives.

But Harney's wrath did not end there; he wanted Twiss's head, and a written complaint from Seth Ward and William Guerrier provided a convenient excuse to rid himself of the recalcitrant agent. Rumors had been circulating for some time that Ward, desirous of protecting his own interests, reported that Twiss was trading with the Indians at the agency camp in violation of Harney's order. The unscrupulous Twiss

---

[10]This notice was sent to Ward & Guerrier, C. Bissonnette & Co., Beauvais, Bordeaux, Richard, and Simero, whose names comprise an accurate list of the traders then operating in the vicinity of Fort Laramie; Twiss to Indian Traders, January 31, 1856, Sioux Expedition Letters.

[11]Capt. Alfred Pleasonton, acting AAG, to Hoffman, February 19, 1856; ibid.

was, in fact, lining his own pockets by offering generous trades in buffalo robes and pelts in exchange for the annuity goods that were to be given to the Indians in accordance with the Fort Laramie Treaty. When Major Hoffman initiated an investigation into Twiss's illicit activities, he found the disadvantaged competitors in the area were only too willing to sign affidavits indicting the agent. James Bordeaux also revealed that the agent was culpable of withholding the two younger Indians involved in the Salt Lake stage attack. Moreover, the traders accused Twiss of extorting "valuable presents" from them by threatening to have their licenses revoked. What Harney did not divulge, and it would prove to be the undoing of his evidence, was that the accusations were biased by the traders' desire to eliminate a competitor.[12]

General Harney lost no time in presenting his case against Twiss to the adjutant general. A few days later, on March 6, he directed Hoffman to inform Twiss that he was to cease all functions as agent until the matter could be resolved. Again Twiss resisted Harney's bullying by suspending his activities, but he took no action to move the agency to Fort Laramie. Moreover, he challenged the legality of Harney's authority over him by declaring his intention to go to Washington to discuss the situation with the secretary of the interior. Penning a note the next day from Pierre Bissonnett's camp near the fort, Twiss advised Hoffman that the Sioux agency was closed forthwith and that he was moving to St. Vrain's post on the South Platte, where he had established the Cheyenne and Arapaho agency the previous fall.

Harney, nevertheless, was determined to get Twiss out of the country altogether. The old dragoon doggedly fired off another missive barring the agent from having anything whatsoever to do with *any* of the tribes. Even though Harney had no official authority over him, neither was Twiss willing to risk incarceration in the Fort Laramie guardhouse. The fact was, Harney had him outgunned if it came to a showdown. Twiss prudently chose to leave immediately for Washington, where he could marshal his own forces from among his many political friends.[13]

[12]Ward & Guerrier to Hoffman, February 7, 1865, ibid.; Hoffman to Pleasonton, February 9, 1856, ibid.

[13]Twiss to Hoffman, March 6, 1856, ibid.; Twiss to Hoffman, March 7, 1856, ibid.; Twiss to Hoffman, March 17, 1856, ibid.; Harney to Cooper, Adjutant General, U.S. Army (hereinafter AGUSA), March 23, 1856, ibid.

While Harney had been jousting with Twiss, the general had proceeded with his plan to meet with the Sioux on the Upper Missouri.
Nine bands were represented, only the Oglalas and Brulés being absent
as the result of Twiss's duplicity. Those two bands ultimately made
their appearance at Fort Pierre in the latter part of April and accepted
General Harney's terms. Thus, in 1856 the Sioux signed a second treaty
with the government, sometimes called "Harney's treaty" or the Sioux
treaty of 1856, based on recent events, stipulating they were to surrender to the military all tribal members guilty of murder or other crimes;
all stolen property was to be returned; and they must not obstruct the
white man's roads or molest travelers. Harney dictated that each band
would name a certain number of chiefs and sub-chiefs who would be
officially recognized by the government, and each band would have a
specific number of "soldiers" to serve as a police force over its people.
The fact that the impulsive actions of Lieutenants Fleming and Grattan had provoked the Brulés to defend themselves in the first place was
lost in the government's zeal to further control all the Sioux. Harney
revealed in his final report that the government's real motive was to
acculturate the Indian to the ways of the whites. Faced with decreasing
food supplies, disease, and white encroachments, Harney observed,
"the character of the Indian is undergoing great modifications," consequently, the tribesmen were recognizing "the irresistible conclusion
that to live hereafter they must work."[14]

Secretary of War Davis agreed with the validity of General Harney's
complaints about Indian traders in general, though he had no authority to deal with agent Twiss and his illicit activities. It was evident that
the government had an inherent mistrust of the old French traders,
who Davis claimed were "irresponsible either through property or
character, and often bound to our government by no sentiment or tie
of allegiance . . . with every opportunity to sell them deleterious articles, and to receive property acquired in marauding expeditions."[15]
Thereafter, he concluded, traders should be confined to the immediate vicinity of military posts as a better way to restrict the traffic in
contraband goods. Indian annuities, likewise, should be distributed at
or near the forts.

---

[14]Harney to Secretary of War, March 8, 1856, in "Council With Sioux Indians at Fort Pierre," *ARSW*,
    1856, 1–4.

Even though agent Twiss was half a continent away by that time, Harney had not heard the last of his nemesis. Once in Washington, Twiss garnered the enthusiastic cooperation of Commissioner of Indian Affairs George W. Manypenny to scuttle Harney's proposed treaty. Manypenny, outraged by the general's haughtiness in presuming to infringe on the authority of the Indian Bureau, had not yet received a copy of the drafted treaty, but acting on rumors of its contents, he directed Twiss to prepare a cost estimate for implementing the treaty provisions. The vengeful Twiss, of course, applied a heavy hand to ensure the price would be shockingly high to members of Congress. Providing teams and farm implements, outfitting a police force for each band, in addition to supplying food and other annuties, he claimed, would cost no less than $62,000 annually. When the Interior Department reviewed and adjusted Twiss's estimates, the total skyrocketed to $100,000. Manypenny and Twiss succeeded in their deception and could not have been more pleased when the Senate failed to ratify the new treaty. The salt in Harney's wound came when the Indian Bureau not only exonerated Twiss of the allegations made against him, but reinstated him as Indian agent and sent him back to the plains.[16]

Good to their word, representatives of several Sioux bands came to Fort Pierre on May 20 to turn over both the stolen livestock and the warriors guilty of past misdeeds. Twelve chiefs came, among them High Forehead, known by then also as "The Man Who Killed the Cow" sparking the Grattan affair. In an uncharacteristic gesture of clemency, Harney was persuaded by the chiefs to release the Indians on their promise of future good behavior. Thus, all was forgiven for the man whose act, rightly or wrongly, had fanned into flame "the first Sioux war." For his own part, General Harney closed the campaign by declaring the end "of all our difficulties and grievances with the Sioux." He little knew it was but a prelude to many years of violence and bloodshed on the northern Great Plains.

---

[15]Jefferson Davis to the President, May 31, 1856, ibid.

[16]Twiss to George W. Manypenny, June 24, 1856, 10–11, ibid.; Manypenny to secretary of the interior, June 25, 1856, 11, ibid.; Sec. of the Interior R. McClelland to President, June 26, 1856, 11–12, ibid.; Utley, *Frontiersmen in Blue*, 119.

CHAPTER FIVE

"THE CHEYENNES ARE
AN UNRULY RACE"

The conflicts of 1854–55 immediately deterred emigration to Utah and the Pacific Coast, with scarcely eight thousand people risking the journey during the summer of 1855. Californians clamored that there were not enough troops and not enough forts to adequately protect travelers on the overland trail. Some thought the government should also provide more supplies and repair stations, and even special rescue parties to aid stragglers. Once again the army considered whether routine mounted patrols would be more effective than infantry garrisons.[1]

Although the army took no immediate steps to send cavalry to the posts on the Oregon Route, the commanding officer at Fort Laramie, Major William H. Hoffman, effected operational changes to bolster security along that segment of the road. He began by detailing escorts composed of an officer and twenty men to protect the "downward" mail as far east as Ash Hollow, where they met a similar party from Fort Kearny escorting the "upward' mail. Above Fort Laramie, troops also escorted the westbound mail coaches over the most dangerous stretch of road from Upper Platte Crossing, approximately 130 miles west of the post, to Independence Rock, or even as far as Devil's Gate.[2]

In 1853 John Richard (pronounced "Reeshaw"), a swarthy, slightly built Missourian of French descent, had constructed a toll bridge over the river at Upper Crossing, a strategic point where the main road

---

[1] Unruh, *Plains Across*, 120, 221.
[2] *Orders No. 35*, June 10, 1855, and *Orders No. 36*, June 23, 1855, Orders, FL.

departed from the North Platte to follow Sweetwater River to South
Pass, where emigrants would begin the ascent over the Rockies. At his
toll-bridge site, Richard built a compound of several buildings, including a store, a blacksmith shop, and a house.[3] Major Hoffman began
posting twenty-five-man guard detachments there because of the
importance of keeping the bridge in operation.

Time revealed that the Horse Creek Treaty had been only marginally effective in fostering peaceful relations among the tribes inhabiting the plains. Even if they intended to respect their neighbors' hunting territories and stop warring against each other, full cooperation
would take time. Although most of the raiding occurred among the
tribes, rather then against the Americans, continuing conflict nevertheless threatened to affect emigrant travel on the road. In fact, at the
very time that Harney was forging his treaty with the Sioux, trouble
erupted with the Cheyennes and Arapahoes, who had been growing
increasingly belligerent toward both the Pawnees and whites. Tensions were strained even further when parties of Crows, hunting as far
south as the Platte and supplied with gun powder by agent Twiss,
threatened to collide with the Cheyennes and Arapahoes.[4]

Major Hoffman sensed the growing animosity of several tribes, a
situation aggravated by the breech in Indian relations with Twiss, and
by General Harney's insistence that agent Twiss have no contact with
any of the tribes in the region. Responsibility for local Indian-white
relations therefore devolved on the military, a situation anything but
acceptable to the tribesmen. Hoffman met with several headmen representing Cheyenne and Arapaho bands in March 1856, coercing them
into promising they would restrain their warriors. They, in turn, sent
their tribal runners to the bands camping on the South Platte and even

---

[3]The enterprising Richard had been engaged in the fur trade since the mid-1830s, operating for a
time on the South Platte and later moving to the North Platte. By 1840, he resided near Fort
Laramie and afterward was employed at nearby Fort Platte. By the time Francis Parkman
passed by in 1846, Richard was the proprietor at Fort Bernard, approximately six miles downstream, established in 1845. The decline of the fur business forced Richard to turn to the market for buffalo robes and he discovered lucrative profits could be made by trading supplies for
footsore animals belonging to passing emigrants. McDermott, *Frontier Crossroads*, 7–9; Sunder,
Fur Trade, 9–10.

[4]Brevet Second Lieutenant Robert C. Hill to Lieutenant E. N. Latimer, Fort Laramie, Neb.,
March 7, 1856, Selected Letters Received, Sioux Expedition Letters.

to groups as far away as the Arkansas River, urging all leaders there to maintain the peace. But the leaders feared that war parties from those groups had already gone north to raid the Pawnees, prompting Major Hoffman to insist that messengers be sent to bring them back. The Cheyennes, he warned, must stay away from the Pawnees until a more binding peace among the tribes could be negotiated.

The Cheyennes retorted that the Sioux, particularly the Oglalas, habitually crossed the North Platte and trespassed into the designated Cheyenne bison range along the South Platte. Hoffman assured the Cheyennes that General Harney's order that the Sioux stay north of the river was still in force, and that they were allowed to cross the river only to visit Fort Laramie for trading purposes. He appealed to the Cheyennes to be patient until Harney met with the Oglalas and reiterated his orders. "The Cheyennes are an unruly race," Hoffman observed, adding that he had little confidence in their promise to be peaceful unless they were "kept in dread of immediate punishment."[5] Harney's timely decision to strengthen the garrison at Fort Laramie served to deter the restless warriors, at least temporarily.

In the spring of 1856, the Cheyennes were camped in the Smoky Hill and Solomon Fork country, and by June they were aggressively ranging north to the Pawnee territory along the Platte River. The messengers Major Hoffman had relied on to contact them for some reason did not. The annual migration of overlanders to the Pacific Northwest was now well underway and the wagon trains, with their herds of cattle, posed enticing targets.

A group of Cheyennes waylaid one party on the Big Sandy, demanding they be given a cow, but while negotiations were underway, an impatient warrior summarily shot one of the group's animals. John Tutt, who happened to be traveling on the road at the time, recognized the raiders as Cheyennes, accompanied by a few Sioux. Ostensibly, they had moved into that area to raid the Pawnees, but it soon became apparent their real intent was to harass the emigrant caravans. A few days later the same Indians confronted a train near the crossing of the Little Blue, opening fire unexpectedly and wounding two whites.

---

[5]Major William Hoffman to Captain Alfred Pleasonton, Assistant Adjutant General (hereinafter AAG), Sioux Expedition, Marcy 31, 1856, ibid.

When Cheyenne leader Big Head and a few others came to Fort Kearny shortly thereafter and were recognized as the troublemakers by a member of the emigrant party, the commanding officer had the culprits arrested. When the warriors broke loose on their way to the guardhouse, the soldiers opened fire, mortally wounding one of the Cheyennes. Yet all managed to escape. Wharton immediately sent dispatches to the commanding officers at Fort Laramie and Fort Riley warning them of potential danger along the road and suggesting that cavalry from Fort Riley begin patroling it regularly. The army did not know, however, that Big Head had convinced his people to overlook the shooting incident.[6]

Soon after the Indian attacks on whites moving through Nebraska Territory, most of the Cheyennes gathered at the great tribal encampment on the headwaters of the Republican River to observe the annual sun dance and to discuss what they should do about the interlopers. Well aware of the punishment the army had inflicted on the Sioux at Blue Water Creek a year earlier, most of the leaders favored peace with the Americans. Even though the chiefs warned the young warriors not to further provoke the whites, they were unaware that war parties in the Pawnee country had already done that.

General Harney enthusiastically supported patrolling the road with cavalry to discourage any war parties that might still be active along the Platte. He also directed Colonel Edwin V. Sumner, commanding the First Cavalry at Fort Riley, to assemble an expedition that would march to Fort Laramie for the same purpose. Harney underscored his resolve to quell the Cheyennes immediately by granting Sumner discretion to take action against any recalcitrant bands he might encounter along the way.

In permitting military force against the Cheyennes, Harney reasoned that according to the Horse Creek treaty, they had no business being in that region. But he had again overstepped his authority. Major Hoffman, in fact, advised Harney that the Cheyennes with whom he had spoken disclaimed any knowledge of a treaty; indeed, they had not even attended the Fort Pierre council. Harney, admittedly, had no

[6]Captain H. W. Wharton to Pleasanton AAG., Sioux Expedition, June 7, 10, and 11, 1856, ibid.; Chalfant, *Cheyennes and Horse Soldiers*, 36–39.

legitimate authority over the Cheyennes and Arapahoes; still, he was "of the opinion that the Cheyennes have been for so long a time in the commission of outrages and insults upon the whites, and their bearing has been so haughty and defiant that it will be necessary to chastise them severely for their misdeeds before they become tractable."[7] His proposed campaign, however, was postponed when the slavery controversy along the Kansas-Missouri border demanded that troops be diverted there to maintain order between northern abolitionists and pro-slavery southerners.

If any hopes remained for a peaceful resolution of the Cheyennes' aggressions, they were soon dispelled. Following the annual encampment, the bands once again separated to continue the summer hunt, with some of them immediately resuming raids in the Pawnee country. On August 24, 1856, when a Cheyenne war party, camped on Grand Island below Fort Kearny, spied a mail wagon coming upstream, two of the young warriors went out to beg tobacco from the employees. The driver mistook their actions as hostile and opened fire on the pair. His shots missed, but one of the arrows the youths fired in return grazed his arm as the coach sped past.

That same afternoon Captain George H. Stewart led a reinforced company of the First Cavalry out of Fort Kearny in search of the Cheyennes. They found tracks of two warriors on the road where they had intercepted the wagon and after a pursuit of fifteen miles, caught up with the Indians, killing six and capturing most of their equipment. Twiss later testified that the tribesmen had signaled that they did not wish to fight by laying down their bows, but the troops had opened fire anyway. The army's disproportionate reaction to this mail coach incident was perhaps the most serious in a series of clashes that together became the catalyst for several years of active hostilities between the Cheyennes and the army.

The Cheyennes, now convinced that the army wanted war with them, unleashed their fury on all whites they found in their path. Thirty-three miles northeast of Fort Kearny, for example, they swooped down on a small train on the Council Bluffs Road, killing

---

[7]Harney to Cooper, Adjutant General (hereinafter AG), Headquarters of the Army, July 5, 1856, Sioux Expedition Letters.

four whites. In another incident, relatives and friends of the warriors killed in the recent fight on the Platte descended on an emigrant train camped about eighty miles west of Fort Kearny, killing a woman and carrying off a four-year old boy. A week later they attacked a party of Mormons, killing four men and capturing one woman. Another party of emigrants was reportedly attacked and murdered on the Little Blue River.[8]

In the midst of the Cheyennes' rampage, Almon W. Babbitt, secretary of Utah Territory, insisted that he reach Salt Lake City to intervene as quickly as possible, despite advice against travel beyond Fort Kearny because of the recent trouble. Babbitt and two companions, lightly armed but carrying a great deal of money and government papers, continued up the road, determined to press on to Utah. The Indian war party operating in the area soon spotted Babbitt's party and ambushed them at their noon camp near O'Fallon's Bluff, killing all three. When their bodies were discovered three weeks later, the press and the American public screamed for retaliation.

At about the same time, an army surveying expedition commanded by Lieutenant Francis T. Bryan was working its way back to Kansas from the Continental Divide in Wyoming, having mapped a potential new route from Fort Riley to the Platte, and westward along the South Platte and Lodgepole Creek to Bridger's Pass. Rather than returning by the same route, Bryan elected to explore down the Republican, thinking it might be a more direct route. But in setting out he failed to consider that it would take his party through the very heart of Cheyenne country. The Indians by now had seen enough surveyors to know that they presaged more roads and more white intruders. While the engineering party was on Rock Creek, a minor tributary of the Republican, a large band of Cheyennes rode into sight, threatening to attack. Fortunately for them, Bryan's dragoon escort caught up at the critical moment, causing the tribesmen to withdraw.[9]

Harney officially terminated the Sioux Expedition in July 1856 and by early August Thomas Twiss was back from Washington and in

[8]Twiss to Commissioner, September 25, 1856, ARSI, 1856–57, 650–51; Wharton to Cooper, AGUSA, September 8, 1856, ARSW, 1856, 109–10.

[9]Jackson, Wagon Roads West, 127–29; Goetzmann, Army Exploration in the American West, 368–70.

business at the Upper Platte Agency. This time he headquartered at the post of veteran trader Andrew Drips, nineteen miles below Fort Laramie. Twiss, the record shows, did everything he could to allay army concerns that the Cheyennes were bent on a general uprising. In October he announced that "the Cheyennes are perfectly quiet and peaceable and entirely within my control and obedient to my authority." Twiss, never reluctant to criticize the army, placed the blame for the recent trouble squarely on the shoulders of the military authorities. "It is clearly evident to my mind," he wrote, "that the exasperation, excitement, and hostile feelings of the Cheyennes, have been caused, in the first place, by the measures adopted and carried into force by the military authorities at the North Platte bridge early last spring; have been kept up and increased in virulence, subsequently, by those others at Fort Kearny." He explained in cogent detail how the late August "attack" on the mail party had been unintentional over-excitement by the Indians, and that if the war party had wanted to kill the mail party they easily could have done so. Animosities were aggravated when Captain Stewart persisted in attacking the warriors after they had professed their desire not to fight. The killing of the six warriors, in Twiss's words, had caused "an excitement and exasperation in the Indian mind beyond control," leading to the retaliatory murders of whites along the Platte.[10]

Higher military authority nevertheless had already determined that the Cheyennes were to be punished for their actions, regardless of the circumstances. Just a few days after Twiss dispatched his assurances that the tribe would uphold the peace, Secretary of War Davis announced that a campaign, the Cheyenne Expedition, nevertheless would be launched against the Indians the following spring. The objective was to subdue them and force the release of any captives and property they had seized.

Colonel Edwin Vose Sumner, First Cavalry, was again assigned to command the expedition. Sumner, a hard-bitten veteran of nearly four decades, had spent most of his career serving in the dragoons on the western frontier. To ensure that *all* Cheyennes were made to pay for the wrongs of a few, Sumner laid out a two-pronged advance from

---

[10]Twiss to commissioner, October 13, 1856; *ARSI*, 1856, 652–54.

Fort Leavenworth to sweep the region between the Platte and the Arkansas, either by driving the Indians off or killing them in battle. Major John Sedgwick would lead four companies of the First Cavalry up the Arkansas River, while another squadron, directly under Sumner, would march to the Platte. Sumner would be reinforced by two companies of the Second Dragoons at Fort Kearny, and from there the column would advance to Fort Laramie, where three companies of the Sixth Infantry would round out his force. The dragoon companies would be left at Fort Laramie where they could join their regiment as a component of another expedition then being organized to quell rebellious Mormons in Utah.[11] Sumner hoped that the mere presence of the two columns in the region would cause the Cheyennes to withdraw from both the Santa Fe Trail and the Oregon-California Route, after which he and Sedgwick would join forces on the South Platte. The combined columns would then march southeast down the Republican, hoping to lure the Cheyennes into a decisive encounter.

During the winter, all forces prepared for the spring expedition. Departing from Fort Leavenworth in mid-May 1857, Sumner's dragoons rode up the Platte and arrived at Fort Kearny in early June. There, Companies E and H, Second Dragoons, augmented his battalion. When Sumner reached Fort Laramie on June 22, a hundred recruits who had recently marched afoot up the trail brought the post's infantry units up to full strength. The resident companies vacated their barracks and moved into the field camp for a brief period of training before the column took up the march. Sumner placed Captain William Scott Ketcham, who had come to Fort Laramie in 1849, in command of the infantry battalion. Its role would be to establish and guard a supply base, while light columns of mounted troops scoured the surrounding country to locate the Cheyennes. On June 27 the troops formed up and proceeded nearly due south to form a juncture with Sedgwick's battalion near the mouth of Cherry Creek on the South Platte, then struck eastward toward the upper reaches of the Kansas River. Cheyenne scouts watched the approaching troops. Although there were more bluecoats than any of them had ever seen

---

[11]Colonel E. V. Sumner to AAG, Headquarters of the Army, September 20, 1857, *ARSW*, 1858, Pt. 2, 98.

in one place, a medicine man assured the warriors that because they had dipped their hands into the waters of a particular small lake, they would be protected from the soldiers' bullets.

Arrayed in line of battle, the Cheyennes confronted Sumner at the South Fork of the Solomon River on July 29. The warriors, outfitted in full regalia, made a magnificent sight as they slowly advanced to the accompaniment of a war song. They had enough experience with the army to expect that the troopers would open fire with their single shot carbines. But after the first volley, the warriors would charge, employing bows, lances, and war clubs before the soldiers could reload.

Sumner, however, saw in the Cheyenne's compact formation an opportunity to take advantage of the sabers his men carried—a weapon the Indians had not previously encountered on the plains. A First Cavalryman recalled the scene: "We were armed with muzzle loaders [carbines] raised, the Cheyennes seemed to treat them with the contempt they deserved, but when they were dropped, and the sabres of, I think, seven companies flashed in the sun, the effect was magical."[12] In the only documented saber charge made during the western Indian campaigns, the cavalry raced at a full gallop toward the massed warriors. Suddenly, the Cheyenne line broke. The soldiers pursued them in a running fight for seven miles as they fled toward their camp on the Saline River. During the fight, the cavalrymen killed nine warriors; two cavalrymen were killed. Ten soldiers suffered arrow wounds. The Cheyenne villagers departed hastily, abandoning most of their lodges and supplies, including their winter's supply of buffalo meat. The troops destroyed the village and its contents the following day.[13]

Leaving behind a company of infantry to protect the wounded soldiers in a hastily erected sod enclosure, dubbed "Fort Floyd," Sumner followed the Cheyenne trail toward the Arkansas River. Failing to catch up with the warriors after a pursuit of several days, he turned upstream to Bent's Fort where he found Indian Agent Robert Miller waiting to distribute annuities to the southern tribes. Sumner demanded that the portion intended for the Cheyennes be divided among the other tribes, except for the guns and ammunition, which he destroyed.

---

[12]*Army & Navy Journal*, August 17, 1878, p. 27 (hereinafter *ANJ*).

The Cheyennes, although humiliated in battle, were by no means defeated. Sumner fully intended to prosecute the war into the autumn, but demands for more troops to accompany the expedition to quell the Mormons cut short his plans. In the aftermath of the recent fight on the Solomon, the Cheyennes retaliated by attacking "Fort Floyd," isolated in the vastness of the Cheyenne country. The soldiers who got away sought refuge at Fort Kearny. Indian raiding parties also appeared along the Oregon Trail, where they harassed army supply trains bound for Utah. The Cheyennes, nonetheless, had been dealt a bitter lesson in confronting regular cavalry in a pitched fight. Their reluctance to engage troops in combat during subsequent years became evident as gold seekers bound for the new strikes in the Rocky Mountains of Colorado swarmed across their territory. Despite flagrant incursions by the whites, the Cheyennes, and their allies the Arapahoes, refrained from retaliating for six years, when events in what had become Colorado Territory again provoked them to challenge the United States Army.[14]

During the interval, Sumner's Cheyenne Expedition had proven to be a boon for Fort Laramie by confirming its strategic worth as a base for operations against the plains tribes along the eastern fringe of the Rocky Mountains.

---

[13]This account of Sumner's Cheyenne Expedition relies heavily on the definitive work by Chalfant, *Cheyennes and Horse Soldiers*; Indian Agent Robert C. Miller to John Haverty, superintendent of Indian Affairs, October 14, 1857, *ARSI*, 1857, 429–36.

CHAPTER SIX

"A State of Substantial Rebellion"

Lingering uncertainty in army circles about the necessity for permanent posts on the Oregon Route was reflected in Fort Laramie's small garrison and limited physical development until after the clash in which Grattan was killed. The construction of new buildings had all but ceased as initial needs were met during the first two years of the army's occupancy. Even though Major Hoffman's arrival with two additional companies of the Sixth Infantry in November 1854 created a critical need for more quarters and support buildings, the army was reluctant to expand facilities at a post that might be abandoned at any time. Having been issued only tents to shelter his men, Major Hoffman suspended all drills and dress parades to devote his troops' full attention to sawing lumber and constructing economical adobe buildings as temporary quarters until the high command decided the fate of Fort Laramie.[1]

Even so, progress was slow and it was obvious that new barracks could not be completed before cold weather set in. Hoffman, in a practical adaptation of local culture, concluded that the hide lodges used by the Indians would make better shelters for his men than canvas tents. He immediately negotiated with traders Ward and Guerrier to obtain the requisite number of tepees from friendly Sioux who remained in

---

[1]Hoffman was of the opinion that adobe was the best and most economical building material available. Although southeastern Wyoming was generally considered to be north of the region where adobe construction predominated, its low humidity and rainfall made the area marginally suitable. Hoffman may have looked to Fort John as a practical example, and he also may have been influenced by his own observations of such buildings during his service in the Mexican War.

the area, and who were disparaged as the "Laramie Loafers" by soldiers at the post.

By the mid-1850s Fort Laramie reflected a bizarre combination of architecture, including a walled fort with bastions, a southern plantation-style house, southwest adobes, frontier slab jacals (structures with walls made of posts set vertically in the ground), simple frame cottages and stone buildings, and now Plains Indian lodges. By the end of December, one company also occupied a portion of the ramshackle commissary storehouse near the river, while two others were crowded into the rickety, two-story frame barracks at the north end of the parade ground. Even that building had never been completed, and now the roof leaked. "In consequence of its unfinished condition this building is very open, and those quartered in it suffer much from cold during the winter," Hoffman reported.[2]

Those were not the only problems facing the commanding officer. In the spring, he reported that the portion of old Fort John that had been adapted for use as a hospital was "in a very ruinous condition and must fall down in a few months." Comfort aside, the sick and injured subsequently were moved into tents for safety. The adobe fort was so dilapidated, in fact, that Hoffman had his men raze the north and west portions soon thereafter to prevent the walls from falling on someone.[3] A month later, the shaky two-hundred-foot-long building used as a stables and storehouse *did* collapse, although miraculously the half-dozen animals inside at the time escaped uninjured. Hoffman alerted his superiors that that the pine-slab mate to that structure, then being used as a barracks, was just as old, and added, "there is no telling how soon it too may fall down. The soldiers quartered in it are possibly in some danger, and I shall probably be obliged to put them in tents dur-

---

[2]*Orders No. 55*, Fort Laramie, August 7, 1855, Orders, FL; Major William Hoffman to Major T. S. Twiss, Indian agent, October 20, 1855, LS, FL; "Annual Report of the Inspection of the Public Buildings at Fort Laramie, N. T., June 30, 1856," CCF.

[3]Hoffman to Captain Alfred Pleasonton, Acting Assistant Adjutant General (hereinafter AAAG), Sioux Expedition, April 18, 1856, LS, Fort Laramie, transcribed copies in library, FLNHS; Hoffman to First Lieutenant James L. Corley, AAAG, Sioux Expedition, ibid. In the only known photograph of Fort John, taken in 1858, it is evident that major portions of the north and west walls are missing, suggesting that the first post hospital had been located in that section. Author's note.

[4]Hoffman to Pleasonton, AAAG, Sioux Expedition., May 21, 1856, LS, FL.

ing the summer."[4] By June, the men were able to erect two adobe brick buildings, each measuring 72 feet by 21 feet, behind the two-story barracks. Company C, one of the hapless units that had spent much of the winter in tepees, moved into one of those, while two companies shared the other as a kitchen and mess hall. Hoffman intended that the new adobe structures would be remodeled at a later time to serve as mess halls for permanent barracks he envisioned in the future.[5]

The officers' quarters were only slightly better than those of the rank and file, with company commanders occupying the four apartments in "Bedlam." Since the original construction of the imposing structure, wings containing kitchens had been added at the rear corners, but the piazzas had never been finished. The notoriously hard winds roaring down the Laramie Valley had quickly damaged its shingle roof and a new one was needed. Eventually, Hoffman hired an experienced civilian builder to oversee the work of some fourteen soldier-carpenters, ten masons, and three plasterers to complete and repair the buildings. Another crew cut timber and operated a sawmill in the hills thirty-five miles west of the fort, however, doors, windows, and other millwork had to be transported from St. Louis.

With enough labor now, work progressed more rapidly, and by August the men had completed a new adobe officers' quarters immediately north of Bedlam to accommodate four subalterns. Standing to the south, between Bedlam and the river, was a row of three two-room houses. Chaplain William Vaux, a civilian, continued to inhabit a decrepit three-room adobe shack covered by a mud roof.

By the fall of 1855, the garrison had erected an icehouse and two temporary granaries, and had enlarged the bakery to serve the larger garrison. Troops also constructed a footbridge over the Laramie at a point just east of Fort John to facilitate crossing to Ward and Guerrier's new temporary trading post and the camping ground frequented by both emigrants and Indians. Major Hoffman, however, closed down the "self-serve" blacksmith shop that Van Vliet had established several years earlier as an accommodation to emigrants, thus depriving travelers of repair services for the entire 460 miles between Fort Kearny and Richard's station at Platte Bridge.[6]

---

[5]"Report of Inspection, 1856;" Hoffman to Corley, August 19, 1856, ibid.
[6]First Lieutenant John C. Kelton to Major George H. Crosman, October 28, 1856, CCF.

Hoffman's decision to close the shop may have been rooted in rumors circulating once again that Fort Laramie would be abandoned and the garrison transferred to the Pacific Northwest. Campaigns against the Yakima tribe in Washington Territory during 1856 brought a tentative peace to that region, but the army established two new forts near the Yakimas to maintain stability between the Indians and white settlers. With its mission on the frontier expanding yearly, the tiny regular army was stretched to its limits. Consequently, troops in comparatively quiet areas like Fort Laramie were shuffled to scenes of more urgency. While Army Headquarters was pondering the fate of the Fort Laramie garrison, the Cheyennes' retaliation for Stewart's attack on the party at Grand Island forced the commanders to reconsider abandoning the post because it was the only available supply point in the entire region capable of supporting campaigns against the Indians.

Meantime, events in Utah were taking shape that would also cast Fort Laramie in a new light of importance. Both the Grattan incident and the recent Cheyenne troubles along the Platte had motivated William M. F. Magraw to request a release from his mail contract. Further, unusually heavy snows during the winter of 1854–55 all but stopped mail and passenger service to California. Passenger service ended entirely in August 1856 when the government finally freed Magraw of his obligations as a result of Hockaday's partnership in the overland stage line. In Utah Territory, disgruntled Mormons, already frustrated with Magraw's irregular service to them and the resulting collapse of their communication with the East, took the initiative and made their own bid for the route to Utah.

In the fall, as the Cheyennes along the Platte were coexisting with whites without incident, the government issued a new mail contract to Hiram Kimball of Utah. Kimball served as agent for Mormon leaders who had plans to secure, and thus control, service to the territory. This scheme originating with Latter-day Saints leader and ad hoc territorial governor Brigham Young. Young calculated that relay stations along the route would serve as seed for future Mormon trading posts and eventually new communities, thus spreading the influence of the Latter-day Saints across the frontier. Left unsaid was the potential for wielding control over the road, and thus communication with Utah. The mail firm came to be known as the Brigham Young Express & Carrying Company, commonly shortened to "the B. Y. X."

The Mormons, who had begun migrating to Utah in the 1840s to escape religious bigotry in the States, covertly desired to establish a powerful territorial government controlled by their church. Those plans were bolstered by the failure of Magraw's mail contract, as the resulting interruption of communications with Utah worked to the advantage of Mormon leaders desiring more authority over territorial affairs. When rumors of these objectives filtered back to Washington in early 1857, government officials were alarmed at the perceived threat to federal authority as well as to the constitutional tenet separating church and state. In Washington circles, conditions in Utah quickly assumed the dimensions of an open Mormon revolt.

A. O. Smoot, the mayor of Salt Lake City and designated agent for the B. Y. X., was in the States during February when he learned of the federal government's reaction to the news of a Mormon rebellion. When postal authorities at Independence refused to allow Smoot to carry the mail back to Utah, and summarily terminated the B. Y. X. contract, it became obvious to Smoot that the government distrusted the Mormons. U.S. concerns about their activities in Utah suddenly resolved the question of whether or not Fort Laramie, the United States military post closest to the Utah territory, should be abandoned.[7]

Magraw may have given up the mail business, but he soon reappeared on the frontier in another capacity. A personal friend of President James Buchanan, the ex-stage man used his relationship to secure an appointment as superintendent of a federal survey of the central Overland route, part of a larger ongoing effort by the Department of the Interior to build and improve wagon roads on the frontier for their ultimate use as supply routes during the construction of the transcontinental railroads. Magraw assembled a crew of one hundred men, equipped to remain ten months in the field to improve the overland road between Fort Kearny and Independence Rock. The expedition,

---

[7]Fort Hall, the third post established on the Oregon Route, would have been closer, but it had been abandoned in 1850 because of lack of forage and the cost of supplying the garrison. Frazer, *Forts of the West*, 44–45.

operating under the grandiose title of the Fort Kearny, South Pass, and
Honey Lake Wagon Road Survey, carried with it letters of authoriza-
tion to draw supplies at military posts along the way. Frederick W.
Lander, considered by many to be a more competent supervisor than
Magraw, was appointed both the engineer and the crew foreman.[8]

Lander left Fort Leavenworth with a reconnaissance party of fourteen men in June 1857 and camped at Fort Laramie in early July, a few
days after Sumner's column left for its rendezvous with Sedgwick on
the South Platte. Lander found several places along the road in need
of work, but his most notable contribution was his discovery of a better crossing over the South Platte, along what had become known as
the Fort Laramie Route. When the new ford was completed, emigrant
and army freight trains coursed along the south side of the Platte, past
the forks, until they reached the Upper (or California) Crossing.
There they turned due north cross-country over the divide to intersect
the North Platte. The new ford, nine miles below the other crossing,
shortened the distance between the branches of the Platte by an entire
day's travel.

Lander's work was timely because plans were already taking shape to
move an army expedition toward Utah Territory to restore order
among the Mormons. Writing from Army Headquarters, General
Winfield Scott justified the expedition on the grounds that the populace and the civil government there were "in a state of substantial
rebellion against the laws and authority of the United States."
Although Brigham Young had been the duly appointed territorial
governor in 1850, his term expired in 1854 and the office was left vacant
thereafter. Young, boasting that he needed nothing but divine authority to rule his people, continued to serve as governor without presidential approval. President Buchanan decided that a new Utah territorial
government, composed primarily of selected federal authorities, would
be installed to regain control over the wayward Mormons. The army
would enforce the president's edict.

On June 10, the Quartermaster Department of the army notified the
freighting firm of Majors and Russell, already under contract to haul

---

[8]The activities of the federal Wagon Road Office are fully elaborated in Jackson, *Wagon Roads
West*, 192–201, 206–17.

military supplies to Fort Kearny, Fort Laramie, and forts in New Mexico, to be prepared to transport two-and-a-half-million pounds of provisions urgently needed to support the forthcoming military expedition to Salt Lake City. Owner William Russell objected to the army's demand because most of the company's trains were already committed to fulfilling the existing contracts. To meet this unanticipated requirement, Russell argued, his firm would be forced to purchase scores of extra wagons and over three thousand oxen to pull them. In addition, the company would need to hire hundreds more teamsters, and at higher wages than provided under the current contract. The prospect of such a great investment seriously risked overextension of both their capital and credit, spelling financial ruin for the freighters. Nevertheless, the army insisted that it was an emergency and assured the owners that they would be adequately compensated in the end. Trusting the government's word, Majors and Russell brought to bear all of their experience and resources to organize numerous wagon trains, load them with tons of military supplies, and quickly send them up the trail, despite the lateness of the season.

General of the Army Winfield Scott, meanwhile, directed General Harney, who had warred against the Sioux two years before, to lead the expedition to quell the Mormons. Colonel Edmund Brooke Alexander, an aging forty-year veteran, was put in command of the first Utah-bound contingent, composed of eight companies of his own Tenth Infantry (the other two would catch up later), the entire Fifth Infantry, the light battery of the Fourth Artillery, and a battery of twelve-pounder field guns manned by an ordnance detachment. The units began the long trek across the plains toward Fort Laramie piecemeal, in the latter part of July, each one departing a few days after the other.

Assistant Quartermaster Stewart Van Vliet also was dispatched from Fort Leavenworth with an escort, to ride ahead to Salt Lake City to arrange for quartering and supplying the Army of Utah once it arrived there. The federal government was still under the false impression that the Utah rebellion involved only certain Mormon factions, rather then the entire population. Believing the engagement, if any, would be relatively limited, Van Vliet paused for three days at Fort Laramie, where he had served at the beginning of the decade, to requisition a number of teams and wagons to haul the forage he intended to purchase from Mormon farmers once he established an office in Salt Lake.

Upon Van Vliet's arrival at there, Brigham Young and his associates extended a courteous, though cool reception, informing the captain that the army should make no attempt to enter the territory. Van Vliet was stunned by Young's demeanor and was astonished to find the community of Saints so strongly united in their opposition to federal control in any form that they would make nothing whatever available to the invading army. Van Vliet informed Young that while the Mormons might defeat the first battalion being sent against them, a much larger force was already scheduled to follow in the spring of 1858. Church leaders responded by boldly challenging the troops to invade Utah; they would find nothing to support men or animals once they arrived. If necessary, they threatened, they were prepared to conduct a scorched earth policy: the entire territory would be laid waste—fields, orchards, storehouses, even homes would be burned.

Captain Van Vliet reported this intelligence to headquarters at Fort Leavenworth, adding his observation that for fifty miles east of the Salt Lake Valley the road wound through narrow canyonland. Such terrain would make it easy for a comparatively small force to repel Alexander's advancing column. The coming winter, already evident at that altitude, would soon choke the canyons with deep snow, effectively preventing any further field operations that season. Van Vliet then suggested that it might be prudent to winter the troops at Fort Bridger, at a trading post on Black's Fork, and at another temporary camp he would establish on Ham's Fork, thirty miles away, to await reinforcements and the coming of spring.[9]

During Van Vliet's reconnaissance, President Buchanan had bowed to a request by Kansas Governor Robert J. Walker to retain General Harney at Fort Leavenworth to deal with continuing troubles between anti-slavery and pro-slavery factions in the territory. General Scott therefore summoned Colonel Albert Sidney Johnston, commanding the newly organized Second Cavalry in Texas, to head the Army of

---

[9]Captain Stewart Van Vliet to Captain A. Pleasonton, AAAG, Army of Utah, September 16, 1857, ARSW, 1858, 24–27.

Utah. Since his forces were already on the march west, Johnston, with an escort of dragoons, hurried to catch up to them. Bringing up the rear were six companies of the Second Dragoons under Lieutenant Colonel Philip St. George Cooke, a distinguished veteran of the Battle of the Blue Water, and several federal civilian officials, who would be installed as the nucleus of the new territorial government. Among them was Governor Alfred E. Cumming, a Georgian and former commissioner of Indian affairs.

Meanwhile, Colonel Alexander's advance battalion reached Bordeaux's trading post on the last day of August and went into camp, probably on the same ground once occupied by Conquering Bear's village. From their bivouac, the soldiers could easily distinguish the ominous mound of rocks covering the remains of Grattan's men. The advance elements of the long column wound their way into the Laramie Valley late the next morning and established a bivouac on the lowlands north of the post. Over the next few days, nearly 1,500 men comprising the various elements of the battalion arrived on the floodplain, making the largest body of troops to visit Fort Laramie up to that time.[10]

Captain John W. Phelps, commanding the light battery, noted in his diary that the fort was "one of the prettiest outposts I have seen. It has been furnished with a steam sawmill and enough lumber has in consequence been made to enable the commanding officer to put up passable quarters and store houses. . . . But by far the neatest and most elegant and comfortable quarters are those which the commanding officer has designed and executed in adobes. There is a neatness, simplicity, and architectural effect about them that is really classical."[11]

The following day, Major Hoffman extended the hospitality of the post by inviting the recently arrived officers to dine at his quarters. They learned from him that Johnston had recently been placed in charge of the Army of Utah, a command that now included Forts Kearny and Laramie to facilitate the coordination of troop movements and supplies. The officers of the column privately rejoiced in the decision to supplant the aging Alexander. "The old woman feels it sensibly," Captain Jesse

---

[10]Gove, *Utah Expedition*, 50; Hafen and Hafen, *The Utah Expedition 1857–1858*, 122–23.
[11]Ibid., 123.

A. Gove confided, mocking the colonel in a letter to his wife. "He grows more worthless every day he lives." A more robust Alexander had received two brevets for gallantry during the Mexican War, but now his long years of military service left him little energy and even less enthusiasm for a rigorous campaign on the frontier.

At four o'clock on the morning of September 4, assembled drummers rattled out reveille, summoning the troops of the expedition to continue the advance on Utah. In truth, Captain Gove too lacked inspiration for the operation and probably echoed the sentiments of others in the officer corps when he wrote, "They [Mormons] will offer no resistance. . . . we are to go and have it done with . . . the sooner it is over the better."[12]

Slowed by heavy rains and deep sand, Colonel Johnston and his escort did not reach Fort Laramie until a month after Alexander and the main body had left. Lieutenant Colonel Charles F. Smith, commanding the two tardy companies of the Tenth Infantry, had just passed the fort, trying to catch up with the main column. Smith left a large detachment of soldiers at the post to reinforce the escort accompanying Johnston. Johnston drew off two companies of dragoons from the garrison, which Sumner had left behind. With Johnston's departure, only two companies of the Seventh Infantry remained at the post.[13]

The long-suffering companies of the Sixth Infantry had recently been ordered to rendezvous with their regiment at Fort Leavenworth in preparation for a welcome transfer to the Pacific Coast. Two of the companies were therefore assigned to join Sumner's Cheyenne expedition, destined to return to Leavenworth via Fort Riley, while the remaining two, led by Major Hoffman, marched eastward, encountering Johnston en route to Utah. It was an unfortunate meeting for Hoffman and his men. Colonel Johnston, in retrospect, anticipating the potential vulnerability of his supply line with only two companies

---

[12]Ibid.

[13]*Orders No. 20*, Battalion of the Tenth Infantry, September 26, 1857, LR, FL; *Orders No. 21*, September 28, 1857, ibid.; Johnston to Major Irvin McDowell, Headquarters of the Army, October 5, 1857, reprinted in Hafen and Hafen, *Utah Expedition*, 145–47; Returns for August and September 1857, Seventh Infantry, Returns from Regular Army Infantry Regiments 1821–1916, R. G. 94, roll 80, Microcopy 665, NA.

left at Fort Laramie, ordered Hoffman to turn back and resume command of the post. Hoffman's disappointment was bitter indeed.

The Mormons, meanwhile, took the offensive by sending out parties of guerillas to strike Johnston's army before its components could be assembled. During the night of September 24 raiders attempted, unsuccessfully, to stampede the mules belonging to the Tenth Infantry's baggage train. Another Mormon attack on October 5, however, was more successful. Discovering two army supply trains on Green River, Mormon raiders plundered and burned them. The next day they attacked and destroyed another train on the Big Sandy, thus depriving the Army of Utah of 150 tons of critical supplies.[14]

As noted, Johnston paused only briefly at Fort Laramie before hastening on in pursuit of the advance battalion of his army. Fearing Mormon rangers might attempt to capture or assassinate Cumming as he made his way to Salt Lake City, he detached twenty-five dragoons from his own escort to bolster the governor's bodyguard, now numbering about two hundred men. Johnston urged the officer commanding the escort to take Cumming in tow upon his arrival at the fort and to catch up with Smith and himself as quickly as possible. Colonel Cooke, Governor Cumming, and the six companies of the Second Dragoons did not ride into Laramie until October 20, their march also having been retarded by the same bad roads Johnston had encountered.

Two couriers sent by Alexander met Johnston at Three Crossings on the Sweetwater River, informing him of the Mormon raids on the supply trains, as well as of Alexander's plan to reach Salt Lake City via the Bear River, thus avoiding the potential dangers to be met in Echo Canyon. Johnston cautiously ordered a countermarch to Black's Fork, where all the troops and trains rendezvoused for the winter. A handful of Mormon raiders thus thwarted the army's first grand effort to invade Utah, bringing the effort to an abysmal end in the snow.

Although the tents, blankets, and most of the other camp equipage had not been aboard the supply trains burned by the Mormons, food was in extremely short supply. The well-stocked Fort Laramie thus

---

[14]Colonel E. B. Alexander to Colonel Samuel Cooper, AGUSA, October 9, 1857, ARSW, 1858, 29; Rodenbough, *Army of the United States*, 536; Carroll, "The Wyoming Sojourn of the Utah Expedition, 1857–1858," 11.

became critical to the Army of Utah's very survival. The Commissary Department had amassed an enormous quantity of supplies at the post, including nearly 150 tons of flour, 24 tons of bacon, and over 10 tons of coffee. The problem now was how to get it to Johnston's army at Black's Fork. Major Isaac Lynde, then commanding Laramie, had only half-dozen poor mule teams available, and those were needed for hauling wood to the post. So, while Johnston and his army endured short rations, a mountain of food sat idle at Fort Laramie for lack of transportation.

Supply problems were compounded when, in 1858, with no public explanation, Forts Kearny and Laramie were placed back under the authority of the Department of the West, headquartered in St. Louis. This move left Johnston in command of the new Department of Utah, which had been carved from the western portion of the Department of the West. It reduced his ability to provide for his army, because most of his supply line now lay outside his personal authority. Johnston argued to have the order rescinded, but army headquarters in Washington stood firm.[15]

While Congress debated the wisdom of the intended Utah invasion, the army advanced its plans to mobilize reinforcements for Johnston. A circular promulgated in January 1858 directed the entire First Cavalry to assemble at Fort Leavenworth in preparation for joining the Utah Expedition in the field. To them would be added two companies of the First Dragoons, the remaining ten companies of the Sixth Infantry, ten companies of the Seventh Infantry, and two light batteries of the Second Artillery. The combined forces would number over 5,300 men, a disproportionately large percentage of the United States Army, which at the time numbered only 17,000 men. General Harney, relieved of his duties in Kansas, would lead the reinforcements, marching out from Leavenworth in six separate columns, and would assume command of the entire Army of Utah upon his juncture with Johnston at Black's Fork.

Major Hoffman, who had since joined his regiment at Fort Leavenworth, was put in charge of the supply train and a herd of some three-hundred replacement mules. The army would not repeat its mistake of

[15]Ibid., 48; Thian, *Notes Illustrating the Military Geography*, 100, 105.

allowing unguarded trains to fall prey to Mormon attack. This time, two companies of the Sixth Infantry, along with the two Dragoon companies, would serve as escort. The train would take the established route west via Fort Laramie, where the two remaining companies of the Sixth and one of the Seventh stationed there would join Hoffman, leaving only F Company, Seventh Infantry to man the fort.[16]

The intrepid freighters, now operating under the name Russell, Majors, and Waddell, prepared to send additional trains to Utah to supply Johnston's burgeoning forces. Although the reinforcements were responsible for carrying three months' rations with them on the journey, Harney wanted another eight months' worth for the entire expedition to be stockpiled at Fort Laramie prior to winter. To achieve this, it was necessary to haul some three thousand tons of supplies up the trail from Fort Leavenworth, a feat that challenged the freighters to hire all the available wagons, teams, and men in the vicinity of Leavenworth. Russell, Majors, and Waddell eventually hired over four thousand men and launched almost that many ox-drawn wagons up the trail, traveling in trains of twenty-five wagons each. The partners also requested and were granted permission to construct depots consisting of shops, storehouses, and corrals at Forts Kearny and Laramie to support their part of the ambitious operation.[17]

To ensure the delivery of adequate supplies of grain for the draft animals, without having to allocate any of their own vehicles for that purpose, the company cleared land, planted seed, and established farms near both posts. At the post, however, although he was instructed to plant fields for feed, Lynde dragged his feet designating a place on the military reservation for those operations. He ordered the freighters to keep their haying activities at least forty miles away from the post, to preserve the available grass for the army's herds. Lynde continued to stall on the field work until July, provoking the freighters to complain directly to Secretary of War John B. Floyd about Lynde's failure to help meet the demand for livestock feed. Rus-

---

[16]Hoffman to AAG, Department of Utah, June 10, 1858, *ARSW*, 1858, 177–81.

[17]This endeavor eventually bankrupted the firm after the partners lost thousands of oxen to freezing temperatures and lack of forage. As a result, they were forced to sell wagons that cost from $150 to $175 each for as little as $10 to Mormons, who salvaged them for iron to make nails. Majors, *Seventy Years On the Frontier*, 142–43.

sell, Majors, and Waddell suspected that post sutler Seth E. Ward, appointed the previous year, viewed their interests as competition with his own, since he held the government hay contract. Late in July, Floyd directed Scott to demand that Lynde comply with his earlier directive.[18]

The army continued to maintain an interest in finding a more direct westerly route to Utah Territory from the Upper Crossing on the South Platte River across Cheyenne Pass to Fort Bridger in southwest Wyoming Territory. While most of Harney's columns would follow the traditional overland route west, one battalion was ordered to take the alternate trail to test the feasibility of Bryan's trail, a passage mapped in 1856. A special detachment, led by First Lieutenant William P. Carlin, Sixth Infantry, and accompanied by Bryan himself, would develop a primitive road to facilitate the passage of wagons.

The winter months, however, provided time for diplomacy. Before Harney's column was fairly underway, President Buchanan rushed two emissaries to Utah bearing a compromise proposal for Brigham Young. If the insubordinate Mormons would promise to respect federal authority and would not oppose Governor Cumming, all would be forgiven. When the president's commissioners arrived at Salt Lake City near the end of May 1858, Brigham Young agreed to step aside and to demand that his people avoid a war that would only ravage the territory. With those conditions met, Alfred E. Cumming was installed as territorial governor in mid-June, and soon thereafter Colonel Johnston marched into the capital city at the head of his army. The troops, under strict orders not to molest the populace or cause trouble of any sort, passed through without incident and soon established Camp Floyd some forty miles south of the city.

With such a large part of the U.S. army detached to Utah, and the posts between there and Fort Leavenworth so meagerly garrisoned, Scott finally relieved the Fourth Artillery from its police duties in Kansas and redirected the "red legs" to protect the overland trails. In late July three companies took up station at Fort Kearny, two more

---

[18]*ARSW*, 1858, 797; Russell, Majors, and Waddell to Secretary of War, February 26, 1858, LS, FL; Samuel Cooper, AGUSA, to Commanding Officer, Fort Kearny (copy to Fort Laramie), March 26, 1858, ibid.

camped on the new trail across Cheyenne Pass, while the regimental headquarters and three companies occupied Fort Laramie. Because of the vital importance of Platte Bridge on the supply line to Utah, two more companies were sent to that location to reestablish a temporary cantonment that was christened Post of Platte Bridge.[19]

Although the Utah campaign had been as abortive as Captain Gove and some other officers had predicted, it had convinced the army's high command that Fort Laramie could not be abandoned after all. It had proven critical for supplying Johnston's forces; indeed, without it the Utah Expedition would not have been possible. Now that the army had established a permanent presence in the territory, Fort Laramie assumed new importance as an indispensable link in the military supply line to Utah.

---

[19]Rodenbough, *Army of the United States*, 359. The temporary cantonment, named Camp Walbach in honor of deceased Colonel John De Barth Walbach, Fourth Artillery, was established east of Cheyenne Pass on Lodgepole Creek on September 20, 1858. U.S. troops were withdrawn April 19, 1859. The site is about twenty miles east of present-day Laramie, Wyoming; Frazer, *Forts of the West*, 186. Besides being the home of John Richard, Platte Bridge was the site of the "Mormon Ferry," also called Mormon Station, established in 1847. In December 1857, troops from Fort Laramie were sent to that location, as well as to the station at Deer Creek Crossing, to search for caches of Mormon weapons and munitions that might be seized by the rebellious settlers in Utah. The site was also known variously as Camp Platte, and Camp Payne, but was abandoned in the spring of 1859. In May 1862 it became the site of Fort Caspar, ibid., 179. Lieutenant John L. Marmaduke to Commanding Officer, Fort Laramie, N. T., December 16, 1857, LR, FL; McDermott, *Frontier Crossroads*, 16–17.

CHAPTER SEVEN

"The Mail Line Is Indispensable"

T he apparent cessation of hostilities with the Cheyennes and the quasi-peaceful resolution of the Mormon rebellion inspired a new surge of westward emigration toward the end of the 1850s. Also, rumors of gold discoveries in the Rocky Mountains in late summer 1858 fueled the passions of adventuresome Americans as nothing had since the California rush a decade earlier. Initial reports from the Pike's Peak region proclaimed that gold could be found simply by sticking a shovel in the ground. But prospectors arriving there the following spring found to their dismay that unscrupulous merchants had inflated the magnitude of the strike as grossly as they had their prices for supplies.

In January 1859 George Jackson, a prospector working alone in the mountains above the new settlement of Denver, serendipitously stumbled upon a gold-bearing gravel bed in Clear Creek. Marking the spot but taking the precaution to cover any signs of his digging, Jackson spent the rest of the winter in Denver before returning to his claim, along with several eager partners, the following spring. Although the bonanza turned out to be less promising than Jackson had anticipated, it was nonetheless impressive.

As this news renewed hopes of fortunes to be made, the backwash of Pike's Peakers receding from the Rockies suddenly reverted to a fresh wave across the plains. Once again, hoards of would-be prospectors, spurred by visions of instant wealth for the taking, hurried west to Colorado. Many took the established Platte River road as far as Upper Crossing, but instead of turning northward at that point, they proceeded directly up the South Platte to Denver. Others pioneered an alternate route leading from the Missouri River at Atchison, Kansas, directly to Denver, going almost due west along the Smoky Hill River. Although about ninety miles shorter than either the Platte road or the old Santa Fe Trail, the track along the Smoky Hill passed directly through Cheyenne hunting grounds, a dangerous gamble few of the "Fifty-niners" were willing to take.[1]

The overland route itself also underwent improvements, including the completion of a new bridge by Louis Ganard over the North Platte about six miles above John Richard's original crossing near Red Buttes. The Pacific Wagon Road Office also sponsored improvements on the trail by spending fifty thousand dollars to upgrade the segment from Council Bluffs to Fort Kearny, a project that included bridging several streams. The government invested an additional three hundred thousand dollars for a Fort Kearny, South Pass, and Honey Lake Wagon Road survey, conducted by Frederick Lander two years earlier.

Meanwhile, communications between the western territories and the Pacific Coast began to improve. After the cancellation of the B. Y. Express mail contract in June 1857, John M. Hockaday acquired the contract to provide monthly service over the central emigrant route from St. Joseph, Missouri, to Salt Lake City. He proposed to utilize the six stations that Magraw had built and to keep three wagon trains in motion to the fort, where the mail would be transferred to connecting trains running to Salt Lake City.

Since both President James Buchanan and Postmaster General Aaron V. Brown hailed from the South, special interest groups exerted intense pressure on the Buchanan administration to designate a southern mail route as the primary transcontinental artery. The visionary Brown, ever a staunch advocate of western business and settlement, was convinced that expediting the mail across the continent was the key to that growth and expansion. He therefore awarded par-

---

[1]Although the Smoky Hill Trail was not heavily used by gold seekers, it possessed undeniable advantages as the most direct route across the plains to Denver. It was officially surveyed in 1860, starting at Leavenworth, Kansas. But, an ever-present Indian danger discouraged most people from taking the road until David A. Butterfield established both freight and mail service over it in 1865. It was largely abandoned after the Kansas Pacific Railroad was completed five years later. Oliva, *Fort Hays*, 1–3.

ticular businesses with generous mail contracts that would subsidize their costs for providing passenger service and for building the additional stations required for picking up fresh animals that would ensure rapid trips. Not only would an eastern mail terminus at St. Louis be of economic benefit to the South, it would have the strategic value of placing the entire cross-country route within southern territory if the slavery controversy led to war. Moreover, rich gold deposits in California and in the southwestern territories would be critical to financing a southern war effort.

Thus began a sectional struggle between political factions that favored the central route via South Pass, some 2,100 miles, and those supporting the Ox Bow route, as it came to be called because of its circuitous U-shaped course from twin termini at St. Louis and Memphis, via El Paso and San Diego to San Francisco, a total distance of 2,795 miles. On the score of distance alone, there was clearly no contest between them. But southern advocates argued that travel over the northerly road was limited by severe winters and sometimes hostile Indians. In the end, Postmaster General Brown succumbed to regional favoritism and awarded the new contract to the Butterfield Overland Mail Company, based in New York, in 1857.

Northern factions immediately cried foul, causing Brown to appease them by contracting with Hockaday & Liggett to continue their service between St. Joseph and Salt Lake City, and with Hockaday's other partner, George Chorpenning, to establish a connecting line from the Utah capital to California. However, Brown, who had sole control over the contracts, awarded dramatically lower sums to Hockaday and his partners to preclude any serious competition with Butterfield. Brown calculated, accurately, that less compensation for the central route would translate into correspondingly slower service, as Hockaday would not have the capital to build the optimum number of way stations, nor could he afford enough coaches and teams to produce faster deliveries. Thus, for example, despite the shorter distance, the Hockaday-Chorpenning line required thirty-two days to complete the trip to California, and then only on a semi-monthly schedule.[2]

---

[2]Gray, "The Salt Lake Hockaday Mail," 1: 14–17; Frederick, *Ben Holladay*, 50–54.

A short time later, Russell, Majors, and Waddell bought out Hock-aday & Liggett's interests in the line to form the Central Overland California and Pike's Peak Express Company (coc & pp Ex. Co.). The company now had the resources to construct dozens of additional stations on the central route, allowing daily stages to make runs in both directions simultaneously in only ten days. At that, Brown saw to it that the only through mail (mail going all the way to California) they handled consisted of newspapers and official government correspondence, thereby preserving Butterfield's near-monopoly with the Ox Bow Route. By the end of the decade, the nation's regular Pacific mail totaled nearly ten tons per month, making it clear to the postmaster general that the only practical solution to efficient mail delivery was a transcontinental railroad.[3]

Russell, Majors, and Waddell apparently discontinued their use of the Magraw change station just below Fort Laramie in favor of establishing a station at Gemenian P. Beauvais's trading post (formerly the American Fur Company post) five miles farther down the North Platte. The coaches followed the usual road paralleling the river before crossing over the Laramie River bridge to swing through the fort. There they paused briefly at the post office, located in the sutler's store, while Ordnance Sergeant Leodegar Schnyder, the designated postmaster, exchanged the incoming and outgoing mailbags. The meticulous Schnyder, appointed to his position in 1859 and serving until 1876, became legendary for his autocratic management of the post office. On one occasion, the prickly sergeant physically ousted a superior officer from his domain for daring to sort through the mail looking for his own letters.[4]

Although Hockaday provided reasonably reliable delivery over his portion of the central route, Chorpenning's operations on the western segment were not so well managed. Repeated failures to deliver the mail on time led the Post Office Department to reconsider his contract early in 1860. This fortuitous circumstance played into the hands

---

[3]Majors, *Seventy Years on the Frontier*, 165–66; Gray, "Hockaday Mail," 1: 17; *Annual Report of the Postmaster General*, 1859, 1409–10 (hereinafter cited as *arpg* with year).

[4]*Chicago American*, February 10, 1901, transcript in vertical files, FLNHS; Gray, "Hockaday Mail," 1: 19; McDermott, "Fort Laramie's Silent Soldier," 128.

of Russell, Majors, and Waddell. Having previously acquired Hockaday's Utah mail contract as part of the arrangement to buy out his interests, Russell and his partners already controlled the eastern half of the line. After Postmaster General Brown died, his successor, Joseph P. Holt, did not continue his predecessor's favoritism for the Ox Bow route. In fact, the new postmaster general was dedicated to making the department financially self-sustaining, rather than paying express companies exorbitant subsidies as inducements to carry the mail over routes that were otherwise unprofitable. Holt therefore annulled Chorpenning's contract and granted it to Russell, Majors, and Waddell, thus consolidating mail service over the entire central route.[5]

Even though the Post Office Department had pieced together a transcontinental mail route, the government still paid only for semimonthly service, a legacy of Brown's biased administration. The hopes the Central Overland Express Company held for securing a lucrative line to the new El Dorado at Denver vanished almost as suddenly as the opportunity had arisen. Neither the Smoky Hill route across Kansas Territory nor a new road up the South Platte to Denver had materialized for them. Because of the peculiar way in which the company had obtained its separate contracts—literally by picking up the crumbs of its predecessors—the Central Overland was now desperate to secure a more profitable contract for new daily service from St. Joseph, Missouri, to Placerville, California. With the COC & PP Ex. Co. staring bankruptcy squarely in the face, something had to be done, and quickly, to rekindle the federal government's interest in a central route via Fort Laramie.

California Senator William McKendree Gwinn, who adamantly opposed the circuitous Butterfield route, demanded that his state receive better mail service, especially in view of its wealth, influence, and the talk of war. Impressed by Russell, Majors, and Waddell's experience and excellent reputation for turning their plans into reality, the senator approached Russell with a daring proposal for a new system of couriers that would carry mail from St. Joseph to San Francisco in only ten days. The flamboyant Russell was intrigued by the idea, but found his ever-cautious partners less enthusiastic about such a

---

[5]Much of the information presented in following sections relies on Hafen, *The Overland Mail*, 156–57.

wild gamble. Russell eventually prevailed, nevertheless, by convincing them that in this instance there was more to consider than short-term financial gain. If they could demonstrate that a daily mail could reach California via the middle route in only ten days, at all times of the year, pressure would mount in Congress to abandon the Ox Bow as the principal transcontinental route. Considering their existing capital investments, familiarity with the region, and established reputation in the transportation business, Russell was certain their company would be favorably positioned to acquire a new postal contract.

To implement the Pony Express, the firm purchased five hundred well-bred horses and hired eighty courageous riders of small stature at the unheard-of salary of $125 a month. Russell, Majors, and Waddell built additional relay stations ten to twelve miles apart as needed to fill the gaps between the existing ones that offered coach service, thereby conserving the horses. Fort Laramie, despite having a post office, was not a practical location for a relay because the company would have required special authorization to erect quarters for a station keeper and livestock corrals within the military reservation. A station within or near the garrison also would have forced the post's nighttime sentinels to challenge the identity of riders as they approached, thereby endangering them. Express stations therefore were established a few miles distant from the fort, though the riders did cross the Laramie River bridge to continue their journey along the south side of the North Platte. Russell, Majors, and Waddell therefore elected to utilize its existing station at Beauvais's ranch and to construct another at Register Cliff, a few miles beyond Fort Laramie.

Living up to their reputation, after making the decision to proceed, the partners completed preparations in only sixty days. Each courier typically rode three segments between "swing" stations, an average of thirty-three miles total, before handing off the mail to another. Circumstances, however, frequently required the express men to endure considerably longer distances between "home" stations where riders were quartered.

To reduce weight, messages were written on tissue paper; the Pony Express fee per half-ounce was five dollars. The riders carried a maximum of ten pounds of mail, secured in locked leather pockets of the *mochila,* a special removable saddle cover that was transferred from one horse to another during the journey. The first rider left Sacramento on April 3, 1860, and, as promised, the mail arrived at St. Joseph just ten days later, a reduction of eleven days under Butterfield's best record. The theory of providing express mail was proved, though as Majors and Waddell had feared, the income for the company amounted to only one-tenth of the operational costs. Nevertheless, the feat itself, and the unfailing consistency of the service, vindicated William Russell's confidence and made compelling evidence for the argument that the central route was superior to the southern.

Although the postmaster general still harbored reservations about the year-around feasibility of relying on the central route, certain members of Congress, influenced by a number of powerful Wall Street magnates, became convinced it would be the cheapest and fastest way to get mail service to California. Even more importantly for the government, the entire link from the Missouri River to the Pacific Coast would lie within northern territory. Ignoring Holt's reluctance to fully endorse the central-route proposal, federal legislators passed a bill in March 1861 terminating the Ox Bow contract and transferring Butterfield's assets to the Central Route. An appropriation of one million dollars included not only compensation for the Butterfield line's damages against the existing contract, it purchased a contract for daily regular mail service on a twenty to twenty-three-day schedule, adjusted to the season, with a branch line serving Denver. Additionally, the fledgling Pony Express, conveying urgent mail, would operate separately on a semi-weekly basis until the transcontinental telegraph line was completed to the Pacific.

Delivering the mail to Denver, however, posed a problem. That community lay some two hundred miles off the main line. Extending a connecting star route southward afforded the most obvious solution, yet it would be expensive and service would be scheduled no more than once every three weeks. Moreover, when the transcontinental telegraph line was later completed, Denver was also serviced only by a branch line. Conversely, were Denver situated on the primary route, it would have benefited by having daily mail, the Pony Express, and eventually, contact with the States by telegraph.

That the rapidly growing town on Cherry Creek stood to become the great halfway point between New York and San Francisco was not lost on its business community. A director of the coc & pp Ex. Co. took advantage of this potentiality by proposing that the residents of Denver underwrite the construction costs to build stations on the line of the Cherokee Trail running northwest from the city to the Laramie Plains, thence to Fort Bridger.[6] Marshall and partners, in turn, would not alter its proposed main line to depart from the old emigrant trail at the California Crossing, and the nearby settlement of Julesburg, to continue westerly from that point. Denver, with fast, reliable express service of its own, was thus assured of a bright future. Russell, Majors, and Waddell reduced considerably their expenses by creating a more direct route to Salt Lake City, thereby also avoiding having to develop an expensive star line link with Denver to comply with the terms of the postal contract. Mail coaches began plying the usual Salt Lake–California road via Fort Laramie and South Pass on July 1, 1861.

The South seceded from the Union during the early months of that year. With sectional hostilities especially intensifying in Missouri, the postmaster general judiciously authorized the establishment of an alternate route westward across Iowa to Omaha, there connecting to the recently established Overland Stage Line at Fort Kearny, and when Confederate incursions began threatening the mail in eastern Kansas and Nebraska, Russell, Majors, and Waddell arranged to rendezvous the westbound coaches there. During following months, however, Indian raids spurred Postmaster General Holt to again modify the route, this time more significantly, noting that "the mail line is indis-

---

[6]Fur trader William H. Ashley is credited with first exploring one segment, known specifically as the Cherokee Trail, during the 1820s as a route to the annual Green River rendezvous. The track, extending from Pueblo to Fort Bridger, was also followed by a party of Cherokee Indians migrating from Indian Territory to California in the 1840s, hence its name. John C. Frémont probably conducted the first formal examination of the lower portion of the route during his 1843 expedition to the West. Proceeding northwest across what is now Kansas, Frémont divided his party at St. Vrain's Fort, one group traveling southward to the site of modern Pueblo, Colorado, then retracing its steps to join Frémont on an excursion up the Cache la Poudre River into the Laramie Mountains. Frémont and a small handpicked party attempted to find a way through the mountains, and eventually did, coming out on the Laramie Plains. Benjamin F. Hall to President of the United States, October 26, 1861, *Official Records of the Union and Confederate Armies*, 2nd ser., vol. 115, no. 5: 120 (hereinafter cited as *OR*); Goeztmann, *Army Exploration*, 89–90, see also map no. 71; Hafen, *Overland Mail*, 230–31n 490.

pensable, and every needful protection and support should be given to the company."[7] The Indian menace along the middle portion of the once-crowded emigrant road induced Holt to move the line south to the South Platte, where it would eventually intersect the Trappers Trail at the Cache la Poudre. From that point, mail traveled to Denver over a spur route, while the through coaches traversed the Cache la Poudre Valley before turning northwest to make the long monotonous haul across what is now southern Wyoming to Fort Bridger.

Service over the new route started July 21, 1862, thus bypassing Fort Laramie and bringing to a close its role in protecting the "Great Overland Mail." Nevertheless, with thousands of emigrants still using the well-worn road to California, and discoveries of rich gold deposits reported in western Montana Territory, the impact of events in Colorado was not felt immediately at Fort Laramie. Moreover, the government's decision to construct the transcontinental telegraph along the North Platte ensured the strategic value of the post. As the only major U.S. military garrison between Fort Kearny and Fort Bridger, the troops at Fort Laramie soon had their hands full, protecting both the emigrants and that critical thread connecting the North with the distant Pacific Coast, the transcontinental telegraph line.

---

[7]*ARPG*, 1862, 127.

CHAPTER EIGHT

"We Are Holding This Territory by a Thread"

Fort Laramie might have reached its zenith in 1860 had not the citizens of the Colorado Territory been so niggardly with their hard-earned gold. The superintendent of the Western Union & Missouri Telegraph Company, Edward Creighton, made the territorial offer similar to that advanced by the stage men. He proposed that if the populace would invest twenty thousand dollars to subsidize the construction of the main line, he would route it through Denver. When the measure failed to muster the necessary public support, Creighton elected to build the telegraph line along the familiar Oregon-California road. At that time, Postmaster General Holt had not yet decided to reroute the transcontinental mail via the South Platte River and Bridger's Pass. The army probably influenced Creighton's decision by reminding him that a line through Denver would be extremely vulnerable because there were no military posts along the more southerly route between Forts Kearny and Bridger, a distance of some 600 miles. Furthermore, the nearest garrison to Denver, Fort Laramie, would be circumvented by more than 150 miles and thereby deprived of vital telegraphic communication. The Western Union construction crew, consequently, strung wire through Fort Laramie during late summer 1861 to complete the army's eastern connection with the States, and on October 24 the two lines were joined at Salt Lake City. The Pony Express subsequently succumbed to a quick death, having lost as much as a half-million dollars during its meteoric life. Yet true to Russell's prediction, it had proved the feasibility of year-round travel over the Central Route.

The previous spring, a pony rider from the East had arrived at Fort Laramie bringing news of the state of war existing with the Southern Confederacy. For the garrison at Fort Laramie, like others all across the frontier, the issue of secession had been a topic of heated debate for months, causing the officer corps, composed of both Northerners and Southerners, to divide into Unionist and secessionist camps. The two factions eyed each other suspiciously, often boasting about what they would do were war to break out. With the April firing on Fort Sumter, South Carolina, individuals hailing from the South were suddenly faced with backing their words by action. For most, it was a very personal choice between upholding the oath they had made as officers in the United States Army, and loyalty to the political positions taken by their respective native states.

As elsewhere in the nation, political passions ran high at Fort Laramie in the wake of that momentous news. Although the post commander, Captain John McNab, was a Vermonter, he had publicly expressed his pro-secessionist sentiments at the sutler's store and to other officers of the garrison. When sutler Seth Ward's manager, William G. Bullock, "dared to proclaim his intention to hoist the secession flag at the post," McNab looked on without taking action. However, the enlisted men serving at the post were predominantly Northern-born Americans or European immigrants lacking regional biases and all were army regulars duty-bound to defend the United States. Offended by Bullock's plan, the troops threatened to hang him from the flagstaff if he attempted to raise the Stars and Bars. Bullock prudently reconsidered. That Captain McNab conspired against the federal government was revealed when he granted furloughs to three subordinate officers, all of whom had resigned their commissions and were awaiting appointments in the Confederate service. McNab deepened his culpability by providing the traitors with arms and falsifying the ordnance records concerning the disposition of the weapons.

Adjutant General of the Army Lorenzo Thomas was alarmed to learn that not only was McNab's "very weak and ineffective" leadership creating an atmosphere of "disorder and lack of discipline" at Fort Laramie, but that an avowed Confederate sympathizer was in control of that important western post.

The former post commander, Colonel Edmund B. Alexander, had been transferred to St. Louis in late April 1861 to replace General Harney as head of the Department of the West. General Scott directed Alexander to return immediately to Fort Laramie to assert federal control. Arriving there on June 10, he initiated an investigation into McNab's conduct, which the latter attempted to thwart by making "use of trickery and falsehood to prevent said investigation." Upon receiving this report, Commanding General Winfield Scott had heard enough. He peremptorily dismissed McNab from the service.[1]

That the Confederacy was casting covetous eyes on the trans-Mississippi West was revealed in a plan for annexing the Southwest territories concocted in summer 1861 by Henry Hopkins Sibley, a West Point graduate and former Second Dragoons officer, now a Confederate general. Early in the war, Sibley convinced Confederate President Jefferson Davis that by acting quickly and aggressively in a campaign moving from Texas northward up the Rio Grande, Sibley's forces could brush aside the small regular garrisons in the region and occupy the territorial capital at Santa Fe. From there, Sibley could move against Fort Union, the southern anchor of the Santa Fe Trail and the central quartermaster depot supplying all of New Mexico Territory. The capture of Fort Union would eventually starve the other southwestern forts into submission and, in the same stroke, would provide a bounty of supplies, enabling Sibley's column to invade Colorado, snaring the gold and silver mines for the Confederate treasury based at Richmond, Virginia. On the diplomatic front, Sibley assured Davis, a successful offensive would do much to persuade England and France to assist the Confederate States.

Once the initial plan had been accomplished, Sibley envisioned an even more grandiose movement against California to secure the state's

---

[1]McNab swore his innocence and attempted to be reinstated, but corroboration of Captain Mix's testimony by Lieutenants Gooding and Mizner sealed his fate; Captain S. H. Starr to Adjutant General Lorenzo Thomas, June 27, 1861; John McNab to Senator J. Colamer, Woodstock, Vt., September 24, 1861; Sarah McNab to "My Dearest Aunt," September 14, 1861; First Lieutenant Oliver P. Gooding to Thomas, January 29, 1862; Captain Joseph K. Mizner, Second Cavalry, to Thomas, February 9, 1862. These and other letters bearing on the McNab incident are in John McNab file, Box 905, Letters Received (Main Series), AGO, RG 94, NA; Captain Seth Williams to Colonel Lorenzo Thomas, April 29, 1861, OR, I, 3, 489. Despite the incriminating evidence, the author found no record indicating that McNab defected to the Confederate States Army.

resources and coastal ports. With the Southwest under his control, Sibley claimed, the land area of the Confederacy would be doubled, "with . . . plenty of room for the extension of slavery, which would greatly strengthen the Confederate States." Although Sibley expressed no specific concern about resistance from the forts along the Oregon-California road, he apparently neglected to consider the potential threat Forts Laramie and Bridger posed to the ultimate success of his plan.

Another Southern strategy, less well known, was a proposal advanced by Missouri secessionist leader F. J. Marshall to attack the western territories from the east. Marshall, like Sibley, coveted the great mineral wealth of Colorado Territory. Similarly, he too was under the impression that because Southerners had pioneered the gold discovery there, a telling segment of the population would side with the Confederacy to control the mines. Writing to Davis on May 20, 1861, Marshall outlined his plan to "seize and hold Forts Laramie and Wise, and Fort Union, if necessary, and take possession of all military stores and munitions of war at the other forts in Kansas and Colorado, and [to] destroy what will be of no utility, establish headquarters near the Cheyenne Pass, and with the possession of Forts Laramie and Wise, cut off all communication between the Northern States and the Pacific coast; and at the same time, acting in conjunction with Missouri, . . . seize Forts Leavenworth and Riley, and expel from Kansas the horde of Northern vandals that now infests it."[2] This was an ambitious scheme, certainly, but not so far-fetched considering that only four under-strength companies garrisoned Fort Laramie, and at that very moment a Southern sympathizer commanded those troops.

With Southern forces threatening Washington, D.C., in the spring of 1861, the Federal army's high command had no time to ponder the strategic importance of the western territories. Secretary of the Interior Caleb Smith was more familiar with the natural resources of the region than were most other Washington officials, but when he alerted the War Department to the necessity of defending the frontier against Confederate invasion, War Secretary Simon Cameron curtly

---

[2]F. J. Marshall to Jefferson Davis, May 20, 1861, *OR*, I, 3, 579; The Confederacy's broad strategy to conquer the Intermountain West is discussed in Colton, *Civil War in the Western Territories*, 3–9 and Josephy, *The Civil War in the American West*, 17–30.

informed him that the military would consider action appropriate to the situation.

In fact, a large portion of the Army of Utah, including the Fifth Infantry, Seventh Infantry, and part of the Tenth, had already been siphoned off to counter an uprising among the Navajos in New Mexico and southwestern Colorado. In May, Winfield Scott ordered most of the remaining federal forces in Utah and New Mexico to concentrate at Fort Leavenworth, preparatory to their transfer to the eastern theater of operations. Union forces in the West were weakened still further when Confederates captured the bulk of the Eighth Infantry in Texas. The combined effect of these events cleared the way for Sibley to make his thrust toward Colorado almost unopposed.

As the Texans marched up the Rio Grande that summer, Colonel Edward R. S. Canby, commander of the Department of New Mexico, prevailed on the territorial governors of New Mexico and Colorado to raise companies of militia to stem the Confederate advance. Although Colorado volunteer units ultimately played a critical role in defeating Sibley, Canby initially envisioned them as a reserve force to support Fort Wise, situated on the Arkansas River. Because of its position on the Mountain Branch of the Santa Fe Trail, the post was of key importance in maintaining communications with St. Louis and Fort Leavenworth.

However, the newly appointed territorial governor, William Gilpin, viewed his Colorado militia merely as a constabulary, raised to maintain order in the event Southern factions of the population rebelled and to defend the citizens against Indian attack in the absence of federal troops. Regardless of his divergent viewpoint of troop use, Gilpin began recruiting men to fill ten companies of the First Colorado Infantry in July.

As beleaguered authorities in Colorado attempted to respond to the dual menace of both secessionists and Indians, General Sibley achieved several early successes as his forces thrust from El Paso into New Mexico. In rapid succession, the Texans defeated Union forces at Mesilla and Val Verde, enabling Sibley to occupy Albuquerque and then Santa Fe, the territorial capital, without further opposition. A complete southwestern victory seemed within his grasp as the Confederate juggernaut moved up the Santa Fe Trail toward Fort Union, the prize that would open the way to seizing Colorado.

But in late March 1862, a hastily organized Union force of regulars and Colorado volunteers defeated Sibley's brigade at Glorieta Pass, east of Santa Fe, which proved to be the crucial battle of the campaign. After the federals destroyed his supply train, Sibley had no choice but to retreat to Texas.

The Battle of Glorieta Pass marked the crest of Confederate ambitions in the West. Marshall's bid to launch a drive from Missouri failed to materialize, but had Sibley been successful in capturing Fort Union, it is conceivable that Colorado, Kansas, and New Mexico might have fallen to the Confederacy. Just what the fate of Fort Laramie might have been had those plans succeeded can only be speculated. Had Sibley captured Denver, his forces would have been in a position to threaten both the transcontinental telegraph and mail lines, thus disrupting communication between the North and Unionist California. Sibley's campaign, for all its inherent implausibility, had been a close call that at last awakened Washington to the vulnerability of the Intermountain West and its vital mineral resources.[3]

Appreciation for the economic and strategic value of the Far West had nevertheless been slow to gain acceptance in Washington. In November 1861, Army Headquarters ordered the last two companies of cavalry at Fort Laramie to rendezvous with their regiment, then en route to join the Army of the Potomac. Their exodus left only two companies of infantry at the post, a precarious situation reminiscent of the Grattan days, but now with potentially more serious consequences. Marauding Cheyennes had descended on sutler Seth Ward's horse herd only the previous May and rumors abounded that southern operatives were on the plains inciting the tribes to take advantage of the Union army's current weakness along the overland trails. The govern-

---

[3]Sibley's plan was flawed in several respects, making it unlikely that it ever would have succeeded. He calculated, wrongly, that the Hispanic population of New Mexico would rise up to join him, but Sibley neglected to take into account that New Mexicans harbored a long hatred of Texans after their short-lived republic attempted to annex the territory for themselves in 1841. Likewise, his plan that his men would subsist on the land's edible vegetation demonstrated a lack of practicality on his part, something an officer of his considerable frontier experience should have realized. And, as Alberts notes, Sibley simply was not the man for such an undertaking. His personality was such that he tended to live for the moment and let the morrow take care of itself. Moreover, he had been an alcoholic for years, an abuse that affected his ability to reason and caused him to miss every battle of the campaign. Had his troops had the benefit of a good leader, the outcome might have been different. Alberts, *Battle of Glorieta*, 8–9; Thompson, *Sibley*, 337–39.

ment countered with prompt delivery of annuity provisions in hopes of quelling any predisposition the tribesmen may have to raid along those roads. Three months later, the army took the further precaution of directing the commanding officer at Fort Kearny to "give protection to the stock and property of the Overland Mail Company and not allow any interference in carrying the U.S. mails."[4] Presumably, the same instructions applied to the garrison at Fort Laramie.

California Governor John G. Downey had recognized early-on the importance of security along the overland trail when he requested permission from the War Department to raise a regiment of infantry and five companies of cavalry to protect the mail and telegraph lines from California east as far as Fort Laramie. Pro-Union citizens quickly responded to his call to arms, but before those units could be mustered and trained, General Scott redirected Brigadier General George Wright, commander of the Department of the Pacific, to organize an expedition, primarily of California militia, to march across New Mexico Territory to intercept General Sibley's army on the Rio Grande.[5] Governor Downey was left with no choice but to recruit additional troops to counter the potential Indian menace to the state's northerly lifeline with the East.

Colonel Alexander was aware of depredations west of the Upper Platte Crossing, but had taken no corrective action, probably because of his shortage of cavalry. The Overland Mail Company complained to Secretary of War Cameron that the army was not doing enough to protect its interests, spurring him to prod Alexander to "afford every necessary protection in men and means."[6] Lacking horses with which to mount his men, the colonel sent a detail of fourteen soldiers from Fort Laramie to ride aboard the Overland Mail coach as far west as the crossing of the Sweetwater to investigate conditions. The troops were to remain at the bridge to protect the mail as well as they could until an alternate plan was found. Once there, the commander of the

---

[4]Report by A. G. Thomas, April 24, 1862, *OR*, I, 50-1, 1027.

[5]Although the Oxbow mail route would soon be relinquished in favor of the Central Overland, service to the southwest territories and southern California was eventually restored to flow more directly via the Santa Fe Trail, thence south on the original Chihuahua Trail to Mesilla (and El Paso), where it connected with the road to Tucson, Arizona Territory, and San Diego. Austerman, *Sharps Rifles and Spanish Mules*, 196.

[6]Thomas, April 24, 1862, *OR*, I, 50-1, 1027.

detachment sent word to the colonel that the rumored raids along the road had been greatly exaggerated, yet noted that the route lay exposed to anyone bent on disrupting transcontinental communication. Alexander informed the secretary of war that his reluctance to furnish the Overland Mail with arms and assistance was founded on his distrust of stage-company employees, believing that many of them were secessionists. Colorado's Governor Gilpin echoed that concern in a report to the Commissioner of Indian Affairs. "It is necessary to inform the department that the powerful company (Overland Express Company) is exclusively filled with rebel agents, and that all correspondence with the Territory by mail and telegraph has been handled by the enemy, and, when important, has been intercepted and suppressed."[7]

By the spring of 1862, events in the Southwest, combined with the realization that communication with the Pacific Coast was in serious jeopardy, motivated the army to name Brigadier General James Craig, who had led a unit of Missouri cavalry during the Mexican War, to command all troops posted along the transcontinental route within the District of Kansas, including Fort Laramie.[8] Designating a general officer to oversee that mission ensured better coordination of the available troops to keep the mails running, and more importantly, the assignment was an indication of the War Department's renewed concern for defending the frontier. Craig arrived at Fort Laramie in June to establish his headquarters at that central point.

Reinforcements reached Fort Laramie in May, ahead of Craig, when two companies of the Fourth U.S. Cavalry passed through en route to relieve the infantrymen posted at Sweetwater Bridge. On the thirtieth, Lieutenant Colonel William O. Collins rode into the post at

---

[7]Ibid.; Returns for April 1862, PR, FL, *ARSI*, 1862, 714.

[8]Several adjustments were made in geographical commands at the beginning of the Civil War as the army responded to changing priorities and posted larger numbers of volunteer troops in the West. The original Department of the West ceased to exist on July 3, 1861, when it was merged into the Western Department, an area embracing all the territories between the Mississippi River and the Rocky Mountains, including New Mexico. However, in November 1861 the Western Department was subdivided into three smaller departments, placing Fort Laramie in the Department of Kansas, which also included the state of Kansas; and the territories of Nebraska (including Fort Laramie), Colorado, and Dakota; as well as a large portion of Indian Territory. Just before Craig took command in April 1862, the department was reduced to a district within the Department of the Mississippi. Less than two months later, that order was countermanded to recreate the Department of Kansas. Thian, *Notes Illustrating the Military Geography*, 66–67, 107.

the head of a battalion of the Sixth Ohio Cavalry, dispatched to the frontier specifically to patrol the great thoroughfare. Later that day a company of Kansas volunteers also arrived to augment the garrison. The Ohio troops camped at the fort only long enough to be resupplied before continuing their march west, posting detachments along the way at the telegraph and relay stations between Laramie and the Sweetwater. Collins established a strong point at Platte Bridge, making his headquarters at Pacific Springs, just west of South Pass.[9]

With these troops in place, conditions were somewhat improved for travelers. Yet the Indians—identified by Craig as Snakes (Shoshones), Crows, Cheyennes, and some Sioux—continued raiding emigrant parties west of the Sweetwater, beyond reach of his cavalry. Two men were reported killed by Indians near Rocky Ridge, while six men were wounded and 160 head of stock stolen from emigrants at Ice Springs. In addition to stages being attacked at various points along the route, a company employee was killed while tending the mule herd at Green River. It still would be some time before California volunteers could reach the area.

The recent decision by the Overland Mail Company to move its operations to the new route via Cache La Poudre and Bridger Pass also affected the army's growing sphere of responsibility. By the time the volunteers arrived on the scene at Fort Laramie, those preparations were well underway. General Craig, in fact, authorized small escorts from the post to protect company employees while they transferred the rolling stock, mules, and other property southward to the new route. The through-mail coaches began following the South Platte River west from Julesburg, Colorado, on July 21, rather than turning north to cross the divide between the forks of the Platte. Suddenly, however, the army was faced with protecting not only the four hundred miles of road and telegraph line between Forts Laramie and

---

[9]PR, FL, May 1862, Fort Laramie; Major General H. W. Halleck to Brigadier General Samuel D. Sturgis, April 6, 1862, OR, I, 8, 668; Assigned to the frontier early in 1862, Companies A, B, C, and D, Sixth Ohio Volunteer Cavalry, never served with the remainder of the regiment during the war and were designated as the First Independent Battalion, OVC. The army intended to send the battalion to the Southwest to resist Sibley's invasion, but Indian trouble on the central overland trail caused them to be redirected to Fort Laramie. In summer 1863, Collins was authorized to recruit a second Ohio battalion for service in the Far West, which, combined with the former battalion, became the Eleventh Ohio Volunteer Cavalry. Reid, *Ohio in the War*, 2: 819–20; Jones, *Guarding the Overland Trails*, 15–17.

Bridger, but the mail route through northeastern Colorado as well. Even though he had not been specifically charged with the safety of emigrants, Craig could hardly ignore their welfare. He reported the intensifying situation to his superior at Fort Leavenworth. "I will retain upon the present route the larger portion of the troops to protect the telegraph line and the emigration," he wrote, "at least until the emigration . . . has passed through my district. I do this because the Indians evince a disposition to rob the trains and destroy the wires. Indeed I am satisfied that unless the Government is ready to abandon this route both for mails and emigrants an Indian war is inevitable."[10]

Farther east, escalating Indian-white tensions suddenly exploded. In mid-August, Santee Sioux warriors in Minnesota went on a rampage murdering scores of white settlers and destroying their homesteads. Local militia and regular army forces soon contained the uprising and eventually defeated the Sioux, but reports of the atrocities fueled already pervasive fears, especially in Nebraska, that Indian raiding along the Platte road was but a precursor to a general outbreak. "Indians, from Minnesota to Pike's Peak, and from Salt Lake to near Fort Kearny, committing many depredations," Craig reported in an obvious overstatement of the situation. Nevertheless, the raids in Minnesota served as the catalyst for him to renew his plea for reinforcements. Craig telegraphed the new secretary of war, Edwin M. Stanton, "If I concentrate my force [about five hundred men] to go against the Indians, mail line, telegraph, and public property will be destroyed . . . I am building [a] new post on [a] new mail route near Medicine Bow Mountain."[11]

At Craig's direction, Major John O'Ferrall led a small force of the Ohio Volunteers to establish Fort Halleck at the northern base of Elk Mountain on July 20, 1862. Placing a permanent garrison at that critical point along the route enabled the cavalry to patrol the road for some distance in both directions and to respond to incursions as they arose.

The Indian scare that panicked whites all across the plains following the violent outbreak in Minnesota resulted largely from American settlers' overactive imaginations and ignorance of Indian ways in general. The Santee Sioux, who inhabited the country on the Red River of the North, for example, had little interaction with their brethren

---

[10]Craig to General James G. Blunt, July 11, 1862, *or*, I, 13, 468.
[11]Craig to Edwin M. Stanton, August 23, 1862, ibid., 592.

below the Missouri, and their troubles with whites never escalated into a general war involving the western Teton (Lakota) tribes. In fact, most of the depredations in the vicinity of the emigrant road were probably incidental to intertribal raiding among long-standing enemies and continuing competition for the ever-shrinking buffalo range. The Cheyennes and their Arapahoe allies, for example, raided back and forth against the Shoshones and Utes from Colorado to Utah. Crows occasionally swept down from the Big Horn region to attack both the Sioux and Cheyennes, and vice versa. As it happened, the emigrant and the mail routes passed through the heart of the disputed territory. This broad range had earlier attracted the fur traders for the very reason so many tribal ranges converged there. Although it would appear that raiding parties did not go out of their way to molest whites, at the same time they were not averse to stealing livestock when opportunities arose. Such incidents usually occurred when unfortunate whites happened along at the wrong time. Chance encounters between white travelers and Indian war parties moving through the same country were overblown and misinterpreted by frontiersmen as evidence of a widespread uprising.

The situation was different in Colorado. The many thousands of Pike's Peakers who had settled in the region during the first two years after the discovery of gold attracted other Americans. Farmers eager to take advantage of the rich lands bordering the foothills of the Rockies followed the miners. Soon, women and children joined them, and the formerly raw-boned mining society began to assume a new air of civilization. Late in 1861 Governor Gilpin boasted, "Property in mills, towns, farms, and cattle, has accumulated to the amount of many millions. This is scattered and located everywhere, in the gorges of the mountains, upon the great roads, along the river bottoms, and on both flanks of the snowy Cordillera."[12] Alarmed by this rapid influx of whites and hoping to scare the interlopers into leaving, a few young Cheyennes threatened the settlers and stole their livestock. The Arapahoes, on the other hand, seemed to accept the intrusion and generally got along well with the Americans. Indeed, the 1851 Fort Laramie Treaty had granted the two affiliated tribes the right to roam that very

---

[12]All quotations are from William Gilpin to William P. Dole, June 19, 1861, *ARSI*, 1861–62, 710.

region even though only a few Southern Cheyenne and Southern Arapahoe chiefs had actually signed the document. None of their northern brethren had done so. Although the agreement provided whites
safe passage through Indian lands, it had not granted them the right
to settle there. Indian frustrations toward the hordes of newcomers
increased when the quantities of game were either killed off or driven
far from the Smoky Hill and South Platte roads.

Government authorities had attempted to forestall such trouble in
early 1861 by coercing some Indian leaders, including the prominent
and peaceful Cheyenne chief Black Kettle, to sign a treaty at Fort
Wise. In return for relinquishing the tribe's great range, which
stretched from the Arkansas River to the North Platte and west to the
crest of the Rockies, the leaders in attendance reluctantly accepted a
barren tract of land north of the Arkansas, along Sand Creek, in eastern Colorado. Significantly, however, the Southern Cheyenne Dog
Soldiers did not sign the treaty, nor did many other leaders, including
those from the northern bands.

The change of the mail route in 1861 left Fort Laramie 150 miles
north of the Overland Road and deprived of mail service. The commanding officer attempted to compensate for the loss by periodically
sending a wagon with an armed escort down to Julesburg to pick up
the mail destined for the post. Initially, the detail made only one trip
every two or three weeks going by way of Scott's Bluff and Mud
Springs, Nebraska. Within a year, however, the mails were running on
a weekly schedule. Complaining about the service, an army wife
wrote: "They, the driver and guard, go about 15 miles and camp, which
means they light a fire, make some coffee, spread their blankets on the
ground, picket their mules, and stay all night."[13]

At the conclusion of their summer migrations, the approach of win-

---

[13]Presumably, the first stop was at Drips's Ranch on the south bank of the North Platte, after which
the mail parties camped successively at Ficklin's and Mud Springs, both of which were telegraph
stations, and on Pole Creek. Collins, *An Army Wife Comes West*, 20. Twiss still maintained his
Upper Platte Agency at Drips's Post. With the companionship of Indian women available there,
it is not surprising that the mail drivers camped overnight so near the fort. This was probably the
reason for Mrs. Collins sarcasm. Soldiers assigned as express riders carried the mail by relays from
Fort Laramie to the various detachments posted along the road as far as the Sweetwater; Major
Thomas L. Mackey to Lieutenant Oliver S. Glenn, November 29, 1862, Order Book, October 27,
1862–April 8, 1863, typescript copy in vertical file, FLNHS (hereinafter cited as 11th Ohio Letter
Book); Captain Frank Eno, AAG to Lieutenant Colonel W. O. Collins, November 25, 1862, ibid.

ter 1862–63 found the Indians settling into their camps. They had committed no further depredations in recent months, and it appeared to the army that the increased presence of troops in the region had been effective. When Indians attacked a cavalry detachment at Sweetwater Station on November 24, 1862, however, post commander Captain John A. Thompson responded by sending fifty men of the Sixth Ohio from Fort Laramie to investigate. "We were just beginning to think what a nice time we would have here this winter," wrote an Ohio sergeant, "but all our hopes were blasted yesterday . . . and a damd cold ride it will be too." The raiders, reportedly about 150 Shoshones, had attacked the nine-man detachment at the station during the night, killing one trooper before vanishing into the mountains. Lieutenant Colonel W. O. Collins, commanding the Ohio battalion from his new headquarters at Fort Laramie, ordered each detachment at the stations west of the post to shuffle a few men to those beyond in the event of another raid.[14]

Despite isolated incidents, life at Fort Laramie went on much as it had prior to the Civil War. It was probably by design that the two companies of the Fourth U.S. Cavalry had been recalled to the post from Fort Kearney in June 1862. When the last members of the Tenth Infantry had departed that spring, higher command wanted a core of seasoned regulars to remain in charge of the post until the Confederate threat subsided and the volunteers gained more experience. The regulars subsequently set the tone for dress and deportment at Fort Laramie. "They make the soldiers wear white gloves at this post and they cut around very fashionably," Lieutenant Caspar Collins noted in a letter to his mother. Awed by the military professionalism of the regulars, Collins admitted that "Any of the non-commissioned officers are better than a great many commissioned officers of Volunteers."[15]

With the winter camp of the friendly Sioux, the so-called Laramie Loafers, still in the vicinity of the fort, coupled with the penchant soldiers had for collecting pets, the post soon became overrun with dogs

---

[14]Sergeant Sam R. McCleery to Sam, November 26, 1862, vertical file, library, Fort Laramie NHS. The soldier killed in action was Joseph Good; Lieutenant C. J. Vanada to Lieutenant Colonel William O. Collins, November 25, 1862, 11th Ohio Letter Book; Eno to W. O. Collins, November 29, 1862, ibid.

[15]Lieutenant Caspar Collins to Mother, September 21, 1862, letter no. 8, Collins Papers, DPL.

and cats. Even a tamed antelope wandered about the grounds. Lieutenant Collins cheerily informed his feline-loving mother that with so
many small animals over-running the area, "there are cats enough at
this place to delight you for ten years. I saw several Indians barbecu-
ing a very fine fat one this morning . . . The whole family was gathered around licking their lips in expectation of a treat. Boiled cat was
to them an unusual delicacy which they properly appreciated . . . I
wish they would eat half about the garrison and then commence on
the dogs, not ours however."[16]

Lieutenant Collins's letters captured other vivid aspects of Sioux
customs. Just after Christmas he witnessed a Sioux scalp dance.
Indicative of the deep animosities felt among the tribes in the region
despite the Horse Creek Treaty designating their separate hunting
lands, the young lieutenant recorded: "A war party of Indians have
returned from fighting the Crows and have got 4 scalps. They have
painted some of their ponies and have had several dances . . . They
only danced one scalp. They stick it on a pole and as they dance
around they shake their fists at it and scold it."[17]

Winter typically passed slowly for the inhabitants of Fort Laramie.
"It is as dull as possible here at the fort," wrote Collins. Indeed, little
disturbed the monotony, until February 1863, when some two hundred Cheyennes arrived and set up camp nearby. That evening, two
of the companies hosted a ball for the garrison in honor of the birth-
day of George Washington. The lonely young bachelor regretted that
there were only eleven white women at the post, "and all of them are
married."[18]

---

[16] C. Collins to Fanny, September 21, 1862, letter no. 8, ibid.

[17] C. Collins to Aunt, December 28, 1862, letter no. 11, ibid. This incident contradicts the soldiers'
long-held perception that the local Sioux had settled into a benign existence at Fort Laramie;
Author's note. When the post commissary condemned a large quantity of hard bread, Captain
Thompson suggested it be issued to the Indians over a period of time. But his concern for making the Indians even more dependent on Fort Laramie was evident when he wrote, "I think it
is useless to keep so much of it here and thereby keep so many lazy wretches hanging on the
post." Captain John E. Thompson to Captain Frank Elm, AAG, Dept. of the Platte, December
29, 1862, LS, FL.

[18] C. Collins to Mother, February 23, 1863, letter no. 12, Collins Papers. This band of Cheyennes was
probably among those that had not signed the Fort Wise Treaty and had remained in the Upper
Platte country. There is also evidence suggesting that the Cheyennes belonged to a band headed
by Bull Bear that hunted, not very successfully, along the North Platte that winter. Agent John
Loree hosted some of these same Indians in August 1863, convincing them at that time to join in
the peace council planned that fall; John Evans to Dole, October 14, 1863, ARSI, 1864, 240, 248.

After the Treaty of Fort Wise, the Cheyennes and Arapahoes attempted to subsist on the plains primarily by hunting within their designated reservation lands, but a scarcity of game compelled them to fragment into small independent groups in order to survive. By 1863, young men among these far-ranging parties had become discouraged and angry with tribal leaders whom they felt had again acquiesced to the white man's insatiable greed. From time to time as opportunities arose, the warriors attacked settlements, isolated ranches, and travelers. The very lack of cohesiveness among the northern plains tribes made it all but impossible for the army to identify and punish the guilty parties. Penning a report from his Denver office, the new governor of Colorado Territory, John Evans, summed up the challenge: "Depredations have thus far been committed by single bands, or small parties, on their own account without any general responsibility of the tribes to which they belong . . . the Indians talk very bitterly of the whites—say they have stolen their ponies and abused their women, taken their hunting grounds, and that they expected that they would have to fight for their rights."[19]

Reliable information the military obtained from a band of Arapahoes in spring 1863 indicated that their people, along with bands of Sioux and Cheyennes, planned to hold a council to discuss a united war against the whites, to drive them from the plains. Governor Evans alerted Indian Agent John Loree, who had replaced Thomas Twiss at the Upper Platte Agency, of these developments, suggesting they jointly convene a meeting with the Indians in hope of settling grievances and convincing the Cheyenne and Arapahoe bands to settle permanently on the Sand Creek reservation.

Inducing the scattered bands to gather at a single location proved difficult. The commission, composed of Evans, Loree, and Samuel G. Colley, agent for the Upper Arkansas region, hired as messengers two experienced plainsmen trusted by the Indians. Elbridge Gerry was a reputable trader known for his close relationship with the Cheyennes and Arapahoes, while Antoine Janis had long been a trader, interpreter, and recognized figure around Fort Laramie. Loree and a stand-in for Janis, who became ill and was unable to make the trip,

---

[19]Ibid.; information concerning the raids is found in ibid., 240–41, and in a report by J. H. Jones, Overland Stage Line, July 7, 1863, *OR*, I, 22, 370.

succeeded in convincing several bands to meet on the first of September at Julesburg, where, incidentally, their annuities would be distributed. Even so, only one northern band showed up. The others, hunting buffalo in the vicinity of Beaver Creek in Kansas, informed Gerry that a recent wave of disease had so decimated their children that they could not undertake the journey to Julesburg. Moreover, they were angry because a sentry at Fort Larned had recently killed a Cheyenne man as he attempted to enter the post.

When the bands finally assembled, the headmen flatly told Gerry he could inform the commissioners that the Cheyennes would never sign a treaty and would never cede the country between the Republican and the Smoky Hill rivers. When presented with the proposition of living on the reservation "like white men," one Cheyenne defiantly countered that "they were not reduced quite that low yet." Despite the Cheyennes' initial lack of interest in acquiescing to white demands, agent Loree eventually obtained the signatures of leaders representing many of the bands residing north of the South Platte. In October, Governor Evans informed the commissioner of Indian Affairs, "This will accomplish the design of the commission in securing the general written assent to a settlement of these Indians on their reservation on the Arkansas river, and an undoubted cession of their claims to all other parts of the country."[20] For the Cheyennes and Arapahoes, the agreement effectively nullified the terms of the 1851 Fort Laramie Treaty.

The peace talks, designed to corral the Cheyennes and Arapahoes in the wastes of eastern Colorado, brought temporary calm to the central plains by summer's end. When a party of soldiers gave chase to Ute warriors who had run off a number of horses near Fort Halleck in June, the marauders boldly turned on their pursuers, killing one soldier and wounding four others. However, with the timely return of a delegation of their leaders from Washington, D.C., the warriors finally recognized the ultimate power of the United States government to crush them if necessary. By October, Governor Evans confidently reported, "There seems to be a period of quiet among the Indians, and a general feeling of security from danger in the public mind."[21]

---

[20]The quotations are from Evans to Dole, October 14, 1863, *ARSI*, 1864, 243-44.
[21]Ibid., 239, 243-44.

Despite the governor's optimism, Colonel Collins maintained cautious vigilance over the routes of travel that fall, a job made more difficult after the withdrawal of the two companies of regular cavalry from Fort Laramie in April, along with the Ninth Kansas Cavalry from the Overland Mail Route. Their departure left only Companies A and C, Sixth Ohio, at the post, and two additional companies scattered in detachments along the Pacific Telegraph line. Other companies of Ohio troops guarded the central portion of the stage line from Camp Collins all the way to Fort Bridger. Colonel John M. Chivington, commander of the District of Colorado by that time, informed his superior in September that he believed he had "ample protection, but no more than ample."[22]

The departure of the last regulars from Fort Laramie may have placed an additional burden on Collins, but at the same time it indicated the confidence of the higher command that he and his men had gained the experience necessary to manage the region on their own. Collins earlier received permission to recruit a second battalion for his regiment, which he accomplished during June and July of 1863. After the second battalion was organized, it was combined with the old Sixth on the frontier to form a new regiment, designated the Eleventh Ohio Volunteer Cavalry.[23] When the second battalion arrived at Fort Laramie in mid-October, one of the officers, Lieutenant George C. Finney, was unimpressed with his new home. "Fort Laramie is not much of a place," he wrote, "and Nebraska Try [Territory], what I have seen of it is not worth living in. I would not give the amount of ground occupied by a house in Cadiz for the Territory I have passed over."[24]

With the additional troops under his command, Collins decided to organize some of them into a battery of artillery. "I have gone into an artillery battery called the Mountain Battery," wrote Private Hervey Johnson. "It is composed of forty-eight men from the different companies. Our guns are called Mountain Howitzers. We have but four guns. Have been drilling some with the artillery. Not made much

[22]Colonel John M. Chivington to Major General John M. Schofield, Department of the Missouri, September 12, 1863, OR, I, 22, 529.

[23]Reid, *Ohio in the War*, 820.

[24]Lieutenant George C. Finney to Richard, October 13, 1863, vert. files, library, Fort Laramie NHS.

progress yet."[25] The battery designated as an independent unit until January 1864, when bad weather prevented further drills and forced Collins to order the members to rejoin their respective companies. To his credit, however, the colonel had the foresight to train a cadre of men to use the howitzers should they be needed in the future.

The Christmas of 1863 was observed with an elaborate dinner hosted by Company D and a party for the officers later that evening at the recently completed cottage occupied by sutler Ward's manager, William G. Bullock, the Southern sympathizer who almost had his neck stretched two years earlier. By New Year's night, the temperature had plummeted to 29° below zero. Heavy snows closed the military road to Fort Halleck and the emigrant trail to South Pass for five weeks. Cavalry detachments at the telegraph and stage stations were stranded, forced to hunker down for the winter. Nothing moved over the frozen white wilderness of the plains, and no news reached the fort, except by occasional telegrams, most of which were just routine army business. Johnson lamented, "There is so little to do here, that the boys just lay around and do nothing but wear fine clothes."[26]

That would soon change. Already rumors were circulating on the frontier that the Comanches, Kiowas, Apaches, Northern Arapahoes, some of the Sioux, and all of the Cheyennes had once again met on the Arkansas River to discuss declaring war against the whites. The military learned through Indian channels that the tribes had agreed to take the warpath in the spring when the grass had greened, and arms, ammunition, and other supplies could be procured.[27] This news was yet another ominous indication of what Evans had been predicting for months. Although the army had sent more troops to the intermountain district, the Indians seemed undeterred in their resolve to take back the plains.

---

[25]Unrau, *Tending the Talking Wire*, 59. The Model 1841 12-pounder mountain howitzer had a bronze tube measuring approximately thirty-three inches long with a bore diameter of 4.62 inches mounted on a two-wheeled oak carriage. The gun had a maximum effective range of approximately one thousand yards with shell and about eight hundred yards with the heavier spherical case (explosive) projectile. *Ordnance Manual*, 20, 54, 75, 386.

[26]Uhrau, *Tending the Talking Wire*, 93.

[27]This intelligence was reported by Robert North, a white frontiersman married into the Arapahos. Evans to Dole, November 10, 1863, *OR*, I, 34-4, 100.

CHAPTER NINE

"This Requires Vigorous War"

W hile rancor smoldered in Indian camps from the Platte to
the Arkansas, white prospectors extended their quests for
gold and silver into areas farther north along the Rocky
Mountains. A rich mining area developed in the vicinity of South
Pass, and in 1862 other parties discovered promising gold deposits in
the Boise Basin of Idaho. Later that year, miners examining the country east of the Bitterroot Range announced yet another promising
strike along the Beaverhead River in southwestern Montana. As news
of these discoveries flashed across the West, prospectors disgruntled
with the fruits of their labors in Colorado, Nevada, and elsewhere
began migrating to the new diggings. Adventurers, too, streamed
eastward from Washington and Oregon Territories. And, despite the
Civil War, or perhaps because of it, other hopefuls heading west
jumped off from both St. Joseph and Omaha, taking the Oregon
Route to Fort Hall, where they diverged from the old emigrant road
to follow a new trail directly to Montana. Still others took the somewhat longer Overland Stage Road to the junction at Fort Bridger
before turning north. Within two years, camps at Bannack and Alder
Gulch, Montana Territory, and Virginia City, Montana Territory,
boasted populations numbering in the thousands.

In the spring of 1863, a Montana miner, John Bozeman, set out to
find a shorter, more direct path to the new gold fields. Leaving Virginia City in spring 1863 with only one companion, Bozeman mapped
out an alternate passage, following the Yellowstone River downstream
almost to the Stillwater, then diverging southeast, rounding the Big

Horn Mountains to intersect the North Platte near the mouth of La Bonte Creek. That location, approximately fifty miles northwest of Fort Laramie, provided a convenient connection with the Oregon-California Road and was already the site of a telegraph station. To promote his route, Bozeman camped near the confluence and awaited passing trains, some of whose members he persuaded to form a new party and follow him over his shorter, as yet undeveloped, route.[1]

Aside from traversing difficult terrain, the newly named Bozeman Trail was more perilous than other routes because it passed directly through lands designated for the Crow Nation, including its southern portion, which lay in territory claimed by the Sioux. The trail was made more unpredictable because the Crows and the Sioux remained implacable enemies, the latter having encroached on the hunting lands of their neighbors for decades. This hotly contested region was no place for whites, nor did they have a legal right to be there, because the 1851 treaty permitted only the government to establish new roads within recognized Indian territories. In breaking his trail, John Bozeman, through his own ignorance, unwittingly combined the ingredients for another conflict on the plains.

At Fort Laramie, Lieutenant Colonel Collins correctly anticipated that an even greater number of gold-seekers would pass through Fort Laramie during the 1864 season. Considering the undercurrent of unrest among the Indians, he also predicted that the prospectors would need escorts. The Eleventh Ohio was still not up to full strength, and yet Collins was charged with protecting both the Overland Stage Line and the emigrant road via South Pass. Collins's rationale for providing artillery training to some of his men was proved justified when department headquarters assigned additional mountain howitzers to defend the garrisons along the mail route. Thus armed, more cavalrymen could be shifted to escort duty on the Oregon and Bozeman routes.[2]

---

[1] Famed mountaineer Jim Bridger had established a rude ferry near the site of La Bonte Station in 1857, which probably influenced Bozeman to make his departure point for his newly acquired party's trail to Montana. Hebard and Brininstool, *The Bozeman Trail*, 1: 81.

[2] Major General S. R. Curtis to Lieutenant Colonel William O. Collins, March 5, 1864, *OR*, I, 34-2, 511.

Recruitment of the new regiment continued unabated back in Ohio, and by January the garrison at Fort Laramie had grown to five companies. One melancholy soldier wrote home, "Fort larama is ver[y] nise plase, but very lonsom."[3] Observing that the mercury in the thermometers froze each night during January, some of the men conducted an experiment by pouring a quantity of whiskey in a tin cup. "It froze solid in twenty minutes, and was tossed about like a brickbat," a recruit wrote. The soldiers calculated that the temperature had reached 50 to 60° below zero.[4]

Isolation, overcrowding, and the notoriously long winters of that region stressed the self-discipline of some of the new arrivals to the breaking point. When two companies were ordered out on March 9 to patrol the road above the post, the men of Company E instead got drunk and rebelled. Attempting to restore order, a sergeant shot and seriously wounded one enraged soldier who attacked him with a knife. As the officer of the day, First Lieutenant Edwin L. Pettyjohn, rushed from the guardhouse to confront the men, Private John Sullivan, mounted on his horse, fired his revolver at Pettyjohn, missing him, but then striking the officer with his pistol and causing a bloody scalp wound. An alarmed Collins, expecting the rest of the drunken mob to join the fray, ordered the other four companies to assemble under arms. The confrontation failed to materialize, although Sullivan remained out of control, riding about the grounds and threatening all comers with his pistol. As the Irishman galloped full-tilt across the parade ground, Collins ordered the entire battalion to fire on him with their Spencer repeating rifles. A soldier who witnessed the affair scoffed, "Something near a thousand shots were fired at him but he being mounted, and his horse running at a full gallop only received one shot which took effect in his thigh . . . several balls passed through his clothes, and one wounded his horse very badly . . . and that before he got halfway across it [the parade ground]." A seriously injured Sullivan, however, was taken to the hospital, where he died several days

---

[3]The first quotation is from George C. Finney to Richard, October 13, 1863, vertical files, FLNHS; the second is in William Henry Cowell Journal, typescript in library, FLNHS (hereinafter cited as Cowell Journal). Cowell was a sergeant in Company B, Eleventh Ohio.

[4]Reid, *Ohio in the War*, 821.

later.[5] Besides pointing up a serious lack of discipline among his men, the incident also demonstrated to Collins that they needed more target practice before confronting Indians in combat. He issued an immediate order directing the garrison to conduct target practice for ten consecutive days.[6]

Collins and his Eleventh Ohio may not have fully appreciated what they would soon be up against, but senior commanders did. Major General Samuel R. Curtis, commander of the Department of Kansas, recognized the potential for open warfare when he predicted on March 18 that "an immense emigration . . . concentrating in the Platte Valley en route for the Bannock mines . . . [is] liable to create trouble with the tribes northwest of Laramie, whose territory they will undoubtedly invade."[7] Writing from his Milwaukee headquarters two days later, Commander of the Department of the Northwest, Major General John Pope, advised that the eastern and western Sioux bands had reportedly formed a powerful alliance on the upper Missouri River "and will, in all likelihood, concentrate on the upper Missouri . . . to obstruct navigation and prevent the passage of emigrants up the river or across the plains . . . There is little doubt that such is now the intention of these bands."[8] Robert North, who lived with his Cheyenne wife's tribe, told authorities that Sioux warriors vowed to resist any attempt by whites to make a road through either the Yellowstone or Powder River regions.

Despite its various detractions, Collins advocated opening the Bozeman Trail on the rationale that it reduced the distance to Bannack by two hundred miles compared to the Idaho route. He admitted, however, that emigrants making the journey would require strong military escorts. Whether or not the Ohio lawyer-turned-soldier was familiar with the provisions of the 1851 Laramie treaty, he accurately predicted there would be trouble when large numbers of whites began

---

[5]Firsthand accounts of this incident are found in Unrau, *Tending the Talking Wire*, 103 and Cowell Journal.

[6]Cowell Journal.

[7]Major General Samuel R. Curtis to Pope, March 18, 1864, ibid., 653.

[8]Pope to Halleck, March 20, 1864, *OR*, I, 34-2, 678; the Department of the Northwest, created in June 1862, was composed of the states of Wisconsin, Iowa, Minnesota, and the territories of Nebraska and Dakota. Thian, *Military Geography*, 82.

penetrating the last prime hunting grounds east of the Big Horn Mountains. The army, he strategized, should control the migration by accompanying the emigrant parties along a single designated route. General David D. Mitchell, on the other hand, doubted that the emigrants could be controlled under *any* circumstances and considered them numerous enough to protect themselves.[9]

In Colorado, meanwhile, the Cheyennes continued to foment dissent among other tribes. Governor Evans responded to the threat of an uprising by requesting federal authority to raise an additional regiment of cavalry for one hundred days' service, to reinforce troops already posted along the Santa Fe Trail and the Overland Stage Line. He also established "safe" camps for friendly Indians at Forts Lyon and Larned, and on the Cache la Poudre, and at the same time notified those bands that they must rendezvous at those places or face punishment. Evans further suggested that Sioux who wished to remain peaceful should go to the Upper Platte Agency below Fort Laramie for government protection. If some went, he believed, "others will join them, and we will bring it to a close. This requires vigorous war and it can be effected soon."[10]

As the vanguard of the spring migration reached Fort Laramie in early April, General Mitchell made a direct attempt to mitigate the number of Indians his forces might have to face in a war that by then seemed unavoidable. The Sioux of southern Nebraska Territory and northern Kansas, remembering the drubbing Harney had dealt them in 1855, thus far remained largely on the sidelines. Mitchell invited leaders of the Ogalala and Brulé bands to meet with him on the Platte at Fort Cottonwood, later renamed Fort McPherson.[11]

---

[9]Curtis to Mitchell April 28, 1864, *OR*, I, 34-2, 330; Captain Eugene F. Ware reinforced the view that many of the westbound emigrants in 1863–64 were "either deserters from the army, North[;] or South, were out for cash only." He added that most did not care whether or not the federal government won the war. Ware, *Indian War of 1864*, 55.

[10]Governor John Evans to Curtis, June 16, 1864, *OR*, I, 34-4, 422.

[11]Camp Cottonwood, founded by Major George M. O'Brian, Seventh Iowa, on September 27, 1863, was located on the right bank of the Platte River, eight miles above the juncture of the North and South Platte Rivers. The post was initially named Cantonment McKean in honor of the current district commander, Brigadier General Thomas J. McKean, but was changed in February 1864, and again on May 18, 1864, to Fort Cottonwood. Two years later, it was designated Fort McPherson. It was officially abandoned by the army in 1880, though the national cemetery established there in 1873 is still active. Frazer, *Forts of the West*, 88.

Mitchell and his adjutant arrived at the post on April 16 to find the Sioux already close by. Also on hand were three skilled interpreters, and it was said that one of the Natives in the camp also had a working knowledge of English. Seventeen Sioux chiefs, with an escort of approximately eighty warriors, rode to the council site the next day. They were met by General Mitchell, a large, bearded man in full dress uniform, complete with cross sash, who looked "like a king," according to one witness. The council began amicably enough, until Mitchell responded to Spotted Tail's inquiry as to why he had asked them to come there. Mitchell responded bluntly that the government wanted them completely out of the Platte Valley and away from wagon trains on the Oregon Route. The chiefs summarily rejected his demand, stating that they had already agreed to allow whites to travel that road unmolested. Furthermore, they added, they had always traded at posts in the valley, including Fort Laramie and neighboring civilian establishments, and they would not concede that right. If the whites wanted them to surrender the Platte Valley, they continued, the government would have to negotiate a formal treaty and compensate them accordingly. Additionally, the Indians countered with demands that whites abandon the Smoky Hill route, and stop work on a new road being surveyed up the Niobrara River to further shorten the journey from the Missouri to Montana.

The Sioux's refusal to concede clearly frustrated Mitchell, who threatened to send many soldiers to enforce his words. Brulé Chief Spotted Tail, now also rankled, rose to his feet and assured the officers that the Sioux were not afraid of the whites. The Sioux, he added, had uncovered the white man's game. The same people who went up the Platte, he said, returned by the Smoky Hill. Scouts watching the emigrants had concluded this was one group of people, moving constantly in a great circle to make the Indians believe they were outnumbered by whites. At a loss for words, Mitchell adjourned the council, which was set to meet again in fifty days.

The general unrest in the region also became evident at Fort Laramie that spring. "Emigration continues to pour along in a continual stream," one soldier observed. "A great many have big letters painted on their wagons such as 'Bound for Bannick' [*sic*] or bust."[12] Colonel Collins again assigned some of his men to drill with the mountain howitzers, thereby arousing the curiosity of the garrison. Sergeant William Cowell recorded in his journal, "They are busy fixing up the artilry. I my self are not abel to do duty so I do not no any thing about the business . . . the fort at this time is all most with out troops, but i think there is no dainger of the fort being atacked by the enemy at this time, at least I hav not saw any signs of it yet. The Indians that are at this post has not shone any hostile apearance yet, but there may be other tribes coming near . . . that have created this exsitment."[13]

General Mitchell convened a second council with the Sioux at Fort Cottonwood on June 8, 1863, with what he considered more positive results. The intervening weeks had given the Indian leaders time to rethink their previous counter demands after considering the potential consequences of joining in the coming hostilities. Spotted Tail and the other chiefs agreed their people would remain on the sidelines in any new conflict and stay away from the roads—with the proviso that periodically they would be permitted to enter the Platte Valley to trade. They feared, however, that they might be mistaken for hostiles by troops the area, and so requested that a reliable white man be sent to live with them until the war with the Cheyennes was over. Finally, they wanted their annuity goods delivered to a point northwest of Fort Cottonwood so they would not need to come to the Platte Valley. Mitchell readily agreed to all their terms.[14]

---

[12]Unrau, *Tending the Talking Wire*, 124, 163.

[13]Cowell Journal. That the local Indians were on friendly terms with the army at Fort Laramie was further evidenced when a band, probably Oglalas or Brule Sioux, came to the post on February 4, 1864. Colonel and Mrs. Collins observed their approach from the rear upper veranda of Old Bedlam, their residence and post headquarters at that time. The Indians came into the post and staged a dance on the parade ground, after which the officers took up a collection to purchase flour, meat, and rice to give to them. Collins, *An Army Wife Comes West*, 18–19.

[14]Transcription of council proceedings as part of Mitchell to Major C. S. Charlot, Dept. of Kansas, June 19, 1864, *OR*, I, 34-4, 459; By 1864, the Upper Platte Agency, known locally as the Woc-a-pom-any agency, was located on the north bank of the North Platte River approximately twenty-eight miles below Fort Laramie, near the present-day Wyoming-Nebraska state line. Apparently, it was not occupied by anyone at that time. Captain Eugene Ware described the site as "a little grassy flat consisting of several acres of land on the Platte river, susceptible of irrigation. In fact, there were old ruins of the irrigation ditch." Ware, *Indian War of 1864*, 219.

It was none too soon, because despite the professions of peace, Sergeant Cowell recorded in his journal soon afterward that "The indians is getting quite troublesome." Much of that trouble, however, was in the form of recurring intertribal warfare. The army identified the principal troublemakers in the immediate area as the Utes, Cheyennes, Shoshones, Arapahoes and Sioux bands that frequented the area to raid on each other, and to prey on Old Smoke's resident Loafers at Fort Laramie. The other bands considered the peaceful "Laramie Sioux" as weak and disloyal to their own nation. A member of the garrison wrote, "They are fighting among themselves. The Missouri Sioux say they are going to kill all the Laramie Sioux that stay among white men."[15]

Raiders indeed ran off several horses belonging to a former soldier named Foote, who now operated a tailor shop about five miles from the fort. Foote and two others gave chase and overtook the party after riding approximately one hundred miles. When they met, the Indians killed one man outright and hit Foote six times—though none of his wounds proved fatal. About three weeks later, on May 25, 1864, the Indians returned to Foote's ranch bent on finishing the job, but the veteran killed one of the attackers and wounded two others. The more seriously injured of them was Robert Smoke, son of the old chief, and a former friend of Foote. A day after the shootout at Foote's ranch, the Utes also waylaid a Laramie Sioux man twenty-five miles from the post.[16]

By late June, Ute raiding parties were openly attacking the tide of emigrants moving west of Fort Laramie. They ambushed and killed two men en route to Bannack and stole livestock from other parties, including eighty head of horses from one especially hard-hit train. Cowell probably echoed the feelings of his comrades when he wrote, "It appears just at this time that the indians is dertemed [determined] for to go to war. I hope we will hav a chance to giv thim a small brushing. I think it wood do thim a great deal of good to get a nother good whipping. Thare getting very sausey."[17]

---

[15]Unrau, *Tending the Talking Wire*, 136; Sergeant Cowell shared the same view, stating "They are at ware with each other killing each other and steeling stock from each other." Cowell Journal.

[16]Hull, "Soldiering on the Plains," 13–14; Cowell Journal; Unrau, ed., *Tending the Talking Wire*, 91, 135–36.

[17]Cowell Journal; Private Hervey Johnson corroborated the increasing frequency of Indian depredations, including the murder of the two men and the sacking of their wagons. Unrau, ed., *Tending the Talking Wire*, 135.

The situation grew worse in Colorado and western Kansas as well. A reliable report confirmed the fears of Governor Evans and the army: the Cheyennes had already formed their proposed alliance with other tribes and intended to conduct an all-out war for control of the central plains.

More ominous for Fort Laramie was a rumor that the Cheyennes intended to intensify raids in the Platte Valley, destroying ranches and murdering emigrants to capture more arms and ammunition. Meanwhile, the Kiowas and Comanches would conduct similar attacks along the Arkansas River, though because of its reduced traffic and fewer ranches, that route offered a less lucrative source of booty.

Although no hostiles appeared in the immediate vicinity of Fort Laramie during early July, raiders struck emigrant parties along the road above the post, and on July 15 a party attacked Ficklin's Station while a train of approximately sixty emigrants was encamped there. The telegraph company employees living there joined in fending off the attackers. The Indians failed to cut the wires, so the operator was able to send a message requesting help from Fort Laramie. Company B, Eleventh Ohio, was immediately dispatched to the scene, while Colonel Collins took the precaution of moving the quartermaster beef and mule herds closer to the post and placed heavier guards over them.[18]

With too few troops available to escort the passing trains, emigrants began banding together for mutual protection, just as Collins had suggested. Even though small detachments were sent to scout the countryside, the Indians easily eluded the troops to strike the trains. In one incident on July 12, hostile Indians posing as friendly approached a train below Deer Creek Station and begged for food. After obtaining what they wanted and riding off a short distance, the warriors turned and opened fire on the unsuspecting whites. They killed most of the men and captured the two women and two children traveling with the party. A trooper passing over the scene of the attack a few days later described what he saw: "the road was strewn for miles with arrows, clothing, beds, flour, bacon, salt, and other plunder, six dead men, one of them a negro . . . all of them had been killed by arrows. The indi-

---

[18]Hyde, *Life of George Bent*, 16.

ans were piling the plunder together and burning it; the wagons were not destroyed, the harness was all cut to pieces by the indians to get the mules out."[19]

Just a week later, two soldiers from Deer Creek Station were on their way to deliver several cases of ammunition to a party of Eleventh Ohio recruits marching up the road when they encountered a war party. Fortunately, both men were armed with Spencer repeaters, and had an abundant supply of cartridges. The pair fired about eighty rounds, enough to discourage their attackers. Learning of this, along with the report of a raid on the herd at Deer Creek, Collins sent two hundred men, with two mountain howitzers, to the telegraph station to await further orders. A few days later, he directed the officer in charge to leave forty men to guard the station and take the rest to search for the Indian village. During the five-day scout, in order to cover a larger area, the command was divided. Forty to fifty Indians surprised and attacked the smaller group near Powder River, mortally wounding Second Lieutenant John A. Brown. Believing Brown was dead, his men made good their escape. A force sent to recover the lieutenant's body the next day found to their amazement that Brown was still alive, though he died two days later.[20]

Working through the council, General Mitchell and Governor Evans had done everything within their means to segregate the warlike Indian factions from those who did not want conflict. Mitchell now acted upon the suggestion Collins had made earlier in the spring that the district commander move his headquarters from Omaha to Fort Laramie, where he would be in a better position to assess the situation and direct operations. Accordingly, Mitchell left Omaha early in July with an escort of the Seventh Iowa Cavalry, bound for Laramie via Forts Kearny and Cottonwood. He paused at Fort Kearny on the eleventh, and then directed a change of commanders at Fort Laramie, perhaps the most critical station in the region. Colonel Collins had proven himself to be an able administrator, but Mitchell was of the opinion that the middle-aged lawyer might not be equal to the challenges of what was shaping up to be an extended campaign. Some of

[19]Unrau, *Tending the Talking Wire*, 147–49.
[20]Indians had also raided the herd at Deer Creek Station a few days earlier; ibid., 148.

his troopers also lacked confidence in Collins, as Private Johnston confided in a letter to his parents: "If we were to get into a skirmish with them [the Indians] he would run and hide tell us to let them alone they are too strong for us, or give them some bacon and flour. The Col might make a good farmer but he aint fit to command a regiment. He might make a good private if awkwardness was any help. The boys have to laugh at him often at 'dress parade.' he draws his sabre so gracefully, handles it with such skill, gives the commands with such accuracy, then returns his sword to the scabbard, the wrong side foremost and works half an hour to get it out to put it in right. I don't want any more Col Collins in mine if I can help it."[21]

On July 25, just two days prior to Mitchell's arrival at Fort Laramie, warriors gathered in threatening numbers in the vicinity of Platte Bridge. The officer in command, First Lieutenant Henry C. Bretney, led a small force that engaged the Indians in a running fight all the way to their camp. The troops destroyed their lodges and captured a number of women, as well as thirty ponies, which Collins ordered brought to Fort Laramie and returned to the Indians. "Just what we expected," a disgruntled Private Johnson wrote. Demoralized by the perceived weakness of their commander, Johnson and his comrades swore that in the future they would not go out of their way to fight Indians and would shoot any ponies that might fall into their hands. "Not another captured pony shall go to the fort," Johnson declared, "We think that if the Indians can kill white people, take their horses, burn their property &c., we have the right to retaliate, to play the same game if it is a dirty one."[22] His comment reflected the no-holds-barred attitude taken by many combatants on both sides during the Indian campaigns.

General Mitchell subsequently issued orders assigning Collins to "general supervision of all posts and detachments west of Julesburg in the District of Nebraska, including both lines of communication westward."[23] Mitchell may have revealed a lack of confidence in Collins by

---

[21]Mitchell to Curtis, July 11, 1864, *OR*, I, 41-2, 141; Unrau, *Tending the Talking Wire*, 136.

[22]Unrau, *Tending the Talking Wire*, 156, 158–59.

[23]*General Orders No.* [left blank] (hereinafter cited as *GO*), District of Nebraska, July 28, 1864; letter no. 80, Collins Family Papers.

limiting his authority to make any decisions necessary along the roads without first securing the district commander's approval. Relinquishing command of Fort Laramie on August 8, 1864, Collins rode out of the post with a strong escort to inspect the troops at Cache la Poudre and Fort Halleck, a tour that spanned five weeks.

The general replaced Collins with thirty-nine-year-old Major John S. Wood, Seventh Iowa Cavalry. Unlike Collins, Wood, viewed as a modest man, claimed some practical frontier experience, having crossed the Great Plains en route to California in the rush of 1849. During his trek to the Pacific Coast, Wood was engaged in at least one Indian skirmish, in which he claimed to have killed a Pawnee warrior. In the first months of the Civil War, Wood had so ably led Company A that he was singled out to command the regiment's third battalion when that unit became operational. Mitchell directed Wood, by then serving at Fort Kearny, to take one company from that post and proceed to Fort Laramie. En route he was to pickup Company F at Fort Cottonwood to serve as the general's escort.[24]

A salute of seven guns announced Mitchell's arrival at Fort Laramie on July 27. Among those on hand to greet him was Indian Agent John Loree, armed with a complaint about the recently reassigned post commander. Some of the Ohio troops, he reported, had mistakenly killed a friendly Sioux when they attacked a party on Rawhide Creek two days earlier. Loree claimed that now the local Indians were threatening revenge. Although Loree's criticism of Collins only reinforced Mitchell's earlier decision, Loree may have had his own motives for casting Collins in a bad light. Friendly Laramie Sioux, who had gone out with another detachment the day after the attack, had plundered what was left of the Indian camp and apparently showed no remorse over the scalped corpse. John Richard, the toll-bridge owner at Upper Crossing, denounced the purported Indian war as a "humbug," but escalating depredations throughout the region contradicted his assessment of the situation.[25]

Farther south, warriors raided the overland route near American Ranch, located about midway between Julesburg and Denver, murder-

[24]Reed, *Roster of Iowa Soldiers*, 1261; Ware, *Indian War of 1864*, 14.
[25]Hull, "Soldiering on the Plains," 17; McDermott, *Frontier Crossroads*, 36.

ing three whites and running off a large number of horses and mules. Governor Evans attributed the incident to Sioux who had reportedly come down from Fort Laramie about two weeks earlier. General Curtis responded by instructing Collins to take one company from a less dangerous part of the line to reinforce Frémont's Orchard and Camp Collins should they be hit next.[26]

Mitchell concluded that the situation was even more serious than he had imagined. The hard-pressed Eleventh Ohio, fragmented in detachments scattered across five hundred miles, was spread too thinly to adequately protect the district. Three of its companies were stationed along the mail route southwest of Julesburg. Mitchell informed Curtis that he could guard the mail, emigrants, and the telegraph line only by mounting constant patrols on both lines of communication in hope of either deterring the Indians, or being in the right place at the right time, intercepting roaming war parties. Virtually all of his cavalry was constantly in the field. Learning from local mountaineers and friendly Sioux that there were a thousand lodges of warlike Natives within seventy miles of Fort Laramie, Mitchell warned Curtis to expect a widespread outbreak at any moment.[27]

Military authorities scrambled to concentrate all the available troops on the overland routes. Pouring over the district's post Returns, Mitchell discovered there were more than three hundred furloughed veterans of the First Nebraska Cavalry who could be recalled to active duty and sent out on the roads once they received horses. Governor Evans also urged Curtis to field the two regiments of Colorado Volunteers immediately, and to authorize the enlistment of five thousand additional men. Fearing for the safety of its employees because of the inadequate military presence, the Overland Mail Company temporarily suspended all service on the line.

Back at Fort Kearny, Mitchell penned a subsequent report to Curtis apprising him of the alarming conditions he found along the road on his return trip. "I find the Indians at war with us through the entire District of Nebraska from South Pass to the [Big] Blue [River] a distance of 800

---

[26]Evans to Curtis, July 18, 1864, *OR*, I, 41-2, 256; Curtis to Evans, ibid., 302. For Frémont's Orchard refer to note 39.

[27]Mitchell to Curtis, July 23, 1864, ibid., 370; Mitchell to Curtis, July 27, 1864, ibid., 429.

miles and more, and have laid waste the country, driven off stock, and murdered men, women, and children in large numbers . . . the only way to put a stop to this state of things will be to organize a sufficient force to pursue them to the villages and exterminate the leading tribes engaged in this terrible slaughter."[28] Mitchell added that twenty emigrants and homesteaders had been killed on the stretch of road between Forts Kearny and Cottonwood, and that all the ranches had been abandoned except those adjacent to Cottonwood and Julesburg. "Unless the Government intends to abandon the Laramie route entirely," Mitchell wrote, "I have taken all the troops off that route that can possibly be spared." To improve administrative control, he divided his district, assigning the First Nebraska Cavalry to bolster the eastern subdistrict from Kearny to Cottonwood, and distributed the Seventh Iowa in the western region between Fort Cottonwood and the strategic road junction at Julesburg. Only one company could be spared to augment the single-company garrison then at Fort Laramie. Collins and the other seven companies of the Eleventh Ohio had the unenviable job of protecting both the stage line from Julesburg to beyond Fort Halleck and the full-length of the emigrant road from Julesburg west to Sweetwater Crossing.

During his march up the North Platte, Mitchell also saw the need for a sub-post to afford greater protection of the road in the vicinity of Scott's Bluff. Troops from Fort Laramie began building Camp Shuman, later renamed Camp Mitchell, in August.[29] General Mitchell also established outposts on La Parelle Creek and La Bonte Creek, west of Fort Laramie; nevertheless, there were pitifully meager forces to contend with such a formidable situation. Even the freighters, who usually were not intimidated by Indian scares, corralled their trains to wait out the trouble, effectively closing the Platte road and cutting off supplies and communication with Denver.

While the army redistributed its forces, the Indians carried out even

---

[28]Mitchell to Curtis, August 15, 1864, ibid., 722.

[29]The site of Camp Mitchell is on the right bank of the North Platte, about three miles northwest of Scott's Bluff and about twelve miles east of the Wyoming-Nebraska state line. Captain Jacob S. Shuman, who established the post, first named it after himself, but within a matter of weeks the name was changed in honor of the Nebraska District commander, Brigadier General Robert B. Mitchell. Frazer, *Forts of the West*, 88–89.

bolder raids. Only a day after Mitchell left Fort Laramie, a war party swooped down on the quartermaster's mule herd as it grazed along the Laramie River about a mile north of the post. They made off with a number of animals before the startled sentries could respond. A detachment of cavalrymen sent in pursuit pressed them so closely, however, that the raiders abandoned the stolen animals.[30] Later the same day, news arrived that marauders had struck a wagon train at Star Ranch, wounding one man and running off all the stock, and, near the mouth of Plum Creek, west of Fort Kearny, a war party killed eleven emigrants, captured a woman and a boy, and fired the wagons.[31]

On August 12 a Sioux raiding party destroyed a civilian camp near Fort Laramie, prompting Major Wood to assign a dozen cavalrymen to serve there as an emergency response force. The detachment was

---

[30] Ware relates the details of a raid on Fort Laramie in which a war party scooped up a number of cavalry horses from the parade ground in late July. Ware, *Indian War of 1864*, 207–208. The author has found no evidence to corroborate the story. The incident was not recorded in the Post Returns, where it certainly should have been noted, nor did Sergeant Lewis B. Hull, present at Fort Laramie at that time, mention such an event. His entry for August 5 simply states: "Indians stole part of the Quarter Master herd a mile above the fort. . . . Iowa boys sent out immediately." Hull, "Soldiering on the Plains," 18. Private Frank Tubbs, Eleventh Ohio, returned to the post on September 14 after escorting Lieutenant Colonel Collins on his inspection tour. Tubbs informed his parents that the magnitude of the "attack" on Fort Laramie—as related in a recent letter written by Frank Armstrong, one of his comrades—was a grossly exaggerated version of the August 5 raid. Tubbs assured his parents that, "it was nothing but 15 Indians stole some Horses from the quartermaster and they was a going to send some men after them but the Indians got scard [*sic*] out and left the horses so they did not go after them. They is no such good news as having a big fight in this Country." Frank Tubbs to Father, September 24, 1864, Frank Tubbs letters. Private Hervey Johnson, posted at Deer Creek, was sent to the fort twice during the period in question, but made no mention in his detailed letters of what would have been an exceptional event, had it occurred. The author has concluded that the usually reliable Ware repeated an apocryphal story based on second-hand information relating to the August 5 raid, an event that occurred the day *after* his company left Fort Laramie. Ware's memory was faulty in that he recorded the date of his departure from Fort Laramie as August 31. General Mitchell, with Ware in command of the escort, actually left the post on August 4, 1864. Ware, *Indian War of 1864*, 217; Post Returns, August 1864, Fort Laramie; Hull, "Soldiering on the Plains," 18.

[31] This unidentified woman was released the following spring and made her way back to the road at Deer Creek Station. There she identified her captor, a Cheyenne leader named Big Crow, who happened to be present at the time. This story is continued in the following chapter. On August 10, 1864, two days after the Plum Creek incident, Cheyennes raided Liberty Farm in the Little Blue Valley of Nebraska. They captured Mrs. Eubanks, Mrs. Roper, and two children. These women figure prominently in the "hanging of the chiefs" episode also related in the following chapter. Grinnell, *Fighting Cheyennes*, 155.

directed to be ready to take the field at all times. He also renewed artillery training by designating a permanent crew to serve the mountain howitzer.

Indian depredations above Fort Laramie subsided rather quickly after the 1864 season's emigration crested in mid-August. With approximately twenty thousand whites traveling over the road that year, it was hardly surprising that the Indians contested the invasion with such fervor. Although wagon trains continued to ply the trail, their formerly large numbers suddenly dwindled to only one or two per week. With the exception of ambushing a lone soldier near Deer Creek Station, Sioux hostiles all but vanished in that area as they concentrated their activity farther down the Platte Valley. By that time, however, the volunteers had become so apprehensive they were ready to shoot at anything that moved. On the night of August 15, for example, outlying picket guards at Fort Laramie fired into the darkness at what they thought were Indians, but which turned out to be nothing. Shots again roused the command from its slumbers on a night about six weeks later. This time an investigation disclosed the attack not only as a hoax, but found that the men supposedly guarding the stock had fallen asleep in a nearby ravine.[32]

Agent Loree distributed out treaty annuities to the local Sioux near the end of August, although the quantity was hardly adequate for their numbers. The summer emigrant migration, along with increased military activity in the region, had scared away the buffalo and other game, making it nearly impossible for the Indians to subsist by hunting alone. Exacerbating the situation, Loree withheld a large pro rata portion of the rations intended for those bands that were unaccounted for and had presumably joined with the warlike factions. Consequently, by late summer the local Indians faced starvation; to survive they resorted to eating the carcasses of dead draft animals that lay along the Platte road. General Curtis expressed his concern that if the peaceful Indians could not be fed, they too would join the hostiles. He urged that no ammunition be issued to any of the plains tribes for fear

---

[32]Hull mentions the "Emigrant Escort," a force, presumably of civilians, organized by the federal government to accompany trains from Fort Leavenworth. He sarcastically notes that the emigration for that year was nearly over by the time the escorts were inaugurated. Hull, "Soldiering on the Plains," 157, 158–59.

it would be used to further the war. Meanwhile, he assured the secretary of war that he was bending every effort to stabilize the region and restore the transcontinental mail service.[33]

While the Sioux continued plundering and pillaging east and south of Fort Laramie, at the fort comparative calm allowed the garrison to resume most of its normal activities. Private W. R. Behymer wrote to his father in September, describing some of their duties:

> there is so many details that takes men out from the post . . . the nearest timber to this post is eight miles back in the bluffs that is the distance we have to haul our wood for this winter. Wood hauling has just comenced there are about thirty teams hauling . . . The hay we get here comes from Scotts Bluffs a distance of sixty miles that is not considered very far in this country . . . hay and wood hauling will continue until cold weather commences & then we will have to pack ice for next summer's use. So the prospect is at present that we will have plenty to do this fall and winter and I am glad of it for when a fellow has nothing to do Camp life grows very monotonous . . . We have a good Library here and a good reading room that is one good thing for a person can get any kind of reading matter we want almost . . . It is not much fun to get into the guard house here and a fellow has to carry himself pretty straight to keep out of it.[34]

The men who enlisted in the Eleventh Ohio were not always dedicated Union loyalists. The proximity of Ohio to the border states of Kentucky and West Virginia made it easy for men to avoid service with the Confederate forces by slipping into the Union ranks, especially with the knowledge that regiments like the Eleventh were being sent to the frontier. Others, natives of Ohio, may have secretly sympathized with the Southern cause and enlisted in Northern units to avoid being drafted to fight against Confederate forces.

In fact, it was not be long before Fort Laramie hosted entire units of ex-Confederates. The army began recruiting Confederate prisoners-of-war by offering them an opportunity to exchange incarceration for service on the frontier, fighting Indians. They would not be compelled to take up arms against Southern forces, and they would be comparatively

---

[33]Curtis to Secretary of War Edwin M. Stanton, August 25, 1864, *OR*, I, 41-2, 857; Continued Indian attacks on the road between Fort Kearny and Fort Laramie disrupted mail service to the post for several more weeks during August and September; W. R. Behymer to Father, September 11, 1864, Behymer Papers.

[34]Ibid.

free in return for their promise to serve in the Union army. For the Federals, recruiting captives offered a means of supplementing their forces to conduct what had become a two-front war. During late 1864 and early 1865, six regiments of so-called U.S. Volunteers, nicknamed Galvanized Yankees by their Union comrades, would be sent west.[35]

Other manpower challenges plagued the campaign against the Indians. There was dissention among the men of the Eleventh Cavalry's old first battalion, formerly the Sixth Ohio. As expiration of their three-year enlistment neared, the men eagerly anticipated returning home, but the army was too hard pressed on the plains to release them from federal service. The situation reached the ignition point on November 1, following an election of officers in which several members of the regimental noncommissioned staff were passed over for promotion in favor of other "noncoms" with less seniority. "The noncommissioned staff and companies A and D want to go home," soldier Lewis Hull recorded in his diary. "They send a remonstrance to the colonel demanding that they be sent home, or they will take the matter into their own hands and go."[36]

On the third, Major Wood ordered the loyal companies to assemble under arms, to intimidate the mutinous element, and to arrest several sergeants who were ringleaders in the rebellion. Major Wood's decisive handling of the situation caused the other malcontents to reconsider their own insubordinate actions. Hull commented, "Dissatisfied men willing to let their remonstrance slide. They did not expect that the matter would prove so serious."[37]

During the fall of 1864, although the Indians moved away from the roads west of Fort Laramie, marauders continued to raid in Nebraska Territory. Near Plum Creek a war party descended on an eastbound train of emigrants who were returning home after having "seen the elephant." The Indians killed one man and wounded two others. On another occasion, a group ambushed a cavalry patrol operating along

---

[35]D. Alexander Brown, *The Galvanized Yankees*, 1–6.

[36]Hull, "Soldiering on the Plains," 27; W. R. Behymer was one of the enlisted men commissioned on November 3, 1864, and confirmed by the adjutant general of the State of Ohio. Behymer served with the Eleventh Ohio for the duration of the war and was mustered out at the rank of first lieutenant in 1866. Reid, *Ohio in the War*, 819.

[37]Reid, *Ohio in the War*, 819.

Elk Creek, killing a lieutenant and wounding a soldier. A week later warriors attacked the Overland Mail eight miles west of Plum Creek, but the employees and passengers were able to successfully defend themselves.

A band of two hundred Indians crossed the Platte fifteen miles west of Alkali Station on October 20, killed an emigrant, and ran off fifty head of oxen. The next day, the warriors returned to attack the troops at Alkali, but were repulsed. Before the end of the month Indians had also skirmished with soldiers cutting wood near Midway Station and attacked a stage-company's haying crew that was working nearby. In a retaliatory attempt to deprive the raiders of forage and hiding places, the troops burned the Platte Valley from Fort Kearny westward to twenty-five miles beyond Julesburg—a distance of some two hundred miles. The flames consumed the vegetation all the way south to the Republican River and for approximately one hundred fifty miles north of the Platte River.

Such harsh, vindictive measures effectively convinced hundreds of Sioux to come as directed by the army to a Fort Laramie gathering during November. Appearing amicable and professing peaceful intentions, the Indians held talks with Colonel Collins and were treated to an entertainment by the garrison. But, although Collins's motives were aimed at reducing tensions, he had blundered seriously in the eyes of some of his men. Frank Tubbs reported the affrontery: "The Boys had a show for the Indians the other knight their was about 100 Indians in it was by the order of the Colonel the soaldiers did not like it mutch the old Colonel let the Indians have the seats and made the Boys stand up. He thinks more of an Indian than he does of a white man."[38]

Meanwhile, the Cheyennes and most of their Sioux allies remained intractable. Their raiding nevertheless diminished with the approach of winter; yet the middle section of the road between Fort Kearny and Julesburg continued to be dangerous. Indians attacked Sand Hills Station on November 9, and shortly thereafter a hundred warriors descended on a train near Plum Creek. Later that month, raiders in the same vicinity intercepted the westbound stage and followed that up by attacking a train the following day.

---

[38]Tubbs to Father, November 15, 1864, Tubbs Letters.

In Colorado Territory, meanwhile, things had remained comparatively quiet. After the fight on the Solomon in 1857, the Cheyennes had remained at peace with whites. There was the occasional appropriation of an unguarded animal, but even the rush of Pike's Peakers in subsequent years failed to arouse them to hostile acts. They and their close allies the Arapahoes seemed content enough to hunt buffalo on the high plains of eastern Colorado and western Kansas—at least until 1861, when the Fort Wise Treaty restricted their forays to within the comparatively tiny Sand Creek Reservation. Making matters worse, their agent, Samuel G. Colley, was suspected of diverting government annuities through his son, who sold them back to the Cheyennes. By the summer of 1863, Colley reported that there were no buffalo within two hundred miles of the reservation and precious little other game within its boundaries. Driven by hunger, and without recourse, some of the younger warriors began demanding, or simply stealing, food from emigrant trains headed toward the mining camps.

Colorado's Governor Evans had made it plain all along that Indians had no place in the emerging civilized society and that he wanted nothing more than to dispossess the Cheyennes and Arapahoes of their remaining lands. By spring 1864, accusations began arising that some Cheyennes were stealing stock from ranches and travelers, thus providing Evans's accomplice, Colonel John M. Chivington, an excuse to take military action against the Indians. Chivington, who had recently distinguished himself against Sibley's Texans at the Battle of Glorieta Pass, had been appointed commander of the District of Colorado. With political ambitions of his own, Chivington was well aware that having a record as an Indian fighter would place him in good stead with western voters.

In mid-April, a rancher residing along the South Platte reported that Cheyennes had run off some of his mules. Without first verifying the truthfulness of the claim, Lieutenant Scott Dunn, First Colorado Cavalry, led forty troopers out of Camp Sanborn and caught up with a party of Southern Cheyenne Dog Soldiers late the following afternoon, just as they were crossing the South Platte near Frémont's Orchard. The lieutenant later claimed that when he attempted to approach them, the Indians showed a disposition to fight, a claim the

Cheyennes afterward denied. According to their version, which held to the evidence, the soldiers charged them without warning and opened fire. The Dog Soldiers lived up to their reputation as fighters by felling four troopers, two of them mortally.[39]

A week later, someone reported that a ranch on the South Platte had been attacked, but when Major Jacob Downing and a detachment of cavalry went to investigate, they found nothing. Nevertheless, the Colorado Volunteers afterward took it upon themselves to punish the first Cheyennes they encountered, killing more than two dozen people inhabiting a small village and completely destroying the camp.

Other skirmishes occurred during the weeks that followed. On May 16, Colorado cavalrymen, led by Lieutenant George S. Eayer, allegedly searching for stolen cattle, discovered Lean Bear's band of Cheyennes on the Smoky Hill River, well beyond the eastern boundary of Chivington's district. Undeterred by "minor" details, such as the legality of their action, the troops approached the camp under a pretense of peace. As the two parties approached each other, the soldiers opened fire at close range, killing Lean Bear in the first volley. A fight ensued that the Cheyennes probably would have won had it not been for the level-headed intervention of Black Kettle. In deference to Black Kettle's stature in the tribe, the Dog Soldiers reluctantly allowed Eayre and his men to withdraw without further bloodshed.

Reports of these events prompted Colonel Collins to order patrols in an attempt to intercept the Cheyennes. Captain Peter W. Van Winkle led a hundred cavalrymen south from Fort Laramie in pursuit of raiders reported to be near the Denver road, but failed to find them. Collins, however, was unaware that the Indians had been so surprised by Lieutenant Dunn's attack at Frémont's Orchard that part of the group became frightened and returned to their village on Beaver Creek in northern Kansas. The others, perhaps fifteen warriors, were spotted a few days later near Pine Bluffs, moving toward Crow country and bent on carrying out their plan to avenge the death of a

---

[39]Frémont's Orchard was named for a grove of trees along the South Platte that appeared much like an orchard when the explorer John C. Frémont viewed it at a distance during his reconnaissance to the Rocky Mountains in 1843–44. It was located approximately eighty miles northeast of Denver. Grinnell, *Fighting Cheyennes*, 137–42, 140n5; see also William H. Goetzmann, *Army Exploration in the American West 1803–1863*, 101; Collins to Chivington, April 18, 1864, *OR*, I, 34-3, 219.

Cheyenne killed in combat with the Crows the previous summer. Chivington, meantime, struck the main trail and dogged the rest of the group back to the Republican without further incident.[40]

The summer of 1864 passed with comparatively little violence in Colorado Territory. Nevertheless, the populace for months had lived in a state of terror anticipating an Indian war. Some Arapahoes had accepted Governor Evans's June summons for peacefully inclined bands to congregate on the reservation near Fort Lyon. But few Cheyennes had yet come in to surrender. The lack of any meaningful response to his invitation, combined with loud public outcry for retaliation for the heavy raiding on the Platte, had influenced Governor Evans to alter his former peace policy to take up a stance of unrelenting war against all the plains tribes. Meantime, the adjutant general of the army had approved the governor's request to form another regiment of cavalry to assist in restoring the territory's commerce and protecting the populace. It took time, however, to arm, equip, mount, and train the unruly mob designated as the Third Colorado Volunteers. Chivington was placed in command of the new regiment. His men, who could hardly be classed as soldiers, were enlisted for only one hundred days—and much of that time had already passed without any field service. The members of the "Bloodless Third" craved a chance to kill Indians. And their colonel desperately wanted another military victory on his record.

While an impatient Chivington sat out the war in Denver, department commander Curtis organized a six-hundred-man column at Fort Kearny to drive the raiders away from the Platte. His command drove south into western Kansas, the haven of the Cheyennes, when the column divided, one scouting east, the other west. However, neither group saw a single hostile.

While Curtis was campaigning in Kansas, Black Kettle and a delegation of Cheyenne leaders arrived unexpectedly at Camp Weld, seeking the government protection extended earlier by Evans. As evidence of their sincerity, the chiefs turned over four white captives. At a sub-

---

[40]Cowell Journal; First Lieutenant George W. Hawkins to Lieutenant G. H. Stilwell, AAAG., Dist. of Colorado, April 25, 1864; OR, I, 34-3, 292; Chivington to Collins, April 21, 1864, ibid., 252; Grinnell, *Fighting Cheyennes*, 142.

sequent council, however, Evans curtly informed the Indian leaders that their delay in responding to his offer now prohibited him from making peace. While the Cheyennes were welcome to go to the reservation at Fort Lyon, he informed Black Kettle that the fate of his people would rest in the hands of the army. Evans concluded the meeting by adding several conditions to their surrender, one of which was they would assist the army in subduing the recalcitrant bands, an offer perhaps he hoped they would decline. Black Kettle and the others, however, readily agreed to abide by all the new terms; thus Evans had no choice but to allow them to proceed to Fort Lyon.

In October, a band of over one hundred Arapahoes, led by Chief Little Raven, camped near Fort Lyon, while Black Kettle circulated on the plains attempting to convince other Cheyenne bands to surrender. The Indians who went to Fort Lyon may have believed that they were at peace with the whites, but Chivington remained determined to grant his men a fight, and boost his own reputation, before their term of service expired.

When Black Kettle and his people arrived in early November, Chivington instructed them to camp on Sand Creek, northwest of the post, until he received permission from General Curtis to issue their provisions. He took advantage of the trumped-up delay to march the Third Colorado to Fort Lyon, where it arrived on November 28 and took up positions to attack the village.

In an ensuing massacre, Chivington's volunteers swept down on the sleeping village, slaughtering some two hundred men, women, and children in a wild melee lasting several hours. Afterward the troopers scalped and mutilated most of the bodies, some even collecting severed body parts as grisly souvenirs of their handiwork. Hailed initially as a great victory by the Denver citizenry, the truth of the atrocity was soon exposed. A congressional investigation followed, and the name Chivington would forever be synonymous with the heinous Sand Creek Massacre—an event the Cheyennes and other plains tribes would never forget.[41]

---

[41]The foregoing discussion of events occurring in Colorado during fall 1864 is synthesized from Utley, *Frontiersmen in Blue*, 284–99; Hoig, *The Sand Creek Massacre*; Hyde, *Life of George Bent*, 139–63; Grinnell, *Fighting Cheyennes*, 153–80.

CHAPTER TEN

"WE ARE GOING TO HAVE
A WARM TIME"

The Cheyennes lost no time in exacting retribution for Chivington's treachery at Sand Creek. Those who survived the massacre fled eastward to the headwaters of the Smoky Hill, where they joined their relatives to wage all-out war against the whites. Although the news of Sand Creek galvanized most of the Indians, some, notably Black Kettle, remained peace advocates despite the outrage recently perpetrated on his band.

Among the Americans incensed by Chivington's actions was Major Edward W. Wynkoop, commander of the First Colorado Veteran Cavalry and appointed a designated agent for the Southern Cheyennes and Arapahoes. Wynkoop predicted that Sand Creek would be the harbinger of hostilities unlike anything yet witnessed on the plains. Writing from Fort Lyon on January 15, 1865, he recounted recent events:

> . . . up to the date of the massacre by Colonel Chivington, not one single depredation had been committed by the Cheyenne and Arapahoe Indians. The settlers of the Arkansas Valley had returned to their ranches from which they had fled, had taken in their crops and had been resting in perfect security under the assurances from myself that they would be in no danger for the present. . . . Since this last horrible murder by Colonel Chivington, the country presents a scene of desolation; all communication is cut off with the States except by sending large bodies of troops, and already over 100 whites have fallen as victims to the fearful vengeance of these betrayed Indians. All this country is ruined; there can be no such

thing as peace in the future, but by the total annihilation of all the Indians on the plains. I have the most reliable information to the effect that the Cheyennes and Arapahoes have allied themselves with the Kiowas, Comanches, and Sioux, and are congregated to the number of 5,000 or 6,000 on the Smoky Hill.[1]

Even as Wynkoop was writing, the combined tribes were moving west to Cherry Creek to await the return of small war parties that had been probing along the South Platte. When all the leaders were present, a second council convened to plan their strategy for a general attack. Taking advantage of the approximately one thousand warriors in the combined camps, they decided to launch their initial raid on the principal settlement, Julesburg, where there were not only stage and telegraph stations, but massive stockpiles of supplies. Only one troop of cavalry was stationed at adjacent Camp Rankin, a mile west of the town.[2]

On January 7, 1865, the Indian force moved north from the camps and descended on Julesburg. Warrior decoys lured the troopers out of their fort, killing fifteen soldiers, as well as four citizens, in a running fight. Other Indians encircled the stockade and kept it under fire to contain the white inhabitants, while the rest of the warriors sacked and looted the settlement.

Later that month war parties conducted simultaneous and constant attacks throughout the South Platte Valley, burning stage stations and ranches, destroying the telegraph line, and ransacking every wagon train they encountered on the road. At Harlow's Ranch, west of Julesburg, they killed all of the men and burned the buildings. One woman

---

[1] Major E. W. Wynkoop to Lieutenant J. E. Tappan, AAAG, District of the Upper Arkansas, January 15, 1865, OR, I, 48-1, 959.

[2] George Bent, who was with the Cheyennes at the time and participated in the raids, described the settlement: "Julesburg stood some distance from the river bank, out in the level sandy valley, which at this point was several miles broad, closed in on the north and south by low sand hills and bluffs. . . . here the company had a large station house or 'home station,' with an eating house, a big stable, blacksmith and repair shop, granary, and storehouses, and a big corral enclosed by a high wall built of sod. Besides the stage company's property, there was a large store selling all kinds of goods to travelers and emigrant trains, and the Overland Telegraph Company also had an office at this point. Altogether, Julesburg Stage Station was quite large place for the Plains in those days and there were at the place forty or fifty men—station hands, stock tenders, drivers, telegraph operators, etc. The buildings here were partly built of cottonwood logs and party of sod." Hyde, *Life of George Bent*, 169.

was taken captive. At Washington's Ranch, fifty miles upstream from Julesburg, Indians stole five hundred cattle and set fire to a hundred tons of government hay. A cavalry detachment guarding nearby Valley Station prudently chose not to interfere with them. For the Cheyennes, the daily raiding victories, celebrated with nightly scalp dances, did much to raise morale after the tragedy of Sand Creek.

As the great village moved toward the North Platte, the warriors again swept down on Julesburg. Although they attempted to induce the soldiers to fight them again, the troops had learned their lesson and remained inside the protective stockade. Some Indians harassed the bluecoats by firing into the fort, but most rode on to Julesburg and again plundered the store and warehouse, then fired the buildings in a last unsuccessful attempt to draw cavalrymen into a fight.

Two days later, the combined villages camped on a tributary east of the Fort Laramie route, ten miles east of Mud Springs Station, which by 1865 was the only place then inhabited by whites in the whole distance between the north and south forks of the Platte. Mud Springs was one of the stage stations established by John M. Hockaday when he took over the central overland mail route in 1858. Hockaday avoided using the old emigrant road that crossed the South Platte at Upper, or California, Crossing, near present-day Big Springs, Nebraska.

Lieutenant Francis T. Bryan's 1856 expedition had discovered a better crossing farther upstream at the later site of Julesburg. From that point, the trail followed Lodgepole Creek west approximately seventy miles before turning directly north to enter the North Platte Valley a few miles below Courthouse Rock. Although Bryan's trail was not immediately popular with travelers, the need for more direct mail service to Denver made Julesburg the logical point at which to divide the mail bound for Salt Lake City from that destined for Colorado. Russell, Majors, and Waddell later utilized the Mud Springs Station as a relay for their short-lived Pony Express venture. In 1861 the Pacific Telegraph Company became a tenant, sharing the station with Ben Holladay's mail line until the central route was shifted again two years later.

Considered a "home" station, one where drivers and passengers overnighted, Mud Springs afforded meals and lodging, such as they were, though one passenger described the station as "a dirty hovel, serving tough antilope steaks, fried on a filthy stove, with wooden boxes serving as chairs at a bench like table." After coaches ceased plying the Jules Stretch, as it was known, the telegraph office remained at Mud Springs and army couriers from Fort Laramie used the place as a stopover en route to and from the Overland Trail. A detachment of soldiers guarded the still-vital station, which consisted of two sod buildings with pole-and-earth roofs, one housing the telegraph office and quarters, the other serving as a combination storehouse and stable, with an adjacent corral.[3]

An advance party of Indian scouts sent out to reconnoiter the station on February 4, 1865, ran off a nearby beef herd belonging to the Creighton & Hoel ranch before the civilians could stop them. The scouts did not, however, attack the station itself. Fully aware of the crisis at Julesburg, the telegraph operator transmitted a frantic message to both Forts Mitchell and Laramie requesting immediate assistance. Any uncertainty over the whereabouts of the Indians after they left the station would soon be dispelled. Mud Springs and its tiny garrison of nine soldiers and five civilians lay directly in the path of the Indian juggernaut.

Captain Jacob S. Shuman at Camp Mitchell, on the North Platte, immediately dispatched Lieutenant William Ellsworth and thirty-six men of the Eleventh Ohio to Mud Springs. Riding nonstop all night, Ellsworth's detachment covered the fifty-five miles to the beleaguered station by dawn the next morning. Soon thereafter the Indians gathered in large numbers about the station, though they maintained their distance when they discovered there were more soldiers than expected. The warriors, some of whom crept down a ravine until they were close to the east side the station, exchanged fire with the soldiers for several hours. George Bent, who accompanied his Cheyenne relatives, later recalled the scene. "The soldiers were all inside the buildings (which were very strong) and were firing out through loopholes. It was a hard place to attack successfully. . . . It was not very interesting, as neither

---

[3]Mud Springs is located a few miles north of present-day Dalton, Nebraska on the west side of U.S. 385. Henderson, "The Story of Mud Springs," 109–14.; Lieutenant Colonel William O. Collins to Captain John Pratt, AG, Dist. of Nebraska, February 15, 1865, OR, I, 48-1, 92–98 (hereinafter cited as Collins report).

side cared to come into the open, and no one could tell what effect was being made by the shooting, as you could not tell whether anyone had been hit or not."[4]

The Indians broke off the skirmish at midday when the whites released the horses and mules from the corral, hoping they would draw the Indians away from the station. But the ruse was only partially successful. While most of the young warriors chased after the animals, others stayed behind to watch the station.[5]

Collins had received the telegram at Fort Laramie at about four o'clock on the afternoon of February 4. He immediately formed a relief column composed of about one hundred twenty cavalrymen from the Eleventh Ohio and the Seventh Iowa. Three hours later, Collins and his command filed out of the post bound for Mud Springs, 105 miles away. The night was bitterly cold and by the time the column reached Camp Mitchell the following morning, several troopers were so incapacitated they had to be left there. Collins himself paused only briefly before advancing with a hand-picked detachment of twenty-five men to reinforce the station as quickly as possible. He assigned Captain William D. Fouts, commanding D Company, Seventh Iowa, to follow shortly with the rest of the battalion.

Colonel Collins and his men arrived at Mud Springs at about two o'clock on the morning of the sixth, Fouts bringing in the rest of the command about six hours later. Shortly after daylight, just as Fouts and his men arrived, large numbers of Indians on the surrounding hills opened fire on the station. "It was evident," Collins wrote later, "that they had come to take the post and expected to do so."[6] The troops found themselves at a distinct tactical disadvantage. The station was situated on a flat terrace just outside the mouth of a long canyon that opened to the northeast. A slow, natural seepage puddled up at the surface near that point, hence the name Mud Springs. Curving below the terrace just a few yards east of the station was a dry streambed. Hills commanded the other three sides, creating gullies across the terrace

---

[4]Hyde, *Life of George Bent*, 188.
[5]George Bent assumed the soldiers were running out of ammunition and therefore released the animals hoping the Indians, who prized horses above all else, would chase them. He stated that no warriors were killed in this action. Ibid., 189.
[6]Collins report, 93.

that provided natural concealment for the tribesmen. According to Collins, it did not take long for his men to follow the Indians' example. "We found it necessary to imitate the Indians, get under banks and creep up to favorable positions, watch for an Indian's head, shoot the moment it was shown, and pop down at the flash of his gun. The men got quite handy at this game and soon made any ground occupied by the Indians too hot for them. It was common to see a soldier and an Indian playing bo-peep in this maneuver for half an hour at a time."[7]

A group of approximately two hundred Cheyennes and Sioux massed behind a nearby hill and in ravines only seventy-five yards south of the station. While the archers remained secluded, they launched showers of arrows high into the air to descend on the troops, wounding a few men and a number of animals inside the corral.[8] Collins telegraphed Major Thomas L. Mackey at Fort Laramie to send down a mountain howitzer to assist in dislodging the Indians, but he had no sooner sent the message than the Indians severed the telegraph line a mile west of the station. Collins quickly organized a counter-attack to break up this concentration, one party of soldiers advancing on foot while a mounted detachment outflanked the Indian positions. In the face of the opposition, the warriors immediately withdrew. Collins's troops fortified the summit with a rifle pit commanding the surrounding area. By early afternoon the Indian fire slackened as the soldiers drove the tribesmen from their vantage points close to the station. Other groups of warriors remained on the bluff tops in the distance until nightfall. Collins estimated the Indian losses at thirty, while his own command suffered seven wounded. However, Collins may have overestimated the accuracy of his men's fire. Contrary to Collins's report, George Bent asserted that no Indians were killed in either of the fights at Mud Springs.[9]

Collins dispatched a detachment to repair the telegraph line at about three o'clock, but the Indians immediately cut it again. A second repair party venturing out just before dark discovered the new

[7]Ibid.

[8]Collins recorded that there were five hundred to one thousand warriors present, all armed with rifles, revolvers, and bows. They had also acquired plenty of ammunition following their recent raids on the South Platte. Ibid., 94.

[9]Hyde, *Life of George Bent*, 190.

break at about the same place in the line, but this time the Indians had also chopped down two poles and taken away a few hundred yards of wire, making the repairs more difficult. With insufficient wire on hand at the station to splice the break, the soldiers took it from the line east of the station, enabling them to restore communication with Fort Laramie. The rest of the troops, meanwhile, fortified the station and prepared for an offensive the next day.

As dawn broke on the seventh, no Indians were visible. Leaving Captain Fouts and a strong detachment to hold the station, Collins led a reconnaissance-in-force to determine the whereabouts of the Indians. Numerous trails on the prairie all led toward Rush Creek, a tributary of the North Platte about ten miles distant, where indeed the Indian village had moved the previous day. Collins and his men returned to the station later that day to lay plans for pursuing the tribesmen.

Early the next morning, after a thirty-four-hour forced march, Captain William H. Brown reached Mud Springs with the howitzer and fifty Ohio troopers to augment Collins's force. The colonel placed Fouts in charge of a guard at the station, then took up the Indian trail with the main body, the howitzer, and a few supply wagons. As he had anticipated, Collins discovered the site of the village at Rush Creek Springs, but to his disappointment the Indians had already abandoned it. It had been a huge camp several miles in length, evidenced by a profusion of empty tin cans, flour sacks, and other debris plundered from the warehouse at Julesburg.

Now hot on the fresh trail, Collins hurried down Rush Creek. As the troops entered the North Platte valley about a mile from the river, they sighted hundreds of warriors scattered across the flood plain on the opposite side. Since there was no sign of women and children, and no lodges, Collins quickly concluded that the noncombatants had fled toward the distant bluffs, while the warriors remained behind to stall the cavalry.[10]

---

[10]Actually, the entire village had marched about ten miles that day, crossing the frozen North Platte by sanding the ice to prevent the horses from slipping, and had camped in the bluffs north of the river. The leaders concluded that the troops were not pursuing them; therefore they had decided to camp for four days on a small stream among the bluffs. However, a Sioux lookout atop a bluff spotted Collins's column moving down Rush Creek and signaled the alarm to the village. The fighting men rounded up their ponies and rode out to meet the soldiers. Confronted by over a thousand warriors, Collins corralled his train and dug in. Ibid., 190–91.

Collins and his men were awed at the sight of the Indians, as well they should have been, for it was a spectacle few white men had ever witnessed—and lived to describe. Arrayed on the prairie, calmly grazing their horses while they awaited the soldiers' arrival, were fifteen hundred to two thousand plains warriors in full fighting regalia. "It was now clear we had underestimated the numbers against us," Collins later conceded. "It was evident that all the hostile Indians that had been committing depredations and holding the country along the South Platte were concentrated here."[11] The troops did not have long to contemplate the precarious situation in which they suddenly found themselves. As Collins began scanning the river for a suitable crossing, the Indians arose almost as one, swung onto the backs of their ponies, and swarmed toward the command. To Collins's amazement, the warriors divided into two groups as if by order and rapidly crossed over the frozen river on both of his flanks. He recalled, "We had barely time to corral our train before they were upon us on every side. The position chosen was the best we could get, but there were many little sand ridges and hollows under cover of which they could approach us. A very great change had come over the men since the morning of the fight at Mud Springs. They were rested and free from excitement, had confidence in their officers, obeyed orders, and went to work with a will. Sharpshooters were pushed out, and the hillocks commanding the camp occupied, and rifle-pits dug upon them."[12]

The volunteers opened fire on the attacking tribesmen, some of whom rode almost into their lines. After their initial charge, the Indians began sniping at the soldiers from more distant positions. A dozen or so warriors crept along and under cover of the river bank to occupy a strategic knoll about four hundred yards from Collins's men. Although the howitzer detachment attempted to shell the Indians' position, the ammunition was so old that most of the projectiles failed to explode. In return, the warriors began firing with such accuracy that

---

[11]Ibid. Although Collins maintained in his report that 2,000 warriors opposed him, the Post Returns for that month recorded 1,500 to 2,000. It was, in any event, an impressive number of hostile bands concentrated in one place. Post Returns, February 1865, Fort Laramie, PR, FL. For a more detailed treatment of these events, see McDermott, "We Had a Terribly Hard Time Letting Them Go," 78–88.

[12]Collins report, 95.

a detail of sixteen mounted troopers under the command of Lieutenant James Patton was sent out to dislodge them. Following Collins's specific instructions, Patton's men formed in line and charged round the hill, dispersing the enemy sharpshooters. But dozens of other warriors, previously unseen on higher ground back of the hill, in turn engaged the detachment in hand-to-hand fighting before the soldiers could extricate themselves. Privates John A. Harris and William H. Harstshorn were killed in the brief melee, though Patton and the rest of the men returned safely under covering fire that drove back the pursuing warriors.[13]

Both sides kept up desultory long-range fire throughout the rest of the day. As darkness approached, the Indians withdrew behind the hills and began recrossing the river. Collins's soldiers spent the rest of the night improving their positions and digging rifle pits to be better prepared for the fight the next day.

As dawn broke on February 9, approximately four hundred mounted warriors crossed to the south bank and began exchanging fire with the soldiers in hopes of stampeding and capturing the army's stock. The rest of the tribesmen posted themselves on the north bank beyond the range of the soldiers' guns. During the exchange, the village continued its trek northward toward the Niobrara River and sanctuary in the Black Hills. The attacking party remained behind only a short time before retreating to join their kinsmen on the march.

---

[13]Harris was a member of D Company, Seventh Iowa, and Hartshorn belonged to C Company, Eleventh Ohio. Both bodies were taken back to Fort Laramie for burial; ibid. Bent claimed that Private Hartshorn, mounted on a very fleet horse, rode through the body of Indians heading west. Several warriors pursued and finally killed the trooper a long way from the area of the fight. According to Bent, a message was recovered from Hartshorn's body and was brought to him for interpretation. It was an appeal from Collins to Fort Laramie, calling for further assistance to extricate him from his situation. Although Collins later failed to mention the dispatch, Bent said that a Sergeant MacDonald, who was in the fight, verified the information to him many years later. Hyde, *Life of George Bent,* 193. Collins later stated that the howitzer ammunition was defective because it had been in storage at Fort Laramie for eight to ten years; Collins report, 97. Bent apparently was one of several white or mixed-blood men who joined with the Indians in these encounters. Collins mentioned "there were white men or Mexicans among them," Collins report, 94. This soon became common knowledge among the enlisted men, and their resentment is reflected in Private Hervey Johnson's statement, "Woe be to the white man that is ever taken by soldiers in an indian fight, his 'hide wouldent hold shucks." Unrau, *Tending the Talking Wire,* 216.

Collins, whose losses thus far stood at twenty-eight men, nine of whom were wounded and ten who were severely frost-bitten, chose not to pursue. "With their [the Indians] numbers," he wrote, "they could at any time compel our small party to corral and fight. We could drive them off and follow again with the same result but could not afford to give them the least advantage."[14] Faced with continuing the pursuit into unfamiliar territory in the middle of winter, with a force that was both outnumbered and ill equipped for such an expedition, portended disaster. The soldiers' only practical choice was to return to Fort Laramie.

Conditions had been tense at the post during Collins's absence. In his zeal to strike a decisive blow on the enemy, he had left only a hundred men at the post. Because the Sioux and Cheyennes had shown no reluctance to overrun Julesburg, Major Mackey, who remained in command at the post, was confident they would not hesitate to attack Fort Laramie. He therefore took immediate steps to bolster his defenses should the Indians outmaneuver Collins and turn upriver. But the post was difficult to defend, especially with so few soldiers. Their status deteriorated even more when Lieutenant Brown was called out on February 6, taking fifty men and one of the howitzers to reinforce Collins.

The fort itself was penetrable. A stockade planned in the early 1850s to enclose the parade ground area had never come to fruition.[15] During its years of military occupation, the fort had been expanded to meet the needs of increasingly larger garrisons, without much thought to their defense. A hospital stood northwest of the enlarged sutler's store, and nearby was a new gingerbread-trimed cottage for the manager. East of the store, near the Laramie River, were frame warehouses and a number of huts for civilian teamsters and laundresses. Cavalry stables and corrals were located some distance northeast of the sutler's

---

[14]Ibid., 96.

[15]A plat of Fort Laramie, drawn by the Corps of Engineers on February 12, 1851, showed a proposed wall connecting the magazine with the guardhouse, thence running south to a proposed blockhouse on the riverbank near old Fort John. The trading post was to be incorporated into the defenses, forming a bastion on the south side. The stockade was to continue west to a point on the bench south of Old Bedlam, where it would have turned north to the magazine to complete the enclosure. All of the main buildings at that time, including the officers' quarters, barracks, stables and storehouses, would lie within. Plat of Fort Laramie, library, FLNHS.

store and on the same terrace. Now sorely missed was Fort John, the last vestige of which had been razed in 1862. Mackey, like the traders before him, may have considered the river winding around the east and south sides of the fort to be a reasonably effective barrier against attack. Also, riflemen posted in the officers' houses could command the lowland behind Old Bedlam.

The major authorized Post Quartermaster H. E. Averill to furnish sacks of corn "to form suitable barricades" at strategic points within the garrison. One of those breastworks presumably connected the officers' quarters with the magazine by filling some of the intervening gaps between the buildings. If not actually manned, the barricades might at least have prevented mounted warriors from entering the interior garrison. Mackey also erected makeshift parapets of sacked corn atop some of the buildings.[16]

The north perimeter of the fort was clearly the most vulnerable. Hardly more than a hundred yards north of the sutler's store was a low plateau about twenty feet higher than the parade ground. The point of the plateau nearest the fort, embracing the cemetery, afforded a near-perfect position for Indian sharpshooters.

The day after Collins and the first relief column marched from Fort Laramie, Mackey had directed Ordnance Sergeant Schnyder and Quartermaster Sergeant J. C. Cummings to oversee the construction of two earthen field fortifications on the plateau as emplacements for two of the three remaining cannons at the post. The lunettes, appropriately christened "Battery Schnyder" and "Battery Cummings," were situated near the west and southeast edges of the elevation, respectively. The men worked feverishly and within a day the batteries were ready and manned. Mackey positioned the third howitzer in a lunette constructed on the gentle slope descending toward the confluence of the Laramie and the Platte. "Battery Harrington," as it was designated, would command the flood plain between the two streams. That Mackey ordered all teamsters, with their mules, to report for duty, suggests that rifle pits were excavated to shelter supporting riflemen on the flanks of the gun

---

[16]*Orders No.* (unidentified), February 7, 1865, Fort Laramie, N.T., Post Orders, FL; Unrau, *Tending the Talking Wire*, 218. The upper verandah along the west side of Old Bedlam was likely one of the fortified points. Author's note.

emplacements. At that, Mackey was at a distinct disadvantage by having too few men to defend such a long perimeter.[17]

As the combined bands of Cheyennes and southern Sioux moved northward, bypassing Fort Laramie, area traders feared that the appearance of these Indians, with their captured plunder, would incite their kinsmen in the Powder River country to join them. G. P. Beauvais, who still occupied the former American Fur Company post below Fort Laramie, sent one of his men with three wagonloads of goods to the Sioux village to attempt to dissuade them from joining the hostile factions. At about the same time, sutler Bullock also dispatched Nick Janis to Powder River with goods. Beauvais's representative was intercepted en route by the Cheyennes, who killed him and appropriated all the goods. Janis was more fortunate, perhaps because his wife was related to the Sioux. Even though the Indians were implacable and refused to trade with him, neither did they molest him. A party of Spotted Tail's Brulés, in fact, escorted him all the way back to Deer Creek to ensure his safety. Writing to his employer, Seth Ward, Bullock blamed "Old Collins" and Agent Loree for the recent and ominous change among the Sioux: "Their [*sic*] is such a want of discipline and judgment that I deem it unsafe for even myself to remain here. But after the departure of Col. C we will feel much more secure as his imbecility and total want of judgment with Loree's peculation of the indian goods is the whole cause of the disatisfaction of the Sioux . . . nearly all the old men in the country are moving over to 'Cache La Poudre,' and Denver. Bordeau [*sic*] is going to the former place and we will be left alone. It is the impression of Bordeau & Bis-

---

[17]A detailed treatment of this topic, based on Fort Laramie primary sources, is found in Chappell, "The Fortifications of Old Fort Laramie," *Visions of a Grand Old Post*, 69–71. Mackey instructed the post quartermaster to have all teamsters, with their teams but without wagons, to report to Sergeant Powell, C Co., Eleventh Ohio, on February 6. The author concurs with Chappell's deduction that their only purpose would have been to operate slips, that is, animal-drawn scoops for moving earth. Using the slips, entrenchments, known either as shelter trenches or rifle pits, could have been constructed easily and rapidly across the flat tableland, and perhaps down to the Laramie River. The most basic type of rifle pit was made by scooping out earth to form a shallow trench five feet wide and with a depth of approximately one foot at the rear of the trench. The excavated soil was carried forward and heaped on the side facing the enemy, to form a breastwork approximately fifteen inches high and two feet thick. This defense would adequately protect a rifleman in the prone position from small arms fire. J. B. Wheeler, *The Elements of Field Fortifications*, 200–203.

sonette that this will be a general combination of the Sioux and Cheyennes in the spring."[18]

Just a few days after Colonel Collins returned from his expedition, welcome news arrived announcing that five companies of Nebraska Volunteer Cavalry and two from Iowa were on their way to relieve the First Battalion. The disgruntled Ohioans, retained in federal service for more than three months after their enlistment had expired, finally received orders to proceed to Omaha to be mustered out. Sutler Bullock, for one, had no regrets over their departure:

> I felt some apprehensions for a while that an attack would be made on the Fort as Col. Collins when [he] left here with the Old Battalion left only about 100 men all told here . . . the discipline here was so imperfect that the Indians could have come in at any time without resistance. In fact, no mob could be worse. Sentinels sleeping on their post[s] was not infrequent. Major Mackey has improved discipline somewhat . . . I know I would have to defend the Store for my personal safety. The Cheyennes have had and still have small war parties around here for the last two weeks and have run off all the Government horses and many other persons in the country.[19]

---

[18]Bullock's displeasure with both Collins and Loree, not surprisingly, was seated in business. First, agent Loree had used an order issued by the District of Colorado, prohibiting unlicensed sutlers from trading with Indians, for denying a license to Ward, Bullock's boss. By excluding his principal competitor from the trade, Loree forced the Indians to bargain exlusively with him for their annuity goods. Second, Ward failed to renew his appointment as post sutler when it expired in March 1863. Collins apparently discovered the oversight and allowed Herman Kountz to serve as sutler for the Eleventh Ohio, under the authority granted by Army Regulations. That provision permitted regimental commanders to appoint a sutler for "troops in campaign, on detachment, or on distant service" at the rate of one per regiment, corps, or detachment. Accordingly, Collins did not have to seek approval from the secretary of war, a legal requirement for post sutlers, though Kountz's appointment was upheld by the assistant secretary of war. Joseph H. Burbank also secured an appointment as sutler on January 6, 1865, but Ward, taking advantage of political influence in Washington, managed to get the appointments of both Kountz and Burbank revoked in March 1865, and to reestablish his own place as the legitimate post sutler at Fort Laramie. Bullock to Ward, February 20, 1865, Seth E. Ward Papers, Western History Collections, DPL; ibid., March 10, 1865; ibid., March 25, 1865; *Revised United States Army Regulations of 1861*, 37; William P. Dole, commissioner of Indian affairs, to John Loree, November 9, 1863, Box 1, LR, FL; S. F. Chalfin, AAGUSA, to Joseph H. Burbank, March 6, 1865, ibid.; Register of Post Traders, Box 1, volume 1, ACP Branch, RG 94, NA.

[19]Companies A, B, C, and D, Eleventh Ohio, received the muster out order on February 17, and left Fort Laramie the very next day. Post Returns, February 1865, Fort Laramie; the First Battalion was mustered out of service at Omaha on April 1, 1865. Reid, *Ohio in the War*, 820. Bullock was so concerned that he sent "Eliza," presumably his wife, to a safer locale. Bullock to Ward, March 10, 1865, Ward Papers.

Shortly after Collins left, Lieutenant Colonel William Baumer, First Nebraska Veteran Volunteer Cavalry, was assigned to head the subdistrict, though Mackey remained in charge of the Fort Laramie garrison. Baumer and five companies of cavalrymen arrived at the post in March. Bullock characterized the new commander as "a very pleasant gentleman," but was hardly more impressed with his three hundred rough-hewn troopers than he had been with the Ohio volunteers. Still worse, hundreds of Kansas troops were expected to arrive at Fort Laramie in the near future. "I do not know how things are going to result here," Bullock complained to Ward. "There is no order or discipline, and [I] would feel much better with the hostile Indians than the friendly troops."[20] Baumer nevertheless distributed his Nebraskans in small detachments along the roads east and west of the post in an effort to maintain telegraph communications with Denver, Salt Lake City, and the Pacific Coast.

With Confederate forces in retreat in the South, and the outbreak of a full-blown Indian war on the frontier, the army implemented significant organizational changes to better cope with the situation on the central plains. A general order promulgated on February 17, 1865, altered the boundaries of the Department of the Missouri to include Missouri and Kansas, as well as the territories of Nebraska, Colorado, Utah, and the western portion of Dakota.[21] By unifying this enormous geographical area under a single commander, army headquarters hoped to achieve a greater concert of action and effectiveness against the Indians, who freely crossed the military's invisible jurisdictions.[22]

---

[20]Bullock to Ward, March 25, 1865, Ward Papers.

[21]Because Idaho Territory was of such immense size, the growing population in the gold camps of western Montana petitioned for improved representation in Congress. Montana Territory was carved out of Idaho by legislation enacted on May 26, 1864, and by the same stroke of the pen most of what we know today as Wyoming, including Fort Laramie, was encompassed within Dakota Territory. Thian, *Military Geography*, 120–21.

[22]The antebellum Department of the West had been abolished and merged into the Western Department on July 3, 1861. Four months later, the army again adjusted its administrative boundaries by creating the Department of Kansas, embracing that state, as well as the territories of Nebraska, Colorado, and Dakota, and the Indian Territory. The Department of Kansas became a part of the Department of the Missouri as a result of General Orders No. 11, Adjutant General's Office, January 30, 1865. Major General Dodge commanded the department from December 9, 1864 until July 21, 1865, when he was replaced by Major General John Pope. Ibid., 67, 75, 106–107.

Major General Grenville M. Dodge, who had been appointed the department commander in late 1864, immediately implemented his own internal changes to facilitate field operations. The most significant of these was his authorization of a vast new District of the Plains, encompassing all the territory outside Kansas and Missouri. Dodge selected an aggressive and no-nonsense Irish immigrant, Patrick E. Connor, to command that sector. Connor's experience included an enlistment in the U.S. Dragoons in the early 1840s, followed by service during the Mexican War, in which he commanded a unit of Texas volunteers. He later joined the gold rush to California, settling in Stockton, where he became a leader in civic, military, and fraternal affairs. At the outbreak of the Civil War, Connor was appointed colonel of the Third California Infantry. Having spent his entire adult life on the frontier, he acquired an uncompromising attitude toward Indians, and a keen understanding of the independent westerners he commanded. Two years later, he gained the stars of a brigadier in recognition of his vigorous activities against the Indians in his District of Utah, particularly for his decisive winter victory over the Shoshones at Bear River.[23]

Connor reorganized his command into new geographical subdistricts, designating Fort Laramie as headquarters for the North Subdistrict. Dodge had previously ordered the Eleventh and Sixteenth Kansas Cavalry Regiments, recuperating at Fort Riley following the 1864 Missouri campaign against Confederate General Sterling Price, to march up the Platte to reinforce the garrisons weakened by the withdrawal of Collins's battalion. Colonel Thomas Moonlight, the ranking officer in the subdistrict, was appointed to relieve Baumer.[24]

The Cheyennes and the warlike Sioux bands did not observe their customary winter hiatus. Most of the Sioux were Oglalas from the South Platte, united with Chief Little Thunder's Brulés, the same people Harney had overpowered on Blue Water Creek a decade earlier.

---

[23]Heitman, *Historical Register* 1: 321–22; Hafen and Hafen, *Powder River Campaigns*, 23n10.

[24]Connor organized the District of the Plains into four subdistricts. In addition to those mentioned in the text, the South Sub-district encompassed Colorado Territory as well as Fort Halleck in Dakota, headquartered in Denver. The West Sub-district comprised Utah Territory, with headquarters at Camp Douglas near Salt Lake City. GO No. 4, April 8, 1865, District of the Plains, OR, I, 48-2, 54.

William Bullock became so concerned for the safety of the firm's sizeable oxen herd that he sent his train with all the cattle back to Fort Leavenworth for safety. Indians nevertheless attacked the train just east of Julesburg, but with the help of nearby troops the teamsters were able to repel them and recover most of the stock.[25] Other attacks occurred west of Fort Laramie at Poison Creek, where a war party fell on a supply wagon, and at La Bonte Creek, where raiders swooped down on a herd of cavalry horses grazing near Camp Marshall. Indians also raided a government supply train traveling along the North Platte approximately seventy miles above Fort Laramie, escaping with all the livestock. Two other soldiers, driving a wagon to Camp Marshall on April 21, 1865, were ambushed and killed on LaPrele Creek, a tributary of the North Platte twenty miles downstream from Deer Creek Station.[26]

Although four hundred lodges of Sioux were involved in these recent conflicts along the South Platte, Little Thunder sent word to Bullock that his Brulés had not, and did not intend to, support the rampaging factions. Thus, at Bullock's behest, both Little Thunder and Spotted Tail brought their bands to Fort Laramie for protection and food in mid-April. But, concerned about the growing number of Sioux camped around the fort and the potential for a confrontation with his soldiers, Mackey arranged with agent Vital Jarrot, Loree's successor, that in the spring the recent arrivals, along with the Laramie Sioux, would be moved downstream to Bordeaux's Trading Post. Although the chiefs professed their peaceful intentions, Bullock clearly had his doubts. "The reason 'Little Thunder' came in" Bullock

---

[25]The exact date of this attack has not been determined, though Bullock stated that Gillespie, his employee, left Fort Laramie on April 6, 1865. Considering the time necessary to travel to the South Platte, with Bullock's instructions to move slowly so as not to wear out the cattle, the raid probably occurred around the 20th. Ward Papers.

[26]Unrau, *Tending the Talking Wire*, 233, 238–39. The graphic description of this soldier's death was told to sutler William Bullock, who in turn related it to his employer. Bullock to Ward, April 30, 1865, Ward Papers; McDermott, *Frontier Crossroads*, 43–44. Some sources also list a skirmish between Sioux and a detachment of the Eleventh Ohio in which Captain Levi M. Rinehart was killed. However, contemporary accounts agree that Rinehart and his men were drunk when they attempted to arrest some Sioux they had accused of stealing horses in the vicinity of Deer Creek. When Rinehart emerged from a tepee he had entered a few moments before, one of his own men accidentally shot him. Rinehart was probably the officer to whom Ware referred as having bought a Sioux woman for one horse. The woman immediately ran away from him. Unrau, *Tending the Talking Wire*, 218, 222–23; Ware, *Indian War of 1864*, 213; Bullock to Ward, April 30, 1865, Ward Papers.

wrote, "is because he is old and very infirm and cannot fight or he would be at it now, as nearly all the Brules are for war."[27] Charles Elston, a Virginian described as "high-toned" yet charming, who claimed three Indian wives and forty years' experience among the Sioux, was placed in charge of a sixty-man Indian "police force" to maintain order and act as a buffer in the event problems later arose.[28]

Major Dodge proposed to strike the renegade bands near the Black Hills in early spring, before they could move south to resume raiding in the Platte Valley. Connor, accordingly, prepared to amass provisions and forage for the stock at Fort Laramie in anticipation of such a movement. The logistics of moving large numbers of troops from the East onto the plains, however, immediately frustrated his plan. Connor also discovered to his dismay that there were no more than four hundred serviceable cavalry horses in the entire district. The Eleventh Kansas, for example, could mount only two-thirds of its troopers. The Sixteenth Kansas, for reasons an infuriated Dodge was unable to fathom, took two months to reach its destination. Other units had to move long distances overland and by steamer to reach the rendezvous point at Fort Leavenworth. As it turned out, most of the troops Dodge intended to use for his spring campaign failed to arrive on the Missouri until early June, still six hundred miles short of Fort Laramie. Even then, most of the cavalry traveled on foot.

The supply trains were another matter. They required an average of six weeks to cover the distance between Leavenworth and Fort Laramie, and the bureaucracy of the Quartermaster Department had delayed letting the freight contracts until May 1. Next, the deadline for delivery was extended to December 1. Barely able to conceal his anger in an official communication, Dodge wrote: "The supplies went forward slowly; trains loitered on their way . . . and in many cases requi-

---

[27]Bullock to Ward, April 10, 1865, and May 8, 1865, ibid. Bullock claimed to have been instrumental in convincing Moonlight to organize the Indian company. They were at least partially garbed in army uniform and may have been armed by the government as well. Bullock to Ward, May 22, 1865, ibid.; *Roster of Iowa Soldiers*, 1254.

[28]The name is found spelled in several ways, including Elston, Ellison, and Elliston. The author uses the form found in Moonlight's official report of May 26, 1865, as well as Ware's *Indian War of 1864*, 201; George Bent and others spelled it "Elliston." Hyde, *Life of George Bent*, 208. The policemen, sometimes referred to as scouts, were uniformed, armed, equipped, and rationed by the army.

sitions for stores did not arrive until late, the staff officers not appearing to have appreciated the necessity for early action."[29]

During the first week of April, the Eleventh Kansas passed through Fort Laramie en route to what the men anticipated would be a major expedition. The Kansans camped on the flood plain below the post, drew rations at the fort the next day, and moved on to a new bivouac upstream. Late in the afternoon of April 9, 1865, came the momentous news that General Robert E. Lee had surrendered his army of Northern Virginia. "What a time," one veteran exclaimed. "No sleep that night. Officers and men lost all control of themselves and did many foolish things."[30] No doubt there was a raucous celebration at the post, too, in observance of the war's end.

The Confederate capitulation notwithstanding, Connor faced insurmountable logistical problems that forced him to conclude there would be no spring campaign against the Cheyennes and Sioux. The best he could do was reestablish the lines of communication, in hopes the expedition yet could be launched during the summer. In the interim, Connor distributed his available troops along the roads, providing a guard detachment at every stage station and sending escorts to protect the stages and supply trains.

As Moonlight was proceeding toward Fort Laramie, Connor learned of the deaths of the soldiers at La Bonte and La Parele Creeks. Incensed, he was determined to exact vengeance, campaign or not. One Indian, Big Crow, a Northern Cheyenne, happened to be a convenient target for Connor. Just before Collins left for Omaha in February, Big Crow had been camped at Deer Creek Station.[31] Coinci-

---

[29]Major General G. M. Dodge to Brevet Lieutenant Colonel Joseph McC. Bell, AAG, Department of the Missouri, July 18, 1865, *OR*, I, 60, 332; Connor also reported that "the troops at Laramie and vicinity are nearly out of ammunition." Connor to Dodge, May 1, 1865, *OR*, I, 48-2, 287.

[30]Charles Waring, "The Platte Bridge Battle," ms., typescript in vertical files, FLNHS.

[31]The man hanged at Fort Laramie should not be confused with a Southern Cheyenne by the same name. The latter was war chief of the Crooked Lance Soldier society and had led the ambush party at Julesburg during January 1865 in which Captain O'Brian and a number of soldiers were killed. George Bent, who was well acquainted with the Southern Cheyenne, clarified the distinction between the two individuals. George Bent to George E. Hyde, May 30, 1905, George Bent letters, Colorado Historical Society, Denver (hereinafter cited as Bent letters); Grinnell, *Fighting Cheyennes*, 183. Two sons of Big Crow had been induced by Catholic missionaries and former Indian Agent Twiss to attend school in the East. After their departure, Big Crow resided near the station, thus accounting for his presence there when Mrs. Morton passed through. William Garnett interview, Camp Notes, typescript 651, BYU.

dentally, a woman named Mrs. Morton, a recently released captive who had been taken on Plum Creek during the previous summer's raids, was making her way back to Fort Laramie.[32] Recognizing Big Crow as her captor, she pointed him out to the detachment commander, who seized him and sent him in manacles to Fort Laramie. On February 8, Major Mackey confined the chief in the guardhouse until Collins returned to decide his fate. But Collins no sooner returned from the field than orders arrived directing his unit to proceed to Omaha for muster out. Big Crow, therefore, remained imprisoned for three months because no one knew what to do with him. But because the Indian had already been charged with murder, kidnapping, and mistreatment of a white woman, Connor decided to make an example of him. He would demonstrate to the Indians that future violations would be dealt with equally harshly.

Connor immediately directed Colonel Baumer by telegram to "Take Big Crow to [the] place where soldier was killed yesterday, erect a high gallows, hang him in chains, and leave his body suspended." Connor obviously did not appreciate the distance to La Parele Creek until Baumer informed him of the impracticality moving Big Crow that far. At that, the general responded curtly: "Execute him where you please."[33]

"Last first day [Sunday] . . . the 'religious ceremony' of hanging an indian chief was performed at Fort Laramie," wrote Private Hervey Johnson. In reality, that "ceremony" was a ghastly lynching done on an improvised gallows of two uprights supporting a crossbeam, over which a harness chain was tossed and the end looped around Big Crow's neck.

---

[32]Bullock stated that Mrs. Morton had been extracted from the Cheyennes by local traders Jules Ecoffey and young Joe Bissonette, son of the senior Bissonnette, a Fort Laramie-area resident since the fur trade days who had served as interpreter for Colonel Stephen W. Kearny during his 1842 visit. "Joe deserves great praise for getting this woman as he risked his life in going to the village after her as several attempts were made to get her before he succeeded. She is from Iowa, about twelve miles from Nebraska City." Bullock to Ward, February 20, 1865, ibid.; Jules Ecoffey (sometimes spelled Ecoffy, Ecoffe, or corrupted into "Coffey") was a guide of French descent who had been in the Fort Laramie area for many years. By the mid-1860s, he had established a ranch and saloon five miles east of Fort Laramie on the south side of the North Platte River. In the early 1870s, Ecoffey formed a partnership with Adolph Cuny to run the Three Mile hog ranch on the Laramie north of the post. Ware, *Indian War of 1864*, 201; Vaughn, "The Fort Laramie Hog Ranches," 40.

[33]Telegram, Brigadier General Patrick E. Connor to Lieutenant Colonel William Baumer, April 22, 1865, Robert S. Ellison Papers, DPL (hereinafter cited as Ellison Papers).

The guards fired two volleys into his writhing body for good measure. The corpse was still "waving in the air" within view of the post when Sergeant Lewis Hull arrived from Fort Halleck two weeks later.[34]

Bullock knew full well that the execution of Big Crow would only exacerbate Indian hostilities. "We are going to have a warm time here this summer," the trader predicted. "All the Sioux and Cheyenne are going to war and are splitting up into small war parties and have commenced their depredations . . . a large war party has started out from the Sioux village to depredate upon the road and posts."[35] Connor had also received intelligence that the Cheyennes were then about two hundred miles north of Fort Laramie, actively coercing the so-called northern Sioux to join them.

---

[34]On April 27, in a letter home, Johnson mentioned the hanging as having occurred on April 23, 1865, but he was at Sweetwater Station at the time, so it can be assumed he received his information secondhand. Unrau, *Tending the Talking Wire*, 218, 243. The date recorded by a Seventh Iowa officer present at the execution agrees. His matter-of-fact notation of the event stated: "I helped hang an Indian Chief today ('Big Crow')." Captain John Wilcox to Mary Wilcox Stalnaker (sister), April 23, 1865, copy in vertical files, library, Fort Laramie NHS. Walter M. Camp cited a Fort Laramie "Guard Book" containing notations that Big Crow was confined on February 8 and executed on April 24. However, Camp did not provide the location of that document. The author failed to locate the Guard Book, if it still exists. Based on Camp's wide reputation as an exacting researcher, the author has no reason to question the validity of his claim to have examined it. Camp letter No. 1, Ellison Papers. Strangely enough, William Bullock made no mention of the incident in his April 30, 1865, letter to Ward. Big Crow led the ambush party to lure Captain O'Brian and his troops away from Camp Rankin in January 1865. Grinnell, *Fighting Cheyennes*, 183, 185. The scaffold stood on the plateau north of the post. Hull, "Soldiering on the High Plains," 35. An aging Sixteenth Kansas Cavalry veteran repeated a secondhand story that said the hanging was botched initially and that Big Crow slipped through the chain noose. He then climbed overhand to the cross bar of the scaffold. A large, powerfully built soldier went after him and wrestled him to the ground, where he was tied up again and hanged a second time. The story has not been verified in other sources, though the man's company did arrive at Fort Laramie within a few days of the incident. Related by R. Bayles in "Adventures in Indian Country," *National Tribune*, January 26, 1911. An ex-sergeant major of the Eleventh Ohio added that Big Crow had been confined a short time before the Collins expedition to Mud Springs returned to Fort Laramie. He stated that Major Mackey ordered the chief chained by one leg to half a wagon axle to prevent his escape. In a foul mood after being bested in the Indian fights, some of the men went to the guardhouse, forcibly removed the Indian, and attempted to lynch him. Colonel Collins intervened and had Big Crow taken back to his cell. Credence is given to this story because a number of details, including names, throughout the account are accurate. The lack of discipline among the men also agrees with Bullock's observations. J. J. Hollingsworth, "Adventures in the Indian Country," *National Tribune*, January 26, 1911; William Garnett, son of Lieutenant Richard Garnett, Sixth Infantry, who lived with his mother's people and acted as interpreter for them, witnessed the execution and saw a squad of soldiers fire twice at the body. Camp notes, typescript 652, BYU.

[35]Bullock to Ward, April 30, 1865, Ward Papers.

Colonel Moonlight arrived at the post shortly after the execution of Big Crow, relieving Baumer of command of the North Sub-district. Within days of his appearance, Moonlight assembled a force of about five hundred cavalry, supported by two hundred pack mules, at Platte Bridge for an offensive against the Cheyennes. Even with famed mountain man Jim Bridger as their guide, the expedition proved to be a cold, fruitless search. Unable to locate any signs of a village, Moonlight turned back to the North Platte and reported to Connor that there were "no Indians nearer than the Bighorn and Powder River."[36] What he failed to realize was that the Indians had been observing him all the while and they dogged his trail to renew their raiding along the road west of Fort Laramie.

During Moonlight's absence in the field, Connor made further dispositions of the available troops to protect the old Oregon-California road, although Bullock was of the opinion that the new district commander cared less about that route than he did that of the Overland Mail. "I fear Connor will prove a humbug . . . From all I can learn he will do nothing this summer except serve Ben Holladay," he informed Ward.[37] Bullock's principal concern, however, was not so much the safety of the country as it was the potential decline in business that would result if traffic were diverted from the Laramie route. Indeed, Connor had little choice. Without enough soldiers to adequately guard both routes, he properly gave priority to protecting the transcontinental mail. With the bulk of his troops distributed along that line, Connor instructed the officer at Julesburg to advise emigrants to also travel via Fort Halleck as the safer of the two avenues. Beyond posting a token force along the Oregon Route, there was little more Connor could do.

---

[36]AAG, Dist. of the Plains to Connor, May 20, 1865, Camp letter No. 1, Ellison Papers; Major General G. M. Dodge to Major General John M. Pope, June 3, 1865, OR, I, 48-2, 751. A pack train was sent to Moonlight from Fort Cottonwood. AAAG, Dist. of the Plains, April 27, 1865, OR, I, 48-2, 227.

[37]AAAG, Dist. of the Plains, April 27, 1865, OR, I, 48-2, 227; Bullock to Ward, May 8, 1865, ibid.

CHAPTER ELEVEN

"We Have Caught Mr. Two Face"

Other events unfolding at Fort Laramie during the spring and summer of 1865 would further tarnish the record of the volunteers. In early May, Oglala subchiefs Black Foot and Two Face were moving southward through the sand hills of northern Nebraska with six lodges of their people when they encountered the Corn Band (of Brulé Sioux) on the Niobrara River. The Oglalas had with them two captives, Mrs. Lucinda Eubank and her son, taken the previous August in a raid on Liberty Farm on the Little Blue River, thirty miles east of Fort Kearny.[1]

During the months of their captivity, Mrs. Eubank and her son had become separated from the other prisoners in the course of being traded from one warrior to another. Eventually, Black Foot and Two Face purchased them from the Cheyennes.[2] When word circulated

---

[1]Lucinda Eubank has been consistently misidentified as the wife of Joseph Eubank, who was actually her father-in-law. Apparently Joseph was a widower at the time of the raid. The family members killed in the attack were his sons William, Frank, James, Henry, daughter Dora, and Belle, a granddaughter whose crying attracted the Indians to the family's hiding place. A fifth son, George, was employed by a government freighter and was not present at the time of the attack. Mrs. Eubank's son William Jr., was about three months old when he was captured. William Eubank [Jr.] to W. M. Camp, June 5, 1917, letter No. 86, Ellison Papers; Minnie Hough (niece) to Camp, July 26 [1917], letter No. 87, ibid.

[2]Heap of Birds, a Cheyenne, was credited by his band for capturing Mrs. Eubank. He later gave her to his sister, then living with the Sioux, who in turn sold her to Black Foot. George Bent to Hyde, May 5, 1905, Bent letters; Bent to Camp, September 1, 1917, letter no. 89, Ellison Papers. A highly suspect version of the Lucinda Eubank story was given by O. H. P. Wiggins, who claimed to have spoken to Lucinda Eubank at Alkali Station following her release at Fort Laramie. The author recognizes that Wiggins's story contains elements of fact, but considers it largely apocryphal. Walter M. Camp Papers, Lilly Library, Indiana University (hereinafter cited as Camp Papers, Indiana University). Another even more fictionalized ac- (continued, next page)

that the whites were offering a ransom for a white woman, some Indians assumed it made no difference which one. The two Oglala sub-chiefs were among those unaware that the reward was specifically for the return of an emigrant named Mrs. Fanny Kelly, who had been captured when Miniconjous raided a train west of Horseshoe Station during July 1864. Mrs. Kelley's family members had deposited the cash equivalent of nineteen horses with the commanding officer at Fort Laramie, and publicized the "reward" through the Loafers in hope that she would be returned alive.[3]

The Brulés informed their kinsmen that Little Thunder and Spotted Tail were already camped near the agency at Fort Laramie for protection. Black Foot and Two Face, also desirous of staying out of harm's way, saw an opportunity to curry favor with the officials at Fort Laramie by surrendering Mrs. Eubank and the child. To convince the whites of their sincerity, they decided that Two Face would take the captives to the post in advance of the rest of the band. Once it was deemed safe, the others would come in. Swift Bear and his Corn Band decided they, too, would go to the agency.[4]

Early on the morning of May 15, Two Face, with Mrs. Eubank and the baby, arrived on the North Platte a few miles below the mouth of the Laramie River, opposite the camps of Spotted Tail and Little Thunder. After making his intentions known to the Brulé inhabitants, the Indians constructed a crude raft and floated it across the swollen river to transport their captives. Once on the south bank, Two Face proceeded to Bordeaux's trading post, where a woman gave Mrs. Eubank, clad only in sparse Indian garb, a dress and other items with which she could properly attire herself before going to the fort. As a

---

(*continued*) -count is in David, *Finn Burnett, Frontiersman*, 30–43; see also Root and Connelley, *The Overland Stage to California*, 353–56; Charles Gereau had clerked for the American Fur Company at least as early as 1854 at their post located five miles east of Fort Laramie on the North Platte. He may have been employed at Fort John prior to the army's purchase of the place. In any event, he had been in the Indian country for some time and was accepted among the Sioux. Frank Salaway interview, Jenson, ed., *Ricker Interviews*, 334–35 (hereinafter cited as Salaway interview).

[3]Kelly, *Narrative of My Captivity*, 22–25; McDermott, *Frontier Crossroads*, 36.

[4]Black Foot was also known as Thunder Bear, according to his son. It was not uncommon for Plains Indians to have more than one name during their lifetimes. Unclassified Envelope No. 9 (typescript 264), Camp Papers, Indiana University.

precaution, Two Face prevailed upon Big Mouth, sergeant of the agency police and head of the Laramie Sioux, to accompany them. Uncertain of the best course, Big Mouth consulted with agent Jarrot and James Beauvais, expressing his reservations about going to the fort alone. The two men agreed to accompany him and speak to Colonel Moonlight. Before the matter could be resolved, however, the over-reactive commanding officer relieved Two Face of his hostage and peremptorily confined the Indian in the guardhouse.

Mrs. Eubank, now liberated, was eager to avenge her family. She informed Colonel Moonlight that Black Foot and his band were not far from the fort, awaiting word to come in. The officers decided to send Big Mouth and an Indian police detachment to assure Black Foot that all was well, and that they would welcome him at the fort. But when the Indians reached Platte ferry on May 24, they were met by post interpreter Charles Gereau and a number of Sioux policemen and soldiers. Gereau told the Lakotas that Moonlight had deceived them as to his real intent. The soldiers, on prearranged orders, then arrested Black Foot, his son Thunder Bear, and five other men. The women and children were ordered to remain on the north side of the river, while the men and teenaged boys were escorted to the post. Once there, speaking through Gereau, Black Foot struggled to convince Colonel Moonlight of their honorable intentions regarding Mrs. Eubank. In fact, contrary to the colonel's impression, he emphasized, he and Two Face had rescued her from the hostiles and were now returning her to her own people. Moonlight ignored Black Foot's pleas and ordered the officer of the day to place the Indians in irons—except for the two youngest members, whom he released. The colonel assured them that the men would be freed in a few days. Now, though, Moonlight directed the remainder of the band should move down to Bordeaux's and camp with the Brulés.[5]

---

[5]Those individuals taken into custody at the ferry were: Black Foot (aka, Thunder Bear), his two half-brothers, Standing Cloud and Red Dog; Calico (his nephew), Long Legged Wolf (step-son), Yellow Bear, and young Thunder Bear (son). When Gereau told the colonel that the latter two were only eighteen years old, Moonlight had them weighed on a platform scale, and was convinced of their youth. He provided them some rations and sent them back to the band. This account combines later statements by Black Foot's son, who was present at the time, and Frank Salaway, the man of French-Sioux ancestry, noted in an earlier chapter, (continued, next page)

In a letter, sutler Bullock described the arrest of the Indians: "We have caught Mr. 'Two Face' and his five lodges who run off our cattle and killed 7 head, and shot 20 more full of arrows," he wrote, in reference to their attack on his train the previous April. "He and his warriors are now sweeping the parade ground with a Ball & Chain to their heels. And I think ere long will be dancing between heaven and earth."[6]

Indeed, despite having promised their freedom, Moonlight staged an informal trial to legitimize his decision to execute the men. He had decided that their deaths would stand "as an example to all Indians of like character and in retaliation for the many wrongs and outrages they have committed on the white race."[7] Lucinda Eubank, the only witness for the prosecution, provided grim details of her captivity. Some of her statements no doubt reflected her treatment at the hands of the Cheyennes, with whom she had been for eight months, yet it was ruled most of the offenses against her were the actions of the Sioux men Two Face and Black Foot.

Mrs. Eubank recounted that the Cheyennes had taken her to the Arkansas River, where "the whole village ravished her," and treated her in a "beastly manner." The following spring, when Black Foot's band of Oglalas crossed trails with the Cheyennes, Two Face offered them three horses for her, expressing his desire to keep her "for sensual use." By that time, however, she was pregnant "by the Cheyenne [Big Crow] who had slept with her," according to Woman's Hair, a

---

(*continued*) who witnessed the Grattan fight in 1854. Salaway obtained his information directly from Big Mouth, his brother-in-law and chief of the Indian police at the Upper Platte Agency in 1865; Thunder Bear interview, MSS 57, box 2, Camp Collection, BYU (hereinafter cited as Thunder Bear interview); Salaway interview, 338–39. The Indian testimony differs on several key points from Moonlight's official reports. Significantly, Moonlight stated that Indian police were sent to the village, where they discovered Mrs. Eubank and her son, and that they subsequently arrested Two Face. Upon learning the whereabouts of Black Foot and the rest of the band, Moonlight claimed that he ordered Indian soldiers "to bring them in dead or alive." The commander gave no hint that in fact the Indians had presented themselves at the fort with professions of friendship. Telegram, Moonlight to Captain George F. Price, AAAG, District of the Plains, May 26, 1865, LR, v. 93, Records of the Department of the Platte, RG 393, NA.

[6]Bullock to Ward, May 22, 1865, Ward Papers. Moonlight also claimed that Blackfoot's band had in their possession "a number of Government mules and horses, also some private mules stolen last winter," implicating their involvement in the raids along the Platte road some months earlier. Telegram, Moonlight to Price, May 26, 1865, Dept. of the Platte Records.

[7]Special Orders No. 11, North Sub-district of the Plains, May 25, 1865, transcribed in Camp letter no. 1, Ellison Papers.

Sioux woman.[8] While Mrs. Eubank did not say that Two Face had been particularly cruel to her, the officers at Fort Laramie concluded from her statements that she had been forced to perform hard labor (which, it should be pointed out, was normal for all women in Indian society), was at one time dragged across the Platte River at the end of a rope, and was kept nearly naked for the entire time she was in Indian hands. A Sioux man later admitted that "When they [Black Foot and Two Face] got ready to bring her back they all went into the river with her swimming, and all ravished her." If the accused were permitted to speak in self-defense, the testimony was not recorded.[9]

The evidence, such as it was, was compelling enough for Colonel Moonlight to pronounce sentence on Two Face and Black Foot, while the other four prisoners remained in confinement. Moonlight specified that the two leaders were to "be hung tomorrow at 2 PM. . . . The execution will be conducted in a sober, soldierly manner and the bodies will be left hanging as a warning to others. No citizen or soldiers

---

[8]John Farnham reportedly came to Fort Laramie in July 1867 as a soldier in Company E, Fourth U. S. Infantry. He later married an Oglala Sioux woman, Win Pelim ("Woman's Hair"), and lived on the northern Plains for the remainder of his life. In 1874, he was employed at the Red Cloud Agency near Camp Robinson, and during the Sioux War he served as post guide and interpreter at Fort Laramie. Walter Camp determined that Farnham was present at the Reynolds Fight on the Powder River in March 1876, and was a member of General Crook's Big Horn Expedition later that spring. The Farnhams resided on the Pine Ridge Reservation when Camp interviewed them in 1917. Farnham interviews, unclassified envelope No. 10 (typescript p. 270), Camp Papers, Indiana University; Paul, *Nebraska Indian Wars Reader*, 117.

[9]This description of Lucinda Eubank's treatment is based on and quoted from Thunder Bear interview; Salaway interview; Mrs. John Farnham interview, (1917), unclassified envelope No. 10 (typescript p. 269), Camp Papers, Indiana University; and Moonlight to Price, May 27, 1865, *OR*, I, 48-1, 276–77; A month after the execution, a story was circulating among the soldiers at Fort Laramie that Mrs. Eubank had submitted to having sexual relations with Two Face after another captive woman had refused. That woman allegedly was tied between two horses and dismembered. The tale may have been factual, as the trial proceedings were public knowledge at the post. However, it must also be considered that Mrs. Eubank's virtue as a white woman had to be defended, in the mid-nineteenth century, with an explanation for her presumably unwilling conduct and resulting pregnancy. Cyrus C. Schofield, Sixteenth Kansas Cavalry, to Mary E. Schofield, June 25, 1865, vertical file, FLNHS (hereinafter cited as Cyrus C. Schofield letter). I have been unable to determine whether the half-Indian baby survived. Mrs. Eubank's niece, who certainly should have known its fate, made no mention of the child, though she stated that her aunt had returned to her native Illinois and resided there for about five years after her release. Mrs. Eubank was subsequently married twice more in later years. She eventually moved to Vernon County, Missouri, where she died in 1911. Hough to Camp, July 26 [1917], no. 87, Ellison Papers.

nor Indians will be permitted to visit or touch the dead bodies without permission from these headquarters or that of the post."[10]

On May 26, at the appointed hour, guards removed Two Face and
Black Foot, still manacled with ball-and-chain, from the guardhouse
and placed them in a wagon to take them up to the gallows. Moonlight had intentionally ordered a second gallows erected on the natural terrace three-fourths of a mile northwest of the post, to the right
of the road, beside the one from which still hung the bullet-riddled
decomposing remains of Big Crow.[11]

Earlier that day, an Oglala rode out from the post to alert the villagers at Bordeaux's that the soldiers were going to execute Black Foot
and Two Face. Black Foot's son, Thunder Bear—one of the boys
Colonel Moonlight had released—with a revolver concealed beneath
his shirt, started toward the fort to try to gain his father's release.
Along the way Spotted Tail joined him and accompanied him to the
fort. On the bluffs overlooking the Laramie, the two observed a crowd
gathered on the highlands beyond. They were too late: the execution
was underway. Thunder Bear was determined to ride to his father's
rescue, but the older and wiser chief advised him not to go any further.
"These people [whites] must pay for this. Go back. You cannot do

---

[10]*SO No. 11*, Ellison Papers.

[11]Most eyewitness accounts place the execution site three-fourths to one mile west-northwest of
the fort. Thunder Bear remembered it as "a high hill about a mile N.W. of the fort." Camp
notes, MSS 57, box 2, BYU. An officer passing through Fort Laramie fifteen years later described
the remnants of the gallows: "After a walk of three-quarters of a mile west of the post, and a little to the right of the old Fort Fetterman road, we reached the gentle eminence on which the
gallows stood in plain view of the post. We could see from the rotten debris that the scaffold
consisted of two ordinary uprights about ten feet apart, connected with the usual cross-piece on
the top. On this gallows three Indians were hung at the same time, and, it would seem, in a
most barbarous manner—by means of coarse chains around their necks, and heavy chains and
iron balls attached to the lower part of the naked limbs to keep them down. There was no drop.
They were allowed to writhe and strangle to death . . . We could see their bones protruding from
the common grave under the gallows. We were glad to leave this gloomy spot and wind our way,
by clamoring steep bluffs, to the highest point overlooking the Platte and the beautiful valley of
the Laramie." First Lieutenant James Regan, "Military Landmarks," *The United Service* 2
(August 1880): 159–61; "I remember seeing the cruel savages hanging by the neck on one of the
hills north of the fort," Fairfield, "Eleventh Kansas," *Transactions*, 354. Additional references to
the site were provided by Captain B. F. Rockafellow, Sixth Michigan Cavalry, who saw it on
June 25, 1865, and R. Bayles, a member of Company D, Sixteenth Kansas. See Hafen and Hafen,
Powder River Campaigns, 167; *National Tribune*, January 26, 1911. See also John Davidson interview, Camp notes, envelope no. 10 (typescript 278–79), Indiana University.

anything to prevent it. It is a great wrong to us and we will some time go to war and avenge it."[12]

Colonel Moonlight had hoped to curry General Connor's favor by setting another harsh example of punitive treatment of the Sioux. In his haste, he had committed a grievous error that did nothing to deter the hostiles on Powder River. In truth, the hanging also turned formerly peaceable Indians against the army.

William Bullock, more keenly attuned to Sioux reaction than were the inexperienced officers at the post, lamented two days after the event that "we have now the Indians hanging in sight of the post. This barbarity is only calculated to make them more vicious and determined, and no stock is safe in the country. As soon as Conner arrives I presume their will be another hanging as they have four more Indians in the Guardhouse."[13] In accordance with Moonlight's order, the corpses remained suspended from the gallows for weeks after the execution. A Sixteenth Kansas Cavalryman remembered seeing "two scaffolds with two bodies hanging on one—Two Face and another Indian—while the other had but one, all hung with chains. We understood the hanging took place at two separate times."[14]

The hanging of the two chiefs at Fort Laramie deepened the stain that the Sand Creek Massacre had already placed on the army's reputation. Although both acts were committed by members of the volunteer army, the Indians made no distinction between state troops and the regulars. Blue coats were blue coats. Accordingly, the army's credibility with plains Indians, particularly the Cheyennes, suffered for years to come.

---

[12]Thunder Bear interview, typescript 650, BYU.

[13]Bullock to Ward, May 28, 1865, Ward Papers.

[14]*National Tribune*, January 26, 1911. Another soldier observed the corpses still hanging from the gallows a month after the execution. Cyrus C. Schofield letter.

In the earliest known photograph of Fort Laramie, taken in 1858, the remains of old Fort John can be seen in the left middle ground. Braces prop up the crumbling adobe walls. Directly behind it are three officers' quarters constructed in 1850. Bedlam, the legendary two-story officers' quarters, dominates the center of the view, and immediately to the right is the Sutler's Store. The enlisted men's barracks, a two-story frame structure used from 1850 to 1866, stands in the right middle ground. Barely visible in the right foreground is the Ward & Guerrier trading post, along with a few Indian tepees. *Library of Congress, Prints and Photographs Division, lc-usz62-100354.*

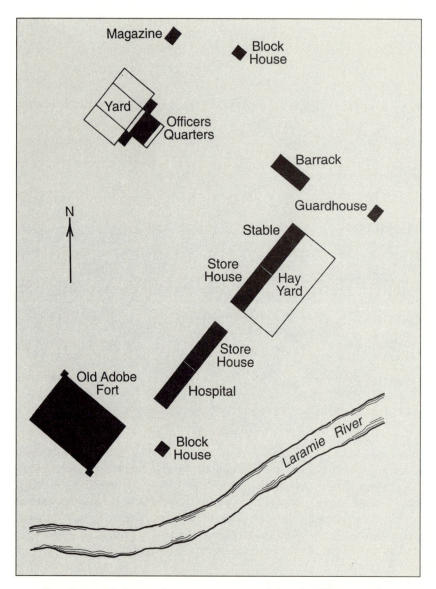

Fort Laramie's layout, late summer, 1854. After the Grattan fight, Fort Laramie's remnant garrison retreated behind the walls of the old adobe post. *Drawing by Dell Darling after Oscar Winship's 1854 sketch. Courtesy R. Eli Paul.*

Partners Seth Ward and Henry Mayer constructed this wagon bridge over the Laramie River about a mile below the post in 1853. By agreement with the government, the owners charged a toll of twenty-five cents for each horse and rider and two dollars for each vehicle with its team. Fees were waived for official military traffic. *Courtesy the Edward E. Ayer Collection, The Newberry Library, Chicago.*

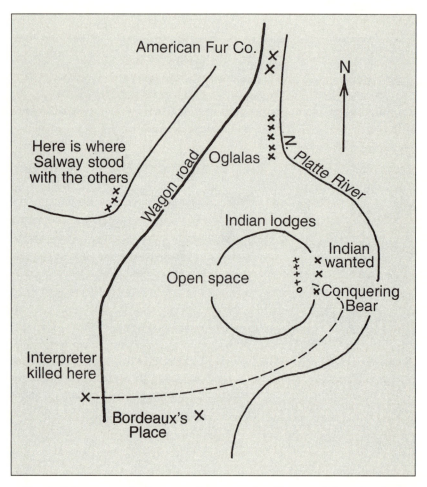

Frank Salaway, an Indian eyewitness to the Grattan fight, sketched important details as he remembered them several decades after the event. *Drawing by Dell Darling after Salaway's 1906 sketch. Courtesy R. Eli Paul.*

Brigadier General William S. Harney had already served thirty-seven years in the army, including the Seminole and Mexican Wars, when he swore vengeance on the Sioux for the killing of Lieutenant John L. Grattan and his men near Fort Laramie. Harney led a decisive punitive expedition against the Sioux during the summer of 1855 that culminated in the Battle of Blue Water Creek. After his retirement, Harney served with the peace commission that concluded the landmark Fort Laramie Treaty in 1868. *U.S. Army Military History Institute.*

Charles F. Moellman, Eleventh Ohio Cavalry, occupied some of his spare time by producing this sketch of Fort Laramie, ca. 1864. *Fort Laramie NHS.*

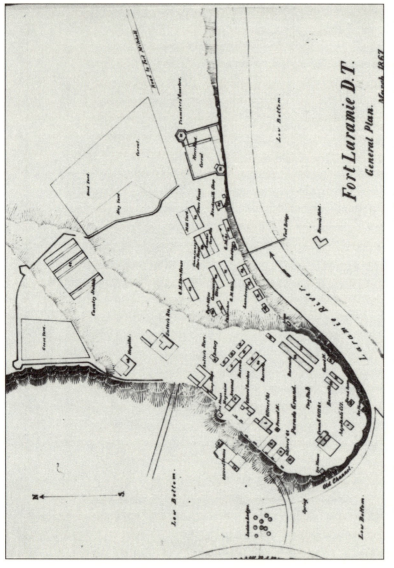

Immediately after the Civil War, the army added many new buildings to Fort Laramie. The corral at the far right was built in 1865 during the peak Indian threat. Designed as a defensive fortification, it incorporated thick adobe walls and two hexagonal blockhouses on opposing corners that actually housed civilian teamsters. *Fort Laramie NHS.*

214

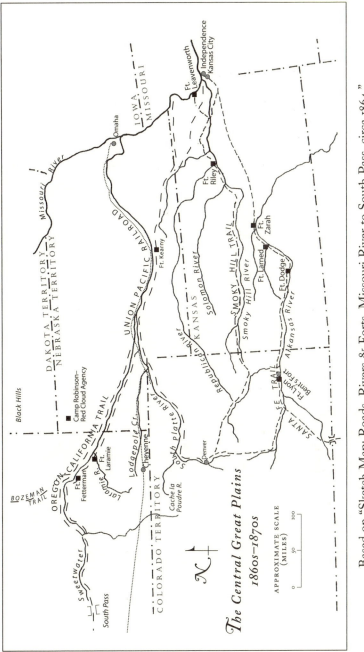

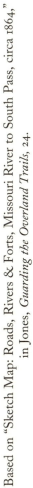

Based on "Sketch Map: Roads, Rivers & Forts, Missouri River to South Pass, circa 1864," in Jones, *Guarding the Overland Trails*, 24.

215

Patrick Edward Connor, an Irishman by birth, began his U.S. Army career as a volunteer officer during the Mexican War and in 1861 was appointed colonel of the Third California Infantry. As commander of the District of the Plains, Connor launched his Powder River Expedition from Fort Laramie in 1865. *Massachusetts Commandery, Military Order of the Loyal Legion, U.S. Army Military History Institute.*

Two men pose beneath an Indian burial scaffold north of the post, ca. 1882. The scaffold is presumed to be the one erected for Miniaku, the daughter of Brulé Sioux chief Spotted Tail, after her death in 1866. If so, the coffin was empty because her father had transferred the remains to the Brulé agency five years earlier. *Fort Laramie NHS, Ivins Collection.*

69. FORT LARAMIE.

Recognizing that Fort Laramie had attained major importance by the end of the Civil War, the army expanded and improved its facilities. This 1870 view shows numerous new buildings erected during the previous four years. Note in the right half of the photograph the many warehouses and offices, along with stables and corrals, needed to support a base for military operations and a distribution point for Indian annuities. *USGS Jackson, W. H. #269.*

217

Spotted Tail, headman among the Brulé Sioux, fought the whites during the 1850s, but adopted a more conciliatory attitude during the following decade. Emerging as a leading peace chief, Spotted Tail grew more confident in the government; he decided to bury his daughter at Fort Laramie in 1866. *Nebraska State Historical Society.*

Oglala Sioux chief Red Cloud was the only Indian leader to deal the U.S. Army a strategic defeat during the plains wars. His steadfast refusal to sign the 1868 treaty until the army withdrew from the Bozeman Trail added to his already great stature among both the Sioux and government officials. *Smithsonian Institution.*

Sioux leaders gather with civilians during the Peace Commission at Fort Laramie in 1868. Included in the group are Post Sutler William G. Bullock (center, gray-bearded) and local Indian trader James Bordeaux (standing, far right). Bordeaux witnessed the 1854 Grattan affair, which occurred near his store on the North Platte River below Fort Laramie. *Courtesy the Edward E. Ayer Collection, The Newberry Library, Chicago.*

Peace commissioners sit in council with the Sioux at Fort Laramie in 1868. *Courtesy the Edward E. Ayer Collection, The Newberry Library, Chicago.*

Photographer Alexander Gardner captured the entire Fort Laramie garrison assembled for dress parade in 1868. The Fourth Infantry, including the band (*far left*) occupies most of the view, while a battalion of the Second Cavalry is visible at the far right. Buildings in the background include (*left to right*) company officer's quarters, post commander's quarters, the three 1850 adobe quarters, and Bedlam, partially visible at the extreme right. *Courtesy the Edward E. Ayer Collection, The Newberry Library, Chicago.*

Fort Laramie was in its prime as a major military installation when German-born artist Anton Schonborn executed this watercolor in 1870. *U.S. Army Signal Corps No. 83150.*

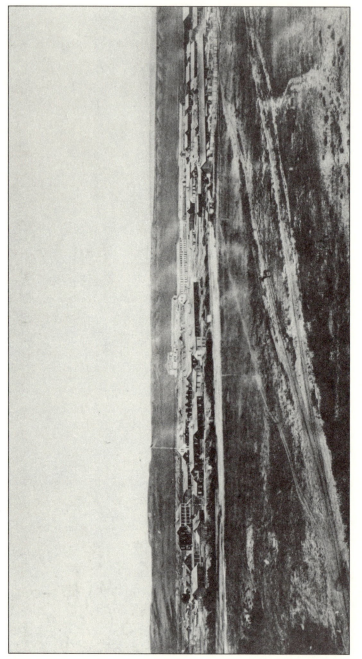

Fort Laramie had grown to a sizeable village by the time this image was taken during the Great Sioux War of 1876. The two-story 1872 hospital overlooks the post, and to the right is the new cavalry barracks, still lacking its porch. Like most of its contemporaries, Fort Laramie had no surrounding stockade, because of its size and because Plains Indians posed little threat to such installations. *U.S. Army Signal Corps No. 100,866.*

This prefabricated iron bridge, constructed over the North Platte River in 1876, was a vital link on the Cheyenne–Black Hills Road. It provided an all-season crossing of the wide, treacherous stream for stagecoaches, miners, and troops passing through Fort Laramie. Pictured here ca. 1900, the bridge remained in use for automobiles until the 1960s and stands today as an American architectural landmark. *Fort Laramie NHS.*

Post trader John S. Collins built the Rustic Hotel at Fort Laramie in 1876 to serve travelers on the Cheyenne–Black Hills Road. Living up to its name, the hotel nevertheless offered lodging, meals, and corrals for horses. *Fort Laramie NHS, Ivins Collection.*

This 1877 image of the Sutler's (or Post Trader's) Store reflects its popularity as a social and recreational center for soldiers and civilians. During the 1850s and 1860s the Sioux frequented the store to exchange buffalo robes for tobacco and manufactured goods. *Fort Laramie NHS, Bolin Collection.*

Soldiers of the Seventh Infantry are formed for guard-mounting on a pleasant winter morning ca. 1883. Beyond them are three recently completed officers' quarters with mansard roofs. *Wyoming Division of Cultural Resources.*

A bird's-eye view depicts Fort Laramie at the zenith of its development in 1888. In contrast to the fort's declining strategic importance, the army continued to erect new buildings, including three two-story officers' quarters (1881), a second commissary storehouse (1883), staff noncommissioned officers' quarters (1884), a second bakery (1885), and a post headquarters and playhouse (1885). *National Park Service.*

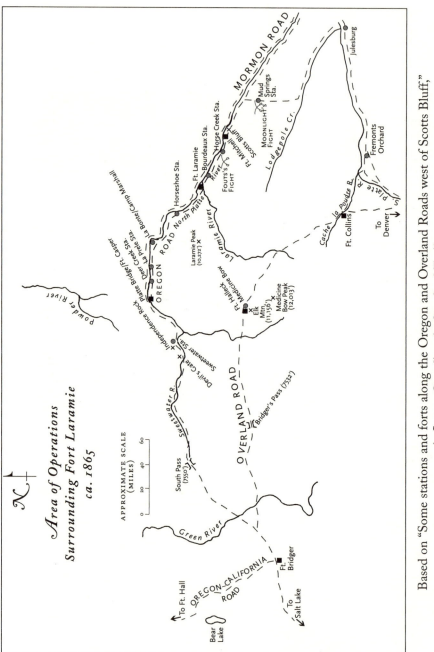

Based on "Some stations and forts along the Oregon and Overland Roads west of Scotts Bluff," in Jones, *Guarding the Overland Trails*, 25.

This view of Officers Row on the west side of the parade ground shows some of the comparatively luxurious quarters added during the 1870s and 1880s, with venerable "Old Bedlam" still occupying a place of honor. *Fort Laramie NHS, Bliton Collection.*

When a photographer captured this image of Bedlam in 1889, just a year before the post was abandoned, the addition of trees, picket fences, vines, and sidewalks gave it a stately air unknown in earlier times. During its forty years, the old structure witnessed the full panorama of Fort Laramie's military occupation, from raucous days as a bachelor officer's quarters, to service as post headquarters and Indian council site, and as home for countless army families. *Fort Laramie NHS, Brininstool Collection.*

John Hunton, pictured here with his wife in 1919, became the living link with Fort Laramie's glory days. First arriving at the post in 1867, he spent his first winter rooming with legendary mountain man Jim Bridger. Hunton served as the last post trader from 1888 until the army left two years later. He continued to reside at the fort until 1920. *Wyoming Division of Cultural Resources.*

By 1932, when this view was taken, the last of Fort Laramie's buildings evidenced their age and long neglect. The effort to preserve the old post was in a race against time and the elements. *National Park Service.*

CHAPTER TWELVE

"We Settle the Indian Troubles This Season"

The warring Indian factions, meanwhile, had not been idle. The northern Sioux bands joined the Cheyennes in a retaliatory rampage on the central portion of the emigrant trail, extending from Fort Kearny to South Pass. On May 20 a force of two hundred warriors descended on the telegraph station at Deer Creek. The Kansas veterans stationed there put up a determined resistance that cost the raiders seven warriors' lives and left one of their men wounded, though they managed to drive off most of the military's stock. The soldiers lost one man.

Lieutenant Colonel Preston B. Plumb gave chase with thirty troopers, but was forced to abandon the pursuit when his command was unable to ford the river. Demonstrating their contempt for the soldiers, another of the united tribes' party stole several mules within eight miles of Fort Laramie. A detachment of forty cavalrymen took up their trail and recaptured the animals. But then, a few days later, Indians interrupted communications by tearing down sixteen miles of telegraph line between Horseshoe Station and La Bonte Creek, and next a war party attacked and burned St. Mary's Station. Indian marauders also stampeded a herd at Sweetwater Crossing on May 26, though they were prevented from getting away with the animals when troopers of the Eleventh Ohio opened brisk fire on them with their Spencers. That same day, warriors boldly attacked a government supply train, escorted by an entire company of soldiers, nine miles below Platte Bridge.[1]

---

[1]Bullock to Ward, May 22 and May 28, 1865, Ward Papers; Price to Connor, May 22, 1865, *OR*, I, 48-2, 554; Connor to Dodge, May 29, 1865, ibid., 670; Price to Connor, June *(continued, next page)*

General Connor had ample reason to renew his requests for additional troops to guard the transcontinental routes, and he would simultaneously launch an expedition into the heartland of the Sioux and Northern Cheyennes, hoping to engage and overpower them. Even Major General John Pope at Division of the Missouri Headquarters in St. Louis was convinced that Connor had to move against the hostiles as soon as possible. He promised to commit all the troops necessary for such an operation, but insisted that the strike must be done before August, lest the column be caught in the field at the onset of winter.

Moonlight, meanwhile, distributed the Eleventh Kansas in battalions at critical points between Fort Laramie and Platte Bridge. But the lack of sacked corn at Fort Laramie, along with a critical shortage of natural hay for the horses, threatened the removal of all cavalry from the road. William Bullock lamented, "Their is no forage here a tall. Not fifty bushels [of] corn and not men enough at the Post to guard a train, and the Indians thick around here, with a determination to take all the stock in the country and they will certainly succeed."[2] Connor nevertheless requested four additional regiments of cavalry and two of infantry to reinforce his district. He also requisitioned hundreds of extra horses and tons of supplies, including grain, to sustain a lengthy campaign against the warring tribesmen.

Connor also emphasized that the cavalry had to leave Fort Leavenworth immediately if the expedition were to take the field before that unit's enlistments expired. Scouring his district for still more troops, Connor also summoned two companies of the Second California Volunteer Cavalry from Fort Bridger. He informed Dodge that he would move his district headquarters to Fort Laramie by about June 10 so that he could personally oversee final preparations for the expedition. Bullock, however, still resented the volunteers and their incompetence in battling the Indians. He admittedly looked forward to the day when they would be withdrawn "and we will once again be blessed with Regular Soldiers."[3]

(continued) 5, 1865, ibid., 718; Lieutenant Colonel P. B. Plumb to Lieutenant I. L. Taber, June 1, 1865, ibid., 724; Unrau, *Tending the Talking Wire*, 249–51.

[2]Bullock to Ward, May 28, 1865, Ward Papers.

[3]Connor to Dodge, June 6, 1865, *or* I, 48-2, 777; Connor to Major J. W. Barnes, AAG, Dept. of the Missouri, May 28, 1865, ibid., 646; Orton, *Records of California Men*, 171; Bullock to Ward, May 22, 1865, Ward Papers.

Bullock's lack of faith in the men was not unwarranted. Connor ordered Colonel Moonlight to conduct the friendly Brulés of Spotted Tail and Little Thunder's Brulé tribesmen, along with Black Foot's Oglalas and the Sioux residing near the fort, all now virtual prisoners of war in the wake of the sub-chiefs' execution, to Fort Kearny to prevent them from joining the hostiles. At the same time, the Sioux already on the warpath would be deprived of supplies and a possible sanctuary provided by their more peacefully inclined relatives at the agency. Selected for the escort was a reinforced company of the Seventh Iowa Cavalry, 139 men total, under the command of Captain William D. Fouts, a veteran of the Mud Springs fight.

The Sioux, particularly those who considered Fort Laramie to be their home, were reluctant to leave. Fort Kearny lay squarely in the territory controlled by their mortal enemies, the Pawnees. Nevertheless, the Indian leaders realized it would be folly to resist in such close proximity to Fort Laramie.

The cavalcade that set forth down the North Platte on June 11 was a memorable sight. The cavalry headed the column, followed by the wagons and a contrasting mixture of some two thousand traditional free-roaming Sioux, the long-dependent fort families, and the attendant menagerie of ponies, dogs, and travois loaded down with all the impedimenta of an Indian village. The company of Indian police led by Elston and Sergeant Big Mouth were charged with maintaining order during the journey. Also in the throng were James Bordeaux, his family, and several wagonloads of trade goods from his store. Bordeaux appreciated that with the exodus of the Indians, he had little choice but to accompany his clientele. Nor was Bordeaux the only white man leaving the confluence area. James Beauvais, as well, abandoned his ranch at the old American Fur Company post, more recently the headquarters for the Upper Platte Agency. He loaded everything he owned in twenty-one ox-drawn freight wagons and drove another fifty head of loose cattle.

Bringing up the rear, under guard, were the four Oglala prisoners, each still bound in chains and weighted down with an iron ball. The magnitude of the exodus is reflected in Bullock's observation that, "All the people of the country have left except [Joseph] Bissonette & Jules [Ecoffey] and they speak of leaving in a few days. . . . We now have no Indians at the fort."[4] Indeed, for the first time in more than thirty years, there were no Sioux villages near Fort Laramie, and in the void an uneasy stillness descended over the valley.

Captain Fouts allowed easy marches down the North Platte for the first two days, to establish order among the assemblage and allow everyone to become accustomed to the routine. When Sioux boys did the natural thing of racing their ponies along the column, Fouts ordered them to stop, threatening to tie any offender to a wagon wheel and lash him with a whip. But while Fouts's attention was focused on discipline, several Indian headmen quietly formulated a plan of escape.

The third day's journey brought the assemblage to Horse Creek, familiar site of the 1851 treaty council, forty miles downstream from Fort Laramie. There they stopped for the night. While the soldiers, including the rear guard with the prisoners in tow, crossed to the far side of the creek before going into camp, the Indians remained stopped on the west side. The leaders secretly directed some of the younger warriors to slip away and locate a crossing above the mouth of the tributary by which the women and children could ford the Platte.

Fouts intended to increase the pace the next day, hoping to make the twenty-eight miles to Scott's Bluff by nightfall. Accordingly, he had reveille sounded at three o'clock on the morning of the fourteenth, with the march to commence at five. Fouts instructed Captain John Wilcox, in charge of the advance guard, to proceed ahead two miles, where he would pause and await the caravan to close up behind him. Discipline notwithstanding, however, in thinking through his march Fouts had inadvertently committed several grievous mistakes at the start. Not only were the warriors permitted to keep their arms and horses on the march, but he allowed the Indians to camp away from the whites, on the opposite side of Horse Creek, thus placing an obstacle between themselves and the troops. He also voiced no objection when the guards allowed the prisoners to ride horseback, rather than compelling them to ride in the wagons. From a self-protection perspective, even more difficult to understand was Fouts's decision not to issue carbine ammunition to the men of his company in the cer-

---

[4]Bullock to Ward, June 12, 1865, Ward Papers.

tainty they would not need it. Wilcox, more cautious, had made sure his mixed detachment of A and B Company men had sufficient ammunition when they left Fort Laramie.

The caravan seemed to be moving smoothly, until Fouts looked back to see the Indian tepees still standing beyond the creek. As the wagons continued down the road toward Scott's Bluff, the captain rode back to hurry the Indians along. Just as he crossed the stream and entered the camp, waiting warriors fired two shots, knocking the dead captain from his saddle. That, in turn, was the signal for the three mounted prisoners with the advance guard to make their escape. The fourth man, who had become lame and was riding in a wagon carrying tentage and equipment for the guard detail, had to be left behind.[5] A messenger quickly returned to Wilcox, informing him that Fouts had been killed and that now the Indian factions were fighting among themselves.[6] The captain ordered his drivers to corral the wagons, with the teams turned to the inside, and the men to prepare a defense. At the same time, he dispatched a rider on a fleet horse to Camp Mitchell, eighteen miles away.

As the men of the rear guard caught up, Wilcox inquired why Lieutenant Haywood and his men had not made a stand where they were. It was only then, and to his great consternation, that Wilcox learned they had no ammunition. He quickly directed them to draw a supply from the wagons, then divided the command into two platoons, one to form a skirmish line outside the perimeter of the wagon corral. He also directed Lieutenants James G. Smith and Jeremiah H. Triggs to

---

[5]The fourth prisoner was reportedly killed by the soldiers during the fight. Antoine Bordeaux interview, envelope no. 72 (typescript 442), Camp notes, Lilly Library. Wilcox may have had this in mind when he later wrote that some of his men "acted badly" during the fight. Captain John Wilcox to AAG, District of the Plains, June 21, 1865, OR, I, 48-1, 324–26.

[6]There was no unanimity among the Sioux for this breakout. During the march down the Platte, the leaders met secretly at night to debate what to do. Apparently, Elston and a few dozen other white men in the camp warned the Indians not to resist the troops. When they did, some of the peace chiefs were killed by their own people for trying to quell the outbreak. Wilcox recorded that his messenger informed him that the Indians were fighting among themselves. Connor also stated that they killed four of their own chiefs "who refused to join them." And, yet another contemporary account reported that Little Thunder himself had been killed in the fray. Wilcox report, 1255; Telegram, Connor to Dodge, June 15, 1865, OR, I, 48-2, 895; Cyrus C. Schofield, Sixteenth Kansas Cavalry, to Mary E. Schofield, June 25, 1865, vertical files, FLNHS (hereinafter cited as Schofield letter); Hyde, Red Cloud's Folk, 120.

have some of the men dig a protective trench just outside the corral. Wilcox and Haywood, meantime, would lead the other seventy men, mounted, back to the Indian camp. There they found Fouts's naked and mutilated body lying on the site of the now deserted village.[7]

When the soldiers found them, the Indians were approximately four miles downriver, swimming the Platte. Mounted warriors riding back and forth on the plain, between the troops and the river, were winding their ponies in anticipation of combat. Assuming that some of the Indians might still be friendly, Captain Wilcox advanced his command to within about six hundred yards of them, and sent Elston forward to communicate with them in hopes of inducing some to return. Suddenly the warriors charged, opening fire on the troops at about three hundred yards. The troops responded with a volley that broke their advance.

Meanwhile, however, other tribesmen were moving around the flanks of the soldiers in an attempt to envelop the command. Still more Indians poured down "like an avalanche" from the hills rising to the left of their position. Wilcox estimated that he was now confronting at least five hundred warriors. Heavily outnumbered and vulnerable on the open prairie, Wilcox mounted his men and turned to retire to the protection of the wagon corral. At that, the soldiers were compelled to fight a rear guard action for the entire distance, while skirmishing with Indians on their flanks and to the front as well. Only when the troopers got within range of the other platoon did the Indians break off the engagement. By that time some of Wilcox's men had already expended all their ammunition.

Wilcox assumed the Sioux would attack his defenses, yet they remained at a safe distance from the wagons. He therefore mounted fifty men on the best horses and again advanced, hoping to detain the Indians long enough to allow his reinforcements to arrive. The cavalry, with the Sioux falling back ahead of them, advanced about three miles down the creek. But when large numbers of warriors appeared on the hills to the west, with still more gathering in around his front and rear, Wilcox concluded that the Indians hoped to lure his little force into a trap. He again retired to await reinforcements from Camp Mitchell.

---

[7]An Indian witness credited Charging Shield and Foam with killing Fouts. Thunder Bear interview.

Captain Jacob Shuman and a detachment of the Eleventh Ohio arrived at the wagon corral at about nine o'clock that morning. Determined to prevent the Sioux from escaping, Wilcox mounted every available man and again advanced toward the Platte. By the time he reached the river, however, the Indian noncombatants had already forded and disappeared over the benchlands on the north side. A rear guard of warriors stood atop the hills, taunting the soldiers to follow, but Wilcox was wise enough not to take the bait. The most he could do at that point was destroy the lodges and other camp equipage they had left behind. Wilcox estimated that his men had killed between twenty and thirty warriors. Besides Fouts, the Seventh Iowa had three troopers killed and four others wounded. The enlisted men were buried on the field, but Fouts's body was taken to Camp Mitchell for interment.[8]

Wilcox's plea for assistance spurred Colonel Moonlight to action. Hastily forming a punitive expedition composed of 234 cavalrymen from the Kansas, Ohio, and California regiments, Moonlight set off down the north side of the Platte on the fifteenth of June in an attempt to intercept the fleeing Indians. Before departing, he telegraphed Wilcox at Camp Mitchell requesting him to cross the river and follow the trail north, in hopes the two forces working in concert could bring the Sioux to bay. However, high water and quicksand cost Wilcox two horses drowned, and very nearly claimed Captain Shuman's life, causing him to abandon any further attempts to form a junction with the Fort Laramie column.

In his enthusiasm to catch up with the Indians, Moonlight pushed his malnourished mounts too hard. By the time he discovered the Indian trail leading from the valley, many of his men were straggling behind. He was unaware that Sioux scouts were constantly observing his movements, waiting for an opportunity to strike. Their chance came on June 17 as the cavalry halted for a mid-morning breakfast on Dead Man's Creek, about 120 miles northeast of Fort Laramie.

---

[8]This account of the clash at Horse Creek draws from the Wilcox report and the Salaway interview. Connor reported that five of the Indians who escaped from Fouts later turned themselves in at Fort Laramie and were incarcerated in the guardhouse. Their fate is not known. Connor to Dodge, *OR*, I, 48-2, 1086.

The colonel carelessly allowed his men to unsaddle their horses and turn them loose to graze. Warriors suddenly swooped down from the adjacent hills and made off with seventy-four prime mounts, all belonging to the newly arrived California companies. With most of his command suddenly afoot, the thoroughly chagrined colonel was compelled to burn the useless horse equipment and hike back to Fort Laramie. News of the blunder was the final straw for General Connor. "Colonel Moonlight has been unfortunate in his dealings with Indians," Connor informed the department commander. "I have relieved him, and will further investigate his conduct."[9]

Despite the mid-June strikes on the Indians and vice versa, preparations for Connor's long-anticipated Powder River offensive began to take shape in June. Government trains and some commercial freight wagons were finally reaching Fort Laramie to begin amassing the stockpile of weapons and other supplies necessary to support the operation. In late May, General Dodge had moved his own headquarters to Fort Leavenworth to be in a more advantageous position to see that both troops and supplies were expedited from that point. "We settle the Indian troubles this season," Dodge emphasized to Connor. "They should be made to feel the full power of the Government and severely punished for past acts."[10]

Guided by Major General Pope's overall strategy, plans were laid to penetrate the Indian stronghold at the headwaters of Powder and Tongue Rivers using four columns converging from the east, southeast, and south. Brigadier General Alfred Sully would strike west from Fort Rice, on the Upper Missouri toward the mouth of Powder River, but that plan was foiled when Santee Sioux made a surprise raid into Minnesota. Army Headquarters in Washington was furious that field commanders there had become so complacent that Indians could

[9]Colonel Thomas Moonlight to Price, AAAG, Dist. of the Plains, June 21, 1865, *OR*, I, 48-1, 325–28; Envelope no. 8 (typescript 261), Camp notes, Lilly Library; Envelope no. 10 (typescript 271), Camp notes, ibid.; Salaway interview; Walker, "The Eleventh Kansas Cavalry," 334; S. H. Fairfield, "The Eleventh Kansas Regiment at Platte Bridge," 355; Nadeau, *Fort Laramie and the Sioux*, 185–86; Connor to Dodge, June 20, 1865, *OR*, I, 48-2, 950; Connor to Dodge, June 19, 1865, *OR*, I, 48-2, 938. In a subsequent telegram, Connor acknowledged that Moonlight's "administration here was a series of blunders." Connor to Dodge, July 6, 1865, ibid., 1059; Dodge to AAG, Military Division of the Missouri, July 18, 1865, *OR*, I, 48-1, 332.

[10]Dodge to Connor, June 10, 1865, *OR*, I, 48-1, 348–49.

move undetected right through their defensive lines. Pope had little choice but to redirect Sully's troops to counter the Santees and protect the northern frontier. He therefore aborted the eastern expedition, ordering Sully to strike them instead at Devil's Lake. Moreover, a few bands of Teton Sioux had recently come to Fort Rice to talk peace, thus diluting the justification for making war against them. With Sully's force thus diverted, Connor had to assume full responsibility for dealing with the combined tribes, thought to be camped east of the Bighorn Mountains.

Another column, commanded by Colonel Nelson Cole, of the Second Missouri Light Artillery, would march up the Loup Fork River in Nebraska to the eastern side of the Black Hills, where a large number of free-roamers were reportedly congregating. From that point, Cole would swing northwest around the hills to the plains beyond to link up with other forces moving north from Fort Laramie. Even if Cole failed to come in contact with the Sioux, it was hoped that his presence in that region would drive them westward, into the path of the other troops.

The so-called Right Column was composed of eight companies of Cole's own regiment, equipped as cavalry, and eight companies of the Twelfth Missouri Cavalry, numbering about 1,400 men in all. A few of the Missouri artillerymen were assigned to serve a section (two guns) of three-inch ordnance rifles.

Cole's troops rendezvoused at Omaha City on the Missouri River in mid-June, planning to set out on July 1. The news of Moonlight's folly still fresh in his mind, Connor admonished Cole to habitually side-hobble his animals, under close protection of sentries, and to throw out scouts on his flanks to prevent surprise attack while on the march. In his final instructions to Cole, the general made clear he wanted a no-holds-barred campaign: "You will not receive overtures of peace or submission from Indians, but will attack and kill every male Indian over twelve years of age."[11]

As Cole finalized his preparations at Omaha, other troops were moving up the Platte Road to flesh out the Center Column then assembling at Fort Laramie. Dodge had put the Sixteenth Kansas Cavalry in

---

[11]Connor to Colonel Nelson Cole, July 4, 1865, OR, I, 48-2, 1048.

motion from Fort Leavenworth toward that point, despite the unit's ill-equipped condition. The horses of the command were undernourished and the men's clothing was threadbare. Because the regiment's term of enlistment would not expire for two more years, he intended to use the Sixteenth as one arm of the expedition, and afterward to employ it along the Bozeman Trail until regular troops became available. Lieutenant Colonel Samuel Walker would lead the six-hundred-man regiment directly north from Fort Laramie along the western base of the Black Hills before turning toward the Powder.[12]

Connor led the Left Column personally, sensing it had the best chance of striking the decisive blow. His command consisted of ninety men of the Seventh Iowa, ninety of the Eleventh Ohio, the two companies of the Second California Volunteers, as well as a battalion of Pawnee and Omaha Indian scouts under the command of Captain Frank North. Augmenting the strike force was the Sixth Michigan Volunteer Cavalry, formerly a component of the famed Michigan Cavalry Brigade of the Army of the Potomac, and only recently dispatched to the frontier by General Dodge. Connor intended to use the Michigan troops to construct and garrison a new post on the Bozeman Trail. The Sixth did not arrive at Fort Laramie until July 25, and when it did Connor discovered that only half of its members were armed. Were that not discouraging enough, he found the men in a decidedly surly mood over their frontier assignment.

Seeing the post for the first time after a tedious march across the plains, Captain B. F. Rockafellow wrote: "Fort Laramie is much the finest station we have seen, One nice Gothic cottage, large H'Q'rs buildings, Bakery, Shops. Quarters for men built of sun dried bricks . . . which buildings Adobes pronounced Dobys. Capt. T. & me called on Mr. Bullock the post sutler who invited us to his house and treated us to ice and sugar etc . . . Laramie River comes in here. Fort like other western so called forts."[13]

---

[12]Connor to Lieutenant Colonel Samuel Walker, July 28, 1865, ibid., 1128.

[13]The "Gothic cottage" was the sutler's residence, situated a few yards northeast of the store. No doubt "Old Bedlam" was the large headquarters building identified by Rockafellow. His observation that Fort Laramie was like other "so called" western forts was a reference to its lack of any sort of defensive stockade. Hafen and Hafen, *Powder River Campaigns*, 167–68.

The Third U.S. Volunteers, along with another of the "galvanized" regiments, the Sixth U.S. Volunteer Infantry, marching up from Fort Leavenworth, would guard both branches of the road to Salt Lake City, thereby relieving the cavalry to join the expedition. Four companies of the Sixth would accompany Connor as supply train and depot guards. Connor himself left Julesburg, en route for Fort Laramie, on June 24, 1865, though his progress was retarded somewhat by six hundred remount horses herded by his men. He promised to keep Dodge informed of his movements once the command was in the field through a system of vedettes carrying dispatches to and from the post.[14]

Dodge sent additional state units to Connor as quickly as they arrived in the Department of the Missouri. But the volunteers, with few exceptions, resented being held in service beyond what they considered to be the end of the war, regardless of the government's justification. They argued that their enlistments had been "for three years, or during the war," but Lee's surrender in April 1865 did not require President Andrew Johnson to formally declare an end to the insurrection—nor would he do so until mid-1866 after some semblance of law and order had been restored in the southern states. The army could ill-afford to lose all its volunteers at once, considering that scattered elements of Confederate forces were still at large and a resentful southern populace had to be policed. Resolving the escalating Indian situation, and reestablishing peace on the plains, were vital to restoring reliable transcontinental communications. The regular army needed time to regroup and refit before its troops could resume duty

---

[14]Connor to Dodge, June 10, 1865, *OR*, I, 48-2, 849; ibid, June 24, 1865, 988; Colonel C. H. Potter to Price, June 27, 1865, ibid., 1010; Connor to Dodge, June 29, 1865, ibid., 1018. Not directly related to Connor's operations was another expedition that played a role in the confrontations on the northern Plains that spring. In March, Congress had authorized a road to be surveyed from the mouth of the Niobrara River (on the Missouri) to Virginia City, Montana Territory. Despite the popularity of the Bozeman route to Montana, army surveys conducted during the 1850s indicated that a logical avenue to the gold fields lay across northern Nebraska. Steamboats could consistently navigate the Missouri River as far north as the Niobrara during most of the year, thus reducing the distance to be traveled overland. The government contracted with Sioux City businessman and former militia officer James A. Sawyers to supervise the expedition, which began its journey on June 15. Sioux City. Although Sawyers eventually reached Virginia City, his route never became popular with emigrants. Hafen and Hafen, *Powder River Campaigns*, 219–81; Johnson, *The Bloody Bozeman*, 168–70; Price to Dodge, August 15 [16], 1865, *OR*, I, 48-2, 1189.

on the frontier. Accordingly, the government had, and exercised, the legal option to retain in service many of the volunteer units up to the full term of their enlistments.[15]

Dissention spread rapidly through the ranks of the regiments bound for the Powder River Expedition. Frequent Indian raids along the routes they traveled made the disgruntled men reluctant to risk their lives. In one instance, the commanding officer at Fort Collins ordered a company of the Eleventh Kansas to relieve detachments of the Eleventh Ohio as stage-station guards on the Overland Mail Road. The troopers stubbornly refused to comply, arguing that they had ceased being soldiers upon the South's capitulation. A detail of the Sixteenth Kansas at Platte Bridge also refused to obey when they were ordered to escort a telegraph line repair party. Connor, not surprisingly, developed a correspondingly low opinion of the regiment. They "are not worth their salt," he criticized, "but I cannot punish them because they are scattered and I cannot dispense with their services at present."[16]

Almost at once, beginning with the Powder River campaign, insubordination and desertion became rampant in the District of the Plains. Writing to his wife, a soldier in the Sixteenth Kansas, whose company was camped a few miles above Fort Laramie, reported rumors that Connor intended to garrison them at a new post far to the north fol-

---

[15]Another of the incongruous units sent west was a combat-experienced outfit that had been reorganized in July 1864 as the Sixth West Virginia Volunteer Cavalry. After engaging Confederates on several occasions, the Sixth went into winter quarters near Washington, D.C., and remained there until spring. When President Lincoln was assassinated in April, the West Virginians were called out to pursue the conspirators, some of whom they surrounded and captured in the Maryland countryside. A sergeant of the Sixth was credited with shooting John Wilkes Booth in that encounter. When the men stood guard duty along Pennsylvania Avenue during the Grand Review a short time later, they no doubt had visions of early discharges and homecomings. But like some other volunteer organizations sent to Dodge for service on the plains, they were legally bound to federal control for up to three more years. An officer described the mood when the men learned they were being redeployed to Dakota Territory to fight Indians: "The boys of the Sixth had fought many severe battles, endured long marches and untold hardships for Uncle Sam without a murmur. Now, the civil war having ended, many believed their duty was done. They declared they had not sworn to do duty against the savages and refused to move from Leavenworth." About a third of the men were coerced to do their duty and proceed to Fort Kearny, while the rest negotiated terms at Fort Leavenworth before finally agreeing to go to Julesburg to guard the mail line. Lang, *Loyal West Virginia*, 228–32.

[16]The quotation is from Connor to Dodge, July 21, 1865, *OR*, I, 48-2, 1113; Potter to Price, July 6, 1865, ibid., 1060; Connor to Dodge, July 15, 1865, ibid.,1084.

lowing the expedition. "They will fail of their plan for wherever I go from one end of camp to the other the talk is the same, nearly every one believes that our Officers are going against orders," he wrote. "If we are kept here much longer, and it is known that we are kept against orders . . . vengeance is sworn on many an officer if we ever get into a fight . . . I would not be in their place for all the world."[17]

Despite the attitude of many of these men, Connor remained determined to prosecute his campaign to a successful conclusion, even if the troops had to stay in the field all winter. Yet, with a desertion rate of nearly 25 percent, many doubted that he would have any troops left by then.

Fort Laramie bustled with activity during July as supply trains arrived almost daily and troops came and went. Private Hervey Johnson wrote: "Fort Laramie reminds me of some of the towns along the Missouri where they are loading and unloading steamboats every day. All around the Quarter Masters Store the big 'bull wagons' (ships of the desert) are thronged from morning til night loading and unloading coming in and going out. The Sutler store is crowded all day long with soldiers, citizens, Mexicans, half-breeds, and Spaniards trading."[18]

Bullock was pleased with the upsurge of business that summer, but found it difficult to manage the stocks of merchandise in the store, "as the troops are passing up and down the road all the time and every twenty-four hours we have a change. Sometimes five hundred men at the fort and in [a] few days only about seventy-five."[19] Human and animal traffic was so heavy in the vicinity of the post that virtually no grass existed within five miles, and no adequate grazing for the animals within ten miles.

Summer was fast slipping away, and Connor's troops had still not moved against the Indians. Despite low morale, there was no lack of soldiers, though Connor wanted still more troops dispatched from Fort Leavenworth. Continuing Indian depredations in the region required that more troops be siphoned off as escorts for mail coaches

---

[17]Schofield letter.

[18]The reader should note that Johnson did not mention Indians being at the fort at that time because the resident Sioux band was still absent. Unrau, *Tending the Talking Wire*, 270.

[19]Bullock to Ward, June 21, 1865, Ward Papers.

and wagon trains.[20] He also inundated the Quartermaster Department with requisitions for additional supplies. Although, the logistical situation was improving, the freight contractors, pausing whenever possible to graze their teams on any scant forage along the trail, were still moving too slowly to suit the district commander. Late summer rains also were turning the Platte Road into a quagmire, further retarding progress of the heavily laden trains.

Impatient officials in Washington, having no report of the expedition's launch, began questioning Connor's inactivity. While Dodge and his headquarter's staff had done everything within their power to support Connor, his excuses for not beginning the strike were wearing thin. Dodge wanted results. In a missive of July 21, Dodge impatiently urged him to "Get your columns off as soon as possible. We have got these Indian matters now in our hands, and we must settle them." Dodge assured Connor that the mutinies at Fort Leavenworth had been put down, and additional troops, including the Michigan and West Virginia regiments, and the Seventh Kansas Cavalry, were en route to join him.[21]

Through mid-summer, the Cheyennes, Sioux, and Arapahoes relentlessly stuck at any travelers along the roads. In July, the allied tribes held a council on Powder River concurrent with their annual summer gathering for sun dance ceremonies. The chiefs reached a consensus to strike Platte Bridge Station, a strategically important point where the wagon trains, once across the river, separated, some going northwest to South Pass, others diverging southwest to follow Bridger's Trail to Montana. The day after Dodge penned his letter to

---

[20]Units ordered from the East and South to the Department of the Missouri included: three regiments of Illinois infantry, the Third Massachusetts Cavalry, Fourteenth Pennsylvania Cavalry, Twelfth Tennessee Cavalry, Eleventh Indiana Cavalry, Seventh Kansas Cavalry, and the Fifth Michigan Cavalry. Even though these regiments were ordered to march to Fort Laramie, the enlistments of nearly all the soldiers expired before they reached Fort Kearny. They simply turned around and marched back to Fort Leavenworth to be mustered out. Such inefficiency and wasteful expenditure of funds brought Dodge his fair share of censure at the close of the campaign, yet the fault lay outside his authority. The administration had begun bending to political pressure from Congress to discharge the volunteers. Dodge to Brevet Lieutenant Colonel Joseph McBell, AAG, Dept. of the Missouri, November 1, 1865, OR, I, 48-1, 335–48. Dodge expressed his views on mustering out volunteer troops in an interesting letter to Pope, August 2, 1865, ibid., 1156.

[21]Dodge to Connor, July 21, 1865, OR, I, 48-2, 1112–13.

Connor, warriors appeared in large numbers in the vicinity of the bridge. They cut the telegraph line below the station, which lured out a repair party. Before the detachment could retreat to safety, they killed one of the men. Then, on July 25, warriors showed themselves on the hills across the river from the station. A detachment of soldiers that went out to drive them off likely would have been cut off and annihilated had they not been recalled to the station just when the Indians were set to spring the trap.

The following day, Second Lieutenant Caspar Collins, popular son of the Eleventh Ohio's regimental commander, led twenty troopers out of Platte Bridge Station to support an approaching supply train on its way in from Sweetwater. His detachment had not gone far beyond the bridge when Indians completely surrounded it. Collins charged through the warriors in a desperate attempt to get back to the station. Although some of the Ohio cavalrymen escaped, the young lieutenant and four others were killed in the engagement.

A few hours later a train approached to within about five miles of the station. The Indians, who had been watching its progress for some time, attacked as it drew near, forcing Sergeant Amos Custard and his men to corral the wagons for defense. Troops from the station attempted to rescue the beleaguered men, but were unable to break through the Indian lines. After fighting bravely for several hours, Custard and his men were finally overwhelmed. After their victories at what would be called the Battle of Platte Bridge, the Indians considered the war to be ended. They began returning to the headwaters of Powder River.[22]

Dodge's prodding finally inspired Connor to order the columns to march from Fort Laramie on July 30. But Walker's Kansans refused to budge from their camp above the post. Connor's quartermaster described the mutiny: "They alleged that their terms of service would be up before the expedition could be terminated, and that they had not enlisted to fight Indians—had not lost any red devils and were not disposed to hunt for any." Connor was furious. He quickly assembled two loyal companies of the Second California, along with the Eleventh Ohio "battery," and boldly marched to Walker's camp.

---

[22] A detailed description of the Battle of Platte Bridge is in McDermott, *Frontier Crossroads*, 61–76.

Deploying his men in a line of battle flanking the two howitzers, Connor announced to the Kansans that they had five minutes to obey his orders, or they would be shot down where they stood. This demonstration of force, accented by the gaping muzzles of two cannons, gave the mutinous men pause to reconsider. "The Kansas boys were smart enough to smell danger and to take the general at his word," an officer recalled. "They fell into line and went out upon the dismal, unprofitable, inglorious hunt after 'scalp lifters.'"[23]

In light of the numerous attacks along the Platte route above Fort Laramie, Connor had become increasingly concerned that the hostiles perpetrating those raids were taking refuge west of the Bighorn range. While the main body of the Left Column proceeded directly up the Bozeman Trail, Connor detached Captain Albert Brown and 116 men of the Second California, with 70 Omaha and Winnebago Indian scouts, to proceed to Platte Bridge, then march northward along the west flank of the Bighorns. Connor hoped these "beaters," like Cole—and Walker on his right—would drive the Indians toward his planned rendezvous in the vicinity of Rosebud Creek.

Connor and his expedition arrived on the upper reaches of Powder River on August 11. Nearby, he found a suitable place to construct the new post, which he modestly named Fort Connor.[24] With axes ringing in the clear air, Connor left the experienced Michigan woodsmen to their work while the rest of the troops marched northwest, still approximating the course of the Bozeman Trail. Captain Brown caught up with him ten days later and reported finding no Indians during his reconnaissance beyond the mountains. The reunited column continued to Tongue River, following that stream northward nearly to its confluence with the Yellowstone before countermarching on his back-trail. Connor, increasingly perplexed, found no signs of Indians.

Then on the twenty-eighth, a group of North's Pawnees rode into camp to report their discovery of a village of about 250 lodges farther up Tongue River. It was later identified as that of Black Bear and his

---

[23]All quotations here are from Captain Henry E. Palmer in Hafen and Hafen, *Powder River Campaigns*, 107.

[24]Fort Connor, renamed Fort Reno on November 11, 1865, stood on table land overlooking the Powder River, approximately twenty-two miles northwest of present Kaycee, Wyoming. It was active for only three years. Frazer, *Forts of the West*, 183–84.

band of Arapahoes. Connor immediately readied a strike force of 125 cavalrymen and 90 scouts to make a night march and attack the village the following morning. At about nine o'clock on August 29, just as the Indians were breaking camp, the troops thundered down on the unsuspecting tribesmen, driving them ten miles in a running fight. By then, however, only three officers and ten troopers had been able to keep up with their commander. When the Indians saw how few soldiers were in pursuit, they turned the tables and chased Connor's party back five miles. The troopers retreated to the Indian village, where the skirmish continued until nightfall. The mountain howitzers of the Ohioans kept the warriors at a safe distance while the rest of the command destroyed the camp.[25]

Connor not only was unable to locate the main Indian camp, he could find no sign of either Cole or Walker, who should have linked up with him by that time. His scouts examined both the Tongue River Valley and Rosebud Creek, but failed to find as much as a hoofprint belonging to either command. And now, the weather had turned bad, with rain and snow making life miserable for the weary troops.

By mid-September, with Cole and Walker still nowhere to be found, Captain North's scouts discovered the carcasses of several hundred cavalry horses in the valley of the Powder, as well as the remnants of saddles and other horse equipment that had been piled and burned. It was an ominous sign that something had gone terribly wrong.

Cole, retarded by his plodding supply train, had followed his instructions to reconnoiter the plains along the eastern base of the Black Hills. Discovering no Indians there, he proceeded to Bear Butte and on to the Belle Fouche River. He and Walker joined forces there on August 18, agreeing to cooperate closely with each other, though their commands would remain separate. Their couriers would provide communications between the two columns.

Cole and Walker's combined force moved northwest up the Belle

---

[25]Connor's official report is reproduced in Hafen and Hafen, *Powder River Campaigns*, 46–48. Although Connor claimed to have killed about thirty-five warriors during the engagement, Captain Henry E. Palmer placed the number at sixty-three. Ibid., 135. An unidentified Indian woman, perhaps a member of the band, came to Fort Laramie later that fall and reported only three men killed, plus twenty-five women and children. Bullock to Ward, December 6, 1865, Ward Papers.

Fouche, then crossed over the divide to discover a well-beaten trail along the Little Missouri River. Cole, with rations running danger- ously low and his horses worn out, elected to return to Powder River in accordance with Connor's instructions. His scouts fanned out to the west but found no evidence of Connor's presence on either Tongue River or Rosebud Creek. Cole had scarcely made his decision to fall back when four hundred to five hundred Indians appeared near his camp and attempted to run off his herd. His men responded quickly, however, and drove off the attackers.

Continuing their trek southward along the Powder, Cole and Walker sighted smoke rising from the valley ahead. They assumed it was Connor attempting to signal them, but they were unable to close the distance that day. That night temperatures plummeted, decimat- ing the troop's already weakened mounts. In the morning the com- pany commanders reported that 225 animals had died during the awful night, setting a like number of his troopers afoot.

On September 4, with the Sixteenth Kansas about fifteen miles in advance of Cole's column, Walker stumbled upon the principal village of the combined hostile tribes. Approximately one thousand warriors advanced to meet the soldiers, initiating a skirmish that lasted for three hours. Again, artillery saved the day. Three days after that fight, on September 8, the troops again engaged the Sioux on the Little Powder River. Walker's men absorbed the brunt of the attack, while Cole corralled his train and advanced the Twelfth Missouri and the 3- inch rifled guns to support the Kansans. Artillery fire finally broke up the Indian concentrations, clearing the way for the troops to advance.

The loss of so many horses was but a precursor to the disaster that befell the troops on the night of September ninth. An early winter storm blew in, freezing to death five hundred additional horses and mules, the carcasses of which were found later by Connor's Pawnees. That loss convinced both Cole and Walker to give up the campaign; there was no choice but to return to Fort Laramie. As the troops wearily made their way up the Powder, Sioux warriors harassed them by taking potshots from the surrounding hills. Connor's scouts finally intercepted the destitute command on September 13, only eighty miles north of Fort Connor. A week later, the troops limped into the fort.

Connor and his men arrived on the twenty-fourth, finally forming the junction of the columns, but not at the place nor with the union of purpose Connor had planned.

The outcome of the campaign was a far cry from the decisive results General Connor had envisioned. And yet, after the troops had had some time to recover, and the horses were reconditioned or replaced, he proposed that he launch a second expedition against the same Sioux and their allies. Higher command had already scuttled his designs, however. Army Headquarters had run out of patience with him, and had succumbed to political pressure to discharge his volunteer forces. Word reached Connor at Fort Laramie that his District of the Plains had been abolished and that he had been reassigned to his former district in Utah.[26] The Powder River Indian Expedition came to an end, as abrupt as it was abysmal, when Connor departed for Salt Lake City.

The failure of Connor's campaign was as much the result of his administrative blunders as those that occurred in the field against the Indians. General of the Army Ulysses S. Grant became particularly disenchanted with Connor when he learned of his orders to reject peace overtures and instead to kill all male Indians over age twelve. Were that not reason enough to fire him, the costs of the Powder River campaign had reached such astronomical proportions that the secretary of the treasury complained to the president that his department would be hard pressed to meet its unanticipated financial obligations.

Generals Dodge and Connor remained convinced that the Indian war either should be prosecuted with determination or the West should be surrendered to the Indians. President Andrew Johnson's young administration had a less clear cut view of how to proceed because the nation was already burdened with the huge costs of the Civil War, and members of Congress were clamoring for state troops to be mustered out. A reasonable compromise, they argued, was to protect the lines of overland emigrant and mail, and allow the Indians

---

[26]*GO No. 20*, Department of the Missouri, August 22, 1865. This document dissolved the District of the Plains and reinstated the District of Nebraska, encompassing the territories of Nebraska and Montana, as well as that portion of Dakota lying west of the Nebraska border. Fort Laramie became headquarters for the new district. *OR*, I, 48-2, 1201.

to occupy and roam uninhabited regions where they would pose no danger to a westward expanding nation.

The invasion of the Powder River country, as the military discovered, had alarmed the Indians to such a degree that most of the Sioux, Northern Cheyenne, and Arapahoe bands temporarily withdrew from the Platte Road. General Connor also contributed significantly to the geographical knowledge of a part of the northern Plains few whites had seen up to that time. Moreover, the establishment of Fort Connor, renamed Fort Reno in November 1865, firmly secured the Bozeman Trail as the only viable route to Virginia City.

CHAPTER THIRTEEN

"There Shall Be No More Treachery"

With the Civil War now over, Major General John Pope, in command of the Department of the Missouri, insisted on reversing Patrick Connor's policy of conducting offensive actions into the Sioux and Cheyenne sanctuaries. His announced purpose was "to return to a purely defensive arrangement for the security of the overland routes to Salt Lake."[1] Pope chose wisely in selecting a new commander for the restored District of Nebraska. Brigadier General Frank Wheaton was an experienced regular officer who had served in the First Cavalry on the plains prior to the war. Soon after the opening of hostilities in 1861, Wheaton, like many of his contemporaries, sought and obtained a commission with the state volunteers. In the rapidly burgeoning army of citizen soldiers, where military experience was at a premium, advancement was considerably faster than in the regular army. Within a year and a half, Wheaton attained the rank of brigadier. By war's end, he had been rewarded with brevet (honorary) rank five times, each time for gallant and meritorious service in combat. Lieutenant William R. Behymer, an Eleventh Ohio officer at Camp Mitchell, probably expressed the view of many others when he wrote, "I am well satisfied with our new commander and I am of the opinion that he is the best commander we have had in the dist. since the commencement of the Indian trouble."[2]

[1]Major General John Pope to Brevet Major General Frank Wheaton, August 23, 1865, *or*, I, 48-2, 1206–08.

[2]Lieutenant William R. Behymer to his father, October 17, 1865, Behymer Papers, Wyoming State Archives. Even the usually skeptical sutler Bullock was pleased with Wheaton's appointment. "Capt. Frank Wheaton is capt. in the now 4 Cav and one of the old set. You can imagine how I set up to him when he arrived," he wrote. Bullock to Ward, September 15, 1865, Ward Papers.

Pope's extensive instructions to Wheaton in August 1865 recognized that most of the state troops had little or no dedication to the army's frontier mission, especially now that the Civil War was over, and he considered it futile to try to hold them in federal service, because they caused more problems than they were worth. Surprisingly, he considered the U.S. Volunteers (former Confederates) to be the most highly disciplined and trustworthy troops then available. Unlike the Union-state volunteers, many Southerners had little incentive to return home to a war-ravaged countryside and decimated economy. Even though soldiering meant serving under the flag they had formerly renounced, at least military service provided food, shelter, clothing, and pay. Moreover, many ex-Rebels saw in the West opportunities for mining, farming, business, and other ventures once their military obligation was fulfilled.

For now, Pope wanted only enough volunteers to protect the routes of travel and communication until the regular army could be recruited up to full strength and troops transferred back to the western frontier. He therefore limited Wheaton to one volunteer cavalry and two volunteer infantry regiments for his district, cautioning him to select only units whose enlistments would not expire until the following spring or summer. Once Wheaton had made his choices, he was to send all the others back to Fort Leavenworth, where they would be discharged forthwith.

Pope emphasized to Wheaton that strict attention to economy must guide his every decision. The excessive quantities of supplies Connor had amassed at Fort Laramie were to be protected during the coming winter, then distributed to Fort Connor (Reno) and other posts, or returned to the general depot at Leavenworth if they could not be used within a reasonable time.

Wheaton followed his superior's recommendations by assigning one company each of the Third and Sixth U.S. Volunteers to serve as the infantry garrison at Fort Laramie, but the choice of cavalry was not so simple. The experienced and long-suffering Eleventh Ohio deserved to be relieved, yet it had not been in service as long as other regiments. Therefore it was doomed to remain on the frontier. It was business as usual for the Ohioans when Wheaton assigned three companies to the post, and stationed others at various points along the overland roads. Other state units held over at Fort Laramie that fall included a few companies of the Sixth Michigan, Seventh Iowa, and the Sixth West Virginia. Trader Bullock, still anxious for the regulars to return, opined: "The 7th Iowa Cavl. a great set of thieves and the 6th [West] Virginian who can beat any Regt. in Kansas."[3] He no doubt rejoiced when orders arrived sending both units home during September and October 1865.

The ragged survivors of the Powder River Expedition hobbled in to Fort Laramie in early October and bivouacked below the post along the Laramie River. The most footsore men in the column had been allowed to ride from Fort Connor in empty supply wagons, while the rest walked. Believing in the adage that an "idle mind is the devil's workshop," Wheaton gave them no rest, but immediately detailed the emaciated Missourians, along with the formerly mutinous Sixteenth Kansas, to improve the earthworks around the northern perimeter of the fort. "The total absence of tools naturally caused some speculation as to the cause of the detail," Cole later wrote. "As the mystery was transparent, it is well enough to add that the ragged and barefooted veterans spent the allotted time at the designated place, tools or no tools."[4] The irksome assignment was mercifully short, however, and within a few days, orders arrived for Cole to march the Second Missouri Artillery to Fort Leavenworth to be mustered out.

Colonel Cole's men were not alone in being assigned to work details. Connor's excess supplies still had to be sheltered before winter. Private Frank Tubbs of the Eleventh Ohio wrote to his father: "I am on detail in the Carpenter Shop we raised a building last week 30 by 120 it is a quarter Master Building we have lots of work to do there is 7 of hand working we having fine weather to work out doors."[5]

With the men of the Sixth West Virginia and Sixth Michigan occupied largely with guarding the mails, the new commander of the West Nebraska Sub-district, Colonel Henry E. Maynadier, a West Point regular commanding the Fifth U.S. Volunteer Infantry, complained to Wheaton that he had only eighty-one men present for duty at Fort Laramie. While Cole's artillerymen were overjoyed at the prospect of

---

[3]Bullock to Ward, December 9, 1865, Ward Papers.
[4]Colonel Nelson Cole to General U. S. Grant, February 10, 1867, Folder no. 10, Camp Papers, BYU, copy at Little Bighorn Battlefield; Unrau, *Tending the Talking Wire*, 294; William Bullock said of the defenses: "Gen'l. Wheaton is enclosing the post with a heavy work & ditch which will ensure the safety of the post for ages to come either from savage or civilized foes." Bullock to Ward, October 21, 1865, Ward Papers.
[5]Frank Tubbs to Father, November 11, 1865, Frank Tubbs letters, copy in vert. files, library, FLNHS.

leaving the Plains, three companies of the Twelfth Missouri Cavalry had to resign themselves to staying behind for the winter. In addition to guarding the telegraph stations and patrolling the road, six-man details functioned as mail parties from the fort to and from the junction of the Overland Road at Julesburg. Cavalry detachments also carried the "up" mail northwest from Fort Laramie to Horseshoe Station, where it was handed off to soldiers posted there.

Travelers on the overland roads, meanwhile, enjoyed only a brief respite from Indian encounters. Connor's troops were barely out of the field before raiding parties once again began harassing wagon trains and mail carriers. Sioux raiders hit the stations at La Bonte Creek and Horseshoe within a matter of days after the columns rendezvoused at Fort Connor. During late September, war parties audaciously struck in the immediate vicinity of Fort Laramie, riding off with fifty animals from the post quartermaster's herd, along with about eighty horses belonging to civilians. On the very day the Sixth West Virginia arrived at Fort Laramie, warriors fired on a Mormon train only nine miles east of the fort, killing two men, wounding seven others, and capturing two women from the emigrant party. And again the next day, as the West Virginia troopers looked on, "a painted band of Sioux filed out of a ravine and succeeded by a bold dash in cutting off a few straggling cattle from a small herd belonging to a transportation train in camp below the fort. There was not the usual war whoop, but the thing was done in five minutes and in a very systematic way. In an instant all was in confusion about the Fort and everybody watched the new Cavalry camp to see what would be done there."[6] Without awaiting orders, the troopers mounted and rode toward the Indians, who fled with the captured oxen. The soldiers chased them for five miles, forcing them to abandon the cattle, some of them shot full of arrows and others crippled in various ways. The raiders, meanwhile, split into small groups and made good their escape.

Corresponding to a peace initiative with the southern Plains tribes, government representatives met with a gathering of Sioux chiefs at Fort Sully during October. Although most of the Teton bands were in attendance, the commissioners somehow failed to recognize that they represented only the peaceful Sioux factions. The views of the groups

---

[6]Bullock to Ward, September 24, 1865, Ward Papers; Holliday, *On the Plains in '65*, 1883, 62. This attack was also mentioned by Bullock to Ward, September 24, 1865, Ward Papers.

involved in the recent war, and still roaming the plains between the Platte and Powder River, were not presented at the council. Therefore, the final accord had no influence on bringing peace to the region.[7]

Proof of this was evidenced at Fort Laramie on November 9, just one day after General Wheaton and his staff left to reestablish his headquarters at Omaha. Corporal Johnson related that they had

> a big Indian scare in the Fort a few days ago, we were all sitting around our fires enjoying ourselves perfectly oblivious to everything without when were suddenly started by the shrill blast of the bugle sounding 'to arms.' Every fellow sprang for his 'shooting irons' wondering what could be in the wind. Were out in line in nearly no time. The artillery was flying about over the parade and being got into position, and 'there was mounting in hot haste the steed' . . . and while were yet in line and awaiting orders, we were informed what the rumpus was about. One of the infantry boys was up the river shooting ducks, he was surprised and fired upon by a party of five Indians which his fertile imagination magnified to a hundred.[8]

As the terrified ex-Rebel ran full-tilt back to the post, the Indians followed him directly to a small train camped just a quarter of a mile from the fort. The muleskinners at the camp fired on the warriors, diverting them toward the bluffs. A mounted detachment from the fort pursued them for fifteen miles, but was unable to catch up with their swift Indian ponies. Later in November, hostiles attacked a party on the road about forty miles west of the fort. Colonel Maynadier himself led the chase after them, but accomplished nothing more than wearing out his horses; the Indians were long gone.[9]

In early December, Spotted Tail sent two women and a boy to the post, professing peace, asking if the band could return to its old agency. They assured Maynadier that the women were even then tanning buffalo robes to renew trading at the sutler's store. The gesture was negated, however, when an unidentified Sioux or Cheyenne war party again stole

---

[7]General Wheaton planned to invite leaders of the hostile factions to a council at Fort Laramie, but the plan never came to fruition. Trader Bullock, however, praised his good intentions by stating, "He will succeed as he is pursuing a different course from Connor, who was nothing more than a murderer of women & children." Bullock to Ward, October 21, 1865, Ward Papers.

[8]Unrau, *Tending the Talking Wire*, 302–303.

[9]PR, FL, November 1865, RG 94, NA, microfilm copy in library, FLNHS. A party of Brulés also attacked one of Seth Ward's trains near Alkali Station, on the South Platte River approximately 225 miles from Fort Laramie, on December 2, 1865. They stole his bell mare and 159 head of mules, for which he later filed a claim against the government. House, 42nd Cong., 3rd Sess., No. 233, (1569).

all the stock from the guards at Horseshoe Station. A dismayed Bullock wrote to his employer: "As long as cavalry is kept in this country the Indians will never make peace they can steal the cavalry horses to easy to ever make peace—and then the commanders that are sent out here are so unfit and worthless as soon as we got one [Wheaton] commander out here who thought of the interests of the Government instead of his pocket he was ordered to Omaha. Are the people of Omaha so turbulent that it takes a General to keep them in subjugation?"[10]

In accordance with the new peace initiative, General Wheaton dispatched the chief of the Fort Laramie Sioux, Big Mouth, along with Big Ribs, Whirlwind, and two others to the Powder River tribes in an attempt to induce them to come to Fort Laramie for talks. Corporal Johnson, who had witnessed the violent deaths of several comrades during the previous two years, and had just returned from two months of utter misery in the field with Connor, was skeptical. "I am neither glad nor sorry to say that the Indian war is about to be wound up by a treaty of peace. Several of the principal chiefs came in a few days ago with a white rag, an order was issued from Head Quarters . . . commanding the men of the garrison to pay them due respect and offer them no violence. I thought I would like to be out somewhere in gunshot of where they would pass. I think I know what respect is due them, and they would get it too."[11]

Connor's withdrawal from the plains, coupled with the unusually harsh winter of 1865–66, which was already exacting a toll on the Indian population, influenced Swift Bear and Standing Elk, chiefs of the peacefully inclined Corn Band, to return to Laramie in mid-January. They had been among the Southern Brulés camped at the Upper Platte Agency the previous spring to avoid being caught up in the war, but had been forced to fall in with the hostile elements after the breakout on Horse Creek. Colonel Maynadier, like his predecessor William O. Collins, believed that treating the Indians with respect accomplished more than could be gained by armed force. Certainly, Connor's dismal performance suggested the need for a different approach. Maynadier gave the Indians a cordial reception at post headquarters, and then discussed in general terms the government's desire for peace. The colonel,

---

[10]Bullock to Ward, December 11, 1865, Ward Papers.
[11]Unrau, *Tending the Talking Wire*, 296.

convinced of Swift Bear's sincerity, invited him to bring more chiefs to the next council so that formal peace talks might be undertaken. After meeting all day on February 1, the Brulés left the post, promising to spread word that the government wanted to end the war and officials would now welcome the Indians back to the Platte on peaceful terms. But, with the plains firmly in the grip of unprecedented winter storms, travel was difficult and it would take time for many to respond.

Indian runners returned to the post in early March with word that Spotted Tail and his band were coming in, but adding that his seventeen-year-old daughter, Brings Water (Mini-aku) had become seriously ill at the big camp on Powder River. The young woman had spent much time at Fort Laramie during her youth and had grown to enjoy the company and customs of whites. She particularly remembered and liked Colonel Maynadier from antebellum days.[12] And now, perhaps sensing her impending death, or wanting the services of a white doctor, Mini-aku had asked her father to take her to the post. Spotted Tail wanted to comply with her request, but by doing so he would lose a voice in the important councils then underway among the tribes. Moreover, since elsewhere on the Plains the Sioux were at war with the army, he could hardly cross the country alone to conclude a treaty. At length, however, the councils ended and his band broke camp to start south toward Fort Laramie. That delay, combined with the midwinter conditions, proved too much for the girl to endure. She died en route, from "exposure and inability to sustain the severe labor

---

[12]Maynadier stated that he knew Mini-aku as a twelve-year old girl in 1861. Colonel Henry E. Maynadier to D. N. Cooley, commissioner of Indian Affairs, March 9, 1866, *ARSI*, 1867, 207–208 (hereinafter cited as Maynadier report); Lieutenant Ware also encountered the girl at Fort Laramie in 1864 and his recollection of her demeanor is worth noting. He also recorded that Charles Elston, mentioned previously in regard to the hanging of Two Face and Black Foot, informed him that Mini-aku had lived in the Sioux camp near the fort for two or three years as a young child. Ware, *Indian War of 1864*, 212, 407–18. For a thoroughly researched exposé of the Mini-aku "legend," contrasted with the actual events surrounding her burial at Fort Laramie, see Clough, "Mini-aku, Daughter of Spotted Tail," 187–216 (hereinafter cited as "Mini-aku"), also available in off-print format. I consider Clough's analysis highly credible; therefore the version presented herein closely follows his work. Any significant departures or additions based on the author's own research are cited as appropriate. The young woman's name has been debated over time, but Clough presents a cogent argument for it being "Mini-aku." He also notes another variation, "Monica," but has been unable to trace the origin beyond George Hyde, noted historian of the Sioux. Clough speculated that the name may have been reported by army officers or their wives. Ibid., 23–24, 29–31. I have found that Maynadier, in fact, referred to her by that name, the only instance in which he used the girl's proper name, in a letter to wife April 8, 1866, vertical files, FLNHS.

and hardship of the wild Indian life," Maynadier sadly recorded.[13] Prior to her death, the girl had asked her father to take her body to the fort for burial, a request he had pledged to fulfill.[14]

The circumstances of Spotted Tail's appearance at the fort were different from those Colonel Maynadier had originally anticipated, yet he immediately saw this tragic new development as a serendipitous opportunity to make a favorable impression on the Sioux, thereby enhancing his chances of winning their confidence. When the chief arrived at the Platte ferry on March 8, 1866, Maynadier and several other officers rode out with great pomp to conduct him to post headquarters. In the conversation that followed, Maynadier invited the grieving Spotted Tail to bring the body of his daughter to the fort for burial at sunset that evening, a gesture of friendship that pleased Spotted Tail and quickly put him at ease. Immediately after the chief left the post to return to his camp, the colonel set men to work hastily constructing a coffin and a scaffold in the cemetery overlooking the fort. At the appointed hour,

> the coffin was carried to the graveyard followed by Pegaleshka [Spotted Tail], his wife, two sons brothers, and sisters. The parapet of the fort, which is run near the graveyard, was covered by Indian braves, squaws, and papooses, and in the graveyard were a large number of soldiers, citizens, and others led by curiosity to attend the ceremony. When all was ready, the coffin was opened and the corpse placed in it, with several articles as presents to sustain her on her journey . . . Then occurred the most impressive scene of all, Rev. Alpha Wright, chaplain of the post advanced towards the open coffin. On one side stood Pegaleshka, and around the coffin the mother, sisters, and brothers of the deceased, Col. Maynadier, and the interpreter, Mr. Jott [agent Jarrot], stood near the chaplain. As the chaplain commenced his prayer every hat in the large assembly was removed, and all assumed an attitude of devotion. The reverend chaplain's prayer was translated by the interpreter, and . . . there is little doubt the Indians understood it perfectly. Taking the whole view, it presented an appearance naturally beautifully . . . Surrounded by the Black Hills, and conspicuously in view the tall front of Laramie Peak, bathed in the glow of the setting sun, the fort presented an aspect of sadness appropriate to the occasion. Within the enclosure of the graveyard stood those engaged in the solemn office of

---

[13]Maynadier to Cooley, ibid. The actual cause of death may have been tuberculosis. Clough, "Mini-aku," 6.

[14]Ware maintained that Mini-aku hoped to be wed to a white officer, which may have been true. At the time of her death, however, she apparently was pledged to a half-blood man known as Tom Dorio. George W. Colhoff to John Hunton, October 28, 1898, Hunton Papers.

the first Christian burial of an Indian in that place . . . The prayer was ended, the coffin raised upon the scaffold, and all slowly withdrew. Thus was the daughter of Pegasleshka consigned to her last resting-place.[15]

---

[15]Untitled article by "Tarsha-Otah," who was probably Maynadier writing under a pen-name to conceal his identity. *St. Louis Republican*, April 2, 1866, copy in vertical files, library FLNHS. Maynadier obviously wanted to make as much political hay for himself as possible, as he disclosed to his wife: "The enclosed account of the burial of Pegaleshka's daughter will answer for a letter, as it has been the important event of the last week . . . if you can get this one published it will be of advantage to me and to the object for which I am striving." Maynadier to wife, March 10, 1865, copy in vertical files, FLNHS (hereinafter cited as Maynadier letters). That "object" was revealed in a subsequent letter in which he posed the question to his wife, "How will you like to be Mrs. Bv't. Maj. Gen'l[?]" Maynadier to wife, May 12, 1866, ibid. The citation read: "For distinguished service on the frontier while operating against hostile Indians, and accomplishing much toward bringing about a peace with hostile tribes." Heitman, *Historical Register*, 1: 699. The date for the action, as given by Heitman, was March 13, 1865 [1866?], which almost certainly is a misprint in view of his service record and his letter of May 12, 1866, informing his wife that he had just received the official notification. The colonel indicated that both Chaplain Wright and the post surgeon, as yet unidentified, submitted draft articles to the press. Maynadier to wife, April 8, 1866. Alpha Wright replaced Rev. William Vaux, who had served as post chaplain at Fort Laramie until spring 1861, when he took leave to his home in London, Tennessee. Because his family was reluctant to return to the frontier, Vaux applied for an extension of his leave, with an option to resign at the end of the year. Meantime, the outbreak of the war prevented him from leaving the Confederacy, which eventually led to the termination of his appointment. William Vaux to Seth E. Ward, April 19 and March 19, 1861, Ward Papers. Alpha Wright, a Vermont native living in Missouri on the eve of the Civil War, served as chaplain with both state and federal volunteers from spring 1863 until he was appointed post chaplain at Fort Laramie on December 11, 1865. He retained his position until his retirement in 1879. He died on November 30, 1888. Heitman, *Historical Register*, 1: 1061. Colonel William O. Collins had the cemetery fenced in late winter 1864. The earthworks constructed in February and October 1865 lay outside the fence, but, as indicated in this article, close enough that spectators had a clear view of the funeral ceremony. Entry for March 22, 1864, Cowell journal, typescript in vertical files, FLNHS. A superb watercolor executed by artist Anton Schonborn in 1868 depicts the burial scaffold standing in the extreme northwest corner of the cemetery. The presence of the earthworks along the west and north perimeters of the cemetery, just outside the fence, correspond to Maynadier's description. The scaffold was undoubtedly moved when a new hospital was erected on the site of the old cemetery in 1872–73. John S. Collins, who served as post trader during the 1870s, recorded that Spotted Tail returned to Fort Laramie on the eve of the Great Sioux War to reclaim the remains of his daughter. According to Collins, the bones were placed in a *new* box lined with calico and wool. "The box was placed in the wagon and they drove away to the agency [near Fort Robinson]." This raises a question about the validity of an 1883 photograph [file no. A-28] of a scaffold burial, purportedly that of Mini-aku, standing a few hundred yards northwest of the New Hospital. Apparently, this or some other scaffold on the plateau was still being identified as Mini-aku's grave when Lieutenant James Regan, Seventh Infantry, saw it "worn and faded" in 1880. Regan, "Military Landmarks," 155–57. It may be that the scaffold and original coffin remained at the second location as a curiosity after the bones were taken away by Spotted Tail, or through time and retelling, another scaffold burial became known as hers. That the scaffolding caught the attention of a photographer indicates that it had become a local attraction, although it was certainly not the only one in the immediate vicinity of Fort Laramie. Others are depicted in a photograph published in Hedren, *Fort Laramie in 1876*, 117.

Maynadier evinced his personal condolences by placing a pair of
ornately beaded gauntlets in the coffin before it was nailed shut, an act
of respect that met with the universal approval of the Indians. The following day, he wrote to the commissioner of Indian affairs expressing
his confidence that the burial of Mini-aku augured well for securing
peace on the northern Plains. He trusted Spotted Tail, in part, he
reported, because "A man of Pegaleshka's intelligence and shrewdness
would never have confided the remains of his child to the care of any
one but those with whom he intended to be friends always. The
occurrence of such an incident is regarded by the oldest settlers, men
of most experience in Indian character, as unprecedented, and as calculated to secure a certain and lasting peace."[16]

Three days after the funeral, following a customary period of
mourning, Spotted Tail, Brave Bear, and Standing Elk, with about
one hundred fifty men, arrived on the Platte early in the afternoon. Of
particular significance to the soldiers at the fort was the unanticipated
appearance of Red Cloud, Oglala leader of the notorious Bad Face
band and one of the foremost proponents of the recent war. Red
Cloud was implacable in his resolve to keep the whites out of the
Powder River country.

Johnson described the arrival of the Oglalas:

> The Indians could be seen crossing the river about a mile and a half from the
> fort, and forming a line along the bank. About a dozen men, including offi-
> cers, mountaineers, and the chaplain went down with a small flag to escort
> them up. When they reached the Indians [about halfway between the post
> and the river] the latter set up a yell that we could hear distinctly. The Indi-
> ans then separated themselves into three divisions, and started towards the
> fort advancing like a regiment in line of battle, the officers in advance of the
> center division. They marched this way till they came to the breastworks,
> when they drew in from the right and left and filed through the passage, then
> spread out again till they reached the entrance to the parade, where the main
> body of the warriors halted, while the officers and chiefs rode on in, to the
> front of Headquarters . . . They all went into headquarters, then at a word
> from Col. Maynadier the warriors dismounted and followed in, leaving their
> ponies in charge of the squaws, of whom there were thirty or forty.[17]

[16]Maynadier report, March 9, 1865.

[17]Unrau, *Tending the Talking Wire*, 322–23; Three other contemporary accounts fix the date as
   March 8. See Maynadier report, as well as an article written by Chaplain Alpha Wright and
   published in the *St. Louis Democrat* under the dateline March 8, in Clough, "Mini-aku," 5–6.

Once inside the fort grounds, the principal chiefs, followed by a capacity crowd of their officers and tribesmen, entered the warm, flag-bedecked adjutant's office (then serving as headquarters) at the south corner of the parade ground, where they would meet with Maynadier, Indian Agent Jarrot, and the post commander, Major George M. O'Brian. Red Cloud, who claimed he had never before been in a white-man's building, was at first reluctant to go in, but was gently coerced by Maynadier. A canvas-over-frame "pavilion," erected nearby as a theater for the "Laramie Varieties," was pressed into service as a shelter for the scores of other Indians who had come. Soldiers congregated on porches and elsewhere around the perimeter of the parade ground, quietly speculating among themselves about the proceedings. Many of the men were irked, feeling that Maynadier had gone too far in appeasing the Indians by hoisting a white flag, "the emblem of humiliation," over the post to fly in place of the Stars and Stripes for the duration of the council. Regardless of their commander's confidence in the peaceful disposition of the Indians, the edgy troops made certain their weapons were at hand in the event of trouble; many even carried revolvers concealed under their coats.[18]

This preliminary meeting, held on March 11, 1866, employed a direct telegraphic connection to Nebraska Indian Commissioner E. B. Taylor, sitting in his office in Omaha. During the council, the Sioux chiefs expressed their earnest desire for peace, but also enumerated their grievances, most of which pointed directly to various failures by the agents assigned to the Upper Platte District. Agents Twiss and Loree had both been infamous for swindling the Indians out of their annuities, for example, at times even trading them to other Indians and pocketing the proceeds. In another complaint, the chiefs objected when the army withheld rations in an ill-advised attempt to deprive the recalcitrant bands. Even Jarrot had to admit that although he had now served for a year as their agent, he had never spoken with the Sioux leaders prior to this occasion. In Jarrot's defense, however, it was noted that he had arrived just as his charges were being forcibly removed to Fort Kearny, and then the Horse Creek outbreak had compelled them to accompany the hostile Oglalas and Cheyennes to Powder River. Nevertheless, Red Cloud exhibited his distrust of Jar-

---

[18]Unrau, *Tending the Talking Wire*, 321–22.

rot by insisting that his close friend, Antoine Janis, who had accompanied him to the conference, serve as his personal interpreter, "for very often the interpreter does not tell you what the Indians say," he admonished, "but this man will tell you all that I am going to say." Jarrot was, however, permitted to speak for Spotted Tail and the other Brulés. The conversation focused on the fact that the Sioux had not received their goods and their people were starving. Large numbers of emigrants and other travelers on the overland roads had both reduced the number of buffalo and driven away the remainder, making it even more difficult for the Indians to subsist by hunting. Spotted Tail summarized their plight. "You know that we are very poor, and have nothing to eat. The buffalo is far off, and our horses are weak, and we have nothing to feed them; we cannot go after the buffalo. We have nothing for our women and children to eat. We hope you will let us have some powder and ball to kill deer and antelope."

Brave Bear pledged that if the government would allow them to trade for ammunition for hunting purposes, "From this time hereafter everything shall be good, and there shall be no more treachery nor no more tricks from any of us."[19] Even Red Cloud acknowledged that both sides had been at fault, and he was willing to sit down with the commissioners with the confidence that all the differences could be settled. With that, the council adjourned. Maynadier conducted the Indians to the commissary storehouse, where rations were doled out, along with a special gift of eight beeves from the quartermaster herd.

The meeting thus concluded on a high note of good will on both sides. The Indians agreed to return by June 1, at which time special commissioners would meet with them to conclude a formal treaty aimed at reconciling the differences between the two races. Meantime, the Indians agreed to would spread word of reconciliation among the other bands, and the officers at the fort pledged to attempt to ameliorate relations between them. Overnight, the Sioux again became a presence at Fort Laramie. In a letter of March 19, Corporal Johnson noted the "homecoming" of the Indians and their mountaineer in-laws: "The Sioux are in here every day buying notions and selling

[19]Both quotations are from the *St. Louis Republican*, March 12, 1865.

robes and moccasins to the soldiers. A small villag came here a few days ago from the south, they have got their 'teepes' stuck up just across the Laramie south west of the Fort. They are getting more familiar every day, and already the squaws smiling countenances are to be seen about the kitchen doors and windows at meal-times."[20]

Momentous changes were in the wind at Fort Laramie. Just as the Sioux seemed inclined to abandon the warpath, the state volunteer units that had come west to fight them were at last being released and sent home. The Twelfth Missouri Cavalry bade goodbye to the garrison only days before the arrival of the Sioux leaders, and by mid-March the last elements of the Sixth Michigan, Sixth West Virginia, and Seventh Iowa followed them down the trail to Fort Leavenworth. The veterans of the last battalion of the Eleventh Ohio were counting the days until June 20, when they too could "get out of that God forsaken Country," as one Michigan veteran recalled.[21]

For the Ohioans, the sudden reversal in Indian relations did nothing to erase the memories of their sacrifices, the bloodshed, and their fallen comrades of the recent Indian war. In preparation for their return to the States, a detachment disinterred the remains of Lieutenant Collins at Platte Bridge Station, which had been renamed Fort Caspar in his honor the previous fall, and brought them to Fort Laramie for temporary burial until they could be transported to the family cemetery plot at Hillsboro.[22] The detachment returned on March 20, and tempers among the men simmered as they witnessed a Sioux dance that Colonel Maynadier permitted them to continue on the parade ground in front of Old Bedlam. "While they were dancing and going on with their powwowing, the body of Lieut. Collins arrived at the Post. They continued their dancing and noise as if in mockery while the remains were being conveyed to Head Quarters. The very same scamps had a war dance over his body once before, and no doubt they remembered it, when they saw the corpse yesterday and

---

[20]Unrau, *Tending the Talking Wire*, 324.

[21]Charles Eberstein to Jay Bliss, June 27, 1936, Wyoming State Archives.

[22]General John Pope ordered the post to be designated Fort Caspar in honor of Lieutenant Caspar W. Collins on November 21, 1865. Frazier, *Forts of the West*, 180.

knew who it was."[23] The garrison attended a funeral with full military honors for Caspar Collins the following morning, with all members of the Eleventh present. Chaplain Wright offered brief remarks and a prayer at the graveside, after which the escort fired the customary volleys and the crowd dispersed to resume their activities.[24]

[23]Unrau, *Tending the Talking Wire*, 325.

[24]This description is taken from the one given by Corporal Johnson, who witnessed the ceremony. It was conducted in strict accordance with the ceremony prescribed in the army tactics manual. Ibid.

CHAPTER FOURTEEN

"Poor Indian Finds Himself Hemmed In"

The Civil War years, coupled with lean congressional appropriations and a parade of indifferent volunteer commanders, had not been kind to Fort Laramie. Major William H. Evans, now the post commander, painted a dismal picture of the place following an inspection in May 1866:

> The Storehouses, quarters, and other buildings . . . are old and worn out. No repairs of consequence have been made for several years much improvement could be made in a new arrangement, and reconstruction of the post. . . . The storehouses are built of yellow pine lumber, very combustible and although sufficient to protect their contents against rain, utterly useless against the decay and destruction produced by the excessive cold of winter and the ardent heat of summer.[1]

Indeed, many of the buildings constructed in the early 1850s, and not very well at that, had suffered the effects of weather, abuse, and neglect. Tumbledown fences and accumulations of trash and cast-off junk about the grounds contributed to the post's forlorn appearance.

Evans was particularly concerned about the water supply. He considered the current method of supplying the fort with water inadequate as well as expensive and time consuming. That essential service alone required the full-time labor of ten to fifteen men using a six-mule team to deliver water-filled barrels from the Laramie River to all

---

[1]Major W. H. Evans to Major Roger Jones, Assistant Inspector General, Division of the Mississippi, May 21, 1866, LS, FL. Additional information relating to the condition of the post is found in PR, June 1866, FL (hereinafter cited as "Inspection Reports" with date).

of the inhabited buildings on the post. He was particularly distressed that the available water would be of little use in combating a structural fire. Wells, he noted, did not answer the need for potable water, because sandy soil at the depth of the water table made for a decidedly gritty drink. He suggested that river water might be diverted above the post and brought down to the garrison via a canal, but the army was reluctant to adopt this relatively simple concept.[2]

By the end of the Civil War, Fort Laramie was more than ever a hub of western transportation routes. "The main road of travel up the North Platte and thence via Salt Lake City and Lander's Cut-off to California and the Northern mines passes the post," Evans noted. "Another road from the South comes from Denver following the valley of the Laramie River. There is every probability that a new road to Montana will be opened this year, which will give increased importance to this Post."[3] That new road to Virginia City, the Bozeman Trail, was destined to become the focal point of events on the northern Plains for the next few years.

Also unleashed by war's end was the effort to construct a transcontinental railroad. After considerable debate in Congress, not dissimilar the controversy surrounding the mail routes to California during the previous decade, a decision was made to use the central route across the Rocky Mountains and the Sierra Nevada. By May 1866, track had already been laid eighty miles west of Omaha. General William T. Sherman, commanding the Division of the Missouri, predicted that the completed railroad would largely overcome the persistent difficulty the army experienced supplying its western military posts. No longer would the Quartermaster Department have to rely

[2]John Hunton, the last post trader who subsequently lived at the fort for many years, formed the Fort Laramie Ditch Company to bring irrigation water to fields at the old post. This topic is discussed in a later chapter. Author's note.

[3]"Inspection Reports," May 21, 1866. Although the development of travel routes across the western U.S. is traditionally viewed in East-West terms, the opening of the Bozeman Trail completed a continuous wagon road all the way from El Paso, Texas, to the Pacific Northwest, via western Montana. The ancient Camino Real from Mexico City to Santa Fe had been in use by Americans as a freight and mail route since about 1850, and the early Taos Trail, used by trappers to travel to the Upper Missouri, developed into a thoroughfare to Denver and Fort Laramie. The North-South route thus intersected the Santa Fe, Smoky Hill, and Overland Trails leading from the East. Author's note.

upon slow-moving wagon trains that were subject to the dictates of weather and were often managed by unreliable, if not unscrupulous, contractors. When Sherman inspected the proposed line of the railroad that spring, he observed, "At the north side of the Platte I found no trains of heavily loaded wagons, but a good many emigrants. The great bulk of travel this season evidently leaves the Missouri river at Atchison and Nebraska City, and follows the old military road by the south side of the Platte."[4] Emigrant parties from Julesburg continued to follow the so-called Fort Laramie Route by way of Scott's Bluff because of the reliable and usually abundant supply of water and forage along the way. As much could not be said for the Overland Mail Route, but because the stage company did not require such large quantities of either, it could contract for forage as necessary. In any event, the railroad was destined to replace them both, though a decision had not yet been made as to which route it would follow westward beyond the forks of the Platte.

In the spring of 1866, with the welcome mat extended at Fort Laramie, the Sioux flooded back to the Platte in droves to meet with the new peace commission. By mid-May, Evans was astounded to see thousands of Indians camped in the vicinity of the post. There had been nothing like it since the great gathering in 1851. Although the Indians seemed to be peaceably disposed, both Evans and Maynadier were alert to potential trouble. It came on the night of May 28, when the sentry at the magazine fired a shot just after taps. The entire garrison immediately tumbled out of their bunks and fell in, partially clad but armed. Soon, one of the soldiers recalled,

> the rattle and flash of rifle and pistol became generally promiscuous, mixed up with shouts of "halt! they're Indians! Shoot the red skins!" We could see them making for the breastworks on the east side of the Fort and as they would near the "beat" of a sentinel, we could hear him open on them with his repeater. It sounded like a regular skirmish. The Indians ran into a lodge a short distance from the fort and the firing ceased. They were followed into the lodge by the Provost Guard and brought out, they brought them up on the parade, and sent for the interpreter. There were four or five of them, one was killed in the skirmish and two wounded.[5]

---

[4]House, "Protection Across the Continent," 39th Cong., 2nd Sess., H. Doc. 23, 2.
[5]Unrau, *Tending the Talking Wire,* 339.

As it turned out, a few Indians, who had been visiting relatives camped along the Laramie River above the fort, had taken the direct route through the post as they returned to their own camp. The Indians, unaware that they were prohibited from crossing through the garrison after dark, became frightened when challenged by the sentry, and bolted, prompting the guards to open fire.

Maynadier, who had served in the West with the Tenth Infantry prior to the Civil War and had gained an understanding of Indians, attempted to diffuse the situation by sending for his friend Spotted Tail, who soon arrived with a number of warriors in full battle array. The colonel explained to the chief that the sentries were obliged to challenge anyone walking about after dark, and to fire if the person failed to heed the sentry's order. The Indians demanded that the guilty soldier be turned over to them for punishment. Maynadier, following an Indian custom, instead offered them substitute restitution in the form of two horses, ten head of cattle, and a quantity of rations. Spotted Tail, already in a conciliatory mood, accepted the Colonel's apology and the matter dropped. Maynadier's adroit handling of the situation prevented what could have turned into a general melee and any hope for a peace treaty would have gone up in smoke.[6]

It was in this tense atmosphere that the first regulars, a company of the Second Cavalry, returned to garrison Fort Laramie after an absence of more than three years. Following General Lee's surrender, the regiment had been recruited to full strength and sent to the frontier to protect the anticipated heavy migration over the Virginia City road. Following close behind this vanguard were B, E, and G Companies of the First Battalion, Eighteenth U.S. Infantry, veterans of numerous actions, including the Battles of Nashville, Chickamauga, Chattanooga, as well as Sherman's notorious "March to the Sea." Like the Second Cavalry, the Eighteenth was being consolidated along the

---

[6]*Montana Post*, July 7, 1866; article by former Eighteenth Infantryman William Wilson, "Army Life in the Rockies," *National Tribune*, June 22, 1899. Henry E. Maynadier graduated from West Point and accepted a lieutenancy in the First Artillery in 1851. He was promoted to first lieutenant in the Tenth Infantry in 1855 and served as regimental adjutant for the next three years. During late summer 1857, Maynadier marched through Fort Laramie as a participant in the Utah Expedition. He was promoted to captain during the Civil War. Heitman, I, 699; Rodenbough, 535–36.

emigrant routes to Utah and Montana. The regulars made an impressive showing as they paraded smartly into Fort Laramie on the first day of June, though the solemn ex-Rebels, now of the U.S. Volunteers, probably eyed them with some resentment.

The commissioners, escorted to the post by the regulars, arrived just two days after the shooting incident. The most prominent member was E. B. Taylor, ambitious editor of the Omaha *Republican* as well as Indian commissioner for Nebraska. Taylor, ever the optimist, possessed an oversimplified view that it would be an easy matter to negotiate a treaty to end the costly Indian-white war of the previous three years, thereby opening the Powder River country to white travelers on the Bozeman Trail. Taylor was accompanied by R. N. McLaren of Minnesota and Thomas Wistar from Pennsylvania, both presidential appointees. Charles E. Bowles, an employee of the Indian Bureau, would serve as recorder, with Frank Lehmer, an Omaha resident, assisting him. Maynadier, now commanding the new District of the Platte, headed the commission.[7] The talks would be interpreted by Charles E. Gereau, longtime Fort Laramie resident and confidant of the Sioux, along with Leon Pallardie, a Frenchman who had formerly worked as an agent for Pierre Bissonette and later worked as Sioux interpreter for Colonel Collins.[8]

----

[7]In the army's transition to a peacetime footing, the Department of the Platte was reconstituted and attached to the Military Division of the Mississippi, effective March 26, 1866. The department initially embraced the states of Minnesota and Iowa, Montana Territory, part of Nebrasaka, and that portion of Dakota Territory lying north of the Platte and Sweetwater Rivers, excluding Fort Caspar. Thian, *Military Geography*, 88.

[8]Although the phonetic spelling "Pillday," rather than "Pallardie," was used by the *Montana Post* correspondent, I consider M. Simonin, a French mining engineer, to be a more reliable source for the name. When Simonin met Leon Pallardie at Fort Laramie in 1867, and wrote his report, in it he related that both Pallardie and James Beauvais had been employed by Joseph Bissonette during the fur trade days. Simonin, "Fort Russell and the Fort Laramie Peace Commission in 1867," 7. Lieutenant Ware also became acquainted with "Palladie," and used that spelling, while stationed at the post in 1864. He described Palladie as having blue eyes, curly hair, and "the happiest disposition of any frontiersman." Ware, *Indian War of 1864*, 202. As previously cited, Charles Gereau also worked as a clerk in the store at the American Fur Company post. Later, the government often employed him as "post interpreter" at Fort Laramie. These men knew each other well and formed an important societal element at Fort Laramie. All of French descent, they had drifted to the Platte Valley during the 1830s and 1840s, and were still living in the area in the late 1860s. It can be safely assumed that all of them had Indian wives. Both the army and the Indian Bureau relied heavily on these individuals as a ready source of interpreters and intermediaries with the Indians at Fort Laramie.

The two-day Fort Laramie council convened on the morning of June 6, with hundreds of Indians present at the fort, while several thousand others remained in camp about twenty miles south where the grazing was better for the large herds of ponies. At one side of the parade, Colonel Maynadier had prepared an arbor of evergreen boughs to shade a large circle of pine board benches. All the principal men were in attendance, headed by Red Cloud, Man Afraid of His Horses, Red Leaf, Spotted Tail, and Standing Elk. Small numbers of Cheyennes and Northern Arapahoes also were present, though without their influential leaders. Following the traditional smoking of a peace pipe, the Indians spoke first, reiterating their desire for new, more trustworthy agents and the delivery of the goods that had been promised by the government.

The Indians also demanded that whites be prohibited from trespassing across lands east of the Big Horns, an area formerly controlled by the Crows, which the Sioux now considered as their own by right of conquest. It was a delicate and volatile issue that Maynadier had carefully, and intentionally, circumvented in previous conversations. More to the point, the chiefs demanded adequate compensation if they were to drop their opposition to the Bozeman Trail.

During the two days of talks, the commissioners continued to evade the subject because they knew full well that the new road was about to be opened officially and occupied by army regulars. The entire Second Battalion, Eighteenth Infantry, under the command of Colonel Henry B. Carrington, was even then en route from Fort Kearny, where it had spent the past winter.[9] Even though the two parties failed to reach a consensus on the issue, the talks nevertheless were amicable. The council concluded after the chiefs announced that they were going to defer signing a treaty until a few other bands were assembled and their views also represented at the council. Their real reason prob-

---

[9]"Report of the commissioners appointed by the President of the United States to treat with the Indians at Fort Laramie," ibid., 209. Patrick relieved Jarrot on September 18, 1866. M. T. Patrick to Taylor, September 20, 1866, ibid. As an interim measure, the army agreed to store any Indian goods that had not been distributed by the end of June. This suggests that Jarrot may have resigned his position during the conference, otherwise the goods would have been placed at the agency five miles down the North Platte. Moreover, storing them at the fort better protected the supplies from being pilfered. Major James Van Voast to Taylor, June 26, 1866, LS, FL.

ably was Carrington's approach, which caused the Oglalas to reconsider making any commitments at that time. Whatever the reasons, Maynadier and Taylor were left no choice but to adjourn the talks for two weeks, while delegates from the tribes went to inform the scattered small bands that their involvement was encouraged.

Carrington's arrival in camp on the floodplain below the post on June 13 could not have been worse timing. It was obvious to Red Cloud's Sioux that so large a force of troops did not bode well for their interests. Word spread quickly through the camps that these soldiers were going to build forts along the Bozeman Trail. There are several versions of Red Cloud's reaction to this development, none of which is considered reliable, but his anger cannot be understated. William Rowland, who lived among the Indians and served as an interpreter at the fort from time to time, was sent to invite the Cheyennes to the council, yet when he attempted to reach the village some miles beyond the Platte, even he met with fierce resentment. Oglala warriors intercepted him, knocked him from his horse, severely beat him, and sent him limping back to the fort. "That is the feeling of the Indians when whites want to go through their country at present," wrote a correspondent to the Salt Lake City newspaper.[10]

A brooding Red Cloud now refused to resume negotiations.[11] On June 28, Spotted Tail and the other Southern Brulé chiefs, who had never claimed any interest in the Powder River country, readily signed the new agreement, allowing the whites a right-of-way through the Powder River hunting grounds. In return, the Indian Bureau would issue supplies at Fort Laramie every six months, rather than annually.

---

[10]As a part of the Regular Army's reoccupation of the plains, the First Battalion, Eighteenth Infantry, was sent initially to posts in Kansas and Colorado in late 1865. Some of those companies were later moved to the Mountain District in present-day Wyoming. The headquarters staff and the Second Battalion were stationed at Fort Kearny for the winter, while the Third Battalion was still being organized at Jefferson Barracks, Missouri. It, too, marched up the Oregon Road to Fort Kearny in early spring. Colonel Carrington was given command of the new Mountain District, Department of the Platte, in May 1866. Rodenbough, *Army of the United States*, 652–53.

[11]*Daily Union Vedette* [Salt Lake City], June 29, 1866, quoting a story filed under a dateline of June 14; this incident is corroborated in Carrington, *Absaraka*, 80. The basic narrative of the book is that of his first wife, Margaret. After her death, Carrington married Frances Grummond, whose previous husband, Lieutenant George W. Grummond, had been killed in the Fetterman fight, December 21, 1866.

Taylor received assurances from some of the Cheyennes and Arapahoes that their leaders would sign the treaty as well, yet all understood that the pact was worthless without Red Cloud's endorsement.

Alluding to Sioux complaints about dishonest agents, Taylor suggested their salaries be increased, so that they would not be "compelled to resort to some other means of making a living." Indeed, within a few months, M. T. Patrick would replace Jarrot at the Upper Platte Agency.[12]

Upon his arrival Colonel Carrington assigned Major James Van Voast to assume command of Fort Laramie, signaling an end to the Eleventh Ohio's long exile on the frontier. The Ohio troopers immediately vacated their dilapidated quarters and moved to the old bivouac ground a mile downstream. They would spend another day there preparing for the homeward march. Carrington and some of his officers, meanwhile, took up temporary residence at the post. The wife of an Eighteenth Infantry officer expressed her initial reaction to the post, recalled, "With all deference to its historic character, Fort Laramie, in my observation and experience, did not impress me as particularly interesting . . . at that season its glory had departed. The parade ground was bare of sod, but in its center 'the flag was still there.' The adobe houses of gray appearance imparted their somber hue to the whole surrounding. The scenery, however, beautiful or otherwise, affected me but little, except in general depression, so great was my concern to escape the ambulance and plant my feet on any kind of earth whatever."[13]

After the arduous journey up the Platte Road, however, the new arrivals appreciated even the simple amenities afforded by a frontier post. Mrs. Margaret Carrington, wife of the colonel, described the scene that greeted her in the Sutler's Store:

---

[12]The stories about Red Cloud's reaction are examined in Olson, *Red Cloud*, 35–37. Olson points out that Taylor and Maynadier were well aware of the approach of Carrington's command and apparently were not concerned about the effect it might have on the negotiations. This suggests that they were confident that the chiefs, including Red Cloud, were willing to sign the treaty, so long as the Sioux were compensated for use of the Bozeman Trail. That Red Cloud may not have even been present at Fort Laramie at the time is suggested in Taylor's statement that "A band numbering perhaps three hundred warriors, headed by Red Cloud, a prominent chief of the Ogalallahs, refused to come in." He made it clear that this was still their status two weeks after the June 6 council. E. B. Taylor to Cooley, October 1, 1866, *ARSI*, 1866, 211.

[13]Carrington, *My Army Life*, 53.

The long counter of Messrs. Bullock and Ward was a scene of seeming confusion not surpassed in any popular, overcrowded store of Omaha itself. Indians, dressed and half dressed and undressed; squaws, dressed to the same degree of completeness as their noble lords; papooses, absolutely nude, slightly not nude, or wrapped in calico, buckskin, or furs, mingled with soldiers of the garrison, teamsters, emigrants, speculators, half-breeds, and interpreters. Here, cups of rice sugar, coffee, or flour were being emptied into the looped-up skirts or blanket of a squaw; and there, some tall warrior was grimacing delightfully as he grasped and sucked his long sticks of peppermint candy. Bright shawls, red squaw cloth, brilliant calicoes, and flashing ribbons passed over the same counter with knives and tobacco, brass nails and glass beads, and that endless catalogue of articles which belong to the legitimate border traffic. The room was redolent of cheese and herring, and 'heap of smoke;' while the debris of mounched crackers lying loose under foot furnished both nutriment and employment for little bits of Indians too big to ride on mamma's back, and too little to reach the good things on counter or shelves.[14]

The Second Battalion did not tarry long at Fort Laramie. Carrington broke camp within a few days to continue his march up the Bozeman Trail. Resuming the tedious journey, Mrs. Carrington lamented, "We surrendered our 'dobey' house, our hospital cots, our sombre blankets, even our tin mirror . . . and with packed mess-chest boarded the everlasting ambulance." Detaching part of his force to garrison Fort Reno, Carrington proceeded northward into the Sioux and Cheyenne stronghold. In mid-July he would establish Fort Phil Kearny on Piney Creek at the eastern base of the Big Horn Mountains, and a month later his men would begin construction of yet a third post, Fort C. F. Smith, on the Big Horn River in Montana Territory.

Red Cloud's Bad Faces and their Cheyenne and Arapahoe allies rejoined the other Sioux bands on Powder River to prepare for the coming invasion. Spotted Tail, hoping to avoid trouble, moved off with his Brulés toward their favorite hunting ground along the Republican River. Big Mouth and the Laramie Sioux, now almost totally reliant on the government, went only as far as the agency at Horse Creek. That small band of Oglalas and Brulés remained near the fort throughout the summer, living on government rations and

---

[14]Carrington, *Absaraka*, 76–77.

getting drunk on the white man's firewater. As garrison life returned to normal, "There were plenty of Indians of the friendly sort visible at any hour of the day, but there was a feeling of perfect security at Fort Laramie itself," wrote an officer's wife.[15]

There was, however, a more tragic side of troop life that she failed to mention. Major Van Voast noted that a "Squaw Camp" had formed near the Platte ferry. It contained, he estimated, about 180 people—mostly women and children—"the deserted [Indian] wives of white men who with the Volunteers have left the Country—and have abandoned their children to the mercy of such charity as might be bestowed."[16] He was saddened to see that the women were reduced to eking out a living by selling moccasins and doing odd jobs around the fort. Even their own tribes exhibited little concern for their welfare. No doubt many continued to resort to prostitution for survival because, as one longtime resident recalled, "The having of Indian women for mistresses and propagating half breeds was such a common thing by nearly all the men of the country at that time that no person thought of taxing his memory with such a thing."[17] Somber evidence of the price paid by the Sioux who attached themselves to the fort was seen in the so-called Papoose Tree, standing just across the Laramie River from the fort. It bore "no less than forty bodies of Indian children wrapped in skins and robes, and lashed to the limbs of the tree with buffalo thongs, at that time the mode of Indian burial."[18]

Within a month after the council broke up, Van Voast observed an increasing number of inebriated Indians coming to the post. He suspected they were trading for liquor at one or more of the "whiskey

[15]Carrington, *My Army Life*, 54.

[16]Van Voast to Major H. G. Litchfield, October 9, 1866, LS, FL.

[17]John Hunton to Mrs. C. F. Byrd, September 24, 1910, Book 21, Box 12, Hunton Papers, University of Wyoming. Hunton knew of what he spoke because he himself had an Indian "wife" for a few years during the early 1870s.

[18]John S. Collins, post trader at Fort Laramie in the 1870s, described the location of the Papoose Tree as on the Laramie River, above the bridge leading into the post. It was "a big box elder that stood three hundred yards from and opposite the quarters called "Dobie Row," its branches covering a space of at least seventy-five feet in diameter." Dobie Row refers to the adobe barracks built in 1866 on the southeast side of the parade ground, evidenced today only by its foundation. Collins, *Across the Plains in '64*, 39. The tree may have been cut down when a cavalry barracks (used as laundress quarters) was erected on that side of the river in the late 1870s. The fate of the human remains is unknown. Author's note.

ranches" that were becoming more numerous up and down the valley. Two of these longtime establishments were Jim Beauvais's place five miles down the Platte, and Bordeaux's post three miles beyond. Joe Bissonette, now old, down on his luck, and nearly destitute, still maintained a farm on the Laramie River above the mouth of Deer Creek, and no doubt still kept whiskey for sale. More recently, Jules Ecoffey had established a saloon and gambling den on the Platte near Beauvais's house. Six miles up the Laramie, near one of the frequently occupied army campgrounds, was another new but disreputable saloon owned by John Hunter.[19] Yet another, known as Nine Mile Ranch, lay northwest of the fort on the Platte. Louis Richard also ranched in the Laramie Valley several miles above the post, and may have been a source of liquor for the Indians.

Faced with the impossible task of trying to single out guilty parties, Van Voast requested permission to simply prohibit the sale of liquor anywhere within fifteen miles of Fort Laramie. Brigadier General Philip St. George Cooke, commanding the Department of the Platte, readily approved his suggestion. On July 27, Van Voast promulgated an order giving area settlers ten days to cease their activities, or be subject to arrest. At the same time, he expelled all the Indians from the military reservation.[20]

Red Cloud and his followers lost no time in displaying their contempt for the army. On August 1, a war party of fifteen to twenty men appeared at the Government Farm, where a large post vegetable garden was maintained, about fifteen miles north of the fort. At dawn, a

---

[19]The Six Mile Ranch was established at a point where the road to Cheyenne diverged from the Laramie River. It was at or near "Camp on Laramie River," a bivouac first used by the dragoons in 1851. Camp Maclin, as it was dubbed at that time, was described by a soldier as "Fit for the gods—one of the most lovely spots I have ever seen." Percival G. Lowe, *Five Years a Dragoon*, 46. Stansbury's surveying expedition probably camped there as well the next year. *Exploration and Survey of the Valley of the Great Salt Lake of Utah*, 52. This bottomland location was used at various times by the volunteers during the Civil War and was the scene of the mutiny by the Sixteenth Kansas Cavalry on the eve of the Powder River Campaign. Cyrus C. Scofield to Mary E. Scofield, June 25, 1865, typescript copy in vertical files, FLNHS. The place is also referenced in PR for October 1858, June, July, and August 1873, FL. The placement of the ranch was probably influenced by the presence of troops from time to time and the business opportunities they brought with them.

[20]Van Voast to AAAG, Dept. of the Platte, July 25, 1866, LS, FL; GO No. 18, July 27, 1866, Orders, FL; GO No. 9, Dept. of the Platte, July 24, 1866, ibid.

short distance from the house there, the warriors scooped up five mules before the five-man detail awoke and recovered from their surprise. The soldiers fired a few shots at the fleeing tribesmen, and then gave chase, but recovered only one animal.

Later that morning, the warriors struck again—this time on the horse herd belonging to their erstwhile friend, Antoine Janis, who was then operating the ferry over the Platte. This was an unusual act, considering that Janis was married to a Sioux and had traded among them for many years. Perhaps because the horses were grazing three or four miles beyond the river, the Indians may have thought they belonged to emigrants. Nevertheless, they made off with twenty-five head. Several friendly Sioux, probably Janis's own relatives, later caught up with the raiders and persuaded them to give up some of the horses. Troopers of the Second Cavalry followed the trail too, more to ascertain the general direction taken by the warriors than with any hope of catching them. However, five days later the raiding party returned, and made up for relinquishing Janis's horses by stealing livestock from Jules Ecoffey's ranch.[21]

In response to these incidents, Van Voast prudently increased security for the twice-weekly mail deliveries to Fort Sedgwick, Colorado. In lieu of the pack mules previously used, the new commander employed an ambulance wagon carrying, in addition to the driver, one or two infantrymen as guards, with two cavalrymen as outriders to defend against ambush. He also posted two troopers at Cold Spring Station, southeast of Laramie (near present Torrington, Wyoming), to serve as the mounted escort over the thirty miles between that point and Camp Mitchell, Nebraska. In this manner, the mail could be conveyed to the main line, 170 miles distant, in thirty-six hours. Detachments of twenty mounted men carried the mail west to Fort Caspar, connecting en route at Bridger's Ferry with couriers from Carrington's Mountain District, headquartered at Fort Phil Kearny.[22]

Coming up the trail behind Carrington were numerous wagon trains loaded with tons of supplies needed for the new forts. Some of

[21]PR, July 1866, FL; Van Voast to Captain Edward Ball, August 1, 1866, LS, FL; Van Voast to AAAG, Dept. of the Platte, August 8, 1866, ibid.

[22]PR, July 1866, Fort Laramie; Van Voast to Lieutenant S. W. Porter, August 2, 1866, LS, FL; Van Voast to Porter, August 4, 1866, ibid.

the trains, particularly those coming directly from Omaha, followed
the old Mormon Road on the north side of the Platte, while those
originating at Fort Leavenworth customarily traveled along the south
bank. With only two companies of cavalry at his disposal, and those
recently filled with new recruits having neither horses nor arms, Van
Voast was unable to provide the escorts that wagon masters began
requesting because of the recent Indian attacks upon them. He
claimed, in fact, that his supply of ammunition was so low the garrison itself would be unable to defend the post in the event of a con-
certed attack.[23] Van Voast therefore advised four trains from Omaha,
two hundred wagons in all, to cross the Platte at Fort Laramie and
join other government trains for mutual protection, assuring the contractors that they would be safe enough if they remained on the south
side of the river until they reached the fork of the Bozeman road at
Bridger's Ferry. From that point northward, he admitted, travel could
be hazardous. Reports had recently arrived that two dozen men, most
of them civilians, had been killed by Indians between Brown's Springs
and Tongue River. There was little more the army could do, except to
station a company of the Sixth Volunteer Infantry at the ferry to offer
whatever protection it could.[24]

If the Galvanized Yankees along the road harbored any resentment
against the regulars of the Eighteenth Infantry, they were undoubtedly
more perturbed to learn that the "devil himself," Lieutenant General
William Tecumseh Sherman, planned to visit Fort Laramie in August.
President Andrew Johnson had recently named Sherman commander
of the Military Division of the Missouri, an enormous area encompass-

---

[23]The volunteer officers in charge of Fort Laramie had apparently been lax in keeping the post
adequately supplied with arms and ammunition. Carrington later recalled that while he was
encamped at the post in June, he had requisitioned 100,000 rounds of musket ammunition for
his command, but was informed that less than 1,000 were on hand. The following month, Van
Voast officially verified that the fort's magazine contained only 1,100 rounds of .58-caliber cartridges. He laid the blame directly on Maynadier, who claimed that he was expecting to be
resupplied at any time, yet Van Voast was unable to find a copy of the requisition in the files.
Carrington, *Absaraka*, 75; Van Voast to AAAG, Dept. of the Missouri, July 18, 1866, LS, FL.

[24]Van Voast to Halse, Treadwell, Hall, and Wood (wagon masters), August 1, 1866, ibid.; Van Voast
to Lieutenant P. W. Harrington, [no date], ibid.; Van Voast to AAAG, Dept of the Platte, August
9, 1866, ibid. The Eighteenth Infantry suffered the first Indian combat death among its officers
when First Lieutenant Napoleon H. Daniels was killed on the Powder River on July 21, 1866. Post
Adjutant to Brevet Colonel G. B. Dandy, August 8, 1866, ibid.; Heitman, *Historical Register*, 1: 353.

ing the entire plains region north of Texas to Canada and from the
Mississippi River west beyond the Rocky Mountains. Sherman was
eager to inspect critical portions of his new domain. He traveled by
wagon with a ten-man escort from Fort Sedgwick, near Julesburg,
arriving on the Laramie on the morning of the twenty-ninth. His
report reflects his surprise at seeing Fort Laramie for the first time:

> Though originally built by the engineer corps, there is no sign of a block-
> house or defense, but a mixture of all sorts of houses of every conceivable
> pattern, and promiscuously scattered about, The two principal buildings of
> two stories [Bedlam and the 1850 barracks] originally constituting the post,
> are now so damaged and so rickety in the high wind that the soldiers of a
> windy night sleep on the parade. Low buildings of adobe, with good roofs
> and not too large, seem better adapted to the climate and circumstances;
> and the commanding officer, Major Van Voast and Quartermaster Dandy,
> are proceeding in all new structures on that hypothesis. Adobes, or sun-
> dried brick, are being made by contract, lime has been burned twelve miles
> off; a saw mill is erected fifty miles off [at Laramie Peak], and wood for
> the use of the post is cut by soldiers and hauled fifteen miles.[25]

On his way up the North Platte Valley, Sherman noted that the area
held great promise for agriculture. He foresaw a day when irrigation
would enable farmers to grow wheat, barley, and other crops in the
rich soil fringing the river but, he thought, "the government will have
to pay a bounty for people to live up here til necessity forces them."
He recognized that despite the extremes of weather and harsh living
conditions, as land grew increasingly scarce elsewhere in the West
homesteaders would eventually settle in the area, and that inevitabil-
ity did not bode well for the free-roaming life of the Indians. "Ever
since the California emigration this road has been traveled as common
as the old national road and the Indians kept clear of it," wrote Sherman. "Since then," he noted, "all the Sioux have been driven from
Minnesota and the Missouri river, and the mountain region of Montana, Colorado, and Utah is being settled up with gold miners and
rancheros, so that poor Indian finds himself hemmed in."[26]

---

[25]Lieutenant General W. T. Sherman to General John A. Rawlins, August 31, 1866, LS, Fort
    Laramie.
[26]Both quotations here are also in ibid.

Sherman concluded his two-day visit at the post by penning a letter to his old comrade-in-arms, Ulysses S. Grant, now General of the Army. In it, he told Grant that, true to his prediction, the transcontinental railroad had been completed to Fort Kearny, and if progress continued apace, the tracks would reach the forks of the Platte by the end of the 1866 construction season. No determination had yet been made as to whether it would follow the North Platte Valley, the South Fork, or even go directly west over Cheyenne Pass to Fort Bridger. That the northerly route was under serious consideration was revealed when a Union Pacific Railroad survey party examining the valley stopped at Fort Laramie later that month.

Sherman considered the telegraph system then in use as unnecessarily duplicative, as the main line to Utah went by way of Fort Laramie and South Pass, while a branch line paralleled the South Platte to Denver and then continued along the Overland Mail Road to Fort Bridger and Salt Lake, ending at the same destination. It seemed to him that a single route, following the railroad, would afford the opportunity to finally consolidate transcontinental transportation and communication. But regardless of the passage selected, Sherman was convinced that a fort on the rail line would be the only logical place from which to conduct future military operations against the Indians. While no one had yet challenged the importance of Fort Laramie in that regard, its fate nevertheless hung on Sherman's visionary comment.[27]

The general, with his entourage and baggage filling five ambulances, set off from Fort Laramie with a twenty-man cavalry escort on the first of September bound for Fort John Buford [later named Fort Sanders], near present Laramie, Wyoming, and Denver. Sherman's visit to the district had not only expedited the discharge of the U.S. Volunteers, thereby leaving Indian matters in the hands of his beloved regulars; his inspection of Fort Laramie gave impetus to the construction program that Van Voast had started shortly before Sherman's arrival. The men were already laying up the ground floor walls of a new stone guardhouse near the river and the major proposed to erect four new barracks, three additional sets of officers' quarters, two cav-

---

[27]Sherman to Grant, August 31, 1866, ibid.

alry stables, and two more storehouses. Van Voast also had Quarter-master George B. Dandy assign men to whitewash and repair the old barracks as a stopgap measure until new quarters could be built. Eigh-teenth Infantryman William E. Kenney, remembering barracks they had built but never occupied in Kansas, wrote that the men went to work on the new buildings at Fort Laramie "thinking it would be our turn in the quarters next winter."[28] In coming months the ramshackle two-story dragoon barracks was razed, before it collapsed of its own accord, and replaced by a 286-foot-long frame building housing three companies. Another two-company barracks, constructed of adobe, was erected on the southeast side of the parade ground.

Captain Dandy, echoing Major Evans, recommended that a water system be constructed that would divert water from the Laramie about one and three-quarters of a mile south and transport it either by pipeline or ditch to reservoirs that would be built on the terrace near the ceme-tery. Dandy prevailed on the visiting railroad engineers to accurately determine the elevations and the point where a diversion dam might be constructed. He emphasized to Quartermaster General Montgomery C. Meigs that fire posed a serious danger to the fort, especially during winter, since the river and the water barrels always froze at that season. Yet the always conservative Meigs would not approve the expenditure.[29]

The recent Indian depredations and concern that more troops should be put on guard caused Van Voast to reconsider the large number of men detailed to the extensive construction activities underway on the post. Dandy, however, convincingly countered that reducing the num-ber of laborers would retard completion of the new buildings, perhaps beyond the onset of winter. More important, the quartermaster had designed two of the structures to augment the post's defenses. The stone guardhouse, well underway by that time, would provide a stronghold near the river on the southeast perimeter, while a quarter-mile down-stream an adobe quartermaster's corral also was rapidly taking shape.

---

[28]Post Adjutant to First Lieutenant Thomas S. Brent, August 8, 1866, ibid.; Van Voast to AAAG, Dept. of the Platte, September 1, 1866, ibid.; Kenney, *National Tribune*, November 4, 1909.

[29]Dandy to Meigs, August 30, 1866, CCF. Regarding the water supply in 1866, Frances Grummond Carrington wrote, "The water used at Laramie was at that time hauled from the river for all pur-poses and was abundant and clear, and yet there was consciousness that you were limited in its use, perhaps on account of the process of conveyance." Carrington, *Army Life*, 56.

Often mistaken by later army residents as old Fort John, the corral had walls two feet thick and ten feet high, surrounding an area approximately 160 by 200 feet. Around the inside perimeter of the corral yard were shed-roof stables to shelter the mules. At opposing diagonal corners, northeast and southwest, stood hexagonal block-houses with firing embrasures in the walls, but under normal circumstances, the corner bastions served as kitchens for civilian teamsters.

The wisdom of Dandy's reasoning convinced Van Voast to suspend all military duties, except guard, and to assign every available man to expediting the construction. Despite these additions, Van Voast recognized that the fort's rambling layout still posed a security problem in view of his limited forces. He wrote on October 6: "This Post is very large and covers ten times to[o] much ground—but it will be in a better state for defence soon than it ever has been."[30]

The major was keenly aware that many of his men were raw recruits, enlisted to replenish the wartime losses incurred by the Second Cavalry and the Eighteenth Infantry. These greenhorns had received only the most rudimentary training at the depots before being sent to the frontier. The major consequently "managed to drill all the men as skirmishers and at target practice, many of the recruits recently received being totally ignorant of the use of the musket."[31] In fact, the post was so destitute of arms that Van Voast was compelled to issue infantry rifle muskets to many of the cavalry troopers until they could be resupplied with first-class carbines. Inexperienced troopers, armed with single-shot muzzle-loaders, hardly made for an effective fighting force, but there was no alternative.

---

[30]Post Adjutant to Captain George B. Dandy, September 13, 1866, LS, FL. Captain John Bourke, who came to Fort Laramie with General Crook in 1877, mistook the corral for "the old sod redoubt that constituted Fort Laramie when it was the post of the American Fur Co., 35 years ago." He did, however, provide a useful description of the structure. He noted that the "lunettes" were "pierced for small field pieces." Robinson, *Bourke Diaries* 2: 247. In 1868, the post surgeon wrote: "It has strong bastions at two diagonal corners and would serve as a stronghold in case of an attack by Indians." Medical History, Fort Laramie (hereinafter MH, FL).

[31]The Eighteenth Infantry, for example, suffered the loss of 39 officers and 929 enlisted men killed, wounded, and captured. So serious were its losses, and regular army recruitment so slow during the conflict, that the First and Third Battalions were temporarily dissolved in 1864 and not reconstituted until late the following year when the regiment was ordered to the plains. Rodenbough, *Army of the United States*, 652; Van Voast to AAAG, Dept. of the Platte, September 1, 1866, LS, FL.

In addition to routine mounted patrols, he also ordered out a company of infantry on a forty-mile reconnaissance to Rawhide Creek, passing through the Government Farm. Although he thought it might be possible for the detachment to come in contact with small war parties ranging in that area, he urged the lieutenant in command to take advantage of the opportunity to condition his men to rapid cross-country marching and to coach them in firing drills along the way. Van Voast expressed his concern about the seriousness of the situation by advising Commissioner Taylor that indications pointed to an all-out war with the Sioux and Cheyennes before winter.[32]

Trouble struck nearby on the evening of September 30, 1866, when a ten-man war party rode through a civilian camp only six miles south on the Laramie. The sole occupant, a man named Lee, was under contract by the telegraph company to cut and prepare replacement poles for the line. The Indians fired a few shots into the camp itself, wounding Lee's friendly Sioux helper, and escaped with twenty-two mules and horses. First Lieutenant William S. Starring, commanding a detachment of scouts recruited from the Laramie Sioux band, and accompanied by Lieutenant Horatio S. Bingham, the post guide, determined the probable route of the raiders and managed to intercept and surprise them in camp. In a brief skirmish, the scouts killed one hostile and successfully recovered all the stock. It was an important lesson that pointed up the value of using Indian auxiliaries.[33]

The Sioux scouts also informed the post commander that the incident was a harbinger of things to come because the hostile bands were finding less stock to steal along the Montana road and were even then returning to their old haunts along the Platte. The scouts also reported seeing two parties, most likely Cheyennes, within five miles of the fort. As a precautionary measure, Van Voast dispatched mounted patrols to occupy certain vantage points to scan the countryside just as dawn broke when the enemy might be moving, but all appeared quiet.

[32]Van Voast to Mr. Lithgow, Telegraph Office, Fort Laramie, September 13, 1866, LS, FL; Van Voast to AAAG, Dept. of the Platte, September 4, 1866, ibid.; Van Voast to AAAG, Dept of the Platte, September 26, 1866, ibid.

[33]The commanding officer requested permission to recruit spies or scouts from among the friendly Sioux in late July. Some of these men were undoubtedly the same ones who had served the army prior to the outbreak the previous year. Van Voast to AAAG, Dept. of the Platte, July 30, 1866, ibid.

The scouts' warnings to Major Van Voast were borne out on the night of October 3 when Indians approached the picket guard at Bridger's Ferry. Sergeant C. H. Gunther, in charge of the station, challenged the intruders, who ignored his warnings. His men opened fire, but the hostiles "seemed not to care." After withdrawing temporarily, they soon returned displaying the same disregard. This time Gunther fired a round of canister from the mountain howitzer emplaced at the ferry. A sheet of flame pierced the darkness as the balls of the shotgun-like charge whizzed across the prairie. When the smoke cleared, not an Indian was to be seen, dead or alive. Gunther later suggested that his stock of canister rounds, quite effective at close range, but useless beyond a few hundred yards, be supplemented with some shells. Van Voast commended the plucky sergeant for his gallant conduct, and rewarded him with a quantity of explosive case shot.[34]

Also, in early October, about a hundred lodges of Cheyennes—those who had earlier promised to sign the treaty—arrived on the North Platte to do so and went into camp near Bordeaux's place. Chiefs Bull Knife, White Clay, Red Arm, and Turkey Leg, along with a retinue of warrior leaders, went up to the fort a short time later and in a three-hour meeting "conducted with dignity and formality," signed the treaty document. Van Voast then gave them provisions and other presents before they left the post riding south toward the Republican River, ostensibly to hunt buffalo.[35]

Despite the conciliatory mood of that band, conditions in the area worsened with each passing day. Van Voast learned there were an estimated two hundred to four hundred hostiles then operating on the road between Forts Laramie and Caspar, and their presence increasing rapidly to the south along the road to Fort Sedgwick. Mail parties traveling that section of the route now more frequently encountered war parties that forced them to seek the protection of the nearest station. "Mud Springs is a dangerous place—always has been," Van Voast informed department headquarters. He recommended posting twelve-man detachments at each of the seven relay stations on the

---

[34]Sergeant C. H. Gunther, Company C, Second Cavalry, to Van Voast, October 3, 1866, ibid.; First Lieutenant William S. Starring to Gunther, October 9, 1866, ibid.

[35]Van Voast to AAAG, Dept. of the Platte, October 12, 1866, ibid. These Cheyennes turned hostile the next spring. *ARCIA*, 1868, 289.

road to Sedgwick to bolster security. The noncoms in charge there were instructed to keep one man on lookout at all times. Noting that Indian spies also had been seen within just two miles of Fort Laramie, the major added, "This post is constantly watched—the hostile Indians all considering it the great source of all their trouble." Word had reached him that the hostile Indians looked upon the Sioux living near the fort as traitors, and that they would rather kill "soldier scouts" than regular troops, though they would delight in giving the soldiers a fight as well. Given the opportunity to attack the Laramie Sioux, the hostile Sioux swore they would not spare even the women. Van Voast gave enough credence to the threat to move the peaceful Indians from the plain north of the ferry up to the fort itself. Well aware of the temptation a feminine presence would present in such close proximity to his men, however, the major prohibited any whites from visiting the village without permission, and posted guards to enforce his order. He also took advantage of the opportunity to require the Indian children to attend school on the post.[36]

True to scouting reports, raiding became common and widespread all along the line during October as Sioux and Cheyenne war parties increasingly made incursions into the area along and beyond the North Platte. On the ninth, raiders stole mules from Nine Mile Ranch, just south of Fort Laramie, and appeared in large numbers in the vicinity of Horseshoe Station on the North Platte River. Only the timely arrival of the mail escort prevented the station from being sacked. During the following week, Indians surprised the herders at the government sawmill at Laramie Peak and got away with several animals. After Indians burned a haystack within half a mile of the post, Van Voast was spurred to take even further precautions by sending out special patrols along both sides of the North Platte to protect Fort Laramie's hay fields in the valley near Camp Mitchell. He urged Dandy to get the hay cut and delivered to the post as quickly as possible, lest the Indians destroy their supply of winter forage. He further

---

[36]Van Voast to AAAG, Dept. of the Platte, October 6, 1866, LS, FL. Several sources refer to the Laramie Sioux camp being situated along the north bank of the North Platte, near the ferry, i.e., the extant historic iron bridge. For example, an emigrant passing by in 1864 recorded: "Arrived at the Ferry. On the banks near the Ferry is situated a Sioux Indian village." "Joseph Warren Arnold's Journal of His Trip to and from Montana," 480.

instructed his quartermaster to ensure that all men accompanying the vital lumber wagons were well armed and to recall an isolated group at work on a limekiln before the Indians preyed on other easy victims.[37]

By the latter part of October 1866, Indian raiders had extended their strikes all the way to the South Platte, destroying several miles of telegraph lines between Forts Laramie and Sedgwick, then sweeping off a few hundred head of animals from the latter post. A cavalry detachment caught up with them north of the Platte the next night and killed or wounded nearly all the unwary tribesmen. Van Voast advised General Cooke that the hostiles were driving most of the stock they had stolen in the area to a point near the Black Hills, and requested permission to organize a small expedition to recover the animals. Cooke approved the proposal and on November 3 Van Voast ordered Captain John Green—having just arrived at the fort with the headquarters, band, and two additional companies of the Second Cavalry—to try to locate the Indian rendezvous. Green returned emptyhanded almost two weeks later; nevertheless he and his men had gained some familiarity with the territory that would benefit future operations.[38]

As winter approached, the free-roaming bands, except for small raiding parties, withdrew to the villages in the north. It came as no surprise to Van Voast when two emissaries from Red Leaf's Brulés arrived at Fort Laramie asking if the band could come in. It was the usual threadbare ploy: fight in summer, repent in fall—and draw government rations all winter. Aware that Red Leaf was allied with Red Cloud, Van Voast told the chief he could do as he chose, but he in fact said he preferred that Red Cloud and the others "stay and fight this winter—that I wanted him to fight till he was satisfied . . . that the Soldiers had given them all summer to make peace but they had no ears—that soon the Soldiers would give them ears."[39]

---

[37]L. F. Harwood, Horseshoe Station, to Van Voast, October 9, 1866, LR, FL; Van Voast to AAAG, Dept of the Platte, October 10, 1866, LS, FL; Post Adjutant to Dandy, October 8, 1866, ibid.; Starring to Captain Edward Ball, November 3, 1866, ibid.

[38]Lieutenant George A. Armes, commander of the detachment from Fort Sedgwick, was later cited in GO No. 20, Dept. of the Platte, November 26, 1866, for his conduct in this affair. ARSW, 1867, 478; PR, November 1866, FL.

[39]Van Voast to AAAG, Dept. of the Platte, October 16, 1866, LS, FL.

CHAPTER FIFTEEN

"RATHER LIVELY TIMES"

In his annual report for 1866, General William Sherman informed Secretary of War Edwin Stanton that the transcontinental railroad had progressed some 275 miles up the Platte by the end of the season, and Sioux resistance notwithstanding, the army had gained a foothold on the Bozeman Trail. The human cost thus far had been twenty-five soldiers and a score of civilians killed, but Sherman was resolute that "this road is necessary to Montana, and must be finished and made safe," adding his conviction that "these deaths must be avenged next year."[1] He suggested that it might be easier to control the aggressive tribes if the commissioner of Indian affairs would restrict the Sioux and Northern Cheyennes to the area lying north of the Platte, west of the Missouri, and east of the Bozeman Trail. He recommended that any Indians found outside those boundaries without a pass issued by a military commander be dealt with harshly.

Red Cloud, however, was just as determined to prevent the whites further from trespassing through the region. Although depredations subsided on the Platte and other overland roads with the onset of another unusually harsh winter, the Oglala leader continued to attack anyone or anything that moved on the route to Virginia City. By that time, he had formed a coalition of tribes consisting of all the western Sioux bands, the Northern Arapahoes, and even some Gros Ventres and Nez Perce. They were reportedly gathered in an enormous village containing as many as five thousand warriors about eleven days' journey north of Fort Laramie. The Crows remained independent, how-

---

[1] *ARSW*, 1867, 21, 32.

ever, and with good reason. While they, too, would have been justified in resisting the white interlopers—more so in fact since the trail
went directly through their homeland—the Sioux posed a more
immediate danger to their existence. Continuing Sioux encroachment, made worse by the expulsion of the eastern Sioux from Minnesota, threatened to drive the Crows out of the Big Horn and Powder River country altogether.[2]

The Sioux and their allies deprived Colonel Carrington of the initiative by laying siege to the new forts on the Bozeman, even as they
were being constructed. The troops could hardly go beyond rifleshot
of the stockades for fear of being ambushed. Attempting several ploys
to draw the soldiers out of the forts, Red Cloud's warriors finally succeeded at Fort Phil Kearny on December 21, 1866. That day, Captain
William J. Fetterman led a combined force of infantry and cavalry out
of the post on a mission to rescue a wood train returning from the pinery a few miles distant. Disregarding Carrington's instructions to the
contrary, Fetterman allowed Sioux and Cheyenne decoys to lure him
beyond the range of any immediate assistance, whereupon his command was quickly surrounded and annihilated.

Having no faster means to transmit news of the disaster, Carrington
induced prospector John "Portugee" Phillips, one of several miners
wintering at Fort Phil Kearny, to carry a message to the telegraph line
on the North Platte.[3] Phillips and a companion, Daniel Dixon, left the
post the same evening bound for Horseshoe Station, the nearest telegraph office. Bridger's Ferry, oddly enough, did not support an operator since the buildings were situated on the north bank of the river,
where as the line was on the south side. When Phillips and Dixon
paused briefly at Fort Reno, the commanding officer, Colonel Henry
W. Wessells, drafted a second note, which he requested Phillips to
deliver directly to his counterpart at Fort Laramie, Lieutenant

---

[2]Lieutenant Colonel Innis N. Palmer to AAAG, Dept. of the Platte, January 2, 1867, LS, FL.

[3]The Phillips episode has been highly fictionalized over the years. The best available analysis is
  Murray, "John 'Portugee' Phillips Legends," 41–56. John Phillips's true name was Manuel Felipe
  Cardoso. Born April 8, 1832, near Terra, on the island of Pico in the Azores, he apparently left
  home about 1850 to join the crew of a whaling ship, which took him to California. There he
  became a miner in the Gold Rush, an occupation he followed to Oregon and Idaho. By 1862,
  he was prospecting in the Boise Basin and moved from there to the strikes in western Montana.
  When those deposits too began to dwindle by 1866, he migrated with a party of men to the Big
  Horn Mountains in search of gold.

Colonel Innis N. Palmer, Second Cavalry, who, upon his arrival at the post just two weeks earlier, had supplanted Van Voast as commander because of his higher rank.[4]

Phillips rode into Horseshoe Station on Christmas morning and handed Carrington's dispatch to the telegrapher, who immediately put it on the wires. Phillips and Dixon rested and warmed themselves at the station for a few hours before striking out on the last forty-mile leg of their journey to Fort Laramie. Arriving at the fort between ten and eleven o'clock on Christmas night, Phillips was conducted by the sergeant of the guard to Old Bedlam, where an officers' party was underway. Phillips conveyed the tragic news to Palmer, "and this created such a gloom over all that the dancing party dispersed early."[5]

The following day Palmer transmitted to Brigadier General Philip St. George Cooke at department headquarters in Omaha his own version of the events at Fort Phil Kearny based on Wessells's note and a subsequent conversation with Phillips. In response to Wessells's request for reinforcements, Palmer suggested that Van Voast lead a relief column from Laramie and that troops from elsewhere be sent to reinforce his own garrison. Cooke adopted the plan and wasted no time in setting troops in motion. The men of the Eighteenth Infantry, having settled into their new quarters just before Christmas, were again thrust into the cold. This time, the weather, averaging more than 20° below zero, promised to be as hazardous as the Indians. Former sergeant William E. Kenney recalled the hasty preparations: "As I was Quartermaster Sergeant it meant much work for me. Our officers remembering the suffering the Winter before, for want of proper preparation, allowed the transportation for two blankets each and one buffalo robe to the man. We had to buy the robes at fancy prices from the post trader's store at our own expense and our company's funds were soon exhausted. The company tailors were put to work cutting them up and making gauntlets for the men."[6]

---

[4]A question seems to have escaped even Murray's careful analysis. Since the telegraph was a "party line" passing through Fort Laramie, why did the operator there not get the news of the Fetterman disaster at the same time, long before Phillips arrived? One plausible explanation for the latter is that the operator at Fort Laramie was not tending the key on Christmas, though presumably he resided at the telegraph office, adjacent to Old Bedlam. Author's note.

[5]Palmer to Brigadier General C. C. Auger, February 2, 1867, LS, FL.

[6]*National Tribune*, November 4, 1909.

With men swathed head to foot in all the clothing they could put on, the column trudged out of the post on January 3, 1867, to begin a punishing 235-mile march across the bleak, snow-blanketed plains. The force was composed of Companies B, C, E, and G, Eighteenth Infantry, and D and L Companies, Second Cavalry. Palmer was clearly under no delusions that the army's job would be an easy one. "This is their last flicker," he predicted, "but this will take a good fellow with them as their power goes out forever." Meantime, Cooke moved quickly to fill the void left in the Fort Laramie garrison by rushing forward three companies of cavalry from Forts Sedgwick and McPherson, along with one company of the newly authorized Thirty-sixth Infantry.[7]

When Cooke made known his intentions to follow up this movement by launching a campaign against the Sioux in February, Palmer hesitated. He assured his superior that although he had faith in the troops, such an expedition would be premature. He argued that "The great mass of our men are new to the service, never before served in the Army, and during the short time they have been in the Service they have been at labor working at building Quarters &c. and they are generally totally without any confidence in themselves, their horses or their arms. Half of our Cavalry men would fall off their horses in a charge and more than half the horses would run away with the men at a firing drill. Few or none of them have ever been drilled at firing the pistol from the horse and as for the sabre its proper use is entirely unknown to them."[8] Palmer added that he expected a late start for such a campaign, predicting that deep snow would remain on the ground until April. At that moment, in fact, an entire train loaded with corn was buried in drifts only ten miles from the fort. "It would take an army to shovel it out," he told Cooke. Grimmer still was Nick Janis's estimate based on rumors circulating among the local Sioux that the opposing warrior force now stood at about ten thousand fighting men. "They will give us a stand-up fight if they think they can whip us," Palmer warned.

---

[7]Post Returns, January 1867, Fort Laramie. The Eighteenth Infantry underwent another reorganization in December 1866 when the army elected to dissolve the three-battalion regiments. Accordingly, the First Battalion became the Eighteenth Infantry, while the companies of the Second Battalion were designated as the Twenty-seventh Infantry, and those of Third Battalion were numbered as the Thirty-sixth Infantry. Rodenbough, *Army of the United States*, 653.

[8]Palmer to Brevet Major General Phillip St. George Cooke, January 18, 1867, LS, FL.

As a precaution against allowing the fort to be infiltrated by hostiles, he issued an order evicting all Indians from the military reservation, except the enlisted scouts, and he gave three days' notice for civilians not employed by the government to also leave.[9]

Cooke, a seasoned old dragoon who had seen much service on the plains, was undeterred in his plans. Despite his certainty of General Sherman's full support of his campaign, Cooke unknowingly had been targeted to shoulder part of the blame for the debacle at Fort Phil Kearny. Colonel Carrington may have been an able administrator, but he had not proven equal to the tense situation then existing on the Bozeman Trail. His vacillating responses to the Indian threat had strained relationships with his subordinates as well as his superiors. Even General Grant had become aware of Carrington's failings as a field commander. When politics dictated that heads must roll, Sherman sacked Carrington and Cooke in the same stroke, since the latter's plan for an immediate campaign was at odds with the division commander's desire to remain on the defensive until the regulars had more time to train and he could augment their numbers on the frontier. Palmer's more conservative views, in fact, were in accord with the stance Sherman had been forced to assume. Carrington was whisked away to command the reorganized Eighteenth Infantry, then headquartered at Fort Caspar, while Wessels took his place at Fort Phil Kearny. And with Cooke gone, Sherman installed Brigadier General Christopher C. Augur at Department of the Platte headquarters in Omaha.[10]

Having received no word to the contrary, Palmer anticipated a campaign into the region of Powder and Tongue Rivers that spring and therefore renewed training his men despite the snow and freezing temperatures. "The companies are all full and we are drilling as hard as we can and I think we will be in good shape when we come to

---

[9] *GO No. 4*, February 22, 1867, FL.

[10] One of Augur's first actions was to distance Carrington even farther from the front lines by establishing his regimental headquarters at Fort McPherson, considered by then to be a rear area. During the trip from Fort Caspar, the hapless officer accidentally shot himself in the groin and was brought to Fort Laramie for treatment. Post Surgeon Henry Saylor Schell successfully removed the bullet, but Carrington was obliged to convalesce at Bullock's home for nearly two weeks until he was able to continue the journey to his new assignment. Carrington, *My Army Life*, 204–205.

leave," he wrote to an officer friend in the East, adding, "We have not had a very gay time here this winter."[11]

Less than a week later, Indians pounced on a four-man detachment carrying the mail from Fort Laramie to Fort Reno, and also wiped out a hunting party near Fort Reno. As winter turned to spring, Indian raiding parties ventured farther southward to wreak havoc at any opportunity. Near Camp Mitchell warriors struck a civilian train and ran off its entire herd of mules, and in April they stole a team from the detachment at Bridger's Ferry. Palmer advised Augur that with the improved weather the Indians were making "rather lively times along the whole route from Fort Sedgwick to Fort Phil Kearney [sic]." With most of the westbound emigrants now turning off at Bridger's Ferry, Palmer questioned if it might not be prudent to abandon Fort Caspar in favor of transferring the garrison to the ferry, a more logical position from which to protect the main road to Montana. His suggestion would lead to the establishment of a new post, aptly named Fort Fetterman, near there the following October.[12]

Sherman still yearned to strike a hammerblow on the Sioux and Cheyennes in the disputed territory east of the Big Horns. In March he directed General Augur to launch a two-thousand-man expedition against them as soon as the weather cleared. But his plans for a spring offensive were frustrated by Washington peace proponents. Both Grant and Sherman had lobbied hard to have the management of Indian affairs transferred from the Department of the Interior to the War Department. They cited numerous instances of conflicting lines of authority and poor communication when both civilian and military officials attempted to deal simultaneously with the same Indian nations. The generals were convinced that a consolidation of authority over the tribesmen was the only feasible solution. Failing peaceful means, or if Indians left their agencies to take the warpath, they believed the army should have full and immediate power to subdue them, thus avoiding the confusion and frequently lengthy delays that occurred when an Indian problem arose. A bill to effect the change passed the House of Representatives early in 1867, but was scuttled in

---

[11]Palmer to Lieutenant Colonel T. F. Rodenbough, February 20, 1867, Rodenbough Papers, DPL.
[12]ARSW, 1867, 54–55; Palmer to Augur, April 20, 1867, LS, FL.

the Senate. Peace advocates within and outside the Johnson Administration prevailed on the president to send forth yet another commission to treat with the Indians.

Sherman had nevertheless set things in motion for the campaign, hoping to field his troops before the commissioners arrived in Omaha, but his plan had to be shelved at the last moment. He could hardly allow Augur to send out troops until the commissioners had been given an opportunity to attempt what Sherman considered to be wasted effort. Brigadier General Alfred Sully, who had actively campaigned against the Sioux in Dakota Territory just a few years earlier, now served a reverse role as head of the peace delegation, designated the Sully Commission. Others included: Judge J. F. Kinney, old-time Fort Laramie trader George P. Beauvais, Colonel Ely S. Parker, John B. Sanborn, and Napoleon B. Buford. Both Sanborn and Buford had served as senior volunteer officers during the Civil War. Sherman could perhaps find some consolation in the knowledge that four of the six commissioners were army officers, yet he had little hope of reviving his offensive anytime soon.

Speeding across Nebraska on the new Union Pacific Railroad, now completed westward to the forks of the Platte, the commissioners planned to first confer with Spotted Tail at North Platte, and interview Colonel Carrington at nearby Fort McPherson. Afterward they would then travel to Fort Laramie to hold a council with all the Indians in the area, then they would secure a strong military escort and proceed to Fort Phil Kearny in hopes of meeting with Red Cloud himself. They, in fact, were so confident that a peaceful solution could be reached that they dispatched a message from Fort McPherson inviting the Oglala leader to rendezvous with them at one of the very posts he was endeavoring to destroy. It should have come as no surprise when Red Cloud spurned the proposal, but Man Afraid and Red Leaf, along with some three hundred of their followers, elected to give up their war plans and go to Fort Laramie to receive treaty goods. When other small bands began to straggle in during early May, Palmer granted the commissioners permission to hold a council within the reservation, a mile or two north of the fort beyond the Platte. Man Afraid arrived within a week, but was disappointed to discover that because army provisions had dwindled to a mere thirty-day supply for the garrison itself, Palmer had terminated distribution of annuities to the Indians until the Interior Department could arrange to feed them.[13]

As the commission began assembling that spring, Red Cloud made clear his intentions to resist the whites by attacking the entire line of travel from Fort Sedgwick to Fort C. F. Smith. "The Indians are at every point in parties varying from ten to some hundreds disputing the roads," Palmer reported. He noted that several soldiers had been killed by carelessly straying too far from their commands. It seemed that raiders were everywhere, never missing a chance to strike. Even a train of wagons laden with lumber returning from Laramie Peak was surrounded until a detachment of the Second Cavalry was sent to rescue it. Virtually every party of civilians moving through the country prevailed on the army for an escort. Palmer complied to the extent possible, but he could not send troops with all of them. However, he did find cavalrymen enough to meet four hundred head of cattle being driven up from Denver as beef on the hoof to feed his garrison. Visiting artist Anton Schonborn heard reports that horses had been stolen from several local ranches around Fort Laramie, and that travelers were frequently chased on the roads, but he doubted the veracity of most of the rumors. "A good many of these Indian stories about chasing people are made up by frightened men, who suppose an Indian behind every bush," he scoffed. "Besides it is hardly considered fashionable to come to the fort without having some Indian story to tell." He conceded, however, that five persons had been killed and scalped in the area.[14]

The presence of the Sully Commission on the Platte, coupled with having to divert troops to protect railroad construction crews, prevented the army from going on the offensive during the summer of 1867. Still, Sherman and Augur were not idle. Sherman had been a vocal proponent of creating permanent Indian reservations with

---

[13]Palmer to Brigadier General Alfred Sully, May 9, 1867, ibid. Apparently Judge Kinney was sent up the Bozeman Trail while the rest of the commissioners remained at Fort Laramie. Palmer made arrangements for a 150-man cavalry escort, but when Kinney found that he could coordinate his trip with a troop movement of the Twenty-seventh Infantry, Kinney decided to accompany them. Palmer to Sully, May 8, 1867, ibid.; Palmer to Judge I. F. Kinney, May 12, 1867, ibid.

[14]Anton Schonborn, May 25, 1867, copy in vert. file, FLNHS.

defined boundaries, unlike the hunting territories prescribed by the 1851 Horse Creek Treaty. Not only would reservations restrict Indian movements, but it would be easier for the army to identify and punish bands bent on making trouble. Aware that the peace commissioners also were inclined toward a reservation system, Sherman used the time to ring the Sioux country with a chain of forts to contain the Indians in that eventuality.

In addition to establishing a line of posts extending from the Missouri to the Yellowstone River in central Montana, Sherman directed General Augur to increase the number of forts in the Department of the Platte, two of which were to be in the vicinity of Fort Laramie. Palmer accordingly sent Major William McEntire Dye, Fourth Infantry, to reconnoiter both sides of the North Platte near the mouth of La Prele Creek, where the Bozeman Trail diverged north. Augur himself would come out to make a final decision.[15]

Augur left his headquarters later that month, following the chosen survey line for the Union Pacific Railroad, directly west from the forks of the Platte. He was familiar with Sherman's recommendations because of his own familiarization tour the previous summer. Sherman had stipulated that if the railroad were built along the shortest route to Salt Lake City, Camp Collins and Fort Morgan could be abandoned and the supplies at those posts transferred to a new one situated along the road tracing Lodge Pole Creek. In addition to providing a central station for as many as twenty-five hundred men, he envisioned a quartermaster and ordnance depot at that point on the railroad to supply all the other posts in the region.

Augur met former general Grenville M. Dodge, now the chief engineer for the railroad, at the proposed crossing of Crow Creek on Independence Day, 1867. While the escorting troops rested on the national holiday, Dodge and Augur scouted the surrounding area and concluded that it was not only a logical site for a military installation, but an obvious division point for the railroad as well. The city of Denver, having grown to sizeable proportions since its humble beginnings as a gold camp, already justified a spur line from that point. The two also envisioned the day when a major north-south line would supply com-

---

[15]For a complete history of this post, see Lindmier, *Drybone*.

munities all the way from Santa Fe to Montana. Augur wired Sherman the next day recommending that the post and supply depot be situated fourteen miles west of the town site to be near timber, water, and abundant grazing—and at a safer distance from the hell-raising boomtown that even then was developing along a tent-lined main street. Dodge, however, saw the military as an underpinning of the future town's economy and argued that the post should be nearer the town to afford protection for the inhabitants, as well as economic benefit to the merchants. In the end, Dodge prevailed and on July 31, 1867, Army Headquarters sent down an order fixing the location of Fort D. A. Russell at the junction of Crow Creek and the railroad. While a military survey team staked the boundaries of the military reservation, railroad surveyors plotted a town site named Cheyenne after the nearby pass over the mountains.[16]

Colonel Palmer concurrently sent out a company of the Second Cavalry from Fort Laramie to explore the shortest practicable wagon route between the two posts. With grading crews already working west of Julesburg, it would be only a short time before the old Oregon route through Scott's Bluff could be abandoned in favor of receiving supplies via rail at Cheyenne.

When the end of track reached Cheyenne late that fall, converging army work crews from Forts Russell and Laramie completed a spur telegraph line connecting the two posts, at once eliminating both the old wagon road up the North Platte and the need for Camp Mitchell. The combination of these momentous developments swiftly redirected the long-established patterns of travel and communication at Fort Laramie, ending its days as a remote station along the western emigrant trail. The Union Pacific Railroad would inaugurate passenger service to Cheyenne in November, with the army establishing a connecting stage line "for mail and military purposes" to Fort Laramie. Twice-weekly mail runs, including deliveries of the newly founded *Cheyenne Daily Leader,* would keep the garrison in timely contact with the world. The Fort Laramie garrison also would enjoy previously unknown comforts provided by comparatively easy access to all sorts of

---

[16]For a more thorough account of the founding of Fort D. A. Russell, the reader is referred to Adams, *The Post Near Cheyenne,* 3–7; Wyoming Territory was constituted on July 25, 1868.

commercial goods, including furniture, clothing, and foods that theretofore had been nonexistent, or at best, expensive luxuries.[17]

Troops also began constructing Fort Fetterman that summer, on a barren plateau bordering the south side of the Platte near where Dye and his men had bivouacked. With Fort Caspar serving no further purpose, its garrison moved downstream to occupy the new site. The troops had hardly vacated the little post at Platte Crossing when warriors arrived on the scene to burn both the post and the bridge. The smoke plume rising over the North Platte Valley represented a symbolic funeral pyre marking the end of the Oregon Route as the great emigrant highway to the Pacific Coast.

The completion of the railroad and the creation of new forts resulted in an even shorter link with the Bozeman road. Government contractors hauling materials and supplies to build Fort Fetterman followed the old Denver Road north along Chugwater Creek to a tributary later known as Hunton Creek. At that point, the road to Fort Laramie continued northeast, crossing the Chugwater to intersect the Laramie River about six miles southwest of the post. However, "old timers" familiar with the area knew that a viable wagon road could be established along a northwesterly course from Hunton Creek, skirting the foothills of Laramie Peak, to reach Fetterman more directly. When that road was established, supply trains, emigrants, and troops bound for Montana thereafter bypassed Fort Laramie, which now lay a considerable distance off the principal artery to the Northwest. Probably few individuals during those hectic times recognized the significance of that subtle change, nevertheless the oldest post in the region had turned a corner toward its ultimate demise.

---

[17]Palmer to Captain E. R. Wells, July 11, 1867, LS, FL. A detail began constructing the telegraph line toward Cheyenne in December. The officer in charge was directed to proceed until he met the crew working northward from Fort Russell. Lieutenant Colonel A. J. Slemmer to Lieutenant J. R. Mullikin, December 15, 1867, ibid. The old route to Fort Sedgwick was officially abandoned effective November 13, 1867, even though communications through Cheyenne did not become fully functional until the following month. The telegraph operator at Camp Mitchell was transferred to Fort Russell as a government employee for the Military Telegraph. Major George W. Howland to commanding officer, Fort Laramie, November 13, 1867, ibid.; Palmer to AAAG, Dept. of the Platte, November 23, 1867, ibid.; *Cheyenne Daily Leader*, November 16, 1867. The mail line was initially operated by the army, probably with ambulances because of their light weight. When enterprising civilians began running stages between Fort Russell and the Chugwater Valley, Post Commander Slemmer suggested it would be more efficient to have the army stage meet them there to exchange the mail. Slemmer to AAAG, Dept of the Platte, January 5, 1868, LS, FL.

James Bordeaux, who had operated his main trading post on the Platte below Fort Laramie since the 1840s and had figured prominently in government-Indian relations for more than two decades, was one of those astute enough to foresee the effect the Fetterman Cut-Off would have on his livelihood. Bordeaux, ever the shrewd businessman, saw an opportunity to offset the loss in trade at his old place by building a store at the forks of the Cheyenne Road to cater to the needs of white travelers. Placing one of his employees in charge of the new establishment, Bordeaux returned to the North Platte Valley to wring out whatever trade might still be had with the Loafer band and other friendly Sioux still in the area.[18]

Regarding Indian-white antagonisms, the region surrounding Fort Laramie was comparatively quiet during the summer of 1867 while the Sioux and Cheyennes concentrated their efforts against the forts on the central portion of the Bozeman Trail. Raiding parties were reported lurking in the vicinity of Laramie Peak and elsewhere, though army detachments scouring the area were unable to find them. While troops farther north fought pitched skirmishes with the Indians, the boys-in-blue at Fort Laramie often turned their attention to the growing number of brothels, so-called "hog ranches," and other vile establishments near the post. William H. Brown, an ex-lieutenant of the Eleventh Ohio, cashed in on the lucrative market by constructing a log hotel and saloon just across the Laramie River.[19] Increased traffic on the road to Cheyenne afforded John Hunter a more prom-

---

[18]Trenholm, "The Bordeaux Story," 121–22. Hugh Whiteside operated Bordeaux's store on the Chugwater until he was killed during the winter of 1867–68. Following his tenure, two unsavory characters, Cy Williams and a man named Swalley, lived at the place for a few months. John Hunton developed a cattle ranch on the site in the early 1870s and maintained property and business interests there until the early twentieth century. Hunton, "Reminiscences," 262.

[19]A Mr. McGamber applied to sell beer on the reservation at fifteen cents a glass in competition with William H. Brown, proprietor of "Brown's Hotel." See Simonin's description in the narrative. William H. Brown had formerly been a lieutenant with the Eleventh Ohio Cavalry at Fort Laramie. His entry in the unit's official history states simply that he was "mustered out," rather than "with the regiment," which suggests he did not accompany his comrades back to Ohio. Notwithstanding repeated orders to close his bar in subsequent years, Brown continued to sell liquor on his premises until at least 1871. Reid, *Ohio in the War*, 818. See also the comments of Ware, *Indian War of 1864*, 213–14; Slemmer to AGUSA, September 10, 1868, LS, FL; Post adjutant to Brown, June 27, August 19, October 27, and November 20, 1868, and January 18 and July 26, 1871, ibid.

ising economic opportunity at the Six Mile Ranch, situated where the road left the Laramie Valley. Its effect became evident almost immediately when a mail party from Fort Phil Kearny dallied there and drank themselves into a stupor. Soon after that a cavalry sergeant appropriated an ambulance from the post and drove to the ranch for a spree that later cost him a fine and his stripes.[20] Jules Ecoffey's place, down the Platte at the former American Fur Company post, had already acquired a reputation for being "a vile den, the resort of the worst characters in the country . . . a grog shop, faro bank, and billiard saloon."[21] A half-dozen murders there bore grim testimony to his statement. When a soldier was killed in a row with "hangers on about the place," on the Fourth of July, the post commander sent a detachment to investigate. Those implicated in the affair had vacated Ecoffey's and gone farther downriver hoping the soldiers would not follow, but they did. Before returning to the post with one suspect in custody, the soldiers took revenge for their comrade's death by pillaging and burning Ecoffey's saloon.

Although no official mention was made of prostitutes at the whiskey ranches, the "soiled doves" were undoubtedly plying their profession at the local dives. The railroad created easy access to Cheyenne, which in turn attracted "all the scum of society," some six thousand people by that first winter, to "The Sodom of the West," as one newspaper dubbed Cheyenne.[22] It did not take long for some of the women, particularly those down on their luck, to recognize the economic potential of offering their services to the garrison at Fort Laramie. Palmer, however, took grave offense when a former post chaplain complained to the adjutant general of the army that Fort Laramie was "a perfect whore house."[23] Palmer did what he could to distract the men, primarily by preparing for a campaign that might still come, by instituting regular target practice with the new breech loading fifty-caliber Springfield rifles that had arrived in mid-summer.

---

[20]First Lieutenant A. E. Bates, to Captain D. S. Gordon, February 26, 1867, ibid.; Brown, *Hog Ranches of Wyoming*, 57–58.

[21]Palmer to AAAG, Dept. of the Platte, July 7, 1867, LS, FL.

[22]Nel, "A Territory is Founded," 2–4 provides a useful overview of the topic. The quotation originally appeared in the *Wyoming Tribune*, October 8, 1870.

[23]Palmer to Brevet Brigadier General H. K. Wessels, July 19, 1867, LS, FL.

During the summer of 1867, the nation's capital witnessed the passage of legislation authorizing yet another peace commission. Although Sherman had prudently refrained from taking an offensive on the northern plains, he had directed General Winfield S. Hancock to conduct a campaign against the southern tribes. Hancock's burning of a Cheyenne village on Pawnee Fork, west of Fort Larned, while allowing the occupants to escape and go on a rampage throughout northwest Kansas and southern Nebraska, reinforced in the minds of peace advocates that military policies only fueled Indian wars. Sherman remained skeptical that the likes of Red Cloud could ever be coerced into surrendering by any measures short of total war. Still, the administration and Congress realized that something had to be done to control the Indians in the interests of developing the country and restoring the national treasury so depleted by the Civil War. An historian summed up the revised Indian policy as one that "anticipated that the plains tribes would be confined on two large reservations, one in Dakota Territory and the other between Kansas and Texas, for the purpose of keeping them away from the settlements and the main travel arteries across the West. All whites would be excluded from the reservations, except for the government employees required to oversee their care. In this protected environment, the Indians would be educated and slowly acculturated into American society."[24]

The army considered the Bozeman Trail vital to those national interests, notwithstanding criticisms in some political circles that both the road and the forts should be surrendered to the Indians. General Augur addressed the issue, prophetically as it turned out, in his annual report: "The question is not a new one. The posts are established, and large sums have been expended upon them for storehouses and quarters for troops. It cannot be supposed that the present Indian troubles along it [the Bozeman Trail] can continue for any very great length of time. They will be terminated, either by treaty or the subjugation of the hostile tribes. When this time arrives, unless this country is abandoned to the Indians, this route substantially must become the great highway between Colorado, Nebraska, and Montana."[25] Members of

---

[24]Utley, *Frontier Regulars*, 130–31.

[25]*ARSW*, 1867, 58. Present-day Interstate 25 traces the Denver Road and Bozeman Trail quite closely.

the new commission included a pious ex-congressman from Tennessee, Nathaniel G. Taylor, the recently appointed commissioner of Indian Affairs. He would be aided in the endeavor by Samuel F. Tappan, who had gained national attention for his investigation into the Sand Creek Massacre; Senator John B. Henderson of Missouri; and former general John B. Sanborn, a member of the earlier Sully commission. Military members included Sherman himself, Brigadier Alfred H. Terry, then commanding the Department of Dakota, and no less a figure than retired General William S. Harney, whose heavy hand had smitten the Sioux back in 1855.

Setting out from St. Louis in August, the commissioners first traveled to the upper Missouri to meet with the tribes under Terry's jurisdiction. They found the Sioux there in a conciliatory mood and easily coaxed them into signing a treaty. The prospects for an early end to hostilities seemed bright to the commissioners as they passed back through Omaha and boarded the railroad cars bound for Cheyenne and eventually Fort Laramie. The troops in the region had previously been instructed to avoid trouble with the tribes if possible, while Indian messengers attempted to coerce Red Cloud into a meeting at the post during September. When their entreaties evoked no response from the chief, the commissioners decided to try again after they returned from a scheduled council with the Southern Cheyennes, Kiowas, Southern Arapahoes, and Comanches, to be held on Medicine Lodge Creek in Kansas.

By November the peace commission was back at Fort Laramie their confidence bolstered by the recent success in getting the southern tribes to accept the plan for being moved onto reservations. Meantime, as both Sherman and Henderson had been recalled to attend urgent business in Washington, Augur filled in for his commander. A French miner and adventurer accompanying the commissioners up the trail from Cheyenne left a graphic description of his impressions of Fort Laramie:

> Seen from the route we followed, the fort more resembled a Spanish-American village than a military post of the United States. The barracks, the warehouses, the offices, the officers' quarters, are all constructed of stone and whitewashed with lime. On one side of the large manoeuver ground is the residence of the general of the fort. With its two-story

veranda or outer gallery, one would take it for a hotel in Panama or Central America. Not far off is a building of a style still stranger for this country, a sort of Swiss chalet, which the sutler, or supply merchant of the post, has built from his profits. This elegant dwelling put to shame the mean appearance of the low, gloomy canteen. By the chalet is the only tree to be seen about the fort. The new barracks and storehouses are built of wood. Along the Laramie river is the corral, a large square enclosure surrounded by a fence. There the hay is kept and the mules enclosed. The angles of the corral on the side away from the river are each defended by an octagonal structure of adobe, or bricks burned in the sun. These defenses were originally built to resist the incursions of the Indians, who usually surprised emigrant trains or military posts by first seizing the mules and horses, so highly prized by them. Today the Indians are far away and the corral forts have been transformed into mess halls for the mule drivers. Instead of weapons there are only kitchen utensils. A wooden bridge connects the two banks of the river, the piles joined by swaying planks. On the left bank is the fort with all its outbuildings; on the right, the one hotel of the country [Brown's], where the officers eat their meals. . . . The hotel is built of adobe and large logs, like the log-house of the American pioneer. There is but one story, but it is most comfortable. . . . Beside the hotel is the indispensable saloon, where ale and whiskey are chiefly sold. As if to temper the effect of these drinks, the dealer also sells books, though his customers apply themselves more frequently to his casks than to his library. . . . Fort Laramie is a fort only in name. No ditch or wall surrounds it. On the side away from the river is a sort of ditch where the dirt dug out is thrown in a heap, with a large circular outline, as if for the foundations of a tower. That is the only work of defense raised against the Indians. Since the fort has never been attacked since its founding, the defense has never been kept in repair.[26]

Upon their arrival at Fort Laramie, the commissioners were disappointed to find that Red Cloud was not there. He had acknowledged them only to the extent of sending a message declaring his intent to make war until the army gave up the forts on the Bozeman. Consequently, only a few Crows were on hand to discuss the treaty, but their consent for Americans to use the Powder River country hardly mattered because the Sioux were already firmly in possession of it. Nevertheless, Palmer arranged a meeting place in an empty quartermaster

---

[26]Simonin, "Fort Russell and the Fort Laramie Peace Commission," 6–7.

storehouse that normally served as a theater for the garrison, in hopes a council might yet be fruitful. Also attending the talks were the Laramie Sioux who traditionally resided near the fort.

The two-day council was filled with the now customary tradition: ceremonial songs, lengthy introductions of prominent persons, the solemn passing of pipes around the circle, and protracted oratories by Indian leaders recounting past grievances and demands for the future. Although the commissioners, speaking through interpreters Pierre Chene and John Richard, tried hard to convince the Crows that the whites wanted only to use a portion of the land—that part already on its way to settlement—the leaders rejected the argument, reminding the commissioners of the failed Horse Creek Treaty. The Crows countered further by echoing the demands of the Sioux, insisting that both the forts and the trail be abandoned. In the end, the Crows refused to sign until the Sioux first "touched the pen" to the treaty, which they did not do at the council.

Having utterly failed in their attempts to bring peace to the northern Plains, the disheartened commissioners were left no choice but to distribute the government's gifts to the Indians and return to the States.[27] It had become frustratingly apparent that the army's occupation of the Bozeman Trail was tenuous at best, but the commissioners were determined to attempt negotiations again in the spring.

---

[27]Simonin stated, "The hall where the pow-wow was held was of considerable dimensions. It was built of wood, and could easily hold 250–300 people; it had *previously* [italics added] served as the quartermaster's storehouse." He added that those in attendance were seated on benches. The most likely building used for this meeting was storehouse no. 43, as indicated on an 1867 plat of the fort. Apparently, this building was converted for use as a theater after new warehouses were constructed closer to the river. Situated only a short distance nearly due east of the sutler's store, it would have been more convenient as a council chamber than facilities more distant, which probably were filled with supplies. Ibid., 8.

CHAPTER SIXTEEN

"My Hands Are Bloody to the Elbows"

I n December 1867, with the Fort Laramie garrison settled in for the winter, Sioux leaders Blue War Club, Red Leaf, and American Horse arrived at the post too late to meet with the commissioners and receive their presents. Winter was always a hard time for the Indians, and relying on the white man's seemingly endless supplies at that season had become a way of life. In view of their peaceful disposition, Post Commander Adam J. Slemmer accommodated them with goods to the extent possible, knowingly violating the letter of Sherman's orders to the contrary. Soon thereafter, Red Cloud's son and nephew approached on the chief's behalf to gain the army's assurance that Red Cloud would be accorded safe treatment if he came to talk to Agent Patrick. Slemmer assured them that his men would take no action against him so long as the warriors behaved themselves by not committing any depredations. During February, Red Leaf's band, still wary, went into camp on Rawhide Creek, some fifteen miles north of the post. About fifty of Red Cloud's own Oglalas soon joined them, but the chief and his principal lieutenants, along with eight hundred lodges of their people, remained on Powder River waiting for the army to abandon Forts C. F. Smith and Phil Kearny. Only then, as his messengers had told the post commander, would Red Cloud consider making a treaty.[1]

---

[1]Lieutenant Colonel A. J. Slemmer to AAAG, Dept. of the Platte, January 16, January 22, February 19, February 27, and March 5,1868, LS, FL.

The countryside in proximity to Fort Laramie had become some-what more settled in the wake of the Civil War and coincident with the arrival of the railroad. John Hunton, an ex-Confederate soldier who had come to Fort Laramie earlier in 1867 to clerk in the store, recalled that about ten whites had settled on three ranches along the North Platte Valley southeast of present-day Guernsey, with another family located at Bridger's Ferry. Other hardy souls had established primitive "road ranches" to serve travelers on Horseshoe Creek, Little Bitter Cottonwood, and on the old emigrant trail at Twin Springs.[2]

The need for railroad crews as well as additional civilian employees at Forts Russell and Fetterman attracted an unsavory element of men with little ability to discern one side of the law from another. Their presence in the area further complicated the army's already difficult task of fixing the blame for recurring thefts and killings of white set-tlers or travelers. In March 1868, at the same time it was rumored that Red Cloud had moved south of Fort Reno, lurking warriors killed two teamsters on the road below Fort Fetterman, and only days later Indi-ans ran off a team of mules near the post sawmill. Slemmer received intelligence through his Indian allies that a small party of disaffected Sioux, operating independently, had committed the deeds, yet Slem-mer was not so sure. "There are a large number of white men refugees and outlaws all through this Country and their thieving acts are often-times laid to the Indians," he explained to Augur.[3] Soon after he made that statement, about sixty Oglalas and Miniconjous, allegedly led by Chief Crazy Horse, attacked Horseshoe Station, killing three civilians and some livestock.[4]

By the time the peace commissioners reassembled at Fort Laramie on April 10, 1868, the government had already shown its hand—agree-

---

[2]Hunton, "Reminiscences," 262. In October 1867, Hunton was joined by famed mountaineer Jim Bridger in the bunkroom used by Bullock's employees. Bullock invited Bridger to stay through the winter, and he did. Hunton stayed at the post until early spring, when he was sent to Fort Fetterman as a guide for troops going to Fort Fred Steele. Hunton to Robert Bruce, May 30, 1923, Hunton Papers.

[3]Slemmer to Brevet Lieutenant Colonel John Green, March 1, 1868, LS, FL; Lieutenant Colonel H. W. Wessels to AAG, Dept. of the Platte, March 13, 1868, ibid; Slemmer to AAG, Dept. of the Platte, March 19, 1868, ibid.

[4]A firsthand account of this incident, perhaps embellished in the retelling, was published in the *Wheatland Times*, August 14, 1952; Heitman, *Historical Register* 2: 430.

ing to yield Forts Reno, Phil Kearny, and C. F. Smith, and declaring that the road to Virginia City, the Bozeman Trail, would be closed to all American traffic within ninety days. The withdrawal of troops from the three forts would commence in spring, starting with Fort Smith and moving south, each successive garrison joining the column en route. Fort Fetterman, standing on the south side of the North Platte, would be maintained in accordance with the treaty provisions.

The loss of the Bozeman Trail was a stunning blow to Sherman's ego, though he consoled himself with the knowledge that he had achieved a more important strategic victory by at last corralling the Indians on defined reservations. So long as they remained there, the army's job would be easy; if they broke out in the future, there could be no question about taking punitive action against them. Besides, it was now clear that the Bozeman Trail probably would have been short-lived in any event, and was certainly not worth the cost and bloodshed that would have been required to keep it open. Further-more, the westward progress of the transcontinental railroad had cre-ated a shorter alternative route directly from Salt Lake City to the Montana gold fields, making the Bozeman Trail a moot issue. And, as the pragmatic Sherman pointed out, "The great advantage to the railroad is that it gives us rapid communication, and cannot be stolen like the horses and mules of trains as of old."[5]

Having won his victory, albeit a hollow one, Red Cloud had only to consent to the treaty. But, what did it portend for Indian-white inter-actions? An examination of the document is worthwhile because it proved to be the single most powerful influence on Plains Indian affairs during the following decade, and is frequently cited even to the present day. Unlike the Horse Creek Treaty, the 1868 accord was designed to channel free-roaming, buffalo-culture tribesmen onto the road of European-style civilization. The Indians could hardly have imagined, much less comprehended, the long-term impact of the Fort Laramie Treaty.

While the document contained familiar provisions binding the gov-ernment to give the Indians food and white man's clothing, as well as to provide mutual justice and reparations for offenders against either

[5]*ARSW*, 1868, 3.

side, the significant distinction was the creation of defined reservations, as opposed to the earlier-established, but failed, hunting territories. The Sioux were to be amassed together on an enormous tract of land comprising the western half of present-day South Dakota. The disputed region lying north of the North Platte and between the Black Hills and the Big Horn Mountains was designated "unceded Indian territory," upon which the Indians would not permanently reside. The Sioux were permitted to hunt there, "and on the Republican Fork of the Smoky Hill River, so long as the buffalo may range thereon and in such numbers as to justify the chase." So far as the Indians were concerned, that would be forever; they could not envision a day when buffalo would not roam the plains. The concept was clear enough to the commissioners, however, because they well knew that hide hunters, with Sherman's blessing, were already beginning the slaughter that would eventually drive the Indians to complete dependence on the government for their existence. That no northern boundary was fixed for the hunting lands only deferred conflicts in that region.

Upon their return to Wyoming to sign the treaty in the spring of 1868, the commissioners were surprised to find that none of the hostile chiefs, notably Red Cloud, were present. It was humiliating for Sherman and the other dignitaries to cool their heels when they had already conceded to all of Red Cloud's demands. Nevertheless, with the entire committee in attendence, meetings got underway immediately with the Brulés. Twenty-five chiefs and headmen, including Spotted Tail, Red Leaf, and Swift Bear, were the first to sign the document, on April 29. A week later, the Crows attached their names to it. The treaty granted them a reservation between the Big Horn Mountains and the Yellowstone River. However, Sherman revealed a surprisingly limited understanding of intertribal relations when he predicted that "in due time, they, too, will find it to their interest to go down the Missouri river and settle among the Sioux."[6] The two nations had been bitter enemies for most of a century—ever since the Sioux had elbowed them from the Black Hills—and in subsequent decades the Crows had resolutely contested their invasion of the Powder River region.

---

[6]Ibid., 2.

The other bands, reportedly, were on their way to the Platte, but they would not arrive for two or three weeks. Sherman, Tappan, Augur, and Terry, impatient to attend to other matters, boarded the military coach for Cheyenne, while Harney and Sanborn stayed behind with authority to conclude the treaty with the rest of the Indians as they came in. Near the end of the month, a large delegation of Oglalas and Miniconjous, including the influential Man Afraid of His Horses, met with the commissioners to sign the documents. Red Cloud, however, was again conspicuously absent. According to the Indians, the chief insisted that he would not make peace until he had personally witnessed the soldiers' exodus from the Bozeman road.[7]

Presuming the rest of the Sioux were still some distance away and hesitant to commit to the treaty, the last two commissioners finally left Fort Laramie on May 28, leaving behind a copy of the document for the others to sign upon their arrival.[8] They also named Charles Gereau "Special Sioux Interpreter" and vested the post commander with authority to act as the government's signatory in their absence. Oddly enough, Harney and Sanborn had been gone only a few hours when about forty-five lodges of Bad Faces, led by Yellow Eagle and Small Hawk, arrived at the fort. Slemmer "rolled out the red carpet" at headquarters, after which the chiefs readily signed the treaty and their people were lavished with gifts of food, blankets, cloth, cooking utensils—even some guns and ammunition.

Word spread quickly to the outlying Indian camps that the atmosphere seemed safe enough at Fort Laramie and that the whites were being most generous. A few days later, Tall Wolf arrived with twenty-six more lodges, and later still 119 lodges of Arapahoes stopped at the fort on their way to join their southern relatives on the Arkansas River. When they left on the twenty-ninth of June, Lieutenant

---

[7]An examination of the treaties reveals the familiar names of Joseph Bissonette, Nicholas Janis, his son Antoine, Lefroy Jott, Charles E. Gereau, and Leon Pallardie as interpreters for the various tribes and bands. Their involvement confirms once again the living link these men of French descent provided to the fort's fur-trade heritage. Kappler, comp., *Indian Affairs: Laws and Treaties* 2: 1004.

[8]John B. Sanborn and William S. Harney to General A. J. Slemmer, May 27, 1868, Records of Sioux Treaty at Fort Laramie, November 6, 1868, RG 393 (hereinafter cited as Sioux Treaty records).

Colonel Slemmer sent Peter Richard to escort them safely through the white settlements that had sprung up along the railroad and across western Kansas. Tensions still ran high on both sides and it would take only a single spark to ignite another war.

Red Cloud by that time was aware of the army's intentions to abandon the northern forts, yet he did not relax the pressure he had exerted from the outset. With the bulk of his warrior force intact, he was able to maintain a virtual state of siege on the Bozeman Trail until the three forts finally were vacated in August. Only then did he move toward Fort Laramie.

Meanwhile, in accordance with the orders of the Indian Commission, agency operations ceased at Fort Laramie on June 5. Agent Patrick thereupon relocated the Upper Platte Agency at the new railroad town of North Platte, Nebraska, to be closer to Spotted Tail's Brulés, who were at that time hunting on the Republican.

Red Leaf and his band of Lakotas were camped on the Niobrara that summer for the same purpose. Many of the Laramie Sioux and the associated white "squaw men" also followed the agency.[9] But the young warriors were difficult to control and a few depredations occurred along the lines of the Union Pacific as well as on the Kansas Pacific route to Denver. Patrick did not admit that his charges had committed any violations of the treaty, if in fact he was aware of them, but he complained to Nebraska Indian Superintendent H. B. Denman that so long as they remained outside the permanent reservation, there could be no progress with farming, no schools, and no acculturation into white society.

Spotted Tail and others in fact had come to discuss these matters with him, at the same time voicing their complaints that no annuity goods had been forthcoming. Both Denman and Patrick knew why—the contract for the soon-to-be-eliminated Upper Platte Agency had already been cancelled. The Indians subscribing to the treaty would be concen-

---

[9]Patrick reported that approximately "600 half-breed white men married to Indian families" from Fort Laramie passed by North Platte on June 30. They were joined by about 150 "similar persons," whereupon the entire cavalcade moved off toward the new reservation on the Missouri. Patrick refers to a detached group as the "Laramie Snipes," a term I have not encountered elsewhere, possibly referring to the Sioux scouts formerly cooperating with the army. M. T. Patrick to H. B. Denman, August 22, 1868, LS, FL.

trated on the Missouri rather than being scattered from the Big Horns all the way to Nebraska and Kansas, and changing the distribution point for their rations was a way to lure them to the desired location.

Sherman used his considerable authority to further hasten that process by closing doors previously open to the Indians. In August, he directed his subordinate commanders to curtail the issue of any supplies "to Indians outside their reservations . . . unless actually in distress and en route to their proper homes."[10] The edict effectively precluded Indians from coming to Fort Laramie because it lay south of the North Platte River and was therefore outside the boundaries of both the reservation and the so-called "unceded territory." As a temporary measure, Denman assigned J. P. Cooper to replace Gereau as special agent for the remaining Sioux, by then numbering only about fifteen families who refused to leave their traditional home at the fort.

Cooper soon learned through them that the larger body of Sioux and the Crows were already fighting each other on Powder River. He predicted the Oglalas and other rebellious factions would refuse to go to the new reservation under any circumstances, and with buffalo already becoming scarce in the region, he felt certain the Indians would again turn to making their living by raiding.[11]

Clashes were frequent enough in the southern part of the department to prompt Augur to cut short the welcome of Sioux bands there. He issued a circular on October 1, 1868, serving notice to field commanders that he was unilaterally nullifying Indian hunting rights in

---

[10]*GO No. 4*, Division of the Missouri, August 10, 1868.

[11]Cooper's arrival at Fort Laramie sparked a minor power struggle with Lieutenant Colonel Slemmer, who claimed authority to deal with the Sioux because Sanborn had left him a copy of the treaty (now in the files of the National Archives) and a letter to that effect. Slemmer also exerted his authority as post commander to issue supplies to the Indians, since the Indian Bureau had none of its own on hand. The treaty stipulated that the army would oversee all issues to the Indians to prevent fraud. Apparently, the conflict was resolved without the need for official intervention from higher authority. J. P. Cooper to Denman, August 27, 1868, LS, Fort Laramie. A few sporadic raids and other incidents continued in the vicinity of Fort Laramie into the fall of 1868. On August 30, for example, Indians ran off seventy mules from a government supply train at Cooper's Creek. Troops followed their trail toward Laramie Peak, but eventually lost it and returned to the post. Just before Red Cloud's arrival, three Sioux boys professing friendship approached a herder over the post's beef cattle eight miles above the fort and mortally wounded him. MH, FL, August 1868, Fort Laramie; Major William McEntire Dye to Lieutenant Colonel George D. Ruggles, November 20, 1868, LS, FL.

that region, thereby expediting the concentration policy favored by Sherman. Since August, he recounted, "their conduct has evinced such general hostility that in the opinion of the proper authority, their further stay between the North Platte and the Smoky Hill rivers is inadmissible. The friendly Indians have withdrawn from that country and you are instructed that hereafter, until further orders, all Indians found there are to be regarded as hostile, and treated accordingly. Commanding officers at Forts Laramie and Fetterman should notify when practicable, the Indians to the north of them, of this determination."[12] As a result, most of the Brulé Sioux and those near Fort Laramie, in addition to many small bands of Cheyennes and Arapahoes in the region, migrated toward the proposed new agency at Fort Randall, in the extreme southeast corner of the Dakota reservation.

Red Cloud, accompanied by Red Leaf, Big Bear, Grass, and his wife, finally made his long-awaited appearance at Fort Laramie on November 4. The chief, who had so recently been the terror of the Powder River country, made a distinct impression on some members of the garrison. "Red Cloud is a plain looking Indian about forty years old, and about six feet high and very quiet when spoken to," wrote an officer's wife after meeting the warriors at Bullock's house. "[He] has a very pleasant smile, and no show or dash in any movement." Unable to resist a more womanly observation, she daringly noted that Big Bear had "the most splendid chest and shoulders I ever laid my eyes upon."[13] Post Commander William McE. Dye, however, looked with less favor on Red Cloud's cool demeanor. He "affected a great deal of dignity and disinterestedness while other chiefs arose, advanced & shook hands with the officers with apparent cordiality, he remained seated; and . . . gave the ends of his fingers to the officers who advanced to shake hands with him."[14] Red Cloud obviously savored his victory over the army and took full advantage of the opportunity to nettle his recent enemies. His was, in fact, the only strategic victory in which the western tribes compelled government forces to surrender both territory and forts. In a

---

[12]*Circular to Commanding Officers*, October 1, 1868, Dept. of the Platte, copy filed in Sioux Treaty records.

[13]Adams, ed., "The Journal of Ada A. Vogdes," 3 (hereinafter cited as "Vogdes journal").

[14]Dye to Ruggles, November 20, 1868, LS, FL.

brief ceremony two days later, Red Cloud signed the Fort Laramie Treaty officially ending the war on Powder River.

Animosities over the treaty arose almost immediately when some of Brave Bear's Miniconjous rode in from their camp north of the river and were told they had no business being at the fort. Dumbfounded, Brave Bear retorted that no one had told them they were no longer welcome to trade at Fort Laramie. With peace established, he was under the impression they could go anywhere they pleased. The Sioux did not comprehend, nor in fact did the document clearly stipulate, that they were prohibited from traveling south of the North Platte for peaceful purposes. The treaty stated only that they would "relinquish all right to occupy permanently the territory outside their reservation." Conversely, it was the whites who were expressly banned from entering their territory.[15] Indeed, it begged the question: how were nomadic people to hunt over thousands of square miles without occupying the country? The Sioux were incensed with what to them was a meaningless contradiction, perceiving it as another example of the white man's duplicity.

When Red Cloud placed his mark on the treaty, he obviously focused on the ouster of whites from the Powder River region, while giving little, if any, attention to the provision requiring his people to live on the Missouri. They had always traded at Fort Laramie; it had become their home. Red Cloud's refusal to abide by key points of the treaty were revealed during conversations with Major Dye in which the chief announced his determination never to go to the reservation on the Missouri and his expectation that the traders would return to Fort Laramie. Now that the contest for the Powder River country was settled in his favor, he expected his people to resume trading at Fort Laramie. He further interpreted the document to mean that it would be the only fort kept open north of the railroad—that Fort Fetterman would be abandoned along with the others.[16]

As the Fort Laramie garrison observed Christmas 1868 with a theatrical performance followed by cups of hot eggnog at Bullock's house, tempers simmered in the Indian camps. Dye reported in mid-January

---

[15]Keppler, ed., *Indian Affairs*, 1002.
[16]Olson, *Red Cloud*, 80–84.

that even though he had not seen any Sioux for more than a month, they had exhibited a decidedly surly attitude and he predicted gloomily, "war was probable, if not inevitable."[17] Concerned that the tensions would escalate if some action were not taken, Dye repeatedly informed the Sioux in the vicinity that they were not permitted to cross the North Platte, although he did relent to the extent of allowing one Indian at a time to cross the river, so long as the individual went directly to Interpreter Gereau's lodge to explain his business. Dye suggested that department headquarters send him some Pawnee scouts to help keep an eye on Sioux movements to the north because rumors indicated most of them were back on the Powder River attending a large council. It was an ominous sign.[18]

Although no other incidents occurred during the depths of winter, Dye dared not relax his vigilance. At the first hint of spring 1869, he advised the post quartermaster to warn his herdsmen to maintain a sharp eye at all times, and when soldiers were available, to post lookouts on high points near the animals. To prevent the theft of teams on the road, Dye insisted that all animals be side-hobbled at night, and that intervals between wagons on the march be kept short to reduce the chances of their being cut off and surrounded.

His precautions were well founded. As if by magic, Red Cloud suddenly appeared at the North Platte ferry with several hundred warriors to challenge the army's authority. With the temperature standing at 13° below zero, the cavalcade slowly crossed over the ice. Ada Vogdes, the wife of a Fourth Infantry officer, witnessed their approach, writing,

> They came in two abreast, singing at the top of their lungs, and as they drew near the post, they formed themselves into a line of battle around one side of the garrison and remained on their ponies for some time. As the Colonel feared their intentions were evil, two companies of infantry were under arms for two or three hours, the artillery was brought to bear, and two cannons were mounted and manned. Everything had a warlike appearance for hours . . . Col. Dye ordered them off, as they had not permission to come in in such large numbers, and [he] told them if they did

---

[17]Dye to Ruggles, January 14, 1869, LS, FL.
[18]Ibid.

not go they would be fired into. Three times they were told before they obeyed, and great was the excitement to see if the last order would be obeyed.[19]

During the standoff, the chief himself rode into the post to speak with Dye. As he passed the sutler's store, his old friend William Bullock came out to greet him. Red Cloud, as proof of his involvement in area hostilities since the previous fall, refused his hand, saying, "Wait, my friend, until I have washed. My hands are bloody to the elbows. I want to wash them before I shake hands with anyone."[20]

His ablution completed, Red Cloud told Dye that his people were hungry; he had come to trade, not to fight. And, since most of the old French traders had already followed their in-laws toward the Missouri, Fort Laramie presented their only recourse. Major Dye, clearly outnumbered by the Sioux, found himself in a difficult situation. He had little room to contest the chief's arguments, yet he had recently received word that Sherman, who had been appointed general of the army on March 8, had issued his own interpretation of the treaty. Drawn up in the form of an edict, Sherman's order read that the Sioux and their allies were to be contained north of the North Platte.

Threatened with the imminent prospect of a new war, in which the first blood would be spilled on his own parade ground, rather than try to stand them off Dye reluctantly consented to permit a few Indians at a time to come to the fort the next day to trade at Bullock's store. Red Cloud, his stature further enhanced by this symbolic victory, strode out and, as Mrs. Vogdes recorded, "made a singular noise and they all mounted their ponies and rode out, scattering in all directions. It was a grand sight."[21]

Abiding by Dye's instructions, small groups of Sioux came back the next day, crowding into the small trade room at the store. Mrs. Vogdes was giddy with excitement as she "rushed around all day to get a blanket worked with beads, which I succeeded in doing for a bag of flour, twenty pounds of bacon, and some coffee and sugar."[22] That

[19]"Vodges journal," 7.
[20]Paul, *Autobiography of Red Cloud*, 191.
[21]"Vogdes journal," 7.
[22]Ibid.

afternoon, in her husband's absence, she naively invited Chief Red Cloud and a few others to dine at her quarters. To the surprise of the garrison, the recent terrors of the Bozeman Trail not only conducted themselves with proper decorum, but showed their appreciation by presenting her with an arrow as a gift upon saying goodbye.

Risking Sherman's wrath, Dye decided to strike his own bargain with Red Cloud. If the chief would promise to keep his young men from raiding south of the Platte River, a trader would be allowed to serve them on the Cheyenne River. Failing that, Dye warned, "swarms of soldiers" would be sent in battle against the Sioux.[23] Dye's threat notwithstanding, several Sioux and Cheyenne bands remained in the vicinity of Fort Laramie during the spring and summer.

Sporadic raids demonstrated that even a respected leader like Red Cloud had limited influence in controlling the warrior societies, especially those of tribes other than his own. A war party crossed the North Platte in early April to attack a detachment of soldiers at La Bonte Creek, killing at least one. A few days later, two companies of cavalry left the post in an attempt to run down the party, rumored to be Miniconjous, who also stole fifty head of cattle between Forts Laramie and Fetterman. Indians subsequently ambushed soldiers repairing the road to Fort Fetterman, killing one man and seriously wounding another. Then on December 2, approximately a hundred Sioux warriors attacked the mail ambulance bound for Horseshoe Station, where the Fort Fetterman mail was transferred to the Cheyenne coach.

Were the Indians not troublesome enough, white outlaws too began stealing stock on the road to Cheyenne. In an effort to combat both problems, Dye posted a company of infantry at Bordeaux's new ranch to patrol the area, and he placed detachments at Chugwater and Horseshoe Stations to prevent the thieves from loitering about those places for the purpose of obtaining information and supplies. Late in August, troops arrested two horse thieves apprehended within the military reservation. Discovering the men were in possession of army animals along with some from ranches as far away as Colorado, the commanding officer turned the rustlers over to the U.S. marshal in Cheyenne.[24]

[23]Dye to AGUSA, March 25, 1869, LS, FL; Dye to Louis Richard, March 31, 1869, ibid.
[24]Second Lieutenant George O. Webster to Non-commissioned Officers-in-Charge, Chugwater and Horseshoe Creeks, April 1, 1869, ibid.; Flint to U.S. Marshall, Cheyenne, W.T., August 31, 1869, LS, FL.

Events in the southeastern part of what had recently become Wyoming Territory, along with incidents farther south, made it clear that the Fort Laramie Treaty had virtually no effect on controlling the Sioux bands having no direct allegiance to Red Cloud. War parties belonging to the bands of Chiefs Pawnee Killer and Whistler, who had refused to go to Fort Randall, were active in the region south of the South Platte. Augur reported that his troops had found large elements of both the Sioux and Cheyennes, the latter led by Tall Bull, willing to defy his orders prohibiting their presence on the Republican River. In fact, he sent Colonel Eugene A. Carr and his Fifth Cavalry to eject them. Carr inflicted a telling defeat on the combined Cheyenne-Sioux village at Summit Spring in July 1869.

Lieutenant General Philip H. Sheridan, now commanding the Division of the Missouri, voiced a bitter complaint to the secretary of war about the inequities of making outlaws account for their misdeeds, while the Indians "run riot along the lines of our western settlements and commercial lines of travel." Referring to white lawbreakers, he said, "If an Indian does the same [thing], we have been in the habit of giving him more blankets." Disgusted with civilian handling of Indian affairs in general, Sheridan characterized the Indian as "a lazy, idle vagabond; he never labors, and has no profession except that of arms, to which he is raised from a child, a scalp is constantly dangled before his eyes, and the highest honor he can aspire to is to possess one taken by himself."[25] The unyielding former commander of the Union army's cavalry division shared Sherman's view that only military force, aimed at complete subjugation of the tribes, could ever resolve the situation and clear the West for settlement.

---

[25]Report of Lieutenant General P. H. Sheridan, *ARSW*, 1869, 70–75.

CHAPTER SEVENTEEN

"I Do Not Want to Be the Only Chief"

Tensions between the U.S. military and the Sioux went unresolved as the decade of the 1870s opened, though a declining number of Indian-white hostilities offered encouragement that Red Cloud was exerting greater restraint over his own Oglalas, if comparatively little over other bands. The first few months of 1870 witnessed no clashes around Fort Laramie, perhaps because the Sioux and Cheyennes were ensconced in their winter camps, away from the routes of travel. Come spring, however, Agent Cooper's prediction that the Oglalas would not accept the reservation anytime soon would begin to prove itself correct.

The citizens of the recently constituted Territory of Wyoming were as dissatisfied with the Fort Laramie Treaty as was Red Cloud, and were as weakly committed to abiding by it. Prospectors from Virginia City venturing southeastward from the Montana diggings into Indian territory spread word that gold was to be found in paying quantities in the Wind River Range, the valleys of the Big Horns, and on the Sweetwater.

During the winter of 1869–70, prospectors with little else to do in the saloons of Cheyenne hatched a plan to launch a mining expedition to the Big Horns. That such a venture would clearly violate the treaty mattered little to the members of the so-called Big Horn Mining Association, who had come to the realization that the treaty placed the entire northwest section of Wyoming Territory off-limits to whites. The group's chairman, W. L. Kuykendall, was convinced that the government must have made a mistake. Certainly, he reasoned, federal authorities would not impede such a venture, "as it must have been the intention of congress in organizing this territory to secure its speedy settlement and development, that having been a consistent government policy in other territories."[1]

Kuykendall conveniently overlooked a significant difference— Wyoming Territory was bound by a preexisting federal treaty at the time it was created. One Red Cloud biographer summarized the dilemma in these words: "As General Augur observed after a hurried trip to Cheyenne to investigate the rumor that an expedition was being planned to go to the Big Horn country, the Government could hardly expect the citizens of Wyoming to acquiesce in a policy which cut them off from a third of their territory for the benefit of hostile tribes. Yet to allow the Big Horn [mining] expedition to start would mean the scuttling of the treaty even before it had been put into effective operation."[2]

The Grant administration proved to be of little assistance when the problem was laid before the cabinet members. Purposefully vague guidance filtered down to Augur that provided him the latitude to allow the expedition to go forward, so long as the would-be prospectors did not enter areas that might result in a collision with the Indians. Some particularly adventuresome, and probably equally inexperienced, men clamored to be permitted free run of the territory; they would take their chances with the Sioux. The prospect that anyone in the government would seriously entertain such a blatant invasion of the newly restricted Indian lands, with the ink hardly dry on the treaty, was preposterous enough, but even more absurd was the administration's directive that Augur allow the expedition to proceed, if *in his opinion* it would not intrude on lands addressed in the treaty. Augur knew full well that, once away from military oversight, the prospectors would go anywhere they desired until the Sioux stopped them. The army would then be obligated to take the field to quell another "uprising." Whatever the outcome, Augur knew that he would be a convenient scapegoat.

---

[1]This opinion appeared originally in the *Omaha Weekly Herald*, January 26, 1870, and is quoted in Olson, *Red Cloud*, 91.

[2]Ibid., 92.

A harbinger of renewed trouble occurred when Indians shot and seriously wounded a civilian within a half mile of Fort Laramie during April. The new post commander, Franklin F. Flint, having no cavalry available, sent out a mounted detachment of Fourth Infantrymen to try to catch the raiders. The soldiers pursued the war party for several miles up the Platte, but were compelled to discontinue the chase when the Indians turned north and crossed the river into the unceded territory. About the same time, Indians attacked a camp owned by cattleman Benjamin B. Mills. Two drovers, John Boyd and William Aug, were in their tent when Indians ventilated it with a volley of shots, narrowly missing both men because they happened to be lying down. The same raiders struck Louis Richard's camp at Point of Rocks a few days later. Familiar with Sioux habits, Richard boldly charged after them and surprised the party, shooting one dead and driving off the others.[3]

Only Red Cloud's unexpected request to visit Washington, D.C., on behalf of the Sioux, prevented a general clash that spring. Although, his interpretation of the 1868 treaty remained unshaken, he now wanted to debate his right to trade at Fort Laramie and to propose new terms. He also indicated that he might be willing to discuss taking his people to a reservation, so long as it was not the one at Fort Randall.[4] His proposal could not have been better timed, for it presented the Grant administration an opportunity to demonstrate to the public the mollifying effects of its new peace policy on one of the most warlike Indian leaders.

For years, the government had resisted pressure from religious organizations to assume a leading role in the management of Indian

---

[3]MH, FL, April 1870; Hunton, "Reminiscences," 265–66. Hunton recalled that another drover, David Cottier, was absent from camp because he had driven a wagon to Fort Laramie for supplies. This represents one of the earliest documented instances of area cattlemen relying on the post for provisions. Likewise, during 1869–70, ranchers in the vicinity of the Cheyenne Road utilized the weekly army mail runs by taking their mail to a ranch situated directly on the road. The driver was authorized to pick up loose mail at such points and transfer it to the coach coming up from Fort Russell or Cheyenne. Ibid., 266.

[4]The impetus for Red Cloud's action may have come from John Richard, Jr., son of the former owner of Platte Bridge and the attendant at the trading post. Richard had killed a soldier at Fort Fetterman in a domestic dispute over a woman. There were implications suggesting he influenced Red Cloud to request the hearing, and in the process, the chief secured his pardon. Olson, *Red Cloud*, 93.

affairs. Although President Grant's own military background biased him toward General Sherman's stance that the army should have total control over all Indian matters, philanthropists successfully prevailed on the new president to allow religious organizations to take a hand in shaping and executing Indian policy. Bowing to their persuasion, Grant established a ten-man U.S. Indian Commission vested with wide-ranging authority to jointly oversee the Indian Bureau's appropriation, formulate policy, and evaluate the performance of agents in the field in hopes of preventing the corruption that had earlier plagued those offices. Sometimes known as the "Quaker Policy" because of that sect's close involvement in its creation, Grant's Peace Policy disrupted the old spoils system members of Congress had traditionally relied on to reward political cronies. His appointment of a significant number of churchmen, along with selected army officers as superintendents and agents blunted congressional opposition to the plan.[5]

When the government's invitation to Red Cloud arrived at the telegraph office at Fort Fetterman, Man Afraid (the younger) happened to be at the post. He swiftly carried the news to the chief, who had planned to take Man Afraid's father, among others, with him on the trip. Red Cloud responded that he would be ready by May 14. At the same time, Grant, having become aware of the Big Horn expedition, instructed Augur to stop the miners at Cheyenne for fear such an intrusion would derail the proposed meeting. Augur undoubtedly breathed a sigh of relief to be off the hook.

About five hundred Sioux were on hand at Fort Fetterman in mid-May 1870 to bid farewell to Red Cloud and his delegation. It was planned that the chief and eleven others would proceed from Fetterman to Fort Laramie to Cheyenne, where they would board the wondrous iron horse for the East. But when their assigned escort, Colonel John E. Smith, met them at Fort Laramie on May 24, Red Cloud insisted that twenty of his chiefs and headmen be allowed to go, along with seven of their wives. The Sioux leader was growing accustomed to getting his way, and after some delicate negotiations, it was agreed that twenty-one

---

[5]A salient provision added to the Peace Policy through the Appropriations Act of 1871 eliminated the status of "domestic dependent Indian nations" that had been inaugurated by Chief Justice John Marshall early in the nineteenth century. According to the provision all treaties then in force would be honored, but henceforth no new treaties would be negotiated with Indians. Utley, *Indian Frontier*, 133–34.

Indians would go, in addition to Fort Laramie locals William Bullock, James McClosky, and Jules Ecoffey as interpreters. The entourage left the post two days later, but rather than going to Cheyenne, they in fact cut cross-country to catch the train at Pine Bluffs, forty miles east, thus avoiding what was shaping up as an ugly confrontation between some of the bands and the residents of Cheyenne.

For several days following the arrival of the Sioux in Washington, officials spared no effort to impress the Indians with the might of the government and the splendor of the capitol city. Meetings eventually got underway with Secretary of the Interior Jacob D. Cox, Indian Commissioner Ely S. Parker, himself a full-blood Seneca, and Felix R. Brunot, Pittsburg steel magnate and head of the Board of Indian Commissioners.[6] Red Cloud, they soon learned, not only rejected the idea of taking his people to the reservation on the Missouri, but he stunned everyone when he claimed to have no knowledge of the Fort Laramie treaty. Since he had refused Dye's efforts to explain its provisions the previous November, he declared, he was therefore not bound by it. He claimed to know only what his runner had told him at the villages, and besides, he was convinced that the interpreters at Fort Laramie had been wrong about its provisions.

The chief's stance, and the new conciliatory attitude engendered by the Peace Policy, caused Cox and his cohorts to "reinterpret" the treaty, and on the eleventh of June they informed Red Cloud that he and his people would not have to go to Fort Randall after all. So long as they remained peaceful, they could live in the region generally north of Fort Laramie near the Black Hills. Secretary Cox further conceded that Red Cloud could submit names of men acceptable to him to serve as agents and traders in the region.[7]

Before parting, the shrewd Oglala chief took full advantage of the situation by convincing the officials to give the chiefs a present of sev-

---

[6]The 1868 treaty placed the distribution of annuities in the hands of the army. The Interior Department, embracing the Indian Bureau, objected strenuously to that arrangement. In passing the Indian Appropriations Act of April 10, 1869, Congress bowed to the secretary's request to have that authority revested in his department. At the same time, however, Congress established the Board of Indian Commissioners as a watchdog over the bureau in an attempt to prevent the fraudulent practices in which many agents had engaged during past years. Ibid., 132–33.

[7]It was probably no coincidence that Red Cloud named Ben Mills as his preference for agent, and Bullock and Ecoffey as traders. Olson, *Red Cloud*, 120.

enteen horses, and to have them available when they detrained at Pine Bluffs so they might ride home in style. Warming to his celebrity status, Red Cloud readily consented to give a speech in New York City before returning to the frontier. He utilized that opportunity to succinctly voice the Sioux plight and publicly appeal for the government to pay fair compensation for the taking of tribal lands. The audience responded with tumultuous applause.

The eastern tour was not only a smashing success for Red Cloud personally, but he had demonstrated to Washington officials his unexpected political prowess by unilaterally redefining the Fort Laramie Treaty, after the fact and in his own favor. The only point he did not win was that of the military abandoning Fort Fetterman. Cox, knowing an attempt to bend the treaty that far would never get past Sherman, was resolute on that point—the troops must stay. The secretary promised to send his representatives to meet again with Red Cloud during summer, at which time the details of their agreement would be worked out.

When the train carrying the Sioux delegation pulled into Pine Bluffs Station, the Indians were pleased to find their gift horses waiting to carry them to Fort Laramie. A cavalry escort also was on hand to conduct them to the post, but Red Cloud declined the offer, saying it was a sign the whites did not trust him. By the time the headmen arrived back at Fort Laramie on June 26, thousands of Sioux were camped in a village at Rawhide Buttes, forty miles north of the river, waiting for the signal to begin trading again. Colonel Smith, however, informed them through the interpreters that President Grant had granted an exception of only ten days during which they could cross the Platte. The free-trading days at Fort Laramie were no more. Despite that disappointment, Red Cloud announced that he would call a council of the combined tribes roaming between Powder River and the Black Hills in which he would exert his influence to bring a lasting peace with the whites. Although he admitted to having no authority over the Cheyennes and Arapahoes, he pledged his best efforts to persuade them to give up the warpath as well.

The great council probably convened in late July on Powder River, and, coincidentally, Commissioner Brunot left Washington about the same time. He was joined in St. Louis by Robert Campbell, a member of the commission whose stature among the Indians was legendary. His experience in the western fur trade could be traced to William Ashley's 1824–25 expedition, which established the fur trade in the Green River Valley of western Wyoming, and nine years later he joined William Sublette to found Fort Laramie. His intimacy with the Sioux and other tribes of the region had also gained him a place on the treaty commission of 1851. Since that time, he had maintained political connections the Interior Department and had kept abreast of Indian relations on the plains.

When Campbell and Brunot stepped off the train in Cheyenne in September 1870 they were met by two companies of the Fifth Cavalry, sent from nearby Fort Russell to conduct them to Fort Laramie. Messengers had been previously dispatched to the Sioux villages to alert them to the coming council, but when the commissioners arrived at the fort on the twenty-seventh, Red Cloud had not yet appeared. However, the massing of large numbers of both Sioux and Cheyennes during the following days presaged the chief's arrival at any time. Massing at the Sutler's Store, meanwhile, was an increasingly inebriated crowd "composed of soldiers off duty, bull whackers, frontier nondescripts, and some citizens from Cheyenne, attracted by the novelty of the expected 'pow wow.'"[8]

Commisioner Campbell believed that Red Cloud's delay was probably orchestrated to insure that all the appropriate leaders from the various bands were in attendance before the start of such an important meeting. The chief's tardiness may just as well have been his penchant for making a grand entrance. But at last, on October 5, an exceptionally large group of Sioux, including Red Cloud himself, made camp on the North Platte about three miles above the post. The commissioners made arrangements to begin the council the next day, while about two hundred warriors made an impressive display by riding en masse to the fort. Bullock laid out a feast for them in front of his store to reinforce the feeling of good will.[9]

The council began the next day in a large open tent that Colonel Flint had erected near the Platte ferry. Before the preliminaries had been spoken, however, Red Cloud voiced objection to the site, stating

---

[8] *Omaha Weekly Herald*, October 19, 1870.
[9] MH, FL, September and October 1870; Olson, *Red Cloud*, 121–22.

his preference that the council meet at the fort itself, ostensibly where his people could gather about to hear what was said. In all probability, his real motive was to achieve another symbolic victory for his people by subtly muscling the government into holding the conference south of the river within the "forbidden zone."

Yielding to the chief's wishes, nevertheless, Flint hurriedly made arrangements to move the meeting to the front porch of his own quarters, a frame house that stood at the south end of the parade ground. When the council reconvened shortly after dinner, the porch was filled to capacity with the Indian delegation, composed of Red Cloud, Man Afraid, Grass, and Red Dog; the commissioners; Flint and his officers; the officers of the Fifth Cavalry escort; and a few army wives. In the surrounding yard stood scores of Indians, soldiers, and civilians, all straining to hear what was said.[10]

After the opening ceremonies, Brunot and Campbell had the unenviable task of once again explaining and debating the stipulations contained in the treaty, tempering them with the modifications made during Red Cloud's recent visit to Washington. When he spoke, Red Cloud said he had only a few concerns, but first he caught Flint and the commissioners off guard by announcing his objection to soldiers whom he had seen cutting hay on "his" land on the north side of the Platte Valley. The commissioners could say little, except to express hope that Red Cloud would not take issue with such a minor thing. The chief responded that he would not go to war over the matter, but he was relying on the Great Father to keep his word and not allow white men in his country on *any* pretense.

Then, Red Dog stood and demanded to speak, insisting that Leon Pallardie, a half-blood Sioux, interpret for him. The Indian audience, predominantly Oglalas, loudly denounced Pallardie as untrustworthy because he belonged to the Brulés who had gone to the Missouri River. Some, in fact, accused him of misinterpreting what had been said at the negotiations in 1868, a significant factor in all the problems occurring since then. The commissioners diffused the tension by sug-

---

[10]Ibid., 123. The commanding officer's quarters at that time was a frame house, insulated with adobe, built in 1868. It stood immediately west of what is known today as Quarters A at Fort Laramie National Historic Site. It was sold at auction in 1890 and stood until sometime later in the decade, when it was salvaged for the lumber. Today, only the foundation remains. See Mattes, "Surviving Army Structures."

gesting an adjournment until the next day, a move endorsed by Red Cloud as a cooling off period to give the opposing Indian factions time to reconcile their differences in private.

The question of a trading post proved particularly thorny. Red Cloud demanded not only that he be given ammunition, he was adamant that the Sioux trading post, which had always been on the North Platte, be reestablished there. Brunot minced words by advising him tersely that the Great Father had promised only that the Sioux agency would be north of the river, not necessarily on it, and that establishing the agency at either Fort Laramie or Fort Fetterman was out of the question. Rather, Brunot suggested, Rawhide Buttes would make an ideal location, and the sooner the Indians agreed to it, the sooner the goods would begin to flow to them. But Red Cloud stolidly insisted that their agency be on the North Platte. Sensing that the meeting had reached an impasse, another chief suggested they allow the matter to rest there; the Indians needed time to consider the new proposals and to talk among themselves about their significance. In the meantime, they made it clear, they wanted their presents. Although no future council date was set, the Indian leaders and the commissioners parted amicably, agreeing that the gift-laden wagon train would go to the village the following afternoon. Thus, another council came to an inconclusive end.

The commissioners took the train directly to Omaha to report their accomplishments to General Augur. Although the question of where to locate the new Indian agency and the trading post went unresolved, the commissioners were of the opinion that Red Cloud now desired true peace and was personally willing to negotiate toward that end. They were not so certain, however, that the young men of the various bands shared his attitude, but so long as Red Cloud was able to maintain his position of near-universal respect among them, and even among the allied tribes, the prospects for a general peace were favorable. Brunot and Campbell concluded the meeting by urging Augur to do everything possible to support Red Cloud, now that the chief was in a cooperative mood. On him hung the best chance for ending violence on the northern Plains.[11]

The government's efforts to appease Red Cloud paid off, resulting in

---

[11] *ARSW*, 1870, 31.

the quietest period in the region in a long while. With the exception of a few isolated incidents near Fort Fetterman and scattered raids along the Union Pacific tracks in southwest Nebraska, the Department of the Platte remained calm during 1870.[12] Augur wanted to keep it that way. He appreciated how vital that iron thread was to the fabric of the nation, "and any interruption to the road by Indians involves also an interruption to the mail and to telegraphic communication, and the whole country, and in fact the world, is affected thereby."[13]

One year earlier, the only cavalry unit attached to Fort Laramie, Captain James Egan's company of the Second, had been sent to establish a camp in northwest Nebraska as a barrier to prevent the Sioux from raiding the Pawnees in the vicinity of Fort Kearny. Its absence left only four companies of the Fourth Infantry at the post, yet a sufficient force under the quieting circumstances. While Egan's men endured the hardships of prolonged field duty, the decline hostilities freed the garrison for other pursuits. But, as one soldier reported to the *Cheyenne Daily Leader*, "The moral condition is very poor, but better since the sutler has been prohibited selling whiskey, which is the worst I ever tasted; and at the moderate price of 25 cents per drink. The 'boys' however, get beer at the same price per glass at Brown's Ranche across the river, which I should judge was fully as poor as the 'Shoe Fly Beer' so graphically described in a late number of your paper."[14]

The Indians, too, were finding they had more time on their hands,

---

[12]Company D, Second Cavalry engaged Indians in possession of stolen stock near Atlantic City, Wyoming Territory, on May 4, 1870. Later that same day, a detachment under Lieutenant Charles B. Stambaugh had a fight with sixty to seventy Indians in which Stambaugh was killed. On May 5, a detachment of Company C encountered a war party on the Little Blue River in Nebraska. These were probably Sioux out to steal horses from the Pawnees in that area. Troops also intercepted large parties of raiders crossing the line of the Union Pacific in the vicinity of North Platte during June. Rodenbough, *From Everglade to Canyon*, 392–94.

[13]Brigadier General Christopher C. Augur to Brigadier General E. D. Townsend, AGUSA, October 25, 1870. *ARSW*, 1870, 33.

[14]*Cheyenne Daily Leader*, July 27, 1870; Brown stopped selling beer when it was impressed on him that he was violating the law granting exclusive rights to the post trader. The post commander issued an order prohibiting the men from thereafter visiting the place. *Circular No. 4*, January 28, 1871, Fort Laramie. W. H. Brown's establishment is clearly depicted in an 1870 watercolor executed by Anton Schonborn. It stood on the east bank of the Laramie River, only a short distance from the end of a wooden foot bridge leading from the fort's warehouse area. The Military Reservation was expanded southeasterly nearly to Scott's Bluffs by GO No. 45, July 21, 1871, Department of the Platte. It is not clear if this was done to protect the haying grounds against the influx of ranchers, or to better control the liquor traffic, or perhaps both.

and the proprietors of local whiskey ranches eagerly took advantage of them as a market for rotgut liquor. Since the Sioux and Northern Cheyennes still had no designated agency, the men often migrated to the North Platte in search of whiskey. Red Cloud found the effects of the liquor trade distressing; it was not what he wanted for his people now that the Powder River war was over. He complained to his friend Colonel Smith, now commanding Fort Laramie, that his men were obtaining whiskey along the river between Forts Laramie and Fetterman and sought Smith's help to eradicate what had been a destructive practice with local traders since the 1840s. Even though Smith sent out patrols, they were unable to locate the responsible offenders. He advised Red Cloud that eliminating the liquor problem required cooperation, and so long as the Indians themselves refused to identify the culprits in the interest of protecting their sources, there was little the army could do.

Nevertheless, the success of Red Cloud's peace efforts became increasingly evident the next spring when Smith estimated that there were at least seven hundred lodges of Sioux, Northern Cheyennes, and Arapahoes drawing rations at Fort Laramie, and more bands were arriving every day. The need for an agency becoming more critical than ever, the Indian Bureau named Major Joseph W. Wham as agent for the Platte River Sioux.[15] Wham arrived at Fort Laramie on March 22, 1871, and arranged a preliminary council with the Indians the next day to acquaint the new agent with Red Cloud and some of the other leaders. By May, most of the Indians had not gone on their usual spring hunts, preferring instead to draw supplies from the government. Consequently, the army was issuing between seven and eight thousand rations daily to the Indians. Fort Laramie, it seemed, had become the Sioux agency by default, a reality not lost on the Indian Bureau.[16]

Chairman Brunot traveled to Fort Laramie in early June to find Red Cloud and some thirty other chiefs awaiting him. At a meeting in the

---

[15]Wham served through the Civil War as an enlisted man in the Twenty-first Illinois Infantry and later as a second lieutenant. After the war, he secured an appointment in the Regular Army. During the reorganization of the army in 1869, Wham was left without an assignment and resigned his commission in 1871 to accept a job as Indian agent. Years later, as an army paymaster in Arizona, he gained modest fame when robbers attacked his detachment in Arizona. Heitman, *Historical Register* I: 1022.

[16]Colonel John E. Smith to AAAG, Dept. of the Platte, March 22, 1871, LS, FL; MH, FL, May 1871.

post theater on the twelfth, Red Cloud, still undecided on an acceptable site for the new agency, informed the commissioner that he preferred to defer the question until he could consult with the leaders of
the absent bands. American Horse, Man Afraid, Red Dog, and the
other principal chiefs present at the time advised Brunot that they
favored locating an agency on the White River, south of the Black
Hills, but they were willing to wait until Red Cloud had conferred
with the other bands before making a commitment. Brunot and Smith
suggested that an agency placed some distance north of the Platte
would reduce the chances of the Indians falling prey to whiskey ped-
dlers in the area.

Fearing that Red Cloud might procrastinate by not returning at all,
Brunot presented the Indians with an ultimatum. He announced that
he would hold another council in fifteen days, at which time they
would be expected to agree on a site north of the Platte. If they failed
to do so, government officials would make the decision for them. Acting on Smith's suggestion to apply some leverage, he further surprised
the chiefs by informing them that rations would no longer be issued at
Fort Laramie; rather, they would be detained at Cheyenne until a decision was made fixing the location of the agency. Continuing distribu-
tions at Fort Laramie, Brunot decided, would only reinforce the Indians ties to the place. For practical reasons, it would also be more costly
to unload and temporarily store the supplies there, only to freight them
to the agency once it was relocated. The meeting ended on that note.
Red Cloud afterward accompanied Smith and Brunot to post headquarters where he disclosed privately his personal support for an agency
beyond the North Platte Valley. Nevertheless, he told them, he was
obligated to consult with "the men of sense," a council composed of
twenty-nine Uncpapas and twenty-six Oglalas, before making a final
decision regarding placement of the agency. Red Cloud confided that
a consensus could have been reached the previous fall, but when the
government withheld arms and ammunition from their annuity, the
Lakota leaders decided to drag their feet. Applying some strategy of his
own, the chief suggested that if he could assure the others camped on
the Cheyenne River that the guns would be delivered, a decision would
be forthcoming. Referring to Conquering Bear, killed at the Grattan

fight, Red Cloud expressed his reluctance to make such a decision unilaterally. "I do not want to be the only chief," he told Brunot. "At the treaty in 1851, we made one great chief, and the white men killed him. Would you want me to say I am the great chief?"[17]

In a subsequent meeting at headquarters the next day, Brunot tried again to pressure Red Cloud for a decision, but the chief counseled patience, saying, "The earth will not move away, it will be here for a long time, and there need be no hurry." While he acknowledged that the whites wanted the agency placed well away from the North Platte and the evil influences there, Red Cloud's own eyes told him that the whites would come anyway. "Every place a white man goes whiskey goes. You can see them here drinking night and day," he exclaimed with a sweeping gesture of his hand. Smith and the others could not rebut the chief's observation, knowing it was all too true. They simply ignored his statement, reiterating instead that the guns would be delivered, but he must give an answer within fifteen days. Assuring them he would do his best to comply, Red Cloud shook hands all around and departed in a friendly mood. It would be the last time any whites would see him for months.

The place finally chosen for the agency represented another compromise. While it was not at Fort Laramie, as demanded by Red Cloud and many of the Sioux, neither was it at the government-preferred site on the White River. Since Red Cloud had failed to make a declaration within the allotted time, Wham selected a site approximately twenty-eight miles down the North Platte Valley. This place, a short distance upstream from the old Horse Creek treaty ground, was acceptable to the Indian leaders present. Wham soon staked out the agency buildings on the valley floor less than a mile north of the river, where they would be sheltered by low hills during winter. By fall, Sod Agency, as it was known among whites, consisted of employee quarters, storehouses, a blacksmith shop, stables, a hay yard, and a cattle corral.[18] Agent Wham also rescinded the moratorium on issuing

---

[17] The account herein follows closely Brunot's June 14, 1871, report published in *ARCIA* 1872, 22–28.

[18] The site is approximately two miles west of present-day Henry, Nebraska, on the north side of Highway 26. The land was later incorporated into the huge Pratte & Farris Ranch, one of the early cattle operations in the area. Accounts of the site by contemporaries who saw it are found in Unclassified envelope No. 8, Camp Collection, Lilly Library, LBHNM transcript 255, 258.

rations, fearing that if the Indians were not fed, the seven thousand then present and disposed to remain at the new agency, would scatter and begin raiding again.

Spotted Tail, meantime, had drifted back to the familiar region lying between the Platte and Republican Rivers. Although he expressed his satisfaction with the placement of the temporary agency and his intention to settle eventually on White River, Spotted Tail ran afoul of Wham when the chief revealed that he was taking his people to the Republican to hunt. Spotted Tail already knew that a train of goods for his Brulés had arrived at Fort Laramie and he insisted they be issued before he left. Wham refused to release the supplies on the Platte, rather he would send the train to White River and Spotted Tail could take possession of them there. The major calculated that once the Brulés were on White River with an abundance of supplies, they would stay there.

The Oglalas, however, objected to the white man's wagon train passing over what they considered to be their lands exclusively, thus revealing a widening breech between them and the Brulés. During the past several years, Spotted Tail and Red Cloud had emerged as arch rivals as a result of the Brulé chief's favored relationship with the whites, countered by Red Cloud's successful showdown with the army. Both chiefs had met with President Grant in Washington on separate occasions, and by the early 1870s both wielded considerable power within the Lakota Nation, creating intense factionalism among the Sioux. When Spotted Tail remained adamant about going to southwest Nebraska, Wham refused to issue the rations, holding them instead for the Oglalas. He further angered Spotted Tail by imposing on him a white chaperone, trader Frank Yates, to serve as his personal informant while the Brulés were hunting on the Republican.

Indian Commissioner Parker had for the most part remained on the sidelines during the debate over the location of Red Cloud's agency, and during that time Parker himself became the subject of an investigation into alleged irregularities associated with Indian annuity contracts. Even though the charges had not been proven, Parker resigned his post rather than suffer continued denigration in the press. Francis A. Walker was appointed to take his place in fall 1871.

Grasping the delicacy of the Sioux situation, Walker made arrangements to meet with Spotted Tail at the town of North Platte on October 25. As was his habit, Spotted Tail spoke frankly about the recent problems with Agent Wham. He afterward learned from Colonel Smith at Fort Laramie that Wham had largely created the situation that resulted in the Oglalas rejecting the wagon train of supplies. Smith believed that it could have gone to White River without a confrontation, but that Wham had magnified ill feelings between the two bands for the purpose of gaining more control over them. The new commissioner took swift action to get the supplies into the hands of the Oglalas at Sod Agency, and to have an equal quantity rushed forward by rail to the North Platte agency for Spotted Tail, thus temporarily satisfying the needs of both bands until more permanent distribution arrangements could be made.

Disgusted with Wham's handling of the situation, and suspicious of his motives, Commissioner Walker subsequently found enough evidence against the agent to have him dismissed from the bureau. The commissioner subsequently selected Dr. J. W. Daniels, an Episcopal agent posted in Minnesota, to replace Wham. Walker's own dealings with Spotted Tail convinced him that the chief was thoroughly reliable and that the government should make every reasonable concession to reinforce its relationship with him. Walker further observed that Spotted Tail's influence was on the rise among the Indians, while Red Cloud, who remained in the unceded territory north of the North Platte, saw his authority waning.

CHAPTER EIGHTEEN

"Indians Have Great Respect for Authority"

W hen Agent Daniels arrived at Red Cloud Agency, as the new site was called, on February 1, 1872, he found waiting there a conglomeration of various Sioux bands, but not all. Spotted Tail and his Brulés were still in southwestern Nebraska, and most of the Oglalas were in winter camp with Red Cloud on the Powder. Daniels, accompanied by Colonel Smith, took the train to North Platte, then rode overland to Spotted Tail's village on Frenchman's Fork to confer with the chief. From everything the colonel could determine, Spotted Tail's people had not been involved in any depredations during their stay on the Republican, yet it was time for them to move to White River.

The Brulés stalled, saying they needed more time to discuss the issue among themselves, but Daniels cut the discussion short, telling them that if they failed to designate their preference for an agency site by early spring, the government would select it for them. Smith's intimacy with the Indians enabled him to recognize the developing intratribal jealousies among the Sioux. Those, in fact, were becoming so pronounced that he thought the most practical solution was to establish separate agencies for the Brulés and Oglalas, and perhaps even a third one for other bands.[1]

Red Cloud, confident that he could still manipulate his white counterparts through stalling and making token concessions, appeared

---

[1]Smith to Francis A. Walker, March 9, 1872, LS, FL.

with about thirty lodges at Fort Laramie on March 12. He announced that he had come to meet with the new agent. Knowing Daniels was not present, this was Red Cloud's way of showing that he refused to recognize any agency other than Fort Laramie. Smith should have established a precedent right then by directing him to the agency, but keeping the president's peace policy in mind, he hesitated to call the chief's bluff. Accordingly, Daniels went to Fort Laramie to listen to the chief's concerns. His previous statements notwithstanding, Red Cloud again announced that he wanted his annuities delivered to the post, and he wanted the agency moved upstream, closer to Fort Laramie. Red Cloud's rant was an all-too-familiar diatribe, and the government was weary of hearing it. Smith and Daniels reminded him that he had not returned and given them the council's decision on where to locate the agency; therefore it had been decided by the government representatives and the chiefs present at that time. There was nothing more to be discussed, they told him.[2]

On the nineteenth, Daniels alerted Smith that young warriors who had ridden down from the Powder River region with Red Cloud were making trouble at Sod Agency, insulting and threatening the employees, and breaking windows in the buildings. Smith immediately put Captain Elijah R. Wells and his company of the Second Cavalry, supported by a mountain howitzer, en route to the agency. The strategy was effective. Two days later the agent reported, "The presence of Captain Wells and Company have had a salutary effect, and all is quiet now at the agency."[3]

The agency may have been quiet enough, but authorities could not ignore the resurgence of depredations coincident with the return of Red Cloud's band there. In one instance, the body of Levy Powell, bearing three bullet wounds and a crushed skull, was discovered on March 18, lying in Fish Creek, a tributary of the North Laramie. Powell had driven a herd of Texas cattle to the region the previous fall, but had chosen to sit out winter 1871–72 near Laramie Peak before moving on to Montana in the spring. Indian raiders also attacked two stock herders at Three Mile Ranch, west of Fort Laramie, on the afternoon of March 21, and a dozen warriors fired on cowboys in Chugwater Val-

---

[2] Smith to AGUSA, March 21, 1872, ibid.
[3] Ibid.

ley the next day, wounding one man. Confronted by Smith about these incidents, Red Cloud promised to return to Sod Agency and attempt to identify Powell's killers. Whatever his intentions may have been when he spoke with Smith, Red Cloud turned his visit to the agency into a public display of defiance by drawing rations for his people, "and to carry his point," Smith reported, "had them brought on [the] south side of the Platte for distribution to his followers." Angered by the recent attacks and by Red Cloud's vacillating behavior regarding the agency site, Smith recommended to Brigadier General Edward O. C. Ord, who had replaced Augur as commander of the Department of the Platte, that the army assert its power by curtailing supplies to the Indians. "I deem it my duty to inform you," he wrote to Ord, "that the temper of many of the Indians is decidedly hostile and that no time should be lost in preparing for any emergency."[4]

Yet it had become obvious even to Red Cloud that it was not good to have the agency so near the travel routes. Just as government officials had warned him long before, the Sod Agency location put his people in constant contact with the growing throng of disreputable whites who were only too willing to sell whiskey to them as well as to the soldiers. Recent experience had demonstrated that the army was largely impotent in curtailing the burgeoning liquor traffic spawned in Cheyenne and Laramie City.[5] Moreover, decades of Euro-American presence in the Platte Valley had practically stripped the region of all mature timber; consequently, finding adequate quantities of firewood was becoming a problem.

Meeting at the agency on April 10, 1872, Red Cloud and several chiefs reached a consensus that some of the headmen at last would accompany Agent Daniels to White River to find a suitable place for the permanent agency. Red Cloud maintained uncharacteristic silence on this occasion, but American Horse and three other chiefs attempted to coerce Smith into making some sort of concessions, oth-

---

[4]Ibid.; Smith to AAG, Dept. of the Platte, March 23, 1872, LS, FL.

[5]Three known whiskey vendors operating in the area were "Curley Jim" Converse, "Jack Nasty Jim" Wright, and Charles Allen. However, the Indians refused to testify against these men for fear of losing their source of liquor. Compounding the problems and further confusing the situation, these whites often stole Indian stock, whereupon the Indians would take revenge on whites other than their liquor suppliers. Smith to AAG, Dept. of the Platte, February 12, 1874, ibid.

erwise they claimed they would not be able to convince their young men to go. Smith did not back down, however, and to reinforce his point, he told the Indians curtly that their warriors had better return to the north side of the Platte or his troops would punish them.[6]

A few weeks later, several headmen accompanied Daniels to White River to examine the area, but Red Cloud was not among them. The reason for his lack of participation became apparent soon thereafter when he arranged yet another trip to Washington. He may have hoped as much to bolster his sagging influence among his own people as to wring further concessions from the government—at a level he considered appropriate to his stature.

The region remained relatively quiet throughout the summer of 1872, even though the Sioux continued to defer making a decision about where they wanted the agency. Small bands continued spurning the treaty by frequenting the region south of the Platte, sometimes to graze their horses, other times to create mischief. Ord, meanwhile, had designated a temporary "District of the Black Hills," embracing both Forts Laramie and Fetterman to better coordinate patrols and punitive actions against the Indians that might be required. Smith, as the senior officer in the region, became commander over the new district. The range of foothills between the North Platte and Laramie Peak was always a haven for lurking war parties, therefore one of

---

[6]Smith to AGUSA, April 13, 1872, ibid. John Richard, Jr., half-blood son of John Baptiste Richard of Platte Bridge fame and a sometimes interpreter at Fort Laramie, was killed in a domestic dispute about this time. It was well known that Richard Junior played both sides of his white-Indian heritage to best advantage. He was indicted for wantonly murdering a Second Cavalryman at Fort Fetterman early in 1870, but was never tried for the crime. When the victim's company was transferred to Fort Laramie two years later, Richard avoided going to the fort, knowing the man's comrades were out to avenge his death. Meanwhile, Richard apparently had taken up temporary residence with an infantry detachment camped about ten miles above Sod Agency as a safeguard during the trouble that spring. In a nearby Indian camp, he became embroiled in an argument with a Sioux over two girls he had purportedly lived with. Richard shot the Indian dead with his Winchester. A friend of the slain man then jumped into the lodge and stabbed Richard to death. He was buried adjacent to the military cemetery at Fort Laramie, near where the Janis brothers were later interred. John Hunton interview, Camp Papers, Lilly Library, typescript copy at Little Bighorn Battlefield, Camp Collection, 258–60. Upon learning of Richard's death, no less a figure than Robert Campbell wrote to his friend Seth Ward: "We have yours of 16th inst. announcing the death of our favorite Richard. The sad news was not unexpected—yet we very sincerely deplore the loss of one, who while a boy endeared himself to us, and to all that knew him." Campbell to Ward, April 19, 1872, Seth E. Ward Papers, Denver Public Library.

Smith's first moves was to direct Lieutenant Colonel George A. Woodward, at the sister post, to station a company of cavalry on the Laramie River near the crossing of the Cheyenne Road. The unit was to continually scout east and north, all the way to Bridger's Ferry, and to intercept any Indians attempting to pass through the region.[7] Late in the season, army hay contractors complained to the acting commander of Fort Laramie that Oglalas were becoming increasingly aggressive in their intrusions on the grasslands south of the river. Troops sent to expel them confronted the warriors in a tense standoff, broken only by Red Cloud's timely intervention.[8]

Only in October was there any other serious confrontation that year. Smith had earlier withdrawn his cavalry from Sod Agency, but when one of the whiskey traders killed an Indian, the tribesmen again threatened the lives of agency employees. Responding to agent Daniels's urgent plea for help, two companies of cavalry marched to the agency, where they found the employees barricaded inside one of the buildings. The Sioux congregated outside were obviously agitated, but tensions subsided upon the arrival of the troops. One company returned to the post, while the other went into camp near the agency as a safeguard against further trouble.[9]

Although winter passed quietly enough along the Platte, the Indian situation deteriorated into complete disarray politically. The Red Cloud faction still waffled over exactly where to place the agency, or whether to submit to agency oversight at all. Other elements of the Sioux, Cheyennes, and Arapahoes began withdrawing their former allegiance to Red Cloud as it became increasingly apparent to some that he had begun giving in to the whites, perhaps for his own aggrandizement.

In March 1873, soldiers reported a sizeable number of Sioux riding south in the vicinity of North Platte, Nebraska. The army assumed they were a war party, but later reports indicated the Indians were Spotted Tail and his men going south to hunt on restricted lands. When Sioux were reported on the river between Forts Laramie and Fetterman, Smith telegraphed Colonel Woodward to send a cavalry

---

[7]Smith to Lieutenant Colonel George A. Woodward, May 8, 1872, LS, FL.
[8]Smith to Secretary of War, October 5, 1872, ibid. Olson, *Red Cloud*, 153.
[9]*ARSW*, 1872, 51–53; Smith to General George D. Ruggles, Dept. of the Platte, October 23, 1872, LS, FL.

detachment down the north side to work in concert with patrols from Fort Laramie that would operate along the south bank as far as Elk Horn Creek. Although the patrols encountered no Indians, Smith nevertheless remained uneasy and watchful through the coming summer as the hostiles focused most of their attention on expeditions escorting the Northern Pacific Railroad survey crew along the Yellowstone River. With Red Cloud and Spotted Tail inclined to follow the white man's road, the recalcitrant factions found new leadership in a figure destined to become a household word in America—Sitting Bull.[10]

Agent Daniels, meanwhile, had reached the end of his patience in coercing the Sioux, as well as Northern Cheyenne and Arapaho bands that had been accorded treaty privileges, to relocate on White River. He telegraphed the commissioner of Indian Affairs in early August 1873 to report that the agency was at last being moved to the new site, and with that accomplished, he was tendering his resignation. His replacement, Dr. John J. Saville, an Episcopal Church appointee then in charge of the Sisseton agency in Minnesota, arrived at Cheyenne on the August 8 and went directly to the new agency. There, on a low plateau at the confluence of Soldier Creek and White River, he found seven thousand to eight thousand Indians gathered, along with "the commissary stores and building material of the agency . . . piled on the ground, covered with paulins."[11]

Agent Saville found his charges in a foul mood, complaining that the guns and horses that had been promised in return for their consent to move to the agency had not been delivered. He did his best to placate them, but the situation worsened late in September when the arrival of the annuity goods attracted bands of Uncpapas, Miniconjous, Sans Arcs, and Oglalas that had not been party to the treaty. The arrival of these bands more than doubled the number for which Saville had rations. Of his dilemma, he wrote, "Many of these people had never been to an agency before, and were exceedingly vicious and insolent. They made unreasonable demands for food, and supplemented their demands with threats. They resisted every effort to count them,

[10]Smith to Ruggles, March 7, 1873, LS, Fort Laramie; Smith to Ruggles, March 25, 1873, ibid.; Smith to Lieutenant Colonel Cuvier Grover, March 25, 1873, ibid.; Smith to Ruggles, April 12, 1873, ibid.

[11]*ARCIA*, 1874, 251.

and as their statements of their number were frequently exaggerated, it became necessary to arbitrarily reduce their rations . . . This caused a constant contention with them."[12] Saville labored through the winter of 1873–74 to convince the Indians of the necessity for the agency to get an accurate census count, often risking his own life in the effort. Finally, late in January 1874, he persuaded the bands that had lived under the agency system for some time that a count was vital for obtaining enough rations for everyone. The hostile factions nevertheless rejected the plan and immediately broke into war parties to prey on any whites they might find.

Indeed, the region immediately south of the unceded hunting lands had become an increasingly tempting target for Indian raids on whites with each passing year. The combination of the 1868 treaty ostensibly confining the Indians north of the North Platte River, and the penetration of the railroad through Wyoming, had begun attracting cattlemen to the vast grasslands in the watershed of Laramie Peak. The commissioner of the General Land Office, in fact, extolled the virtues of that area in his annual report that same year. Before long, Denver banks were lending huge sums for the purchase of Texas cattle to stock the ranges paralleling the railroad both east and west of Cheyenne. Towns like Cheyenne and Laramie, as well as Sidney, Nebraska, were destined to serve as shipping points for cattle bound for eastern markets.

By the early 1870s, the corridor along Chugwater Valley, already the common route of travel from Denver to Forts Laramie and Fetterman, had become a magnet for ranchmen because of its lush grazing and reliable water sources. Its proximity to the lines of communication, especially the Union Pacific Railroad, and the availability of supplies at the army posts represented significant advantages. Not to be overlooked in those unsettled times was the protection the military afforded such operations. The area east and north of Laramie Peak boasted some forty ranches by 1871, most of them small concerns each running a few hundred head of cattle, though two claimed to be grazing nine thousand and twelve thousand head, respectively.[13]

---

[12]Ibid.

[13]Dale, *Range Cattle Industry*, 65, 68–69; *ARSI*, 1871, 294–95.

Among those settling in that area was none other than John "Portugee" Phillips, Colonel Carrington's messenger for the perilous ride from Fort Phil Kearny to Laramie in December 1866, reporting on the killing of Fetterman's forces. Phillips had since married and taken up ranching on the Chugwater. Phillips had given up prospecting in favor of more promising ventures as a government contractor, small rancher, and operator of one of the "road ranches" that marked the way to Cheyenne. Jules Ecoffey, Adolf Cuny, and Louis Richard, all formerly linked with the Indian trade (not to mention the whiskey business), adapted to changing times by combining their resources to establish a legitimate cattle ranch on the Laramie River in 1871. Richard apparently tended the cattle, while the other two partners generated working capital at the Three Mile "hog" ranch just upstream from Fort Laramie.

F. M. Phillips, who had purchased the late Levy Powell's large herd, established a ranch farther up the Laramie at the mouth of Chugwater Creek. And, when the corrupt spoils system of the Grant administration ousted Seth Ward from his long sutlership at the fort that year, his faithful manager, William Bullock, turned to cattle ranching in partnership with Ben Mills. Apparently, Mills, who had profited as an Indian trader, shared with Bullock a common vision of the future potential of the region, as they too combined their resources to purchase cattle soon after the treaty had been signed. Bullock's place lay on the north side of the Laramie, below the Phillips Ranch. Other hardy cattlemen also brought stock to the ranges along Sybille and Horseshoe Creeks.[14]

A new series of Indian attacks began in the vicinity of Fort Laramie on January 24, 1874, when tribesmen first pounced on Callahan's ranch, nine miles up the North Platte, taking several animals. Then, showing no partiality for their mixed-blood relatives, they stole some cattle from Louis Richard as they passed through the Laramie Valley. The renegades also swept through Antoine Renaud's camp the same day, getting away with four horses and two mules, but Richard and

---

[14]Hunton, "Reminiscences," 262–63; Murray, "John 'Portugee' Phillips Legends," 48–49; Murray, *Visions of a Grand Old Post*, 40, 52n85; Vaughn, "Fort Laramie Hog Ranches," 40. General Augur renewed Ward's license on August 2, 1867, but it was revoked in favor of J. S. McCormick's application on May 20, 1871. McCormick, incidentally, was fired from the position on December 28, 1871, on the basis of Colonel John E. Smith's charges of "drunkenness and disorderly conduct." John S. Collins was appointed in his stead on same date. Register of Post Traders, RG 94.

two companions later caught up with the thieves and convinced them to surrender the stock. The Sioux threatened that since they were not getting the agency food promised to them, they would continue to take it from the whites.

A few days later, an army hunting party exchanged fire with four warriors, but neither side suffered any casualties. Raiders also ran off several animals from a small ranch on Cottonwood Creek. Caught unaware by the suddenness of these depredations, Colonel Smith requested that the Indian agent be compelled to report Indian movements before war parties reached the white-settled areas, and that military officers be kept apprised of current Indian policy in order to take appropriate action. It was the usual frustrating lack of coordination between the civilian and military branches of government. Having no other recourse, Smith prepared to send out cavalry patrols in a belated attempt to head off some of the war parties rampaging through the country.

The raids turned deadly in early February when some of the remaining Indians at Red Cloud Agency rebelled, murdering the clerk, Frank Appleton, and threatening to destroy the agency itself. Only intervention by more stable Oglala and Brulé factions prevented them from doing so.

While many of the raiders moved back toward Powder River, some again crossed the North Platte, probably hoping to steal horses from the ranches before rejoining their kinsmen. Unaware of any immediate Indian danger, a cavalry detachment escorting a trainload of lumber left the saw mill at Laramie Peak on February 9 en route for the post. The teamsters driving heavily laden wagons pulled out of camp at about daylight, intending to reach the halfway point to the fort by nightfall. First Lieutenant Levi H. Robinson and Private Frank Noll, Fourteenth Infantry, along with Second Cavalry Corporal James Coleman, all assigned to the train escort, delayed their departure by about two hours.[15] Robinson had decided to take a shortcut through the foothills in hopes of shooting a deer along the way, rather than

---

[15]A native of Vermont, Levi H. Robinson served as a sergeant in the Tenth Vermont Volunteer Infantry from 1862 until February 1865. At that time, he secured a commission as a second lieutenant with the U.S. Colored Troops, and served with them until spring 1866 when he transferred to the Fourteenth Infantry. He was promoted to first lieutenant August 11, 1866. Heitman, *Historical Register* 1: 839.

accompany the slow-moving train on the more circuitous wagon road along Cottonwood Creek.[16]

A combined party of forty or more Miniconjou, Uncpapa, and Sans Arc Sioux, purportedly led by half-blood renegade Tousant Kensler, was moving southward when they spied the train about twelve miles from the lumber camp. Farther out, they also spotted Robinson and his two companions riding across the snowy landscape. The warriors, screened by intervening hills, circled in a wide arc to get ahead of Robinson's party and lay an ambush. When the three were separated from the train by approximately five miles, the Indians confronted them and opened fire. Private Noll, dismounted at the time, returned fire, according to his own account, but Robinson and Coleman turned tail and made for the sawmill. Noll stalled the warriors long enough to gain the summit of a small hill, where he took cover and continued to exchange fire with some of the warriors. The last he saw of his two companions was the men bent low over their saddles, spurring their horses at a dead run. Now alone, Noll remounted and rode toward the safety of the lumber train. Although most of the warriors had gone off in pursuit of Robinson and Coleman, four or five had stayed behind to deal with Noll. The private kept ahead of the tribesmen until an Indian bullet felled his horse just half a mile from the train. But, hesitant to approach any closer, the pursuing warriors allowed Noll escape on foot.

With Robinson and Coleman nowhere in sight, the train moved on to Cottonwood Spring, where it corralled for the night in anticipation of a dawn attack. Meanwhile, Private James N. Connely, mounted on the fleetest horse in the command, rode to Fort Laramie to summon reinforcements. He arrived there about eight-thirty in the evening with news of the attack, whereupon Captain James Egan was dispatched with all the available troopers of Companies E and K.

---

[16]This account of the attack on Robinson's party is a synthesis of information contained in Smith to Ord, February 11, 1874, LS, Fort Laramie; Smith to AAG, Dept. of the Platte, February 12, 1874, ibid.; PR, January and February 1874, FL; Regimental Returns, Fourteenth U.S. Infantry, February 1874, RG 94; Hunton, "Reminiscences," 267–68; *Chicago Daily Tribune*, February 11 and 12, 1874; and Connely, "An Old Campaigner of the 2nd and 4th U.S. Cavalry," *Winners of the West*, July 30, 1928. A questionable account, recalled from memory years later and perhaps embellished to elevate the role of the witness, was told by Young, *Hard Knocks: A Life Story of the Vanishing West*, 103–104. Presumably, Robinson should have been with the train escort, rather than taking a shortcut. He was likely unaware of the present Indian danger, since the outbreak had only recently manifested itself.

Egan's command rode steadily through a windy, moonless night to arrive at the spring shortly before daylight on the tenth. He immediately went in search of Robinson and Corporal Coleman. Following the trail of the two riders, Egan found their bloody corpses about half a mile apart along the alternate road to the saw mill. Both were riddled with gunshot and arrow wounds, yet neither body was mutilated. The corpses were taken back to the train to be transported to the post for burial. The train reached the fort the next afternoon without further trouble. Although Egan again took up the trail of the attackers, he found they had crossed to the north side of the Platte well ahead of him. Prohibited from entering the Indian hunting territory, he had no choice but to turn back to the fort. Another company from Fort Fetterman scouting down the North Platte likewise came up empty-handed.

The Red Cloud Agency was now beyond Saville's control. The Indians had seized his entire operation, and another wood party was reportedly attacked near Fort Fetterman. The Indian Bureau had recently prevailed on the army to establish a new military post near the agency, but Sheridan had declined to reduce his buffer of troops protecting the transportation corridor and the settled regions farther south. Recent events in the vicinity of Fort Laramie, however, caused him to reconsider; clearly the army would have to mount an offensive in a belated effort to contain the outbreak at the agency. On February 18, Sheridan telegraphed General Ord in Omaha directing him to use troops from Fort Laramie to restore order there as soon as possible. Upon receiving those instructions, Smith estimated that the army would face at least two thousand warriors. That in mind, he requested an additional eight companies of cavalry, and half a million rounds of ammunition, for the operation, called the Sioux Expedition.

Aware that matters could quickly get out of hand, Sheridan and an aide promptly boarded a train for "the front" to make a personal assessment of the agency situation. He was joined en route by Ord, who had meantime issued orders for a number of units at Fort D. A. Russell to assemble at Fort Laramie to comprise the expedition. Sheridan and Ord, accompanying the vanguard of troops, arrived at the post on February 22, 1874, to confer with Smith. Demonstrating the benefits wrought by the railroad, just as General Sherman had foreseen back in 1866, companies from Fort Sanders, Fort Fred Steele,

Fort McPherson, and even as far as away as Omaha, along with their horses, were rapidly concentrated at Cheyenne. The column was augmented with five companies of the Eighth Infantry and one of the Third Cavalry from the Fort D. A. Russell garrison, making a total of approximately one thousand men ready to take the field within a matter of a few days. With the necessary supplies already on hand at Cheyenne Depot (Camp Carlin), and more readily obtainable from points east, the operation presented a stark contrast to the days of '65 when Connor had struggled for months to field his army.

Marching in separate battalions up the road to Fort Laramie in freezing weather, the expedition went into camp near the post during the closing days of the month.[17] Agent Saville, notwithstanding wild newspaper reports that he had fled his post, offered encouraging news that all the warring Indians were gone and, in a strange contradiction, Red Cloud's Oglalas were now protecting the agency.

Cheyennes and Arapahoes who had also been drawing rations at the agency had also sent runners to inform Saville that they had fled the territory merely to avoid becoming implicated in the current trouble, and they intended to return. Likewise, some of Spotted Tail's men, as a demonstration of their loyalty to the government, had found and executed Appleton's murderer. They were now guarding their own agency, about thirty miles northeast, in the event any of the hostiles attempted to return. Despite those assurances, Smith had his cavalry intercept a large shipment of guns and ammunition that had been bound for the Indians, to fulfill one of Red Cloud's most ardent demands.[18]

As elsewhere in the West, civilian business interests were ever quick to seize upon and magnify any Indian threat, real or perceived. Local rancher and saloon proprietor Adolph Cuny exclaimed to the editor of the *Cheyenne Daily Leader* that "the Indians are red-hot—as bad as in 1865," though his alarm was probably motivated more by imagining the profits to be made from a large influx of troops than from any fear of an Indian uprising.[19] In fact, the farther one happened to be from the epicenter of the trouble, the less serious it appeared. The members of the Omaha Merchants Club soon concluded publicly that the Indian marauding resulted from conditions peculiar to Red Cloud

---

[17]PR, February 1874, FL; Buecker, *Fort Robinson*, 11–12; Adams, *The Post Near Cheyenne*, 51–52.

[18]Smith to Ord, February 12 and 16, 1874, LS, FL.

[19]*Cheyenne Daily Leader*, February 15, 1874.

Agency and were not indicative of a general uprising. The distant *Chicago Tribune* offered an even more considered view: "It is a strange, but stubborn fact, that the Territorial citizen has a peculiar knack of augmenting trivial matters; and, in anything relating to Indian affairs, he is sure to make the most of it, especially if he can gain anything by it . . . Next to a stolen horse, nothing rejoices the heart of a 'Sage-Brusher' like a breech-loading musket, and, if he can only get ammunition with it, he is in the seventh heaven. There is nothing that he won't do to get one and while he could send East and buy the same kind for $15, he prefers to pay a deserter $75 for one."[20]

As an added precaution against false or inflammatory reporting, the army took possession of the telegraph line from Fort Laramie to Cheyenne. There would be no sensitive information "leaked" to the press, where educated mixed-bloods might read it and pass troop strengths and other vital military information to the warring bands.[21]

Smith divided the expedition into two columns for the march to White River. Major Eugene Baker, the officer who had led the infamous and much publicized attack on a Piegan village on the Marias River in 1870, was delegated command of the cavalry, while a veteran Eighth Infantry officer, Captain Henry M. Lazelle, led the infantry battalion. Smith sent with the column a Gatling gun as added muscle. His troops clad in overcoats, fur caps, and gauntlets, Major Baker broke camp on March 2, 1874, followed the next day by Lazelle's doughboys trudging northward following in the trail the horsemen had broken through wind-drifted snow.[22]

The appearance of troops prepared for engagement had an immediate effect in subduing the Indians. The northern Sioux still in the area vanished to join their relatives, while those with personal allegiance to Red Cloud and Spotted Tail sullenly viewed the blue-coated soldiers with uncertainty. Whatever their feelings, agent Saville found the Indians suddenly cooperative, including submitting to the census. Smith left part of his command in proximity to the Oglalas, and took the remainder downstream to patrol Spotted Tail's agency.

---

[20] *Chicago Tribune*, March 13, 1874.

[21] *Cheyenne Daily Leader*, March 4, 1874; Buecker, *Fort Robinson*, 14.

[22] The troops followed the old Fort Laramie–Fort Pierre Trail, once recommended by the Quartermaster Department as an alternative supply route. It will be recalled that this was a segment of the longer trappers' trail from Taos, New Mexico, to the Missouri. Author's note.

Two weeks after the army's arrival on White River, the Indian Bureau became involved and sent a four-man Special Sioux Commission to investigate Sioux grievances, and to resolve the internal bickering that had immediately arisen between Saville and Smith. Again, it was the familiar dispute over whose authority was supreme: civilian or military. Whereas the agent was satisfied at having gained the Indians' cooperation, albeit at gunpoint, he attempted to use the troops as his personal police to enforce bureau regulations and his own rules. Colonel Smith rejected Saville's attempts to exercise civil authority over his soldiers by continually impressing on the good churchman that the army was there only to protect life and property, not to administer the policies of the Indian Bureau. In that, the commission failed. Although the members supported a continued military presence to suppress further Indian revolts, the lines of authority between the two government departments could only be reconciled by the president.

Incredibly, a sanctimonious agent Saville gave the army no more than passing credit for its role in quelling the uprising. Ignoring the influence the troops' very presence, which may have saved his life, the agent claimed full credit for himself. "The excitement . . . soon subsided," he later wrote, "and I commenced a registration of the people . . . since this has been accomplished there had been little or no difficulty, as they readily comply with almost any request I make." Without acknowledging the military force that was present to back up his requests, Seville conceded that "Indians have great respect for authority."[23]

After visiting the Red Cloud and Spotted Tail agencies during late summer, the commissioners recommended adopting a suggestion made by Colonel John H. King, commander of the military district. King and the commissioners thought that the two agencies could be combined under a single agent. It would be an advantageous move, they thought, because the two neighboring tribes were virtually indistinguishable in culture and language and there was constant interaction between the Oglalas and the Brulés, many of whom shared family ties. Moreover, consolidating the two agencies would promote unity in the Indian Bureau's policies and the administration of its affairs. A fringe benefit would be an absence of rivalry between agents competing for supplies, facilities, and employees. From the army's

[23]*ARCIA*, 1874, 252.

perspective, it would be easier and more economical to have a single post oversee one large agency than to maintain two separate garrisons to guard two agencies situated forty miles apart. Bishop William H. Hare, chairman of the commission, opposed the plan because he thought it would be virtually impossible to find an agent competent enough to manage such a large number of Indian people.[24]

Disappointing to military authorities was the commission's avoidance of relocating the Red Cloud and Spotted Tail agencies somewhat farther north. The army had contended for some time that the new sites selected actually lay within Nebraska, and were therefore "illegal," even though the northern boundary of the state had not yet been surveyed officially to verify that claim. The Indian Bureau was just as convinced that the Sioux agencies were already situated north of the line, within the designated Sioux reservation. The official survey completed that summer was to prove the army correct.[25]

Nevertheless, Sheridan complied with the Interior secretary's request that the army maintain a strong presence at the agencies. In consideration of the coming warmer seasons and the additional expense of moving a new garrison there, Ord simply cut orders on March 24 acknowledging the permanent transfer of some of the troops—four companies of infantry and one of cavalry—already on the ground. Initially called Camp at Red Cloud Agency, Colonel Smith shortly thereafter renamed it Camp Robinson, in honor of his recently killed lieutenant.[26] Forage was at a premium at that time of year, therefore Baker and the rest of the cavalrymen were sent back to Fort Russell to reduce expenses.

General Sheridan's decisive response to the Indian uprising and takeover of the agency with a display of overwhelming force had narrowly averted another war. At last, Chiefs Red Cloud and Spotted Tail had been convinced that for their peoples' good they must stay at their agencies. The army was now there to make certain they did.

---

[24]Ibid., 88, 96.

[25]Buecker, *Fort Robinson*, 22–23.

[26]The agencies would remain on the White River, much to the displeasure of Nebraska citizens and politicians, until the Sioux were forced to move to a new location on the Missouri in October 1877. Thus, compliance with the 1868 treaty was finally achieved. Buecker, *Fort Robinson*, 118–20. A more detailed account of initial activities at the agencies, the conflicts between Smith and Saville, and the accomplishments of the special Indian commission is found in ibid., 14–19.

CHAPTER NINETEEN

"THE SIOUX WAR . . . WILL BE OVER FOREVER"

By the mid-1870s, Fort Laramie had grown to sizeable proportions, but its age and the work completed under a long succession of post commanders were reflected in its rambling amalgamation of buildings. A visitor to the post in 1874 remarked:

> It is an old post. . . . It is as old and dirty as it is ancient, piles of refuse matter are found everywhere, and in warm weather aromatic savors are inhaled everywhere. It is not only old, dirty, and sweet-scented, but very peculiarly built. There are wooden houses, and adobe houses, and concrete houses. There are new pretentious looking houses, and good, substantial looking houses, and tumbledown, dilapidated looking houses. . . . I suppose the greatest combination of the grotesque, the filthy, and the ill-arranged in the department is here at Fort Laramie. They talk of cutting a canal through it. It would be well to run both rivers, the Laramie and the Platte, over its site and wash the whole mess from the plains.[1]

He also might have mentioned, as Post Surgeon Hartsuff noted in an inspection report, that the aromas of the post were made all the more pungent by "the very offensive condition of the Company Sinks [toilets], [which] besides being liable to produce disease are disgusting to all who are brought into proximity to the same."[2]

In the army's defense, however no one in the service in 1849 ever imagined that troops would still be occupying Fort Laramie a quarter

---

[1]*Omaha Weekly Herald*, October 20, 1874.
[2]Major Albert A. Hartsuff to Post Adjutant, June 30, 1875, LR, FL, copy in vertical file, FLNHS.

century later. At that time, the low plateau above the river appeared to be more than adequate to accommodate foreseeable military needs, and old Fort John provided a readymade facility that could be supplemented with a few outlying buildings. However, changing needs during the following years resulted in an evolutionary process that continued throughout its entire military era. By the third decade of military occupancy, nearly fifty buildings crowded the flood plain and the two terraces rising above the Laramie River. Added to those were several dozen privies, chicken coops, officers' stables, sheds, fences, and other minor structures, creating an appearance more like a frontier settlement than a military installation.

Old Bedlam, constructed during the first year of the army's presence, still presided over the parade ground, though a coat of dark red paint detracted from its former white splendor. On its flanks were the more modest adobe officers' houses built later in that first decade, but now suffering from the ravages of time and exposure to the elements. With the exception of the stone magazine, most of the other early buildings had disappeared from the perimeter of the parade ground. In their places stood the substantial frame-and-adobe infantry barracks, along with the stone guardhouse erected by the regulars just after the Civil War. A frame two-story officers' quarters, designed for the post commander but converted at the last moment into a duplex for two families, stood at the south end near the former site of Fort John. Adjacent to it, alongside the river, was the frame headquarters, or adjutant's office. On the opposite (west) side was the adobe-lined frame commanding officer's quarters where some of the meetings with Red Cloud had been hosted. An assortment of quartermaster and commissary storehouses, mechanics' shops, and rude quarters for laundresses and other civilian employees were arrayed on the lowland east of the parade ground.

By the time John S. Collins secured his license as post trader, the original adobe store had been expanded by several frame, stone, and log additions. The store itself formed the south corner of a rectangular complex comprising a post office, soldiers' billiard room, storage areas, and a corral in the rear enclosed by wagon sheds and repair shops. A separate officers' clubroom, constructed during the war, stood a few feet southwest of the store.[3]

The larger garrison, averaging five companies of infantry and two to six companies of cavalry by the mid-seventies, had demanded that more barracks be constructed. To meet that need, an additional frame quarters for cavalry was built just across the Laramie River early in the decade, and an imposing two-story concrete barracks was erected a few yards northeast of the sutler's residence. The original hospital, standing behind the sutler's gingerbread cottage, was converted to other uses after a new concrete hospital and steward's quarters were completed atop the plateau in 1872, on the former site of the post cemetery. That expansion required the burial ground to be relocated a few hundred yards farther north.

Fort Laramie was anything but a pretty place at that time. Another visitor, Laura Winthrop Johnson, one of a party of half a dozen ladies out on a summer lark in 1874, was as taken aback by its desolation as she was the face of its oldest resident, Ordnance Sergeant Schnyder. "No grass, no gardens, no irrigation, no vegetables nor anything green is here. One good sized cottonwood, perhaps coeval with the post, seemed as much of a veteran as the old artilleryman [Post Ordnance Sergeant Leodegar Schnyder], a character always pointed out to strangers, who has lived at the post ever since it was a post, and is distinguished as the ugliest man there. . . . Another distinguished character is the pet elk . . . who abuses his privileges by walking into houses and eating up hats, shoes, window-curtains, toys—anything to satisfy his voracious appetite."[4]

Seth Ward's toll bridge, in use since 1853, had been salvaged for its timbers by William Bullock in 1871, and the planking used to construct his ranch buildings a few miles up the Laramie.[5] The army had replaced

---

[3]Mattes, "The Sutler's Store at Fort Laramie," *Visions of a Grand Old Post*, 20–52, presents a useful chronology of the trader's complex.

[4]Johnson, "Eight Hundred Miles in an Ambulance," 693.

[5]Hunton, "Reminiscences," *Annals of Wyoming* (January 1930): 263; Mattes, "The Historic Approaches to Fort Laramie," typescript, National Park Service, 1947, 42, 48–49; The skeletal remnants of "the bridge on the old California trail" were destroyed by a flood in June 1884. *ANJ*, June 4, 1884.

the bridge with a substantial wagon bridge spanning the Laramie just above the quartermaster corral. The new bridge signified that the axis of travel had shifted from east-west to north-south. Although Ward's bridge, just above the confluence, had been ideally situated to serve the traffic on the old emigrant road, it was now too far off the route leading to Cheyenne, Fort D. A. Russell, and the railroad. It was only logical that a bridge over the Laramie should directly access the fort.

During his brief visit to the post in February 1874, Sheridan's keen military eye had perceived the need for an additional bridge at Fort Laramie—one spanning the North Platte. It was obvious to him that with the Sioux agencies now established on White River, Cheyenne would be the obvious and most economical point from which to supply them. Troops also would be quartered at the agencies for some time to come, perhaps permanently; thus it would be necessary to have a direct, all-season link with the army depots at Fort D. A. Russell. The antiquated ferry with its single barge at the crossing of the North Platte, having been in service continuously since the early 1850s, was no longer up to the magnitude of the task.

When Sheridan made this observation to the editor of the *Daily Leader* upon his return to Cheyenne, it was just the boost needed for an idea that had already caught fire among several of the town's leaders. Many feared that Sidney, Nebraska, might usurp Cheyenne as the Union Pacific supply terminus for the Black Hills. A bridge over the North Platte at Fort Laramie would secure the Cheyenne-Deadwood Road as the primary route into the Black Hills and would enhance the prosperity of that community. Accordingly, territorial delegate W. R. Steele introduced a bill in Congress to provide an appropriation of $15,000 for that purpose. When Secretary of War William W. Belknap and his subordinate generals strongly supported the bill, Congress passed it almost without challenge on June 23, 1874. Belknap directed General Sheridan to have the Quartermaster Department prepare engineering plans and cost estimates immediately.

In his desire to develop a connection between the transcontinental railroad and Fort Laramie, Sheridan was motivated by broader strategic considerations than he revealed to the press. For the past few years, in fact, he had been soliciting General of the Army Sherman and President

Grant for permission to ring the Sioux reservation with military posts as a buffer against further outbreaks and, conversely, to prevent whites from encroaching on Indian lands. The attacks on the Northern Pacific Railroad survey crews, coupled with depredations south of the Platte, had done much to strengthen his argument that the Indians had to be confined to their assigned areas so that the economic development of the West could continue unimpeded. The so-called "unceded lands," as the government recognized from the outset, were hardly of any significance because the plan had always been to confine the Sioux and Cheyennes on a reservation where they would be dependent on the Indian Bureau for their existence. For Sheridan, continuing depredations during the years following the Fort Laramie treaty only proved the need to abolish the hunting territory once and for all. He wanted to do anything within his power to encourage white settlement of the Bighorn and Powder River country, thereby curtailing its use by the Indians and achieving the army's goal of Indian concentration.

By 1874, Sheridan had several new military stations in place, including Fort Abraham Lincoln on the Missouri north of the Sioux reservation, Forts Randall and Sully on the east, and Camp Robinson on the southern perimeter. Older posts like Forts Laramie and Fetterman now formed a secondary line of containment, but were disadvantaged by distance from the reservation. To fully realize his plan, Sheridan wanted to establish two forts in the Yellowstone country, one northwest of the reservation, and another near the Black Hills, "to better control the Indians making these raids toward the south . . . so that by holding an interior point in the heart of the Indian country we could threaten the villages and stock of the Indians, if they made raids on our settlements."[6]

---

[6]*ARSW*, 1874, 24 (hereafter cited as Sheridan report). Sheridan's purpose in establishing forts in eastern Montana Territory was threefold. They would offer protection to the Northern Pacific Railroad as soon as construction resumed in the wake of the Panic of 1873, and they would bar the northern Sioux from hunting in the West's last great buffalo range. Additionally, fort manpower would be used to segregate the Sioux from the Crows and other traditional northern enemies. One might speculate that had Sheridan been granted permission to build those posts earlier, the Great Sioux War of 1876 might never have happened. The year 1877 saw three forts established to guard the western side of the Sioux reservation: Fort Keogh on the Yellowstone at the mouth of Tongue River, Fort Custer at the confluence of the Bighorn and Little Bighorn, and Fort McKinney at the foot of the Bighorn Mountains, near the site of old Fort Reno. Sheridan also would be granted his wish to establish a fort at the Black Hills, named Fort Meade, in 1878. Hutton, *Phil Sheridan*, 289–91; Greene, *Yellowstone Command*, 5–8.

Having secured the blessings of the Grant administration in fall 1873 to conduct a military reconnaissance of the Black Hills, Sheridan looked to Fort Laramie as the logical base from which to launch such an operation; it lay only about a hundred miles south of the Hills and was readily supplied from the railroad. Following a visit to the post in February 1874, however, Sheridan second-guessed himself, and considered the situation at Red Cloud Agency too volatile at that time. The last thing Sheridan needed was to further arouse the already agitated Sioux by marching a large body of troops into the reservation, right under Red Cloud's nose. Instead, he chose to enter the hills "through the back door," from distant Fort Abraham Lincoln, on the Missouri, partially because of the presence there of the Seventh Cavalry, and its commander, Lieutenant Colonel George A. Custer. Sheridan proclaimed that the aggressive cavalryman, who had served him so well during the Civil War and against the tribes on the Great Plains, was "especially well suited for such an undertaking."[7]

The expedition began in summer 1874, and it produced more than military intelligence. In addition to the geologists and cartographers accompanying Custer, two miners also went along to verify the presence of gold, rumored for many years to be plentiful that region. The reconnaissance indeed found gold in paying quantities, although Sheridan played down the claim that one could simply pluck nuggets from the grass roots.

Anxious to release this momentous news to the nation, Custer selected his trusted scout, Charlie Reynolds, to carry the message to Fort Laramie, the nearest telegraph connection. Custer left his base camp on French Creek on August 3 and proceeded south with five companies of the Seventh Cavalry to explore the south branch of the Cheyenne River. Reynolds accompanied the troops for two days before striking out alone on the evening of the fourth to make the ninety-mile ride to Fort Laramie. A soldier noted that Reynolds applied "boots" to

---

[7]The legality of Custer's entry into the Black Hills has often been questioned, and just as often has been attributed to a whim of his own discretion, which it clearly was not. The expedition was conceived by Sheridan, and approved by higher federal authority in accordance with Article 2 of the 1868 Fort Laramie Treaty. As noted here, Custer just happened to be in the right place at the right time to be assigned command of the expedition. Sheridan report, 24.

his horse's hooves to muffle the sound and that the experienced plains-
man rode only at night until he was far away from the Hills.[8]

When the news of a new El Dorado broke in late summer, hordes
of prospectors immediately converged on the Black Hills. This time
not even the lateness of the season delayed the adventurers, as it would
have in former times, because now they could take the train, from
either east or west, or up from Denver. Overnight, both Cheyenne,
Wyoming Territory, and Sidney, Nebraska, became the principal outfitting centers. Local businessmen promoted Sidney as a shorter, more
direct, route for those coming from the East. Tent camps sprang up
throughout the Hills as prospectors searched every stream and canyon
for easy riches.

More urgent than ever was the need for a bridge across the North
Platte at Fort Laramie. Having received fifteen bids for the project,
Department of the Platte Quartermaster Daniel H. Rucker favored
the one submitted by the King Iron Bridge Company of Cleveland,
Ohio. The company promised to supply all of the materials necessary
for a prefabricated three-span bridge at a cost of $10,500. The pro-
posal wound its way through the army hierarchy and was finally
approved by the War Department on November 12, 1874, too late for
the work to commence that season. The bridge materials arrived in
Cheyenne by rail early in 1875, though construction was not completed
until the following December, and the bridge was not approved for
public use until February 1876.[9]

Once the golden floodgates opened, it seemed that suddenly everyone was interested in the Black Hills, the 1868 treaty restricting white
access to the region notwithstanding. Professor Othniel C. Marsh, a
pioneering Yale University paleontologist, expressed scientific curiosity in the region. In fact, Custer was still in the Hills when Paymaster
Thaddeus H. Stanton informed his friend Marsh that in the course of
traveling to Camp Robinson, he had seen abundant evidence of fossils

---

[8]Carroll and Frost, eds., *Private Theodore Ewert's Diary*, 55–56; Liddic and Harbaugh, eds., *Custer and Company*, 60.

[9]The complete story of the army's iron bridge is related in McDermott, "Fort Laramie's Iron Bridge," *Visions of a Grand Old Post*, 133–40. Primary materials are found in Letters, Report and Graphic Materials Received, Department of the Platte Records, RG 77, NA, Chicago, Ill.

and suggested he investigate. Marsh was occupied with other business at the time, but subsequently organized a Black Hills expedition and applied to General Sherman for an army escort that fall.

In early November Marsh and his fellow scientists arrived at Fort Laramie, where they were greeted by Stanton and Post Commander Luther P. Bradley, lieutenant colonel of the Ninth Infantry. Bradley assigned Captain Andrew Burt to command the escort, a combined force of infantry and cavalry. When the expedition paused at Red Cloud Agency to secure what Burt and Marsh were confident would be perfunctory permission to enter the reservation, the Oglalas refused it. They saw no reason for whites to go onto their lands for fossils or anything else. With negotiations at a sudden impasse, the troops made camp for the night while Marsh and Burt discussed their options. In an ill-considered move, Burt elected to slip his men out of camp that night and proceed north before the Indians realized where they had gone. The ploy was successful, though the Sioux quickly caught up with the troops and thenceforth kept the expedition under close surveillance. That they did not attack was a high tribute to Red Cloud's newfound forbearance. Marsh showed his gratitude by meeting with the chief on his way back to Fort Laramie and documenting Sioux grievances about the quality of rations being issued to them. Marsh promised to convey them to influential friends in Washington, and indeed he did.[10]

The rush to the Hills quickly became frenzy. With the nation still in the throes of the 1873 financial depression, thousands of unemployed men, supplemented by the usual throng of footloose adventurers lured to the latest bonanza, saw the strike as their salvation. Men formed mining "companies" for mutual support and protection in towns as far away as Yankton, Sioux City, Omaha, and even Chicago.

Though his personal sentiment lay with the miners, Sheridan was legally bound to uphold the treaty rights of the Sioux. In September 1874, he wired orders to Generals Ord and Terry, in the Departments of the Platte and Dakota, respectively, directing them to use every means at their disposal to halt the miners before they got to the Hills. If they had to resort to burning the wagons and jailing the leaders to

[10]Mattes, *Indians, Infants, and Infantry*, 193–97; Olson, *Red Cloud and the Sioux Problem*, 179.

break up the parties, they were authorized to do so. Bradley subsequently sent out Captain Guy V. Henry with a detachment of the Third Cavalry to try to locate a group of miners rumored to be in the southern part of the range during December. Subzero temperatures and blinding snowstorms soon forced Henry to return empty handed. However, when Captain John Mix was ordered out on a similar mission the following March, he finally found and arrested the men. The members of the so-called Gordon Party were marched back to Fort Laramie before being released, with a stern warning not to return.

During the intervening months, public debate ensued over whether or not Custer had really found gold in the region. The chief geologist with the expedition later denied its existence, as did Samuel D. Hinman, a Christian missionary serving the Sioux. Grant, already plotting a strategy to appropriate the riches of the Black Hills as a solution to the nation's financial woes, demanded confirmation. To that end, he instructed the secretary of the interior to form and dispatch a new scientific expedition to positively settle the question. The party would include a number of qualified geologists, topographers, astronomers, and experienced prospectors who could verify the quality of any mineral deposits found.

The eighteen scientists, headed by geologist Walter P. Jenny, assembled at Fort Laramie for that purpose on May 25, 1875. The escort was composed of eight companies from the Second and Third Cavalry, and two companies of the Ninth Infantry, a total of four hundred men under the command of Lieutenant Colonel Richard I. Dodge.

With the new iron bridge still incomplete at that time, Dodge was compelled to cross his command, and its seventy-five wagons, over the North Platte using the old rope-drawn ferry barge. At length, the column re-formed on the north bank and was set to move, when it was discovered that one member of the scientific group was still back at the fort. Dodge was vexed to learn that Horace P. Tuttle, a Cambridge astronomer, had not finished making celestial calculations of latitude and longitude using the flag staff as a datum point.

Jenny and Dodge remained in the Black Hills area all summer, but in late June the officer sent a dispatch to Omaha substantiating that gold had indeed been found, and in paying quantities. The five newspaper correspondents accompanying the expedition quickly filed their own reports to the nation. Even as the column wound its way through the scenic beauty of the Black Hills, small parties of miners followed along at a discrete distance, for protection, and although Dodge knew of their presence, he was not inclined to arrest them.[11]

The Grant administration seemed unable to make up its mind whether to abide by the 1868 treaty, or bend to economic winds. Just a month prior to Dodge's departure from Fort Laramie, Brigadier General George Crook had replaced Ord as commander of the Department of the Platte. Upon reaching Cheyenne in July, Crook expressed his intent to issue a new directive to field commanders to expel any unauthorized persons found within the limits of the Sioux reservation. The *Cheyenne Daily Leader* echoed the local negative reaction by daring Crook to *try* to keep prospectors out of the Black Hills.

Mirroring his superiors, Crook's sentiments actually lay with the miners, but at the moment he was duty-bound to enforce the treaty. The general and his aides thus loaded themselves into ambulances and drove to Fort Laramie, where they stopped only briefly en route to the Black Hills. Joining Dodge's column at Spring Creek on July 28, Crook posted public notices evicting the miners, but tempered the order with a stage whispered suggestion that they assemble in public forums to secure their claims, in the now likely event the Black Hills were opened to white settlement. A stream of disheartened miners began flowing back to Cheyenne during following weeks.

Grant thereupon attempted a new ploy to resolve his dilemma; the government would offer to buy the Black Hills from the Sioux. In September yet another special commission arrived at Fort Laramie on its way to negotiate with the Indians. Among the members were Senator William B. Allison, Brigadier General Alfred H. Terry, A. G. Lawrence, Congressman Abram Comingo of Missouri, Reverend S. D. Hinman, and W. H. Ashby from Beatrice, Nebraska. Once again, the government called upon one of the former traders, G. P. Beauvais, then retired in St. Louis, to assist as an interpreter and one attuned to the Indian psyche. Post Trader John S. Collins went along as secretary.

---

[11]Dodge's own fascinating account of the Jenny Expedition is published as Kime, ed., *Black Hills Journals*; see also Sheridan's report in *ARSW*, 1875, 71, and Mattes, *Indians, Infants, and Infantry*, 200–202.

The Allison Commission and its cavalry escort arrived at Red Cloud Agency on September 4. Several thousand Indians were awaiting them. Notably absent, however, were the Miniconjous, Sans Arcs, and the Uncpapas. The latter's powerful spiritual leader, Sitting Bull, who had steadfastly rejected the Fort Laramie Treaty, declared that he would never meet with the whites and would roam where he wished so long as game enough existed to support the people.

Meeting with the Indians on September 20 on White River about eight miles east of the Red Cloud agency, the commissioners proposed that the government would either purchase the Black Hills outright for six million dollars, or would lease the mining rights for an annual payment to the Sioux of four hundred thousand dollars. The chiefs present, including Red Cloud and Spotted Tail, showed little interest in striking a bargain, though Red Cloud and a few others indicated they might sell, if the Sioux were promised generous annuities for seven generations. Some witnesses believed that an agreement might have been reached, had the commissioners been more adept and had they paid appropriate homage to the influential Red Cloud. Others claimed there was misinterpretation of the amount being offered, since the Indians had no comprehension of the meaning of sum such as a million dollars. In any event, after a few meetings, some of the Indian leaders declined to participate further and the talks soon fizzled out.

Professor Jenny and his escort arrived back at Fort Laramie in mid-October. During the summer, he had dispelled any doubt about the presence of gold in the Hills by sending messengers to the post bearing dispatches to be telegraphed to the States. During those several months of tramping through the heart of the Sioux reservation, Dodge proclaimed that he had opened fifteen hundred miles of trail passable by wagon and an additional six thousand miles of horse trails. That the region would be thrown open to mining appeared to be a foregone conclusion.

Back in Washington, meanwhile, the Grant administration was growing ever more desperate to seize the land, especially after the failure of the Allison Commission to peacefully negotiate control of the Black Hills. Something had to be done to ease the economic depres-

sion still gripping the nation, and satisfy the growing political pressure
to allow mining in the Hills. On November 3, Grant convened a special meeting of selected officials at the White House, including Secretary of War Belknap, Generals Sherman and Crook, the newly-
appointed secretary of the interior, Zachariah Chandler; and Assistant
Secretary Benjamin R. Cowen.

Grant, now resolved to go to war over the Black Hills, had been
planning this conference for a month and had carefully chosen his
confidants. The plan hatched during this meeting, to acquire access to
the rich hills, was two-fold. First, the existing order prohibiting non-
Indian entry into the Black Hills would remain on the books, ostensibly to satisfy the terms of the treaty. The army, however, would quietly stop enforcing it. Once word spread that the military was not
guarding the entry routes, a flood of miners taking de facto possession
of the region might influence the Sioux to negotiate after all. That
would get the public, and the press, off Grant's back. If, on the other
hand, the Lakotas reacted by mounting raids on the new mining settlements in the Hills proper, or in the Platte River country, public
opinion would quickly support the withholding of Indian rations and
the use of military force to quell uprisings.

The second, and secret, phase of the strategy was to start a war—
and then blame it on the Indians, a concept by no means novel in the
West. The refusal of Sitting Bull and several thousand warriors to
accept the government dole was making it all the more difficult to
coerce the reservation Sioux into parting with the Black Hills. Many
of those at the agencies were drawn back to the hostile camps in summer, but slipped back to the comparatively easy life of the reservation
for winter. Sitting Bull, consequently, had a reserve of warriors to augment his already formidable force on Powder River. Aware of this,
Chandler decided to issue an edict for all the northern bands to report
to the reservation by the end of January 1876, thereby nullifying the
concept of the unceded territory. If, as expected, many did not comply, they would face military action. The timing of this order would
come in winter, when it would be all but impossible for the Indians to
travel, even if they were inclined to obey. When the Sioux failed to
come in, the Secretary of the Interior would hand over the situation to

the War Department, and the army would launch a campaign to round up the tribesmen and force them onto the reservation.

Thus, all the desired outcomes were wrapped in one neat package. The Black Hills would be taken as spoils of war; national economic needs would be served by the new mining wealth; the unceded territory would be abolished; and the Sioux would be confined to a smaller reservation on the Missouri, where they would be out of the way and totally dependent on the government.[12] The "Sioux problem," as many called it, would be resolved at last.

The first phase of the plan went off smoothly enough when miners discovered the doors open to the Black Hills. Getting there was made that much easier with the completion of the iron bridge across the North Platte at Fort Laramie. Soon mining camps with names like Custer City and Deadwood sprang up along streams in the Hills. The Cheyenne road, with mail and telegraph connections as far north as Fort Laramie, became the principal avenue for the surge of prospectors. By February 1876 a new commercial coach line, the Cheyenne-Deadwood Stage, connected the mining camps with the Union Pacific, and within three months coaches were making runs in both directions every other day, a schedule that was soon increased to daily trips. The company established its headquarters in a new log hotel, "The Rustic," erected by J. S. Collins at Fort Laramie, which happened to be the halfway point.[13]

The January 31, 1876, deadline for the winter roamers to repair to the reservation came and went, as anticipated. In response, Crook prepared to send an expedition north from Fort Fetterman to strike the wintering tribes before they scattered. When he and his staff passed through Fort Laramie in late February, they were among the first to enjoy the luxury of crossing over the new King iron bridge. During his brief layover at the post, Crook ordered two companies, I and K, Second Cavalry, to join his column at Fetterman. Three weeks later, his forces surprised and attacked a Northern Cheyenne village on Powder

---

[12]A more detailed account of the political maneuvers preceding the Great Sioux War is found in Gray, *Centennial Campaign*, 24–32.

[13]*Cheyenne Daily Leader*, November 17, 1875; January 21, February 3, March 24, and April 5, 1876. The Rustic Hotel stood on the plain below the Post Hospital, approximately two hundred yards north of the Post Trader's Store.

River. Although the charging troops initially stampeded the inhabitants, the warriors quickly reorganized and counterattacked. At the
end of a five-hour engagement, the mismanaged cavalry under the
command of Colonel Joseph J. Reynolds was forced to withdraw, leaving a number of its dead on the field.[14]

By April, the Indians at the agencies were nearly destitute, partially
because so many people from the northern tribes had come to the
agencies to be fed during the winter, and because Congress delayed
passing an emergency appropriation to make up the shortage. Pre-
dictably, the Indians vented their frustrations on any whites they
encountered. The body of H. E. Brown, a stage company employee,
was brought to Fort Laramie on April 25. He had been mortally
wounded two days earlier when Indians attacked his coach near Hat
Creek. The *Daily Leader* reported a few days later: "The starving Indians from Red Cloud agency, having been supplied recently with a sru-
veit of flour, sugar, and coffee, have recovered sufficient strength to go
on their annual horse stealing expedition, and in their last excursion
south of the Platte have visited Col. Bullock's and John Hunton's ranch
on the Chugwater and relieved these gentleman of thirty-one horses."[15]

The raiders also killed and scalped Hunton's brother, James, near
the Goshen Hole rim as he rode to a neighboring ranch. A cavalry
detachment sent out in search of the war party failed to catch up with
them before they recrossed the Platte. A week later, tribesmen ran off
stock from Hiram B. Kelly's ranch, also on the Chugwater south of
Hunton's place. As a preventative measure, troops from Fort Russell
began regular patrols of the road north of Cheyenne, while Egan's
Company K plied the trail twice monthly from Fort Laramie to
Custer City in the Hills.

Sheridan's grand strategy for the 1876 summer campaign called for
three strong columns to converge on the vicinity of Powder and
Tongue rivers, the suspected haunt of Sitting Bull's northern Sioux and
allied Cheyennes. Colonel John Gibbon would proceed eastward from
Fort Ellis down the Yellowstone, while General Terry would jump off
from Fort Abraham Lincoln and march west. Despite his earlier

---

[14]For a thorough account of the Reynolds Fight, see Greene, comp., *Battles and Skirmishes*, 3–19.
[15]*Daily Leader*, May 7, 1876.

repulse, Crook assembled a second force, soon christened the Big Horn and Yellowstone Expedition, at Fort Fetterman to press the hostiles from the south. While Sheridan intended no particular concert of action by the three columns, he hoped their simultaneous movements would force the Indians into a decisive fight, where they could be bested, and compelled to go to the reservation. He considered any of the three forces strong enough to defeat Sitting Bull, an assumption that drastically underestimated the mood and power of the hostile tribes. Crook was soon out of the summer campaign. On May 17, a large force of Sioux and Cheyennes surprised Crook's column on Rosebud Creek and fought the troops to a standstill in a day-long pitched battle. Much to the displeasure of Sherman and Sheridan, Crook retreated to Goose Creek, where he and his men occupied themselves with hunting and fishing until August while awaiting reinforcements.

Crook's demands for additional troops imposed a heavy draft on garrisons throughout the Department of the Platte, including Fort Laramie. In late May, three companies of the Ninth Infantry and one company of the Second Cavalry marched off to join Crook's forces in the field. Their departure left only Companies E and F, Ninth Infantry, along with Egan's troop, to guard the Cheyenne–Black Hills Road and perform the necessary garrison duties. Soldiers at Camp Robinson patrolled the alternate route from that point to Red Canyon, where a company of infantry established a temporary camp at the southern entrance to the Hills. Crook soon augmented the depleted garrison at Fort Laramie by ordering one company of the Fourth Infantry and another of the Twenty-third at Omaha Barracks to be posted along the road to the Black Hills.[16]

By spring large numbers of angry Indians, inspired by the army's repulse on Powder River, were reportedly slipping away from the White River agencies and going north to join the hostiles. In an effort to curb those defections and better protect the road, Crook requested that the Fifth Cavalry be transferred from its stations in Kansas to his

---

[16]Company H, Twenty-third Infantry established a supply camp on Hat Creek in June, and K Company, Fourth Infantry occupied the camp at Red Canyon. *Daily Leader*, June 25, 1876. This abbreviated record of events during the Sioux War relies heavily on the thorough treatment presented in Hedren, *Fort Laramie in 1876*.

department. Sheridan approved, and early in June the Fifth was on the cars of the Kansas Pacific bound for Denver, where they would transfer to a connecting line to Cheyenne. On the subsequent march to Fort Laramie, a trooper in the Fifth noted how settled Chugwater Valley was becoming. "This valley is full of stockmen, their ranches stringing along its entire length, and only three or four miles apart, Hundreds of cattle could be seen grazing on the side hills."[17]

General Sheridan himself was also bound for the front at that moment. Concerned about the reports of Indians fleeing the reservation, he determined to make a personal inspection of the agencies. He arrived in Cheyenne by train on June 13, two days after the Fifth Cavalry had commenced its northward march. After conferring briefly with Lieutenant Colonel Wesley Merritt, en route to take command of the Fifth, Sheridan hurried on to Fort Laramie where he found the regiment bivouacked on the floodplain below the fort. After an overnight visit, which included a dress parade formed to render the customary honors due a general officer, Sheridan rose early and hurried on to Camp Robinson on the fifteenth.

Sheridan, as it happened, was only one of the notables to visit the post that summer. He had narrowly missed meeting Spotted Tail, the dignified fifty-three-year-old leader of the peaceful Brulés, when the chief passed through Fort Laramie en route to Denver. During his layover at the fort, Spotted Tail recovered the bones of his daughter from their resting place atop the weathered scaffold standing on the plateau near the hospital. Since the Sioux were now prohibited from trading at Fort Laramie, and permanent confinement on the reservation seemed certain, Spotted Tail wanted his daughter's remains to be near him during his advancing years.

Accompanying the Fifth Cavalry to Cheyenne was their old comrade William F. "Buffalo Bill" Cody, who had scouted for Carr during the 1869 campaign and had participated in the Summit Springs battle. Cody was an accomplished frontiersman with extensive experience in the West, but more recently had turned showman, cashing in on his reputation by performing vignettes of his life on the stage before eastern audiences. The famed scout abandoned his current tour

---

[17]Ibid., 111. For General Sheridan's annual report relative to these events, see *ARSW*, 1876, 35–36.

to make a hasty rendezvous with the Fifth at Cheyenne on the eve of taking the field. Cynthia J. Capron, wife of a Ninth Infantry officer at Fort Laramie, recalled her impression of Cody: "I remember his fine figure as he stood by the sutler store, straight and slender, with his scarlet shirt belted in and his long hair distinguishing him as a well known character, so much more widely known since."[18]

Meanwhile, General Terry's Dakota Column collided with the Sioux in Montana, not far from where Crook had been repulsed. On June 22 Terry unleashed Custer's Seventh Cavalry to act as a strike force against what turned out to be a large alliance of Sioux and Northern Cheyenne bands, numbering perhaps two thousand fighting men. The Battle of the Little Bighorn on June 25–26, 1876, is unquestionably the best known, and most widely debated event, in western frontier history and is the subject of literally thousands of books and articles. Suffice it to say that the Indians achieved a great victory, decimating five companies of the Seventh Cavalry, killing Custer himself, and so severely mauling the remaining seven companies that they were of only marginal combat effectiveness for the rest of the summer. By the time Terry and Gibbon joined forces and reached the battlefield three days later, the Indians were gone. Their troops could only help bury the Seventh Cavalry's dead and assist the wounded.

The news of Custer' defeat, received at Fort Laramie on July 5, electrified the tiny garrison, now reduced to only one under-strength infantry company. Crook's previous draft on the troops had left Major Townsend with an alarmingly small force at his disposal. Company E of the Ninth had just left the post as escort to a supply train bound for the intermediate camp at Sage Creek, and Egan's cavalry, kept almost constantly in the field on one mission or another, was presently out scouting for Indians rumored to be in the vicinity of Chugwater Creek. Mrs. Capron, whose husband was then in the field with Crook, expressed her fear that "the Indians could very easily take the post."[19]

Although there was little likelihood of that happening, the Indians still at the agencies became noticeably restless after runners brought news of the great victories over Crook and Custer. Fifth Cavalry

---

[18]Capron, *Indian Border War*, 488.
[19]Previously quoted in Hedren, *Fort Laramie in 1876*, 131.

detachments patrolling the Powder River Trail from their new bivouac on Sage Creek observed an increasing number of small parties traveling through the country, a route known to be the main avenue between the hostile camps and the White River agencies. Officers at Camp Robinson now feared the reservation Sioux would bolt in a wholesale exodus to join their northern kinsmen.

The events at Little Bighorn had provided an intimidated Crook, who had sidelined himself for weeks on Goose Creek, the justification he needed to persuade Sheridan to add the Fifth Cavalry to his command. Crook felt certain that the presence of the veteran regiment would virtually ensure victory over the hostiles. But just as Crook redirected the regiment to join his expedition, a large force of Cheyennes left the agency bound for the hostile camps. When that word reached Merritt, who had just joined the Fifth in the field, he positioned his troops on War Bonnet Creek to intercept them. The Cheyennes, unaware of the troops' presence, ran headlong into the Fifth and after a brief skirmish, peremptorily retraced their trail back to the agency.[20]

While the columns in the field pursued Sitting Bull's bands across eastern Montana, an unprecedented number of miners streamed through Fort Laramie on their way to the Black Hills. A civilian present at the time attempted to describe the menagerie: "There are many outfits going from here to the Black Hills gold country and an immense train leaves here tomorrow. They travel in larger companies on account of Indians. Saw Cap. Egan's Co. of Cavalry start this morning—it was a hard looking mob and with no fuss & feathers but looked like business. . . . Was up town this morning and saw the miserable mob about the sutler store. Every man has either a gun & two revolvers strapped to him or a revolver & knife—all go well fixed for any emergency."[21]

Captain John G. Bourke, Third Cavalry, commented that he considered Fort Laramie to be "the center of all the business, and fashion, and gossip, and mentality of the North Platte country; the cynic may say that there wasn't much, and he may be right, but it represented the

---

[20]This event is detailed in Hedren, *First Scalp for Custer*. See also Hedren, *Fort Laramie in 1876*, 132–34.

[21]Anon., "Diary of a surveying trip from Fort Leavenworth to Fort Laramie, 1876."

best that there was to be had."[22] Contributing to that reputation was a new telegraph line following the stage road from Fort Laramie to Custer City, thence to Deadwood. Hibbard offered to build a line to the agencies, if the army would only supply escorts for the crews cutting and hauling the poles, but nothing came of it, probably because there simply were not enough soldiers to go around. Army dispatch riders made twice-weekly trips between the telegraph station at Fort Laramie and Camp Robinson until March 1877, when troops completed a military extension between Robinson and Hat Creek, the station nearest the Hills.[23]

Even with the large number of troops in the region that summer, small parties of Sioux drifted in and out of the reservation, some blending with Sitting Bull's free roamers, others committing depredations south of the North Platte. On August 1, a party of about thirty warriors attacked a government contract train hauling supplies from the depot at Fort Russell to Fort Fetterman. The owner, A. H. "Heck" Reel, was an experienced freighter in the area, and he had taken the precaution of arming his men with both Colt revolvers and Winchester repeating rifles before leaving Cheyenne. When the Indians ambushed the train on a segment of the old Oregon Route between Coffee and North Elkhorn Creeks, Wagon Master George Throstle was killed instantly. Sylvester Sherman and the drivers quickly corralled the wagons to form a defense and skirmished with the Indians for the remainder of the day. There were no other casualties among the freighters, though the Indians did capture one unit of three wagons in tandem that had straggled and been abandoned a few hundred yards from the corral. Taking as many kegs of beer as they could carry, the warriors set fire to five tons of bacon still aboard. By morning, the Indians were gone and the train resumed its journey.[24]

The campaigns of 1876 were by no means the U.S. Army's finest hour. Sheridan had stood firm in his conviction that heavy, converging columns would be as successful on the northern Plains as they had been in the Texas panhandle and Indian Territory a few years earlier.

[22]Bourke, *On the Border*, 249.

[23]*Daily Leader*, July 2, August 6, and November 4, 1876; Major E. F. Townsend to AAG, Dept. of the Platte, August 24, 1876, LS, FL,; Buecker, *Fort Robinson*, 50.

[24]For more on this incident, see Vaughn, *Indian Fights*, 167–83.

But Crook had been repulsed at Powder River in March, and stopped cold at the Battle of the Rosebud in June. Custer and the Seventh Cavalry, meantime, were mauled by the very same tribes at Little Bighorn a week later. When Crook finally did move again in August, he encountered Terry on Rosebud Creek and the two combined their forces, creating a huge, unwieldy army entirely unsuited for Indian campaigning. The command relationship, moreover, was strained to the breaking point until the two generals mutually agreed to go their separate ways, finally recognizing that such a large force had no chance of catching Sitting Bull.

Terry kept his forces in the Yellowstone country of eastern Montana, while Crook struck east on a trail leading toward the Missouri. His expedition, degenerating into what became known as the "Starvation March," slogged through rain and mud for weeks, existing on reduced rations until the men were compelled to eat the horses and mules as they dropped from malnutrition and exhaustion. Only on September 9 did the troops score a modest success when some of Crook's emaciated cavalry stumbled into an Indian village near Slim Buttes, some distance north of the Black Hills. Saved only by wagonloads of food sent out from Deadwood, Crook's men finally staggered to Camp Robinson, where the expedition was dissolved.[25]

At the time Crook and Terry were conducting their stern chase in Montana, Congress passed special provisions in conjunction with its annual appropriation for Indian annuities. Custer's defeat had galvanized the legislators to take a firm stance in dealing with the Indians, and a resolution passed in mid-August did much to abrogate the Fort Laramie Treaty of 1868. Significantly, the ultimatum declared that the Sioux reservation no longer included the Black Hills. Likewise, the unceded lands no longer existed so far as the Sioux were concerned. The resolution specified that they would live on a much smaller reservation; they would stop fighting forever; and they would submit to having several new roads built across their reservation to access the Black Hills. In return, they would be fed, clothed, and schooled as wards of the government. Even though things had not gone according to plan so far as the military campaign was concerned, the govern-

---

[25]This engagement is treated in Greene, *Slim Buttes*.

ment nevertheless realized the goals outlined in its November 1875 conspiracy.

In the fall of 1876, a seven-member commission, headed by George W. Manypenny, was sent out on behalf of the president to deliver these terms to the Sioux at the White River agencies. Major Edwin F. Townsend, in command of Fort Laramie during that turbulent summer, extended the hospitality of the post to the commissioners when they arrived on September 2. Two days later the commissioners left the Rustic Hotel and, escorted by the weary members of K Company, Second Cavalry, moved on to Camp Robinson to meet with the Sioux. The one hundred fifty Oglala and Brulé headmen in attendance were peremptorily informed of the recent congressional edict, and told, moreover, that in the future their annuities would be delivered at the Missouri River agency. There would no equivocation on that point as there had been following the 1868 treaty.

Sheridan, meanwhile, had his own plans for handling the Sioux problem. To make certain there would be no misunderstanding among his field commanders, the division commander once again journeyed to Fort Laramie, arriving there while the commissioners were still in council with the Sioux. Sheridan had previously notified Crook and Colonel Ranald S. Mackenzie to meet him at the post after summoning Mackenzie's veteran Fourth Cavalry from its stations in Texas to further reinforce the troops in the Department of the Platte.

The three met on September 21 to plan a final strategy for bringing the Sioux War to a quick conclusion. Sheridan fell back on the strategy of his earlier success, when Custer had hounded the Southern Cheyennes in Indian Territory during the winter of 1868–69, by ordering Crook to conduct a similar campaign aimed at striking Cheyenne villages reported to be gathering on Crazy Woman Fork. Mackenzie's cavalry brigade would deliver the blow when the expedition was within striking distance. Determined to muster all the force possible to defeat the hostiles in a grand effort, Sheridan declared that "The Sioux war, and all other Indian wars in this country . . . will be over forever."[26]

Crook, meanwhile, would disarm and dismount the Indians at the White River agencies to preclude their involvement. This time, Sheri-

---

[26]*ARSW*, 1876, 39.

dan wanted to make certain the reservation Sioux would not assist the hostiles, and that the agencies would not serve as refuges for the recalcitrant bands. Evidence of their complicity had surfaced with Red Cloud's refusal the previous summer to camp near the agency, when it was suspected his people had been supplying combatants, ammunition, and guns to the hostile factions, the very arms that Red Cloud had previously insisted were vital for hunting and survival. Sheridan and a party of visiting Japanese army officers left the post the following day to catch the train at Cheyenne, while Crook prepared for another hunting expedition, this time to Laramie Peak, with Egan's well-worn company as his escort.

On October 23, 1876, Mackenzie, surrounding Red Cloud's camps with eight companies of cavalry and a battalion of Pawnee scouts, carried out the disarmament of the Sioux and Cheyennes at the agencies, without opposition. It came none too soon. During the week of October 10, the bodies of no less than three white men had been brought to Fort Laramie for burial. Two were civilians, the other Private W. C. Tasker, of Egan's troop. All had been killed in the vicinity of the Chugwater.

Crook temporarily established his field headquarters at Fort Laramie on the twenty-sixth while he awaited initial elements of his expedition to assemble. Two days later, Merritt arrived with five more companies of the Fifth Cavalry and two companies of the Ninth Infantry. While camped there, the troops were outfitted with fur caps and buffalo overcoats to make the coming campaign as endurable as possible. That done, the column moved to Fort Fetterman where more troops would join them. Eventually, the force totaled eleven companies each of cavalry and infantry, plus four companies of the Fourth Artillery sent from the Pacific Coast to serve as infantry. Mackenzie's Fourth Cavalry, the last large contingent to pass through Fort Laramie, camped on the flat below the post on November 4 before crossing over the Platte bridge en route for Fort Fetterman.[27]

---

[27]The strategic importance of the iron bridge at Fort Laramie was measured not only by its value in moving traffic to the Black Hills and Camp Robinson, but by its ability to facilitate large troop movements during the Indian campaigns north of Fort Fetterman in the late 1870s. Columns could cross to the north bank of the North Platte at Fort Laramie with considerably less effort and in less time than they could at Fort Fetterman, which had only a ferry available. From the bridge, they followed the old emigrant trail paralleling the river. Lindmier, *Drybone*, 38–40.

As Crook advanced northward for the third time that year, his Indian auxiliaries discovered Dull Knife and Little Wolf's Cheyennes camped on Red Fork of Powder River, near the south end of the Big Horn Mountains. In a dawn attack on November 25, the cavalry surprised and routed the villagers, who subsequently took up positions on nearby bluffs and put up stiff resistance while the noncombatants fled to safety. After a hotly contested fight lasting several hours, Mackenzie's men finally dislodged the warriors and took possession of the village. In the lodges, they found plunder taken from the bodies of Custer's men, offering proof of their involvement at Little Bighorn.[28] The destitute Cheyennes struggled northward in bitter cold, eventually finding a haven with Crazy Horse's Oglalas. Although Crook attempted to run them down, he was plagued by supply shortages, finally giving up the chase a few weeks later. The expedition was dissolved and the troops sent back to their home stations for the winter.

The close of the 1876 campaign resulted in Fort Laramie hosting a large garrison—six companies of cavalry and five of infantry, all crowded into its barracks. For the remainder of the season, most of the troops enjoyed the comparative comforts of routine garrison duty. Colonel Nelson A. Miles and his Fifth Infantry by then were posted in a cantonment on the Yellowstone River in eastern Montana, in the heart of the region occupied by hostile remnants, while many of their number had commingled with their brethren back at the agencies. Miles' aggressive activities in the north, meantime, kept the roamers off balance through the winter. In a singularly hard-fought engagement on January 8, 1877, Miles found and defeated Crazy Horse's combined Sioux and Cheyenne bands in the Wolf Mountains in southern Montana Territory.[29]

During the comparatively quiet winter that followed, the troops at Fort Laramie were called upon to mount only occasional patrols in response to reports of Indians having been seen in the area, though few of the rumors could be verified. The only noteworthy incident, in fact, occurred when Corporal C. A. Bessey and four men of A Company, Third Cavalry were sent out to repair the telegraph line to Fort Fetterman. When the detachment encountered a small band of Indi-

---

[28]For a complete account of Mackenzie's campaign, see Greene, *Morning Star Dawn*.
[29]A comprehensive treatment of Mile's activities is in Greene, *Yellowstone Command*.

ans near the mouth of Elk Horn Creek on January 12, the warriors immediately attacked them. In the skirmish that followed, Bessey and Private Featherall were seriously wounded, but the plucky corporal organized such a determined defense that the Indians finally withdrew. Bessey was later awarded the Medal of Honor for his actions.[30]

The majority of purported Indian sightings actually may have been white outlaws, who began preying on ranches and the Black Hills coaches after the Indian danger subsided. And, in a contradiction of roles, numerous bands of thieves began rustling horses from the Indians at the White River agencies. Consequently, some of the Indians seen on the North Platte undoubtedly were parties attempting to recover their own stock. When outlaws ran off thirty ponies from Red Cloud Agency on February 2, Lieutenant H. R. Lemley and a detachment of twenty-five troopers from Fort Laramie were ordered to patrol down the Platte in an effort to intercept them. Lemley caught up with the gang, captured two men, and recovered most of the stolen ponies, but the other members managed to escape.[31]

By spring 1877, due largely to Miles' relentless pursuit of the dwindling number of northern Sioux and Cheyennes, culminating in their defeat at Lame Deer Creek in May, many of the staunchest hostiles followed Sitting Bull to find sanctuary in Canada. The remaining at-large Indians eventually surrendered at Camp Robinson, where Crazy Horse would be killed during a botched attempt to arrest him. The remnants of Dull Knife's Cheyennes would be sent to Indian Territory to join their southern kinsmen on the reservation at Fort Reno.

The Indians had scored the greatest victories on the battlefields of the Great Sioux War, but the army's doggedness, punctuated by a few decisive skirmishes in which large amounts of Indian supplies were destroyed, eventually wore down the tribesmen until they had no place left to hide, and nothing to be gained by further resistance. The Sioux War simply sputtered out.

---

[30] PR, January 1877, FL; MH, FL, January 1877.

[31] Major A. W. Evans to Lieutenant W. S. Schuyler, A. D. C., Headquarters in the field, Dept. of the Platte, February 2, 1877, LS, FL.

CHAPTER TWENTY

"Everything Had Changed"

In the wake of the Great Sioux War, the Fort Laramie garrison soon settled into the familiar routine of post life. Most of the men had eagerly anticipated field service the previous year, but those who were not already veterans learned soon enough that Indian campaigning on the frontier could be a miserable, frustrating, utterly exhausting experience with few rewards. At least the humdrum of guard, drills, and fatigue were compensated by regular meals, the comfort of a barracks, an occasional bath—and the solace found in warm beer. But the regular army was never a soft touch, and officers and noncoms alike moved swiftly to restore discipline and prepare the men for whatever might come. First Lieutenant John G. Bourke, who had been Crook's adjutant during the recent campaign, described the new order: "Every morning, the troops of these two garrisons [Fort Laramie and Camp Robinson] have been put through the school of the Company, dismounted, Manual of Arms, Skirmish drill, and in afternoon mounted drill, besides an occasional setting up exercise and target practice. This severe training is having a very marked effect upon the physique of the recruits."[1]

The officers found life less regimented than did the enlisted men. For the most part, reliable first sergeants supervised the companies on a daily basis. Many line officers visited the orderly rooms only long enough to sign the company morning reports, consult with the first sergeants, and perform other essential duties required by orders or

[1]John G. Bourke Diary, 22: 1837, John Gregory Bourke Collection.

regulations. Bourke painted a picture of life on officers' row that contrasted sharply with that of the rank-and-file.

> The daily routine of our lives at Fort Laramie was rather monotonous. We arose and dressed about 7:30, breakfasted, listened to the music of the Band at Guard Mounting, then visited the Hd Qrs. stables to see that the horses were properly groomed. . . . Returning from the stable, the opening hours of the morning were devoted to whatever business was contained in the mail of the preceding evening; then resumed our books, which were not relinquished until dark, except during the moments that the music of the afternoon open-air concert tempted us to promenade the broad veranda encircling the house. In the evening, the mail was delivered and read, after dinner, which was served at retreat, if we did not pay any visits or receive any callers, the allurements of our book engaged us again until the hour for bed-time, 11 o'clock, approached.[2]

The army may have done its best to maintain the discipline and health of the troops, but other elements at work in the neighborhood proved counterproductive. The "hog ranches" just outside the military reservation experienced a booming business in liquor and prostitution as a windfall of Fort Laramie's large garrison. Lieutenant Bourke described some typical establishments: "Three miles out there was a nest of ranches, Cooney's and Ecoffy's [sic] and Wright's tenanted by as hardened and depraved a set of wretches as could be found on the face of the globe. Each of these establishments was equipped with a rum-mill of the worst kind and each contained from three to half a dozen Cyprians, virgins whose lamps were always burning brightly in expectancy of the coming bridegroom, and who lured to destruction the soldiers of the garrison. In all my experience I have never seen a lower, more beastly set of people of both sexes."[3]

Adolph Cuny himself fell victim to some of those very characters

---

[2]Ibid., 1844–47.

[3]Ibid., 1848–49; According to an old-time resident, Cuny and Ecoffey continued to operate their saloon at the former Beauvais Ranch, five miles down the North Platte, in addition to the newer one at Three Mile. John O'Brien interview, June 18, 1946, FLNHS. Jules Ecoffey reportedly died in 1874. Following Cuny's murder, Posey Ryan purchased the log building at the Three Mile and moved it to his ranch up the Laramie. Charles Charleson reportedly married Cuny's widow and thus became owner of the hog ranch for a short time. John Owens subsequently bought the place, then sold it either to Bob Osborne or Henry Ritterling about 1880 or 1881. Typescript copy of "Minnequa Historical Bulletin No. 8" (1934), FLNHS; Vaughn, "The Fort Laramie Hog Ranches," 41.

later that summer when he assisted U.S. Marshal Charles Hays from Cheyenne in the arrest of Duncan Donald and Billy Webster, two members of an outlaw gang suspected of murdering a stage driver. Cuny, who was a local deputy, joined Hays and his partner on their way to the neighboring Six-Mile Ranch, where the outlaws reportedly had been seen. After making the arrest, Hays and his partner pursued other gang members, while Cuny stayed behind to guard the two prisoners. McDonald apparently attempted to overpower him, and at the same time one of the absent outlaws entered through a side door, shooting Cuny to death.[4]

In a strange turn of events, outlaws had replaced Indians as the major source of trouble in the region. Many of the coaches coming from the Black Hills carried large amounts of gold and other valuables, thus presenting tempting and easy targets for bandits. In a particularly noteworthy robbery, a gang of fifteen road agents waylaid a special treasure coach and made off with $30,000 in gold. A soldier at Hat Creek Station recorded that the bullet-riddled vehicle was later brought there on its way to Cheyenne for repairs. When holdups became fairly frequent during 1877–78, the garrison provided guards to ride aboard the stages between the post and Deadwood. Also, cavalry detachments from Fort Laramie, acting in the capacity of posses comitatus, were sometimes sent out to try to catch the robbers, even though the army's authority for doing so was vague at best.[5]

---

[4]*Cheyenne Daily Leader*, July 22, 1877; Vaughn, "Hog Ranches," 41.

[5]The use of federal forces to enforce civil law was rare in American history, and closely restricted prior to the Fugitive Slave Act of 1850. With the passage of that bill, Attorney General Caleb Cushing authorized the army to enforce that law on those occasions when troops were summoned by civil officials. Over time, and especially in the West where few if any civilian law enforcement officers were available, the law became a loosely interpreted policy. Technically, officers who chose to act under that authority risked becoming the targets of lawsuits, but few were actually charged. The Army Appropriation Act of 1878 included a much more restrictive definition of the posse comitatus provision. It prohibited the use of troops in civil matters, except when specifically directed by the president or Congress. This was promulgated to the army as GO No. 49, July 7, 1878, AGO, although a subsequent order, GO No. 71, issued the following October, gave officers wider discretion in that regard. Most post commanders, it would seem, simply applied common sense in responding to civilian requests for assistance. This topic is fully examined in Tate, *Frontier Army in the Settlement*, 80–110; For specific references to Fort Laramie's involvement in combating banditry, see Commanding Officer to AAG, Dept. of the Platte, June 30, 1877, LS, FL; First Lieutenant J. B. Johnson to anon., July 20, 1877, ibid.; Major A. W. Evans to commanding officer, Camp on Hat Creek, November 25, 1877, ibid.; MH, August 1878, FL; Private George W. McAnulty to Lillian, September 29, 1878, typescript copy in vertical files, FLNHS.

In the span of only a few months, Fort Laramie had slipped from a post at war to a quiet station where the solitude was disrupted only occasionally by an incident of outlawry or an altercation between soldiers at one of the local road ranches. A correspondent to the *Army & Navy Journal* reported the nearest thing to an "attack" in October 1877, when a wild elk ran out from the river bottom and "charged" across the parade ground. The ever-present menagerie of dogs lying around the post immediately counterattacked and chased the frightened elk among the buildings until the animal turned on his pursuers and gored three or four of them. As the dogs engaged the intruder, several officers saddled their mounts and took up the chase, firing a considerable number of shots at the fleeing beast. The elk eventually outdistanced them, whereupon the officers, "returned to the fort, leaving the elk to seek some quiet grazing spot on the boundless plains."[6]

Life became increasingly more relaxed as months passed. The *Daily Leader* commented that the first Christmas following the Sioux War was observed with "Every window in the post . . . brilliantly illuminated with a dozen candles each, the quarters were decorated with evergreen, and in the old band quarters were as merry a set of dancers as ever tripped the 'light fantastic toe.' All went merry as a marriage bell. Wine flowed freely, and many a hearty toast was drank to the happiness of old friends in Cheyenne."[7]

The resolution of the Sioux situation, along with the redefinition of their reservation, negated the army's need for the extensive Fort Laramie Military Reservation authorized in 1872. The Indians no longer posed a threat to the critical hay fields near the present-day Wyoming-Nebraska border, and at the same time the dissolution of the un-ceded hunting territory encouraged a further influx of ranchers to take up lands in southeastern Wyoming.[8]

---

[6] *ANJ*, October 6, 1877, 138. One wonders if this might have been the same pet elk, come home, that Post Trader J. S. Collins kept at the fort in 1874. The commanding officer complained to Collins that the elk had the run of the post and that he should confine the animal in some way. Post Adjutant to J. S. Collins, October 10, 1874, LS, FL.

[7] *Cheyenne Daily Leader*, January 19, 1878.

[8] Nick Janis had settled at Little Moon, a small lake in the North Platte Valley near where the first Red Cloud Agencies had been located. He established a successful haying operation there, which he sold to John Hunton on July 25, 1880. Hunton's diary suggests that Janis finally left the Platte at that time. Hunton sold Little Moon to the burgeoning Pratt & Farris Ranch just three months later for a handsome profit. *Hunton Diary* 4 (1880–1882): 64, 68, 88.

A survey taken in 1876 recorded no less than sixty-eight cattle ranches in the area. Many of the owners, for example John Hunton, were only too happy to secure lucrative contracts for supplying hay and wood to Fort Laramie. Some, like the burgeoning Pratt & Ferris operation, working through political channels, influenced the government to cede to them a large area of prime land considered no longer vital to the army. A congressional act approved on August 14 of that year therefore reduced the military reservation to its 1869 boundaries, an area of fifty-four square miles. The six-by-nine-mile tract lay on a north-south axis with its northern boundary a short distance beyond the North Platte River.[9]

Notwithstanding the cessation of open hostilities, the tribes gathered at Red Cloud and Spotted Tail Agencies continued to be an unresolved problem. Sheridan complained that their presence in the extreme southwest corner of the reservation put them entirely too close to the travel routes, particularly the road from Sidney, to the Black Hills. He confided that the only reason for keeping the agencies there was to benefit the traders and freighting contractors, who made huge profits supplying the Indians. Moving them closer to Fort Randall on the Missouri, as originally planned, would enable the Indian bureau to ship the goods more economically by steamer. Were that not justification enough for relocation, Sherman doubted that "if in the present frame of mind of the Red Cloud Indians the two races can live so closely together without fighting."[10]

The crux of Sherman's objection was rooted in his long-held obsession with exiling the Indians to the wastelands of Dakota, far removed from white settlements and travel routes. Once that was accomplished, he could advance his strategy for consolidating most of his forces in large posts along the rail lines, leaving only a few military stations active near the reservations in the event of trouble. The army could then dispense with many of the older and more remote forts,

---

[9]The Pratt & Ferris Ranch eventually embraced most of the Platte Valley from present-day Lingle, Wyoming, to Scottsbluff, Nebraska, ibid., 71; GO No. 90, August 22, 1876, AGO. By 1879 ranches threatened to overrun the Laramie Peak area where the army had obtained its lumber for many years. The army scouted the area that year to delineate a suitable area that could be protected from encroachment. A timber reserve was authorized by executive order on February 9, 1881, and published to the army as GO No. 5, February 28, 1881, AGO.

[10]ARSW, 1878, 34.

like Laramie and Fetterman, which were at once becoming increasingly expensive to maintain and less useful.

The State of Nebraska lent its full political weight to Sheridan's argument, but for its own reasons. The citizens of the state objected strenuously to having the Sioux and affiliated tribes residing within its borders. The state based its objections on the grounds that as a legally constituted territory at the time the Fort Laramie Treaty was signed in 1868, unlike Wyoming, Nebraska had not agreed to the concept of the hunting territory, nor had it consented to assume a portion of the Sioux reservation within its boundaries. The stance taken by the governor and the congressional delegation, based on the concept of states' rights, was enough to finally sway the Interior Department to move the Sioux to the Missouri in late October 1877. The Arapahoes, who had no designated reservation, agreed to make peace with their old Shoshone enemies and live in the Wind River country.

The Northern Cheyennes, who had been removed to the foreign environment of Indian Territory, did not long remain there. Their people sick and malnourished, Dull Knife and Little Wolf led the survivors on an epic journey all the way back to northwest Nebraska, with troops in hot pursuit the entire way. Even though they finally were arrested near Camp Robinson in early 1879, the determined Cheyennes eventually won a concession to live in their traditional homeland on Rosebud Creek in southeastern Montana.[11]

The busy years following the post–Civil War renewal of Fort Laramie had been hard on the infrastructure of the old post. The continual demands of the Indian situation had once again left little time, and few soldiers, to maintain the buildings. Troops had been kept in the field patrolling the roads from Cheyenne to the Black Hills and to Fort Fetterman, repairing telegraph lines, escorting mail coaches, and guarding key points along the trails. Crook's successive drafts on the garrison to support his thrusts into the Sioux country so seriously depleted the number of men available for duty at the post that much of the time the commanding officer was hard-pressed to carry out essential duties.

---

[11]A thorough treatment of this remarkable story is presented in Monnett, *Tell Them We Are Going Home*. See also Buecker, *Fort Robinson*, 125–48.

The wagon bridge over the Laramie had seen considerable service during those years, carrying virtually all traffic to and from the post. The structure had additionally borne the immense flood of traffic to all points north, including the Cheyenne–Black Hills Stage, trains of annuity goods and supplies bound for Camps Robinson and Sheridan; large numbers of troops and their trains, not to mention the stream of gold rushers. By 1878 the rickety bridge, with its abutments being eroded away by the current, posed a serious danger for heavily laden vehicles. Only a year earlier, the army had constructed a make-shift diversion dam upstream using several old wagons filled with stone and scrap iron to anchor them in place. Major Julius W. Mason, Third Cavalry, pro-posed to the department quartermaster that the bridge be replaced as soon as possible by a new one built somewhat farther upstream. Mason recommended a site about one-half mile southwest of the post, near the existing Cheyenne road. Because the channel narrowed at that point, the bridge would be shorter and therefore less expensive to build. More-over, redirecting the main access into the fort would circumvent the crossing of Deer Creek, a small but sometimes troublesome tributary flowing into the Laramie. Mason's plan was approved and the structure was completed in late summer of 1878. The new route conveniently brought the coaches on the Cheyenne-Deadwood line directly to the station at the Rustic Hotel before coursing past the post trader's store and the two-story cavalry barracks toward the Platte bridge.[12]

First Lieutenant James Regan, Ninth Infantry, first saw Fort Laramie as a member of the Eighteenth Infantry in 1866. Visiting the post again in 1880, he made what is perhaps the most graphic and complete description of Fort Laramie during its military occupancy. Regan's keen appreciation of the fort's remarkable history, probably recounted to him by Ordnance Sergeant Snyder, made his comments all the more poignant:

> The modern Fort Laramie is built in the form of a rectangle; the men's barracks, six in number, in long buildings occupying the north and east sides, post headquarters and officers' Quarters the south side, and officers

---

[12]Bourke diary 22, pp. 1838, 1849; MH, June 1877, FL; Major J. W. Mason to AAG, Dept. of the Platte, April 17, June 20, and August 27, 1878, LS, FL; The old wagon bridge remained in use as a convenient service access across the river, and likely carried the quartermaster trains from Cheyenne Depot because of its proximity to the storehouses. Author's note.

quarters the west side. On the last mentioned side is old 'Bedlam,' which was sent out in finished parts with the first troops from Fort Leavenworth, a distance of six hundred and seven hundred miles. The episodes connected with this old building, were they well known and properly told, would form a volume in themselves. We have ourselves seen every room from lower to upper story brilliantly lighted and filled with card-parties, composed of Officers, some of whom have since become distinguished. This old building is still used as officers' quarters, but it is hardly habitable, owing to its dilapidated condition, its warped boards affording shelter for bats and swallows. An officer's wife, writing to her friends or relatives in the East, who were concerned about her being so far away on the frontier, informed them that she was in less danger, and was dwelling in a $40,000 house, meaning 'Bedlam,' that being the original cost of the house.

The magazine is also located on this side, and although standing by itself in early days, it is now wedged between Officers' Quarters. Some people might be nervous being so near to tons of powder and ammunition, but the people here treat it with the greatest indifference.

The Quartermaster's store-houses, workshops, corral, stables, commissary store-houses, hospital, and a long log building, 'River Side' or 'Venice' which is used as Officers' Quarters, are all on the north side of the post. There are two new buildings on this side of the post, which are built of concrete, a conglomeration of gravel and lime and water. One is a hospital two stories high, with wings extending north and southeast. The other, a long building designed for two companies of cavalry, is two stories. The upper story is divided into sleeping apartments; the lower, into kitchens, dining-room, reading-rooms, orderly and other rooms. Both of these buildings are superior edifices, and reflect credit upon the Government. They are a step in the right direction, it being full time for mud roofs and dingy quarters for troops in garrison to pass from existence. These buildings, however, like most army quarters, are minus the grand essential of bath-rooms and bathing facilities for the men.

We strolled to the grave-yard on the hill, and there saw the elevated grave of Spotted Tail's daughter, which was very much worn and faded . . . Around this old grave-yard, which is now utterly demolished, some of the graves being moved a quarter of a mile further north, can be traced the line of a breastwork, which of old was thrown up to resist the attack of Indians.

The Trader's Establishment was the next place of note . . . It is one of the very oldest adobe and stone buildings at the post. It was in existence long before the arrival of the military. It is now in the possession of a Mr. Collins, a business man of Omaha, and is used as a trading establishment

for the military, civilians living in the vicinity of the post and Black Hillers.
. . .

   From the post-trader's it is but a few steps to the post-office, which is
in one of the primitive adobe buildings. The interior is divided into two
rooms, one of which was used as the postal-room, and the other as the
abode of Postmaster and Ordnance Sergeant Leodegar Schnyder, who
marched here with the first troops in '49, and has been in this one isolated
post ever since.[13]

In a tragic postscript to Regan's description, Post Trader Gilbert H.
Collins died by his own hand on July 10, 1880, shortly after Regan's
visit. John London, brother of First Lieutenant Robert London, Fifth
Cavalry, immediately secured a temporary license to serve as post
trader while he followed political avenues to take over the business. A
post council of administration, convened to fix the value and prices of
goods in the store, allowed John S. Collins, Gilbert's brother and a
former trader, until October 1 to have the buildings appraised. In the
interim, London was appointed permanent post trader, to take effect
February 1, 1881.

By 1880, Cheyenne was both Wyoming's territorial capital and the
unchallenged commercial center in the region. A Union Pacific
branch line extending north from Denver had recently linked those
two cities, and survey crews were already in the Chugwater Valley
staking a route leading toward Montana, with a spur servicing the
Black Hills. Concurrently, a competitive line, the Chicago & Northwest Railroad, was rapidly laying track toward the Hills from the east.
And, with the Indians finally out of the way, the Northern Pacific was
advancing west across Montana to connect the Great Lakes region
with the Pacific. General Sherman took great satisfaction in the
knowledge that his army had done much to make that progress possible. With a network of railroads in the West becoming a reality, Sher-

---

[13]Regan, "Military Landmarks," 151–59. Regan apparently did not realize that officers had indeed
complained about the storage of munitions so near their quarters. In 1876, upon completion of
a new concrete guardhouse, the munitions were moved to the old stone guardhouse near the
Laramie River. The "arsenal," comprised of the old magazine, a frame gun shed, and an adobe
storage building, all joined under a common roof, housed small arms, artillery pieces, accou-
trements, and other equipment belonging to the Ordnance Department. See McChristian,
"Special Report: Magazine."

man reiterated his desire to consolidate troops along the railroads, and to abandon many of the frontier forts: "These railroads have completely revolutionized our country in the past few years, and impose on the military an entire change of policy. Hitherto we have been compelled to maintain small posts, along wagon and stage routes of travel. These are no longer needed . . . the regular stations built for storage at convenient distances afford the necessary shelter for stores and for the men when operating in the neighborhood. We should now absolutely abandon many of the smaller posts . . . and concentrate at strategic points . . . where railroads intersect, so as to send out detachments promptly to the districts where needed."[14]

With all of the western tribes assigned to reservations, and the frontier becoming undefinable, Sherman knew the time had come for the army to consolidate by designating those strategic points. He put his plan in motion by urging Congress to authorize the army to begin divesting itself of posts having no appreciable military value. Not only would it be cheaper for the army to maintain fewer stations, he argued, but larger numbers of troops could be supplied to the region more economically along the rail lines.

Fort Laramie now lay ninety miles from the transcontinental railroad, and Fort D. A. Russell had long since eclipsed it as the largest and most strategic post in the region. Fort Robinson, promoted from "camp" status in 1878, and its new sister post, Fort Niobrara, stood watch over the southern perimeter of the several Sioux reservations to thwart any Indian incursions into the new white settlements sprouting across western Nebraska. The appearance of surveyors for the Fremont, Elkhorn, & Missouri Valley Railroad along the Niobrara River in 1882 presaged a direct east-west rail connection for both of those forts just four years later, at the same time bypassing Fort Laramie by some forty miles.

These developments served as a strong influence for Sherman and Sheridan to place Fort Laramie high on their list for abandonment, and to give it a correspondingly low priority for repairs. The post commander lamented, "Indeed there is not a set of quarters here, that does not need a thorough overhauling, and repairing, in order to make

---

[14]*ARSW*, 1880, 5.

them last a few years longer."[15] The question was whether Fort Laramie *had* a few more years. Even to a casual visitor, it was obvious the post had gone to seed by the early 1880s. "Of all the garrisoned military posts that I have seen," wrote Professor William Berryman Scott during a western paleontology tour in June 1882, "Fort Laramie was the most neglected and ill-kept and I saw there a striking illustration of the incredibly foolish way in which the army administration at Washington mismanaged its affairs."[16]

If frontier forts were kept active longer than they should have been, the fault was not Sherman's. In his 1883 annual report, he had declared the Indian Wars virtually over: "I now regard the Indians as substantially eliminated from the problem of the Army. There may be spasmodic and temporary alarms, but such Indian wars as have heretofore disturbed the public peace and tranquility are not probable."[17] Counteracting his efforts to consolidate the army at fewer posts were congressional representatives who, then as now, resisted all efforts on the part of the military to eliminate stations within their respective districts. Needed or not, the presence of an army garrison always underpinned the local economy. Payrolls added cash flow to area businesses, and contracts to supply the posts with wood, beef, and hay were staples of local enterprise. By the 1880s, with the Indian threat only a memory and the civilian population on the rise, it became common for small ranchers and homesteaders to sell vegetables, milk, and eggs to company messes.

That Fort Laramie was living on borrowed time became clear as other posts in the region fell victim to Sherman's budget knife. He began by lopping off both Fort Hartsuff, in central Nebraska, and Camp Sheridan near the old Spotted Tail Agency, in 1881. Forts Fetterman and Sanders in Wyoming Territory met a similar fate and were closed the following year. In accordance with Sherman's consolidation plan, most of the Fifth Cavalry was transferred to Cheyenne, leaving only two troops of the Fifth, and one company of the Fourth Infantry, at Fort Laramie. The diminutive garrison carried out routine garrison

---

[15]Colonel A. G. Brackett to AAG, Department of the Platte, January 7, 1880, LS, FL.
[16]William Berryman Scott, *Some Memories of a Palaeontologist*, 151.
[17]*ARSW*, 1884, 125.

duties and continued periodic patrols along the Cheyenne–Black Hills Road to discourage bandits, since the daily coaches continued to be the principal link from the railroad to Custer City and Deadwood. Although the Union Pacific Railroad had secured a franchise for a branch line to connect with the Northern Pacific in Montana, unforeseen delays stalled construction of that critical link.

After Crook was ordered back to Arizona to contend with the Apache situation, Brigadier General Oliver O. Howard was assigned to replace him at the Department of the Platte Headquarters in fall 1882. The following spring, Howard conducted a personal inspection of the posts under his jurisdiction to acquaint himself with the country in which troops might conceivably operate. By the conclusion of his tour, Howard was convinced that Fort Laramie should be maintained, at least for a while. Although he considered Forts Robinson and Niobrara to be the first line of defense in responding to problems within the reservations, he believed "posts like Robinson and Laramie, the former for observation, for settling small troubles, and as a nucleus on which to form in case of a more general disturbance, are still too necessary to be dispensed with."[18]

Howard backed his decision to maintain Fort Laramie by assigning to it most of the Seventh Infantry, along with its headquarters, when that regiment was transferred to his department. Four companies were assigned to Fort Laramie in late 1882, with three more arriving in the spring following Howard's visit. The Fifth Cavalry, meanwhile, was shifted to Forts Robinson and Niobrara, thereby drawing down the curtain on Fort Laramie's days as a cavalry post.[19] Only infantry would garrison the post for the remainder of its military occupation.

When Colonel William P. Carlin, who had served at Fort Laramie in the 1850s, took command of the Fourth Infantry at Fort Russell

---

[18]Ibid., 125.

[19]On only one occasion after that did Fort Laramie see any large force of cavalry. Near the end of May 1885, nine troops of the Fifth Cavalry from Forts Robinson and Niobrara prepared for a general change of station by concentrating at the post before marching to the railroad at Cheyenne. The Fifth was replaced by the Ninth Cavalry in late July and early August. One troop arrived on July 28 and departed for Fort McKinney two days later. It was followed by the headquarters and eight troops, which arrived at Fort Laramie on August 4. The black cavalrymen camped near the post for a few days before moving on to their new stations at Forts McKinney and Robinson. PR, July and August 1885, FL; MH, FL, August 1885.

thirty years later, he was awed with how the region had evolved since he had last seen it. "In the meantime," he wrote, "everything had changed. The railroad had been built, Denver was a great city. Cheyenne had grown up. The buffalo had disappeared and tame cattle had taken their places. The Indians had been limited to narrow reservations. Civil government had been established. The country in short had become the home of civilized and refined people with all the arts, comforts, and appliances of civilized life."[20] One of those conveniences was an electric light system, which first illuminated the territorial capital in January 1883. Wyoming Territory was rapidly coming of age.

Carlin's observation that cattle had supplanted the buffalo was hardly an overstatement. By 1883, raising livestock had become Wyoming's chief industry, with at least 800,000 head of cattle and nearly as many sheep being pastured in the territory. Long-held fears that the severe winters would preclude cattle ranching had given way to successful practical trials, the earliest of which were credited to those hardy souls who had settled along the Chugwater and the Laramie in the early 1870s. They discovered that the Texas cattle they brought there to winter not only survived, but actually gained weight by spring. Once the Indian danger subsided, cattlemen from as far away as Oregon and western Montana drove increasingly larger herds to the territory to take advantage of the vast open ranges east of the Rocky Mountains. The railroad even made it economically feasible to ship large numbers of cattle from Iowa and Missouri to fatten in Wyoming before being transported to lucrative eastern markets.[21]

Drovers, ignoring the unfenced boundaries of the military reservation, sometimes allowed stock to graze near the fort, and at other times brought herds there to take advantage of the old emigrant fords across the rivers. On one occasion, an unusually large herd from Oregon, en route to the Sioux agency at Pine Ridge, was driven to South Pass, then along the old Oregon-California Road to Fort Laramie. There the cowboys cut out a thousand head of steers, forded the Platte

[20]Colonel William P. Carlin to H. H. Bancroft, San Francisco, Calif., November 14, 1884, typescript in vertical files, Fort Laramie folder no. 4, Wyoming State Archives; *Cheyenne Daily Leader*, January 13, 1883. Oddly enough, the *Leader* did not acquire a telephone until 1886. Ibid., January 29, 1886.

[21]Report of the Governor of Wyoming, *ARSI*, 1883, 576.

below the fort, and drove them to nearby Goshen Hole to fatten over the winter.[22]

Colonel John Gibbon, who had figured prominently in both the Sioux and Nez Perce Wars, particularly the Battle of the Big Hole in 1877, expressed his concern about roaming cattle soon after taking command of the post late in 1882. Gibbon wrote that he found "this reservation overrun with cattle and I am told by Officers who have spent the winter here that during the winter season, and especially during stormy weather thousands of cattle flock into the post to pick up remnants of food thrown out from the stables."[23] Gibbon was especially concerned about cattle fouling the open ditch that finally had been constructed to supply water to the post from farther up the Laramie. He therefore proposed to erect a fence connecting the North Platte and the Laramie rivers to keep out wandering cattle, and to preserve some grazing land for army animals.

Prospectors, desperate to find another rich strike before the frontier and free land disappeared entirely, discovered modest deposits of silver in the hills along the North Platte above Fort Laramie and at Rawhide Buttes. When local rancher John Hunton stopped by the post on August 1, 1881, he found there was "big mining excitement about the fort," created by the discovery of a promising copper ore deposit in the hills about fifteen miles northwest.[24] Within a short time miners flocked to the area to stake claims, giving birth to a camp they named Hartville. Before long, the thriving little community arranged for mail service via a star route connecting with the main line at Fort Laramie. A little more than a year after the first inhabitants arrived at the mines, Hartville was included on a military telephone line strung between Forts Laramie and McKinney. Prospectors also found iron in the Laramie Range and elsewhere during the early 1880s, as well as large quantities of petroleum, inspiring the territorial gover-

---

[22]In one instance, cowboy John Thompson, drowned while swimming the Platte with a herd. His comrades brought his body to the post hospital, where it was kept on ice until it could be sent to Cheyenne on the next southbound stage. Rollinson, *Wyoming Cattle Trails*, 104–109; MH, FL, June 1882.

[23]Colonel John Gibbon to Major J. H. Taylor, Dept. of the Platte, December 6, 1882, LS, FL.

[24]The quotation is in *Hunton's Diary* 4: 152.

nor to rightly proclaim: "Wyoming is about to enter upon a new era of progress."[25]

While new communications links were being developed across the region, the commercial telegraph line to the Black Hills, now several years old, had fallen into "wretched condition," according to Captain Daniel W. Benham, post commander during the summer of 1884. The telegraph company avoided the costs of maintaining the line by requesting the army to do it for them, though there was no formal agreement in that regard. "Working parties from the post have been out nearly every week for the past year in the interest of this private enterprise," Benham grumbled in a letter to department headquarters. That the line between Hat Creek Station and Fort Robinson had been destroyed and never rebuilt only added to his frustration. Benham pointed out that the line to the Hills was of no benefit, except in the unlikely event he might need to communicate with Fort Meade. The captain concluded his remarks by stating that if Howard had no objections, he intended to cease making line repairs northward, in favor of establishing a government line to Fort Robinson. Howard approved Benham's proposal and construction commenced in late fall with crews converging from both forts. Although winter weather temporarily interrupted progress in late December, a work detail made the final connection the following April.[26]

If Professor Scott thought Fort Laramie reflected Washington mismanagement in 1882, he would have been dumbfounded to see it just

[25]A brief history of Hartville is in Mellinger, "Frontier Camp to Small Town," 259–69; Oddly enough, the Mellinger study failed to discuss the origins of the name Hartville. Journalist and lay historian L. G. Flannery was of the opinion that Hartville was the namesake of B. A. Hart, chief clerk at the post trader's store as early as 1877 and later postmaster and clerk for John Hunton. The supposition is reasonable because, according to Flannery, Hart had many business dealings in the area. However, Colonel Verling K. Hart, Fifth Cavalry and post commander at various times from 1880 to 1882, cannot be overlooked as another possible inspiration for the town's name. It is well-known that army officers often invested privately in business ventures that might secure their financial futures, and the practice of naming places for the influential was as common then as now. The aspect of combining civilian opportunity with military life is addressed by Tate, *The Frontier Army in the Settlement of the West*, 282–303; *Cheyenne Daily Leader*, September 21 and December 19, 1882; Wyoming Governor's Report, 1883, 560–61.

[26]Captain D. W. Benham to AAG, Dept. of the Platte, August 15, 1884, LS, FL; PR, December 1884, March and April 1885, FL; *ARSW*, 1885, 142.

a few years later. Despite official indications that Fort Laramie's days were numbered, the mid-1880s witnessed another building spree. That apparent contradiction of word and deed was probably attributable to a combination of factors. At the head of that list was Howard's decision to quarter seven companies of the Seventh Infantry at the post. Even though Sherman, and his successor Sheridan, were bent on concentrating troops at central posts, the reality was that many of those forts lacked the quarters and other buildings necessary to support those larger garrisons. Fort Laramie, on the other hand, boasted several barracks, most of which were then standing empty.

Also influencing that decision was the fact that two influential personalities—Colonel Wesley Merritt and Colonel John Gibbon—commanded Fort Laramie during the early years of the decade. Both were antebellum graduates of West Point, both had distinguished Civil War records, both had attained the rank of major general of volunteers during the war, and both commanded their respective regiments at the time they came to Fort Laramie. In the absence of any decision to abandon the post, each did his best to enhance living conditions. Also to their advantage were the abundant numbers of soldiers available for construction work, with nothing better to do now that the Indians were corralled.

Merritt's first priority, not surprisingly, was to erect three sets of officers' quarters along the west side of the parade to replace the old adobe units that had stood on that site for decades. The new houses, one designed for the commanding officer and the others as double-quarters for captains, were built of formed concrete with stylish mansard frame roofs. In 1884, troops completed a new bakery, a commissary storehouse, and quarters for staff noncommissioned officers, all of concrete. The following year, they constructed a large L-shaped administration building to house headquarters, the post school, and a theater. The perimeter of the parade ground was now lined with trees, while picket fences, boardwalks, and street lamps graced Officers' Row. A water system, relying on a steam engine to pump water from the river to a reservoir on the plateau, from which it was gravity fed to the garrison, added a touch of previously unknown luxury. That made possible the construction near the river of a large communal privy serving the band, four companies, and the guardhouse. Flushed by running water piped into the building, it was "a marked sanitary improvement" over the pit toilets formerly used. If any further evidence were needed, birdbaths at the corners of the parade confirmed that Fort Laramie was anything but a primitive frontier post during its waning years.[27]

Almost as an acknowledgment of that, Fort Laramie's longest resident, Ordnance Sergeant Leodegar Schnyder, left the post on October 13, 1886. He had established an unchallenged army record—thirty-seven years at the same station. As a young Swiss immigrant, Schnyder had arrived on the Laramie as a member of G Company, Sixth Infantry during the summer of 1849. Over the years, he came to embody the institutional memory of the post because he personally witnessed the pageant of all that had happened at Fort Laramie. Yet, to the everlasting detriment of history, "Fort Laramie's silent soldier" never recorded a single word about his experiences there, nor did anyone bother to interview him for the purpose of extracting his recollections. Honoring Schnyder as "the oldest resident in Wyoming" at that time, the *Daily Leader* reported that the sergeant was accorded a serenade by the Seventh Infantry band as he and wife, "Cross Eyed" Julia, left the post. The entire garrison turned out to see the couple off and wish them well in their new assignment.[28]

With the absence of Indian campaigning in the West by the mid-eighties, save the Apache campaign in southern Arizona and New Mexico, the army was forced to create alternatives to keep the men physically fit and to teach the growing numbers of inexperienced recruits how to get along in the field in the event something did happen. To that end, the service instituted annual "camps of instruction" where the troops from several posts in a department assembled to practice battalion tactics, drills, and field maneuvers. The units involved marched overland to the designated rendezvous to condition the men and provide practical field experience before arriving at the camp. The Seventh Infantry participated in camps held at Pine Bluffs

---

[27]Post Commander Benham also proposed building a bathhouse for the men in 1885, but the request was disapproved. MH, FL, December 1885.

[28]*ANJ*, October 30 and November 13, 1886.

in 1885, near Fort Caspar in 1888, and at Fort Robinson in 1889.[29] Colonel Henry Clay Merriam, who followed Gibbon as regimental commander of the Seventh Infantry, recognized the value of conducting his own practice marches in the absence of a formal rendezvous. In fall 1886, he instructed each of his companies to conduct a ten-day march to Laramie Peak and back, with full field equipment, "in the event of any unpleasantness with Mexico."[30]

General Crook, who resumed command of the Department of the Platte in 1886, preceding Geronimo's surrender, also required his post commanders to conduct target practice at some point at least fourteen miles distant from their respective stations. He specified that they were to camp there for at least six days, again to familiarize the men with caring for themselves in the field.[31] Lieutenant George W. McIver, who served under Merriam at Fort Laramie, remembered that the colonel paid "close attention . . . to the details of post administration, [but] he never allowed anyone to forget that the purely military side of life in a garrison was of the first importance. He paid great attention to close order drills and formal parades and was himself a very good drill master. Under his direction the regiment became very proficient and officers and men came to have a great pride in making a good appearance."[32] McIver added, however, that Merriam, like many older officers, was unable to see the need for changes in tactics as a result of breech-loading arms. Influenced by his experience in the Civil War, Merriam focused on battalion close order drills, and largely ignored the skirmish drills and minor tactics that were of the most value in Indian warfare. Indeed, Merriam's attitude was symptomatic of the army as a whole, and by the end of the decade, it was neither

---

[29]Camps of instruction were inaugurated by GO No. 9, May 26, 1885, Department of the Platte. The order directed troops to participate "for the purpose of military instruction and practice in practical field engineering, outpost duty, escort and defense of convoys, defensive and offensive maneuvers, and, generally, the minor operation of war." In one instance, Merriam marched the entire garrison of five companies, along with the headquarters staff, military band, and medical detachment, 150 miles to a camp near Fort Caspar in August 1888. They did not return until October. PR, August and October 1888, FL; ANJ, July 21, 1888.

[30]ANJ, October 9, 1886.

[31]PR, August 1887, FL; ARSW, 1887, 134.

[32]McIver, "Service at Old Fort Laramie," typescript in vertical files, FLNHS (hereinafter cited as "McIver account").

fish nor fowl—no longer an Indian fighting organization, nor a force fully prepared for conventional warfare.

Most of the time, however, the usual garrison routine continued with little deviation. The Cheyenne & Northern Railroad, formed in 1886 to supplant the Union Pacific's failed effort to lay track northward from the capital city, reached John Hunton's place at Bordeaux, twenty-eight miles from Fort Laramie, during the summer of 1887. That event spelled the end of the Cheyenne–Black Hills Stage and Express Company, after which only a short line coach ran from the railway station at Bordeaux to Fort Laramie and a few points beyond.[33] Significantly, the third railroad to be laid through the region also bypassed the post by a rather wide margin. The cumulative effect was inescapable. Now well off the new lines of communication in both directions, the ageing post had become a metaphorical island within a rapidly developing region. Lieutenant McIver attempted to put the best face on the situation when he wrote, "I found the social life of the post very pleasant. There were more people to associate with than I had known before and the number was increased by occasional visitors. I rather think that the isolation of the post tended to greater sociability among the members of the garrison. Lacking the distractions of a nearby town, the people were more inclined to depend on each other for amusement and recreation and a social atmosphere prevailed there that I had never seen before and have never seen since."[34]

McIver had to admit, however, that the place was suited only for quartering troops and at that, recreational opportunities were few. He noted that there was no longer any wild game in the vicinity, nor any trout in the Laramie River, only a few Pike to offer any sport to the anglers of the garrison.

A Seventh Infantry recruit, arriving at Fort Laramie in May 1888, had a contrasting reaction when he expressed profound disappointment with his new home. "So drear and desolate was the country by which it was surrounded," he lamented, "that in any direction but few habitations would be encountered within a radius of 30 miles. Aside from the yearly visit of a Roman Catholic priest, the appearance of a

---

[33] *Cheyenne Daily Leader*, June 13, 1886; February 20 and June 23, 1887.
[34] McIver account.

distant squatter or cowboy, the sight of a white man, except the soldier in uniform, was indeed so rare a thing that he was absolutely
looked on as a novelty."[35]

The long anticipated directive to abandon Fort Laramie finally
came down in late summer 1889. Most of the garrison was absent,
attending a camp of instruction at Fort Robinson. It was welcome
news, in fact, and as soon as the troops returned to the post in late
September, they immediately began packing in preparation for the
move to their new station at Fort Logan, near Denver. Most of the
residents were glad to be leaving. As Lieutenant Daniel Robinson
wrote to his wife on October 20, "All the families left here last Thurs-
day without any apparent regret."[36]

---

[35]O'Sullivan, "Army Posts On the Plains," *Winners of the West*, May 30, 1927.
[36]Daniel Robinson to wife, October 20, 1889, Robinson collection, FLNHS.

CHAPTER TWENTY-ONE

"The Wind Moans Dismally"

Fort Laramie is practically abandoned," penned a disheartened John Hunton to his diary.[1] Earlier that day, March 2, 1890, he had stood in the doorway of the Sutler's Store and watched as the last two companies of the Seventh Infantry strode briskly out of the post and across the bridge en route to their new station at Fort Logan, Colorado. While the departing soldiers probably were cheered by the prospect of Denver's bright lights, Fort Laramie's last post trader witnessed their exodus with sadness, and a sense of foreboding.

The fort had been the center of Hunton's world since his arrival there as a young man in 1867. A native Virginian, Hunton had served through the Civil War in the ranks of Confederate General James Longstreet's corps, experiencing, among other things, Pickett's Charge at the Battle of Gettysburg. In the wake of Appomattox, Hunton had joined a surge of veterans from both armies migrating west in search of new opportunities. He eventually landed at Nebraska City, one of several points of origin for the Oregon-California Route, where he hired on as a bullwhacker on a freight train bound for Fort Laramie. Shortly after his arrival, sutler Seth Ward offered him a job clerking in the store, a position he retained for the next four years.

As a result of that experience, Hunton learned that the army was a lucrative source of income, prompting him to secure several contracts with the Quartermaster Department during the early 1870s to supply wood, hay, and beef to Forts Laramie and Fetterman. In conjunction with those activities, he established a cattle ranch some twenty-five

---

[1]Hunton diary, March 2, 1890.

miles south of the fort along the road to Cheyenne. Hunton was doing well financially when he applied for the formerly profitable post tradership at Fort Laramie in 1888.[2] Now, just two years later, he was left with a store full of goods on a vacant army post.

The legal procedure for abandoning military posts had been outlined in general orders published in 1884, when Congress foresaw the need to establish guidelines for disposing of the growing number of excess reservations.[3] In the case of Fort Laramie, the fifty-four-square-mile reservation was considerably larger than the physical size of the post might have suggested. Most western forts were surrounded by buffers of government land aimed at keeping undesirable commercial enterprises, such as saloons and brothels, at a respectable distance from the troops. These preempted lands, excluded from homesteading, ensured that the army had adequate grazing lands as well as protected sources of fuel and building materials. The law provided that nonessential military reservations were to be transferred to the Interior Department for some public use, such as Indian schools, or returned to the public domain and opened to homesteading.

Prior to the departure of the garrison, Colonel Merriam had anticipated the need for a civilian caretaker to watch over the buildings and the reservation until final disposition of the property. He therefore approached longtime quartermaster employee and sometimes postmaster John Fields with an offer of employment. Fields, a reliable family man with a wife and four daughters, eagerly accepted.[4]

After the Indian Bureau declined to establish a school at Fort Laramie, probably because of its distance from the reservations and lack of convenient rail connections, the government placed the property on the public auction block. First, however, Captain Taylor, along with a detachment of the Ninth Cavalry, returned to salvage anything that might be utilized at Fort Robinson.[5] "The Post is being disman-

---

[2]Hunton, "Early Settlement of the Laramie River Valley, "MS, Folder HJ-2, vertical files, FLNHS; Lieutenant Daniel Robinson to Greswold & Clayton, Fort Laramie, Wyoming, September 12, 1888, McDermott File.

[3]GO No. 72, AGO, July 17, 1884.

[4]Merriam to AAG., Dept. of the Platte, September 29, 1889, LS, FL, transcript in McDermott File; John O'Brian interview, Folder O/b. j-1, FLNHS.

[5]Orders No. 51, March 18, 1890, Post Orders 1888–1897, Fort Robinson, Neb., microfilm roll No. 8, Fort Robinson Museum; PR, FL March, 1890. Accompanying the detachment was Baptiste "Little Bat" Garnier, one of Hunton's oldest and best friends. Garnier was as- (continued, next page)

tled thoroughly by having doors, windows, and flooring taken out of quarters," Hunton recorded.[6] Taylor and his men spared nothing of any potential value. As he witnessed the final ignominy imposed on the old fort, Hunton could not help but regret "the necessity the military authorities are laboring under regarding the destruction of the Fort."[7]

One evening soon after the troops left, Hunton and others who had been associated with this queen of the plains gathered in the officers' club room for a sort of all-night wake, drinking and reminiscing about her many exciting, tragic, and humorous times. A Cheyenne resident passing through the fort earlier that day informed the *Daily Leader* that "Anyone who loved the old post in the palmy days would almost weep at the sight of the ruins. The windows and doors have been taken from the buildings and the wind moans dismally through the structures."[8]

All the government buildings were put up for sale except Officers' Quarters No. 3, which was reserved as a residence for Custodian Fields and therefore exempted from salvage. The house was an old and not very desirable building, the rear portion of which originated as the stone munitions magazine in 1850. The front section, facing the parade ground, had been constructed of adobe during the Civil War— as an arsenal to house small arms and other ordnance property.[9]

Also excluded from the sale was the flagstaff, which had served as the datum for the boundary survey of the post reservation, and three bridges—the iron bridge built across the North Platte in 1875, the

---

(*continued*) signed as messenger for Captain Taylor because the telegraph lines had been taken down. Hunton diary, March 18, 1890. Addendum notes by L. G. Flannery for the March 1890 transcript, Box 3, Accession No. 9, Hunton Papers. Garnier was born at Fort Laramie in 1854 and remained a resident of the region the rest of his life. He was praised for his ability as a hunter, and had served the army as a scout and guide on numerous occasions, especially during the Sioux War of 1876. During the 1870s, he lived at Hunton's ranch, where Hunton took up residency with Bat's daughter, "Lallee," for seven years. Thrapp, *Encyclopedia of Frontier Biography* 2: 538–39; Hunton to Reverend Johsep Lindobner, January 12, 1904, Hunton Letters, Mattes Collection, FLNHS (hereinafter cited as Hunton Letters, Mattes Collection).

[6] Hunton diary, March 18, 1890,

[7] Ibid., March 19 and March 25, 1890.

[8] *Cheyenne Daily Leader*, March 25, 1890.

[9] Quarters No. 3 stood immediately south of the building now called the Surgeon's Quarters at Fort Laramie National Historic Site. Taylor to AAG, Dept. of the Platte, March 26, 1890, transcript in McDermott File; McChristian, "Special Report: Magazine," FLNHS; "Report of Condition, Capacity, & of Public Buildings at Fort Laramie, Wyo. On 31 March 1888," CCF, photostatic copy in Fort Myer Documents, FLNHS (hereinafter cited as "Report of Buildings, 1888").

wagon bridge spanning the Laramie on the south side of the post, and a light-duty footbridge behind the east barracks. The army initially intended to sell the bridges, until the Laramie County board of commissioners intervened to exempt them for inclusion in the public road system. "With characteristic stupidity," cried the editor of the *Cheyenne Daily Leader*, "some officer or board ordered the sale at auction of these structures, not foreseeing that they might come into possession of designing persons who would have small regard for citizens."[10] Indeed, in its zeal to dispose of the fort as quickly as possible, the army failed to consider the potential for private owners to convert them to toll bridges, and control the only means of crossing those streams on the wagon road running north from Bordeaux. In a successful eleventh-hour effort to reserve the bridges, Commissioner Timothy Dyer traveled to the fort to negotiate with Captain Taylor for their purchase.

Although a late blizzard that hit the day before the auction may have discouraged some prospective buyers from attending, on April 9, 1880, Hunton was gratified to see "a number of people here" and said that "houses sold fairly well."[11] Nineteen persons, most of them local residents purchased thirty-five buildings, resulting in proceeds of only $1,417 for the U.S. Treasury.[12]

The army, however, sold only the structures, not the land on which they stood, since by law the entire military reservation, nearly thirty-four thousand acres, was transferred to the Department of the Interior for eventual return to the public domain.[13] It was therefore incumbent

---

[10]*Cheyenne Daily Leader*, April 8, 1890.

[11]Hunton diary, April 9, 1890.

[12]Since the army had inventoried fifty-six major structures before the post was deactivated, we must assume that Taylor razed a number of them and hauled the lumber to Fort Robinson. Another, though less likely, possibility is that Taylor and his auctioneer, Albert Whipple, grouped outbuildings, such as stables and privies, with the primary structures. That would account for some, but not all, of the buildings. Ruling out the possibility that some structures failed to sell at all was Captain Taylor's verification to the department quartermaster at Omaha that all public property remaining at the post, except the few structures specifically exempted, had been sold. Taylor to Chief Quartermaster, Dept. of the Platte, April 10, 1890, LS, FL, transcript in McDermott File; "Account of Sales," appended to "Memorandum Notes in Connection With Old Fort Laramie Wyoming Buildings," MS, Folder BG-15, vertical files, FLNHS (hereinafter cited as "Account of Sales"). Hunton claimed to have purchased eighteen buildings, but this does not agree with the official "Account of Sales." Hunton diary, April 9, 1890.

[13]Although other land laws, namely the Timber Culture Act of 1873 and the Desert Land Act of 1877, were in existence, Congress specifically restricted the disposal of the Wyoming military reservations to the 1863 Homestead Act. *U.S. Statutes at Large* 666: 227.

upon those acquiring buildings at Fort Laramie to either remove or raze the structures before the land was opened to settlement. Some of the buyers, notably John Hunton, Harriet Sandercock, and Joe Wilde, squatted on the land with the intention of eventually filing on the parcels that contained their buildings. The other individuals who purchased buildings apparently saw no future in the place and immediately began salvaging them for useable materials.

During the days immediately following the auction, freight wagons passed in and out of the fort as Taylor's men loaded them with material bound for either Fort D. A. Russell or Fort Robinson. Completing the work on April 20, Taylor turned over the remaining government property to Custodian Fields and returned to Fort Robinson. On that day, nearly forty-one years after the Mounted Riflemen had first arrived on the Laramie, Hunton recorded, "The last soldier left here today, he being Lt. C. W. Taylor, 9th Cav."[14]

Hunton was not exaggerating when he informed his sister that "The breaking up of Fort Laramie and the sending of the soldiers from there . . . was about the *breaking up of me financially*." In the absence of several hundred soldiers, officers, and civilian employees, he was left with a clientele consisting of only a handful of local cowboys and homesteaders. Cash was scarce, prompting Hunton to complain that there was "no money among them." Not only did sales in the store plummet, but the army cancelled the hay and wood contracts he held, leaving him with piles of cord wood cut and stacked. By mid-summer, with his business in its death throes, a depressed Hunton lamented, "Everyone who I owe [is] howling for pay because they know I have no money & cannot get any. Am dead busted."[15]

Life became difficult for John Hunton. Throughout the 1890s, he survived by raising and selling small numbers of horses from his ranch at Bordeaux, as well as hay he grew in the Laramie valley. He also took advantage of political connections to snare a position as a commissioner for the General Land Office, a job that paid him a subsistence wage. In

---

[14]Hunton diary, April 20, 1890.

[15]Ibid., July 8, 1890. Several officers of the Seventh Infantry departed without settling their accounts with Hunton. In view of his friendships among the officers, Hunton chose to carry their accounts, collecting what he could (usually nothing), rather than turn over those debts to a collection agency. An example is found in Hunton to Major D. W. Benham, September 1, 1891, Hunton Letters, Mattes Collection.

addition to operating a blacksmith shop, where he repaired wagons and farm implements, Hunton occasionally found work as a surveyor on some of the irrigation canals being constructed through the valley. Cash, nevertheless, remained elusive, and Hunton often had to resort to selling used lumber, old furniture, and equipment left at the fort.

The solitude and isolation of the place soon weighed heavily on Hunton. He complained that the nearest access to the railroad was twenty-six miles distant, and that the only sizeable town, Cheyenne, lay seventy-five miles away.[16] John's eastern-bred wife, Blanche, had married him and come to his frontier home in 1881. Initially, she seemed to adapt fairly well to her new surroundings, but when the army left Fort Laramie, so did Blanche. For most of the next thirty years, she traveled about, staying with friends and relatives from one end of the country to the other, while John eked out a lonely existence at the tumbledown fort, worrying about how he would finance Blanche's adopted lifestyle. "I feel very despondent," he once confided to her, "I have no where else to go and you detest this place."[17]

Hunton clearly missed the association of the officers, as well as the hustle and bustle of an active army post. The sudden change was most pronounced on the Fourth of July, when the garrison had traditionally observed Independence Day by suspending all nonessential military duties. The day was an occasion for celebrating with horse and foot races, picnicking, contests, a baseball game, and, of course, the consumption of copious amounts of liquor. Now, all that was just a memory. Still, Hunton reasoned, this was a government reservation and some observance of the occasion seemed appropriate, if only to break the monotony. Therefore, just at sunrise on Independence Day 1890, the ex-Confederate soldier and a friend, Union veteran John Crawford, together raised the colors over the deserted fort in a humble, yet fitting, tribute to the nation's unity. Otherwise, Hunton noted, it was "quite a dull Fourth." A week later, on July 10, Wyoming was admitted to the Union as the forty-fourth state.

But Hunton was not defeated. He began urging a friend in Cheyenne to use his influence with the Burlington and Missouri Valley Railroad to "talk up Fort Laramie . . . see if they will not send some

---

[16]Hunton to Frank S. Hunton, Lima, Ohio, July 22, 1893, Hunton Letters, Mattes Collection.
[17]Hunton to Blanche Hunton, September 4, 1892, ibid.

good settlers here and take up about three sections of land west of the Platte bridge." What was good for the country, would be good for John Hunton. But his appeal was to no avail.[18]

Fort Laramie hung on as one of the few settlements of any consequence in the area, though that was not saying much. The iron mining district at Hartville, active since the mid-1880s, lay about twenty miles to the northwest, and Uva, a short-lived cow town, was situated on the C&N Railroad near the fork of the North Laramie and Laramie Rivers. Fort Laramie, meantime, had degenerated almost to a ghost town.

With the post trader's store closed and Hunton strapped financially, a woman settler who had lived in the area for a time, Mary Wilde, stepped in to establish her own general store to cater to the needs of the local populace. During the army days, she and her husband, Joe, had lived about nine miles west of Fort Laramie. While Joe worked as a government teamster, Mary sold butter and eggs to the garrison through the trader's store. Just prior to Hunton's foreclosure, the Wilde's saw an opportunity to start a new business in the Cavalry Barracks, which they had purchased. The Wilde's therefore purchased a stock of goods from Hunton, who was only too happy to sell, and established a store on the ground floor of the barracks.[19]

The couple's cavernous two-story barracks, adapted to house the store, a saloon, dance hall, shoe shop, and twelve-room hotel, soon became a popular social center for farmers and ranchers in the area. On July 4, 1892, for example, Hunton wrote that there were "quite a few people in the Post," and that the Wilde's hosted a dance that night. Independence Day once again became a time for people to gather at the fort. Wilde's establishment, legendary for its raucous all-night dances throughout the year, remained a local institution well into the twentieth century.[20]

Still to be disposed of were the military and timber reservations associated with Fort Laramie. Legislation passed on July 10, 1890,

[18]Hunton to Hicks, October 5, 1891, ibid.
[19]Hunton to B. A. Hart, May 25, 1891, ibid.
[20]Ranchers and homesteaders continued to avail themselves of the store and saloon until about 1910, when Wilde shut down that part of his operation. For some years after the arrival of the railroad, the Wilde Hotel served passengers who detrained at New Fort Laramie. The hotel and dance hall were closed in 1917, when Joe Wilde sold the property to retire in Lingle, Wyoming. McDermott and Sheire, "1874 Cavalry Barracks," 38–44.

authorized the post reservation to be opened for settlement in accordance with the 1863 Homestead Act, which had been designed as a means for equitably distributing the vast public domain west of the Mississippi. In theory, at least, it was intended to provide and opportunity for farmers and immigrants to secure land and become self-sufficient. The law stipulated that any twenty-one year old citizen, or any alien who had declared the intent to become a citizen, could obtain 160 acres of surveyed public land simply by filing a fee of ten dollars and establishing residence on the tract. Those who filed claims for homesteads were required to actually occupy the land for five years and make basic improvements, meaning construction of a dwelling or cultivation, within six months. If the settler survived for the full five years to validate his claim, "proving up" as it was called, he could pay nominal additional fees and receive clear title to the land.

The 1890 law governing abandoned government reservations in Wyoming acknowledged that squatters already had settled illegally on some of those lands. In other instances, civilians previously associated with the military, like the Huntons and Sandercocks at Fort Laramie, were accorded certain concessions. Therefore, any persons settled within the Fort Laramie Military Reservation as of January 1, 1890, were granted preferential right to file on a quarter section of land, retaining any subsequent improvements they may have made.[21]

Before the land could be opened for settlement, however, the General Land Office was required to establish section lines corresponding with the universal grid system beyond the boundaries of government property. When the military reservation was created in 1869, prior to official surveys, a simple rectangular parcel of land surrounding the fort, six miles wide by nine miles long, was delineated by a series of corner stones and intervening wooden posts. William O. Owen of Laramie, Wyoming, was contracted by the General Land Office to undertake a new survey in May 1891.[22]

Of immediate concern to Hunton was the question of whether any portion of the reservation lands would be withheld by the government, or if the entire reservation would be accessible for homesteading. As

---

[21]*U.S. Statutes at Large, 26*, 227; HR No. 1116, 51st Congress, 1st Session; Dick, *Sod House Frontier*, 118–19.

[22]The contract was awarded March 20, and field work was completed that spring. ARCGLO, 411.

the owner of several buildings, Hunton stood to lose financially were the reservation completely dissolved and the land acquired by others. Hunton had previously conducted his own informal survey, so it came as no surprise to him when Owen established a section corner on the nose of "Hospital Hill," leaving him with buildings in all four sections, spread over an area of about eighty acres. Hunton, apparently unaware that the legislation already contained such a provision, appealed to Senator Joseph M. Carey saying that it would be only fair if those holding title to the buildings were granted special consideration in filing for homesteads.[23]

Hunton also had another strategy in mind. He pointed out to Carey that the government needed a small, exclusive reservation to protect the custodian's residence and the flagstaff, both of which belonged to the Department of the Interior. He suggested that a 160-acre tract would be sufficient for that purpose. Of course, with several of his best buildings situated within that parcel, Hunton had managed to protect his own interests from potential homesteaders. But ultimately, his concerns about losing out to a flood of settlers proved groundless. Unlike coveted public lands elsewhere, the Fort Laramie reservation failed to attract an onrush of settlers when it actually was opened to homesteading on September 29, 1891. With some relief, Hunton informed a friend that there were "No boomers around yet."[24] Indeed, southeastern Wyoming was far from being an agrarian utopia at that time. Perennial drought conditions during the years 1888 to 1892 so disheartened many homesteaders attempting to farm beyond the midwestern rain belt that thousands actually retreated eastward, away from the Great Plains. Those arid conditions, aggravated by the lack of man-made irrigation, probably discouraged many would-be land seekers from migrating to the region surrounding Fort Laramie.

Meanwhile, John Fields resigned his position as custodian. According to Hunton, there were no funds available for the salary, but his recorded recollection failed to reveal the political subterfuge to which Hunton had resorted for his own benefit. Hunton knew that Fields, with a family to support, would be unable to occupy the position if it were not

---

[23]Hunton to Carey, July 15, 1891, Hunton Letters, Mattes Collection; Hunton to Miss [Kate] Friend, January 18, 1892, ibid.

[24]Hunton to Hart, September 3, 1891, ibid. Hunton also recorded in his diary that there was "no excitement." Hunton diary, September 29, 1891.

salaried. Even though Hunton was hardly in better financial condition than Fields, he cunningly offered through his crony, Senator Carey, to take the job without compensation, thus putting Fields out of a job.[25]

Neither was it coincidental that the reservation was again reduced in size—to only forty acres—concurrent with Hunton's appointment as custodian. That tract neatly embraced most of Hunton's buildings, and there can be little doubt that Hunton conspired to displace Fields, to ensure that he was the sole resident on that parcel. According to the secretary of the interior's proclamation concerning the disposition of unclaimed lands within former military reservations, "actual occupants already there, as of January 1, 1890 shall have preference right to make one entry not exceeding 1/4 section."[26] Hunton perceived Fields as a potential threat, since both he and Fields could make legitimate claims for continuous residency since that date. In the event that this last government parcel was declared open to homesteading, Hunton wanted no competitors.[27]

Senator Carey, under the misimpression that the reservation still included one hundred sixty acres, suggested to Hunton that it might be converted to a town site, under the provisions governing abandoned military posts. At that time, only two families resided on the land, Hunton and Fields. In Hunton's opinion, the costs of surveying and acquiring the town lots would be too expensive and, in any event, only about twenty-two acres were suitable for building sites. He reminded the senator that since the reservation had already been reduced to forty acres, it would be best to leave well enough alone. "As the thing stands at present," Hunton wrote, "I am secure in the undisturbed possession of the *most* of the buildings in which I am interested."[28]

No challenges threatened Hunton's possession of the remaining government reservation acreage until 1896, when Antoine "Frenchy" Ducarr attempted to file a homestead based on his temporary residency in one of the Hunton houses. Hunton wrote immediately to Congressman Frank W. Mondell to muster political support. He emphasized to

---

[25]Hunton to Carey, January 22, 1892, Hunton Letters, Mattes Collection. Interestingly, Hunton noted in his diary that he received $50.33 for his services as custodian. Hunton diary, November 19, 1892.

[26]*U.S. Statutes at Large* 26: 227.

[27]Speaking of Fields many years later, John O'Brian confided, "But Hunton got the best of him, and they got him out of here as Post [custodian] . . . Mr. Hunton used to tell me a lot of stuff here about that." O'Brian interview.

Mondell that although Ducarr had rented rooms for about four years, he had never owned any buildings on the reservation. Hunton, in his own defense, candidly revealed that his sole purpose in donating his services as custodian had been "to get the U.S. to allow the 40 acres of land to remain unoccupied so we need not be forced to tear down good and expensive buildings and remove the lumber therefrom or have to sacrifice all at such price as an entryman of the land might dictate. Mr. Ducarr, in my opinion would be a shylock."[29]

Although Ducarr's threat failed to materialize, Hunton nevertheless took action to secure what he already considered to be his property. About a year later, he drafted a bill that would grant his wife, Blanche, the right to purchase the forty-acre reservation at the appraised price of $1.25 per acre. He sent copies of his proposal to Senator Francis E. Warren and to Congressman John E. Osborn, who had won Mondell's seat in the 1896 election. Although the wheels of Congress turned slowly, the scheme worked, and on July 5, 1898, legislation passed directing the secretary of the interior to sell to Blanche Hunton the last quarter-section of the Fort Laramie reservation, including the improvements thereon.[30]

Despite the lack of land "boom" in the Fort Laramie area at the close of the century, new settlers nevertheless trickled into the North Platte Valley and its environs. By 1896, Laramie County School District No. 11, centered at Fort Laramie, could claim a few students and forty registered voters.[31] Hunton, in his role as a commissioner for the General Land Office, recorded that eighty-six homesteads were filed through his office at the fort, along with twenty-three Desert Land Claims.[32] The claims represented homesteads both within and beyond

---

[28]Hunton to Carey, February 22, 1892, Hunton Letters, Mattes Collection; Hunton to Carey, March 17, 1892, ibid.

[29]Hunton to Mondell, December 19, 1896, ibid.

[30]*U.S. Statutes at Large*, 30, 1478; The next spring, Hunton fenced his land to preclude further dispute. Hunton diary, March 8 and 9, 1899.

[31]"List of names of all lawful voters residing in school district No. 11, Laramie County Wyoming on Nov 1, 1896." Hunton Letters, Mattes Collection.

[32]Initiated by cattlemen seeking a way to acquire more land than could be homesteaded legally, the Desert Land Act of 1877 allowed the purchase of 640 acres of arid land at 25 cents per acre, if the claimant could prove that he had irrigated a portion of the property. By doing so, he could gain title to the land by paying an additional $1.00 per acre. The law proved to be an open invitation to fraud, since witnesses could be hired to vouch that they had seen water on the claim, even if was only a bucketful poured on the ground. Billington, *Westward Expansion*, 699.

the former post reservation. Of greater significance were the sixty-nine final proofs that so-called "entrymen" had filed on local lands, indicating that several dozen homesteaders had come to stay.[33] Of course, like homesteaders everywhere in the arid lands of the West, most of the claims were for lands bordering streams and rivers. "All the inhabitants of this section are small ranch men and grangers," Hunton observed, with "good crops being raised wherever irrigated." In fact, by late 1901 the only tracts still available within the old reservation were those having no water.[34]

Concurrent with the influx of homesteaders at the dawn of the twentieth century was the construction of the Burlington and Missouri Railroad (later renamed as the Chicago, Burlington & Quincy, or CB&Q) extending up the North Platte Valley. In 1899, Hunton noted the arrival of a reconnaissance party plotting the route and negotiating rights-of-way. The following year, surveying and construction crews were laying track along the north side of the river, bypassing the fort entirely. That singular event at once signaled a boon of enormous benefit to the economic development of the entire region, and the final downfall of old Fort Laramie.

Before long, a new whistle-stop labeled Fort Laramie Station boasted not only a depot and section-crew house, but threatened to claim the post office as well. Hunton arose in defense of old Fort Laramie by objecting to the removal of that most critical of identity symbols, its federal mail stop. He was particularly peeved that railroad officials had the audacity to usurp the grand old name of Fort Laramie and apply it to what was no more than an undeveloped siding on the Burlington line. Writing to Wyoming Senator F. W. Mondell, Hunton complained that if the department did not want to operate a post office at the fort, then "an office *under another name* may be established on the north side of the Platte River and, that Fort Laramie still remain on its *Historic Ground*."[35]

---

[33]Undated letter fragment, ca. 1897, Hunton Letters, Mattes Collection. Hunton was appointed U.S. Commissioner for the District of Wyoming in 1892. Hunton diary, April 5, 1892.

[34]Hunton to Mrs. H. G. Barton, Tie Siding, Wyoming, April 4, 1898, Hunton Letters, Mattes Collection; Hunton to Mondell, December 11, 1901, ibid. A cursory survey of the patents recorded indicates that much of the land around the fort was homesteaded during the period from the late 1890s to about 1915. Abstract Book, Township 26 North, Range 64 West, Goshen County Records.

[35]Hunton to Mondell, July 8, 1901, Hunton Letters, Mattes Collection; Hunton to Mondell, November 20, 1901, ibid.

To illustrate what Hunton still believed to be the fort's strategic location within the region, he forwarded a map to the senator showing the road network emanating from the military post. As commendable as Hunton's loyalty to the abandoned fort may have been, he failed, or refused, to recognize the changes in demographics and lines of communication occurring all around him. Nevertheless, his efforts to forestall the removal of the post office were temporarily successful, and the Post Office Department did not strip that last element of official identity from historic Fort Laramie until 1907.[36]

The new village of Fort Laramie beyond the river attracted a few merchants and residents, albeit slowly. Even though the railroad provided a convenient shipping point for crops produced by the struggling homesteaders, that accommodation was short-lived. The very next year, the CB&Q closed the depot for lack of business, much to the disappointment of local residents. Within just a few years, the old military post had been bypassed by the railroad, had lost its bid to retain a post office, and now even New Fort Laramie failed to merit a rail station. As the editor of the *Guernsey Gazette* saw it, "it appears . . . almost like a thrust at the power and influence of the once famous old Fort."[37]

---

[36]When Hunton closed his store, which also housed the Fort Laramie post office, Hattie Sandercock, widow of Post Engineer Tom Sandercock, was appointed postmaster. Mrs. Sandercock, who had purchased Officers Quarters "A" situated at the south end of the parade ground, established the post office in a front room of her residence in the spring of 1891. Sandercock retained the position for ten years, at which time she was succeeded briefly by Nettie Rutherford. When Rutherford proposed relocating the office at her home near the North Platte bridge, and only about one-half mile from the whistle-stop, Hunton raised a petition to keep the post office at old Fort Laramie. Surprisingly, even Rutherford was persuaded by Hunton's appeal. She resigned her position and supported the appointment of John Purdy, another local homesteader, who moved the operation to a temporary frame building situated within the angle of the derelict Administration Building. But despite the efforts of Hunton and other residents, the post office eventually was established in the town of Fort Laramie in 1907. Hunton to assistant postmaster general, October 23, 1902, ibid.; Statement by Mead Sandercock (relating to Photo No. 131 in the collections at Fort Laramie National Historic Site) in Mattes, "Surviving Structures"; Meschter, "Post Offices of Wyoming"; *Wind Pudding and Rabbit Tracks* 1: 196; "History of Fort Laramie (Town)" and "Station Closed," *Guernsey Gazette*, January 31, 1908.

[37]"Station Closed," *Guernsey Gazette*, January 31, 1908.

CHAPTER TWENTY-TWO

"That So Much of It
Has Been Saved"

T he twentieth century dawned on a mere remnant of the once-proud military post of Fort Laramie. The decade following its abandonment witnessed the wholesale destruction of most of the principal buildings and virtually all of the minor ones. Where dozens of buildings once stood, only foundations or stark ruins remained. Those few buildings still more or less intact at that time remained comparatively unchanged in subsequent decades because the resident owners, Sandercock, Hunton, and Wilde, found practical uses for them.

Although later preservationists would lament the razing of the fort buildings, no one at that time, with the possible exception of John Hunton, expressed any consideration for saving them for posterity. In their active period, frontier forts like Laramie were by no means unique, and the citizens in the vicinity were still too close to the realities of army days to conjure up any romantic notions about the place. Since many of the area's settlers had worked on the post or lived nearby for some time, it would have been inconceivable to them that anyone in the future might find the place of any particular interest or historical significance—much the way citizens today view many of the nation's more recently abandoned military bases. Everyone was simply too preoccupied with the everyday struggles of life to indulge in nostalgia. The editor of the *Cheyenne Daily Leader* probably came as close as anyone to expressing regret when he referred to "the historical post [as] a veritable deserted village."[1]

---

[1]"Old Fort Laramie," *Cheyenne Daily Leader*, March 25, 1890.

One might speculate that John Hunton had some "higher purpose" in mind when he bought so many of the government buildings. That he intended to sell some of his buildings for salvage purposes, however, is reflected in his own statements.[2] Any notions he may have entertained for saving some of the army structures were quickly dismissed in the face of his own financial crisis. Accordingly, he sold many of his buildings during the first two years after the army left, with no apparent remorse. Hunton needed cash, and needed it badly when his creditors hounded him to settle his accounts.

Nevertheless, questions of intent arise concerning the obvious inconsistencies in Hunton's treatment of the buildings he owned. Some—like Old Bedlam, the trader's store, and the two officers' quarters standing between them—seemed to be inviolable. Certainly, one of his motives was that these particular buildings stood on a parcel of land that he planned to homestead, and eventually did acquire by purchase. Most of the others were on tracts later filed on by his neighbors, Joe and Mary Wilde and Hattie Sandercock. As noted previously, B. A. Hart initially acquired the northwest quarter of Section 28, where several other of Hunton's buildings stood. The division of those lands may have been the subject of a gentleman's agreement, though no evidence has been found to indicate that was the case. Whatever the reason, Hunton divested himself of those buildings through sale or salvage within a short time after the post reservation was thrown open to homesteading.

Hunton lacked the money to maintain the row of buildings on the west side of the parade ground, but he nevertheless saw to it that they were spared from outright destruction. Bedlam, in particular, seems to have held a special, if not sentimental, place with him. This largest of the frame buildings contained more lumber than perhaps any other building on the post, yet he did not salvage it, nor did he permit the use of the building by anyone, except when he rented out rooms to local schoolteachers now and then. The so-called Burt House, adjacent to the sutler's store, served as Hunton's personal residence for as long as he lived at the fort, and he used the former Surgeon's Quar-

---

[2]During the two days prior to the auction, Hunton occupied himself with measuring the buildings and estimating how much lumber they contained. Hunton diary, April 7 and 8, 1890.

ters next door for storage, with a room or two infrequently rented to temporary tenants.

Hunton might have had a perfect opportunity to continue a general merchandise business and even run a saloon—the store building contained two of them in ready condition—had it not been for his indebtedness and the fear that his creditors would seize the assets of any new enterprise he might start. While these circumstances may not fully explain his apparent lack of initiative, there seems to be no other reason for his decision not to revive his store. Others, notably Joe and Mary Wilde, operated successful businesses at the old post for many years afterward. Although Hunton's cluster of buildings stood neglected and largely unused for any commercial purpose for nearly three decades, he neither sold nor salvaged them, which bears moot testimony to his motives.

By the end of the nineteenth century, America began witnessing the first faint indications of a preservation ethic. One authority asserts that "not only were we as a people using historic shrines to assert our legitimacy in an international community of venerable nations, but also, as individuals and groups, we looked to associative history for reassurance."[3] In 1906 Congress passed the landmark Antiquities Act, the first comprehensive federal legislation for the purpose of reserving as national monuments, "historic landmarks, historic and prehistoric structures, and other objects of historic or scientific interest." The legislation reflected President Theodore Roosevelt's obsession for conserving what he considered to be some of America's greatest cultural treasures. The weakness of the law lay in its limitation to properties either already owned by or donated to the U.S. Government. The act was nevertheless important for demonstrating federal interest in land conservation and preservation of cultural resources. Of equal importance, the Antiquities Act laid the groundwork for the extension of an entire system of such reserves and, ten years later, the creation of an agency to administer those sites—the National Park Service.

That same year, coincidentally, Ezra Meeker, who had migrated to California on the Oregon Trail in 1852, recrossed the trail in a personal

---

[3]Mackintosh, *Historic Sites Survey,* 30.

commemoration of that pioneering event. In staging his tribute to the thousands of emigrants who had passed over the combined Oregon-California and Mormon Trails in the mid-nineteenth century, Meeker drove one of his original wagons, drawn by a team of oxen. During his overland journey from Puget Sound, Washington, to Independence, Missouri, Meeker drew public attention to the need for marking the route of the emigrant trail before it was entirely obliterated by modern roads, railroads, cultivation, and towns.

An example confirming his worst fears of historic neglect was Fort Laramie. Meeker was appalled by what he found. "The old place is crumbling away, slowly disappearing with the memories of the past," he despaired. The aging pioneer observed, correctly, that little evidence remained of the post he had seen over a half-century earlier. In fact, he concluded, the ruins visible in 1906 did not represent a fort at all, "but an encampment."[4] Meeker's impression, however, reflected the fact that most frontier army posts had no stockades and, consequently, more closely resembled settlements than fortifications.

In the wake of Meeker's nostalgic reenactment, subsequent interest in memorializing the emigrant route across Nebraska and Wyoming grew rapidly. Despite Wyoming's relatively recent statehood in 1890, and its still-sparse population, the state emerged as a leader in regional efforts to mark the Oregon Trail, as well as in identifying and erecting monuments at numerous other historic sites within its own boundaries. Whether they were conscious of it or not, Meeker and his disciples were expressing a connection of the past with the present—associative history—lest that anchor be lost.

Even John Hunton felt compelled to take action by writing to the secretary of war in 1910, suggesting that "a small monument should be erected at the site of the immense immigration trail or road which is very rapidly passing out of recognizable existence."[5] In 1891, when an army detail returned to the fort to retrieve soldiers' remains from the post cemetery, Hunton had called their attention to the mass grave at

---

[4]Meeker, perhaps unknowingly, summed up the structural evolution of the post from a walled trading post to the scattered array of buildings typical of most western army posts. Jording, *Interested Residents*, 3.

[5]Hunton to Senator F. E. Warren, June 15, 1910, Hunton Letters, Mattes Collection.

the Grattan Battlefield. Now, nearly twenty years later, he thought it was appropriate to place a monument marking the famed trail, which passed near the scene of that 1854 skirmish.[6]

The national preservation movement became characterized by two elements—patriotism bordering on religious zealousness, and women most often assuming the leadership roles. The Wyoming preservation effort reflected those trends. The seeds that Ezra Meeker sowed fell on fertile ground in the state chapter of the Daughters of the American Revolution (DAR). That group initiated a program in 1908 to raise money for purchasing and erecting markers along the trail, and just five years later installed an imposing monument where the emigrant route entered the state near Henry, Nebraska.

The DAR capitalized on that first major success by introducing a bill in the state legislature petitioning for funds to further its efforts. The legislature not only appropriated $2,500 for that purpose, but established an Oregon Trail Commission (OTC) to administer a statewide landmarks program. Among the important places memorialized by the commission were several frontier military posts, including Fort Laramie. Such monuments, the group concluded, were necessary "to do honor to those who endured hardships and privations, encountered dangers and peril, who gave up their lives to make possible the civilization of the great west."[7]

When the OTC contacted John Hunton with a proposal for erecting a significant monument at Fort Laramie, he responded that he and other old-timers associated with fort were willing to contribute modest cash donations and labor. Early in June 1914 Hunton assembled a crew of volunteer workmen composed of Mead and George Sandercock, soldier's son John O'Brian, and Joseph L. Wolf, proprietor of a dry goods and grocery store in New Fort Laramie. A week later, Hunton proudly announced that he and his friends had finished the monument, "a very substantial structure 6' × 6' square at base, tapering to 2' × 2' at top and 12' high."[8] Appropriately, the Fort Laramie monument was strategically placed a few feet northeast of the post

---

[6]This marker was not placed until 1916. Grace Raymond Hebard to Hunton, July 18, 1916, ibid.
[7]Jording, *Interested Residents*, 5.
[8]Hunton to A. J. Parshall, Cheyenne, Wyo., July 18, 1914, Hunton Letters, Mattes Collection.

trader's store, a place Hunton and the others knew had been a key historical road intersection in the fort's heyday.

The monument was formally dedicated in a ceremony held the following summer. Echoing the preservation philosophy of the late nineteenth century, the speakers typically praised the spirit and courage of those white Americans who had "settled the West," yet not one proposed that the tangible remains of the old post itself be preserved for future generations. Even Hunton failed to speak up (perhaps because he had been so instrumental in destroying much of the place) and historian Grace Raymond Hebard gave only a passing nod to the historical significance of the fort. "The part that Fort Laramie had taken in helping to execute this trust," she said, "makes us today, with reverence and sacred memory place a monument on the spot, that more than any other place in the great West contributed to a successful and triumphant march of Western development and expansion."[9] There was, to be sure, a sense of place and its thematic association with the westward movement, yet typical of the times, it was the new artificial monument, not the original structures, that were perceived as the permanent reminder of Fort Laramie.

Perhaps the most significant effect of the ceremony was its initiation of a grassroots movement to save the physical remnants of Fort Laramie. Fired with enthusiasm, James Johnston, editor of the *Torrington Telegram,* published an editorial soliciting support for what he viewed as the higher cause. "Few people realize the importance of Fort Laramie as a historic spot in Wyoming," Johnston wrote, "and to think that the site of the first fort in the state lies within the borders of our own county ought to arouse the patriotism of the present generation to restore the works and make it into a beautiful resort." Betraying considerable naïveté about the complexities of such an undertaking, Johnston attempted to rally public support through the pages of the *Telegram.* "There are a dozen or more of the old buildings in tact, and can be put in shape for use at a very little cost," he urged.[10] He went on to say that because the fort was convenient to

[9]"Significance of Fort Laramie On the Oregon Trail," *Torrington Telegram,* June 24, 1915.
[10]"A Notable Pleasure Resort," *Torrington Telegram,* June 17, 1915.

Wheatland, Guernsey, and Torrington, it made a wonderful spot for picnics and other social gatherings.

Johnston's plea, unfortunately, failed to generate any immediate enthusiasm from the local populace. Even Hebard, apparently satisfied that the needs of commemoration had been served, failed to step forward to champion the cause of saving the last original structures. Historian Merrill J. Mattes later interpreted this to mean that "because it was inconceivable that any agency would preserve an old fort solely as an historical park, all early proposals revolved around various pragmatic uses."[11] While those ideas may not have met modern criteria for historical preservation, they were nonetheless aimed at protecting such sites.

The editor of the Nebraska-based *Midwest Magazine*, Will M. Maupin, advanced an alternative concept, no doubt inspired by the Great War then underway in Europe. Having attended a Wilde dance in 1914, Maupin saw the old fort as ideally suited for a military school. To promote his concept, he proposed a grand picnic at the fort on Independence Day, 1916.[12]

The festive day included picnicking on the grounds, wrestling matches, baseball, and a speech by Judge Charles E. Winter, a champion of land reclamation in Wyoming. True to form, he presented a strong argument for government ownership of the fort. The presence of influential and popular ex-Governor Carey garnered crowds, too, and wider publicity to an event that Maupin's cause alone probably would not have achieved. Of even greater significance, the old-timers' picnic elevated the level of concern from the local populace. One citizen expressed interest in making the fort a tourist resort, while another aspired to the higher plain of federal involvement. Winter's proposal to create a military school on the lands, was timely on one hand, considering America's impending involvement in the new world war. But when the U. S. actually declared war in April 1917, such notions were lost amid more pressing concerns.

---

[11]Mattes, "Fort Laramie Park History," 59.

[12]"A Fourth of July Picnic at Old Fort," *Guernsey Gazette,* July 19, 1916. That Maupin had more than a passing interest in such things was demonstrated by his appointment as the first custodian of Scotts Bluff National Monument in 1919. Mattes, "Fort Laramie Park History," 61.

The two most important figures still living at Fort Laramie, John Hunton and Joe Wilde, were along in years by that time and had made no secret of their desires to sell their Fort Laramie properties. As early as 1913, both men advertised their lands for sale, "either jointly or separately." The Wilde property encompassed the Cavalry Barracks and other buildings north of the New Guardhouse, as well as the meadows below the post on the left side of the Laramie River. Hunton still owned the entire parade ground area, excluding the corner containing Quarters "A," the ruins of the Administration Building, and the Old Guardhouse, which then belonged to the Sandercock family. Hattie Sandercock's sons still farmed the bottomlands around the fort, but after spending the better part of their lives at Fort Laramie, Hunton and Wilde were weary of the place and eager to go elsewhere. At the same time, as the nation expanded and people became more mobile, the West evolved into a destination for those with money and leisure time to travel. For many, Laramie was on the route to scenic wonders.

Joe Wilde, in particular, had "been bothered considerable in trying to provide accommodations to the visitor." Louis Carlson, a contractor who had built irrigation canals in the North Platte Valley, saw an opportunity to take advantage of the increasing flow of tourists coming up the valley en route to Yellowstone National Park and other points of interest. Carlson's plans for improving Wilde's facilities included adding a general merchandise store, and a hotel "equipped to take care of the trade in good shape." As concessions to modern tourism, he also proposed opening an auto route through the fort grounds, and providing travelers with a convenient gas station.[13] Carlson subsequently bought out Wilde's interests through a series of mortgages executed during the years 1917–1919.[14]

In the fall of 1920, Hunton also negotiated a deal to sell all 640 acres he had acquired over the years to Thomas Waters, an Omaha, Nebraska, developer and a former representative of the Pennsylvania Railroad. Waters apparently wanted either to rent out his agricultural land or hire out the farm work. In any event, he seemed unconcerned with the historic structures. In exchange for vacating their longtime

---

[13]"Old Fort Laramie to Undergo Improvements," *Guernsey Gazette,* August 31, 1917.
[14]Lands Records, Goshen County, Wyoming; Mattes, "Fort Laramie Park History," 63.

home in the Burt House, Waters permitted the Huntons to reside in the south half of the adjacent Surgeon's Quarters until 1922, when they relocated to Torrington to spend their final years.[15] John Hunton was gone at last, and with his departure went the last living resident from Fort Laramie's military era.[16]

The 1920s witnessed a series of plans for preserving the structures of old Fort Laramie, but most of those well-meaning efforts were incidental to profitable tourist developments. Local newspapermen L. G. "Pat" Flannery of the *Lingle Guide-Review* and George Houser, editor of the *Guernsey Gazette,* jointly launched a crusade to save the post from oblivion, while Waters concurrently revealed his intention to create a dude ranch at the fort, complete with a hotel, restaurant, rental cottages, and a golf course. Waters' development was actually part of a larger effort to redirect the burgeoning tide of tourist traffic from the interstate Lincoln Highway at Ogallala, northwest to Yellowstone National Park, with Scott's Bluff, Fort Laramie, and other Oregon Trail sites serving as intermediate regional attractions. Although Waters hoped to be on the ground floor of establishing public accommodations along the route, his salesmanship failed to attract enough investors to fund his enterprise and it eventually faded away.

Despite earlier failures at boosterism, local communities were fired by the prospect of economic development through tourism. In 1925, for example, Houser got wind of an impending bill in Congress that would designate an "Oregon Trail Highway" extending from Independence, Missouri, to the Pacific Coast. Houser and Flannery worked tirelessly to mobilize various civic organizations to urge Congress to set aside Fort Laramie through a rider to the legislation. The language of House Joint Memorial No. 4, as it was labeled, reflected for the first time not only broad support for preserving Fort Laramie, but specifically proposed "restoring, preserving, and perpetuating to posterity this historic monument of pioneer days and making it accessible to visitors." For many, the intention to bring what remained of the fort under the protective umbrella of the National Park System was unmistakable. But internal bickering among trail "authorities"

---

[15]Hunton to Ezra Meeker, New York, N.Y., February 14, 1926, Hunton Letters, Mattes Collection.
[16]Wilde died in 1926; Hunton in 1928. Author's note.

over which route to promote, as well as its starting and ending points, eventually defeated the bill in committee.

After a wildfire nearly claimed the last buildings at the fort that same year, Houser and Flannery redoubled their efforts to provide permanent government protection for the place. They were aided measurably by the creation of the Oregon Trail Memorial Association, headquartered in New York, with chapters in each of the states traversed by the route. Bolstered by the influence of ex-Congressman Frank Mondell and historian Grace Raymond Hebard, the association developed additional muscle by unifying several local groups, including the DAR and the Daughters of Pioneers, into a single-minded lobby. Still, the effort failed to gain enough traction to move Congress to action.

Houser and Flannery, all the while, continued to beat the drum for preserving Fort Laramie as a national park area and were successful in gaining both moral and monetary support from numerous organizations in southeastern Wyoming. Fortuitously, the Annual Pioneers' Reunion, held at nearby Guernsey in 1926, attracted Robert S. Ellison, an avid history buff and preservationist from Casper, Wyoming. Ellison's enthusiasm and energy were apparent in an editorial he later wrote in which he claimed that Fort Laramie "outranks in the history of the west any other trading or military post." In a subsequent meeting, National Park Service assistant director Horace M. Albright laid out a strategy that held promise for bringing Fort Laramie into the park system. Albright explained that the Park Service was most reluctant to acquire park lands through the government's power of eminent domain; however, if Wyoming were to establish a small landmarks committee to unify the preservation effort under the auspices of state government, such an entity might better negotiate to purchase Fort Laramie from its private owners. Once in state hands, the property could be readily transferred to the Park Service through legislative authority.

Ellison, who had served as one of the initial board members for the Oregon Trail Memorial Association, immediately spearheaded a successful campaign to create the Historic Landmarks Commission of Wyoming, a group empowered by the legislature to evaluate potentially significant sites throughout the state and to recommend for acquisition those it considered of greatest significance. It came as no surprise when the commission established Fort Laramie as its highest priority in its 1928 annual report.

The concept was simple enough, though bringing the plan to fruition proved infinitely more difficult. A lack of state funds, soon aggravated by the Great Depression as well as owners' unwillingness to sell their lands for the reappraised lower prices, prolonged for another decade the movement to preserve Fort Laramie. A breakthrough finally came in 1936, when National Park Service Assistant Director Hillory A. Tolson happened to pass through the area on his way to Yellowstone National Park. He was given a tour of the fort by Merrill J. Mattes, then serving as historian at Scotts Bluff National Monument. Tolson, the first high-ranking park service official to visit Fort Laramie, was so impressed by what he saw, as well as with what he learned of its historical significance, that the park agency shortly thereafter announced publicly that it would be willing to establish the site as a unit of the park system, if it were donated to the government.

Through unflagging determination by Flannery, Houser, Hebard, and other dedicated area residents, the Wyoming legislature increased the Landmark Commission's budget authority and approved the purchase of additional former fort acreage. The combination of those elements at once allowed the committee to meet the terms of the sellers, and provide a more generous buffer zone surrounding the fort. Members of the Landmarks Commission, acting on behalf of the State of Wyoming, eventually reached agreement with the respective land owners in January 1937. State representatives from eight Wyoming counties joined in sponsoring a bill authorizing the immediate purchase of the fort. The measure flew through the legislative process to enactment the following month. The state resolution not only authorized the Landmarks Commission to purchase the historic site, but to convey it to the National Park Service as well, thus streamlining the acquisition process.

The National Park Service at the same time worked to prepare the way for President Franklin D. Roosevelt to proclaim the fort a national monument by executive order under the authority of the

Antiquities Act. Accordingly, Fort Laramie became a unit of the National Park System on March 31, 1937.[17] Throughout its historic lifetime, Fort Laramie had outlived the needs of fur trappers, emigrants, goldseekers, Indians, and eventually, even the soldiers. But, even in decline, the fort served the needs of cattlemen and homesteaders, although those days, coupled with army salvage and the ravages of time and the natural elements, took a heavy toll on the structures that had once comprised the grand old post. Of the dozens of buildings that once stood there, only a handful survived for posterity, presided over by venerable Old Bedlam. Still, as historian Merrill J. Mattes optimistically put it, "We should not express disappointment that so much of Fort Laramie was lost, but rather surprise that so much of it has been saved."[18]

---

[17]The lengthy campaign to bring Fort Laramie under government protection is detailed in McChristian, "Private Property Era," 62–98.

[18]Mattes, "Fort Laramie Park History," 17–18.

Regiments Represented in the Fort Laramie Garrison, 1849–1890

In most instances, regiments were represented by only a few companies at any particular time and the dates do not always reflect a continuous presence at the post. Accordingly, the entries indicate only that some portion of the unit was stationed there for a period of time during the inclusive years listed.

Regulars, Cavalry

Regiment of Mounted Riflemen—1849–51
Second U.S. Dragoons—1855–56, 1857, 1858–61
Second U.S. Cavalry—1866–68, 1869, 1872–77
Third U.S. Cavalry—1872, 1875, 1876–80
Fourth U.S. Artillery—1855–56, 1858–59
Fourth U.S. Cavalry—1862–63
Fifth U.S. Cavalry—1870–71, 1880–83

Regulars, Infantry

Second U.S. Infantry—1855–56, 1859–60
Fourth U.S. Infantry—1867–71, 1874–75, 1876–77, 1878–82
Sixth U.S. Infantry—1849–58
Seventh U.S. Infantry—1857–58, 1882–90
Ninth U.S. Infantry—1874–77

Tenth U.S. Infantry—1855–56, 1857, 1860–62
Fourteenth U.S. Infantry—1871–74, 1876–77
Eighteenth U.S. Infantry—1866–67
Twenty-third U.S. Infantry—1876
Thirty-sixth U.S. Infantry—1867

VOLUNTEERS, CAVALRY
First Battalion, Nebraska—1865
First Kansas—1865
Sixth Michigan—1865–66
Sixth Ohio—1862–63
Sixth West Virginia—1865
Seventh Iowa—1864–66
Eighth Kansas—1862
Ninth Kansas—1865
Eleventh Kansas—1865
Eleventh Ohio—1863–66
Twelfth Missouri—1865–66
Sixteenth Kansas—1865

VOLUNTEERS, INFANTRY
Third U.S.—1865
Sixth U.S.—1865–66

BIBLIOGRAPHY

MANUSCRIPTS

Brigham Young University, Harold B. Lee Library, Provo, Utah.
  Walter Mason Camp Collection
Colorado Historical Society Library, Denver.
  George Bent manuscripts, Samuel Tappan Papers
Denver Public Library, Denver.
  William O. Collins Family Papers
  O. F. Davenport Letters
  Robert S. Ellison Papers
  Seth E. Ward Papers
  Theodore Rodenbough Letters
Goshen County Courthouse, Torrington, Wyo.
  Records of the County Clerk
    Land Records
Homesteaders Museum, Torrington, Wyo.
  Historical Files
Huntington Library, San Marino, Calif.
  John W. Gunnison Papers
Kansas State Historical Society, Topeka.
  Preston Bierce Plumb Papers
National Archives (Main), Washington, D.C.
  Record Group 92, Records of the Quartermaster General's Office
    Consolidated Correspondence File
      Fort Laramie boxes
  Record Group 94, Records of the Adjutant General's Office
    Letters Received (Main Series)
    Medical History, Fort Laramie
    Post Returns, Fort Laramie

Reservation File, Fort Laramie
Returns from Regular Army Cavalry Regiments 1833–1916
Returns from Regular Army Infantry Regiments 1821–1916
Selected Letters Received Relating to the Sioux Expedition
Record Group 156, Records of the Office of the Chief of Ordnance
    Quarterly Returns of Ordnance and Ordnance Stores in the Hands of Troops
Record Group 159, Records of the Office of the Inspector General
    Reports of Inspection, Fort Laramie
Record Group 393, Records of U.S. Army Continental Commands, 1821–1920
    Fort Laramie Records:
        Letters Received
        Letters Sent
        Orders
        Records of Sioux Treaty
National Archives, Great Lakes Region, Chicago, Ill.
    Record Group 77, Records of the Corps of Engineers (Chicago District)
    Letters, Reports, and Graphic Materials Received, Department of the Platte
National Park Service. Fort Laramie National Historic Site, Wyo.
    Louis Brechemin interview
    Reynolds Burt interview
    William H. Cowell journal
    Robert S. Ellison scrapbook
    Mattes Collection
    McDermott File
    Johnny O'Brian interview
    Vertical Files
Barbour, Barton H. "Special History Study: The Fur Trade at Fort Laramie
    National Historic Site." Typescript. Santa Fe, New Mexico: National Park Ser-
    vice, 1999.
Mattes, Merrill J. "Fort Laramie Park History 1834–1977." Denver: September 1980.
———. "Surviving Structures at Fort Laramie National Monument: A Docu-
    mented History." Fort Laramie, Wyo.: July 1943.
Mattes, Merrill J., and Borrensen, Thor. "The Historic Approaches to Fort
    Laramie," Fort Laramie, Wyo.: October 1947.
McChristian, Douglas C. "Historic Resource Study: Fort Laramie National His-
    toric Site: The Private Property Era 1890–1937." Typescript. Denver: National
    Park Service, 1998.
———. "Special Report: Magazine (HS-14)." Typescript. Fort Laramie National
    Historic Site: National Park Service, 1998.

University of Colorado, Western Historical Collections, Norlin Library, Boulder, Colo.
  William Carey Brown Papers
  Agnes Wright Spring Papers
University of Indiana, Lilly Library, Bloomington.
  Walter M. Camp Papers
University of Wyoming, American Heritage Center, Laramie.
  John Hunton Papers
  Frank Tubbs Letters
Wyoming State Archives, Cheyenne.
  W. R. Behymer Papers
  Jay Bliss Collection
  Thomas B. Brumbaugh Collection
  Fort Laramie Files
  B. A. Hart Papers
  John Hunton Collection
  Charles Logan Papers
  John London Papers
  Harry F. Mayer Papers
  Daniel Y. Meschter manuscript
  McCullough Collection
  Rouse Collection
  Ward Papers
  Works Progress Administration Files

U.S. GOVERNMENT PUBLICATIONS

Annual Report of the Commissioner of the General Land Office to the Secretary of the Interior, 1871, 1891, 1896, 1898.

Annual Reports of the Commissioner of Indian Affairs to the Secretary of the Interior, 1853–1857, 1862–1874.

Annual Reports of the Secretary of the Interior, 1850–1893.

Annual Reports of the Secretary of War, 1840, 1850–1890

General Orders, published annually by the Adjutant General's Office, Washington, D.C.

Heitman, Francis B. *Historical Register and Dictionary of the United States Army From Its Organization September 29, 1789, to March 2, 1903.* 2 vols. Washington, D.C.: Government Printing Office, 1903.

Indian Affairs: Laws and Treaties. 2 vols. Edited by Charles J. Kappler. Washington, D.C.: Government Printing Office, 1904.

Revised United States Army Regulations of 1861. Washington, D.C.: Government Printing Office, 1863.

Statutes at Large
  26 Stat. 227
  30 Stat. 1478

U.S. Congress
  American State Papers: Military Affairs, "Report on the Establishment of a Line of Posts and Military Roads for the Defence of the Western Frontiers Against the Indians," 24th Cong., 1st Sess. (1836) No. 659.

  House. H.R. Doc. No. 23: "Protection Across the Continent," 39th Cong., 2nd Sess. (1867)

  House. H.R. Doc. No. 45: "Inspection Report by Generals Rusling and Hazen," 39th Cong., 2nd Sess. (1867).

  House. H.R. Doc. No. 111: "General Ingalls's Inspection Report," 39th Cong., 2nd Sess. (1867).

  House. H.R. Doc. No. 233, "Claim of Seth Ward for Compensation on Account of Depredation Committed by Brule' and Ogallala Sioux Indians," 42nd Cong., 3rd Sess. (1873).

  House. H.R. Doc. No. 1116, "Abandoned Military Resevations in Wyoming," 51st Cong., 1st Sess. (1889).

  House. H.R. Doc. 1532, "Granting Homesteaders Right to Purchase Land on Certain Reservations," 57th Cong., 1st Sess. (1901).

  Senate. S. Doc. No. 2, "Report of a Summer Campaign to the Rocky Mountains &c. in 1845," 29th Cong., 1st Sess. (1845).

  Senate. S. Doc. No. 231, "Report from the Secretary of War With a Resolution . . . to the Establishment of a Line of Military Posts From the Missouri to the Oregon or Columbia River," 26th Cong., 1st Sess. (1840).

  Senate. S. Doc. No. 174, "Report on the Exploring Expedition to the Rocky Mountains in the Year 1842 . . . by Brevet Captain J. C. Frémont," 28th Cong., 2nd Sess. (1845).

War of the Rebellion, The: A Compilation of the Official Records of the Union and Confederate Armies. Washington, D.C: Government Printing Office, 1886.

BOOKS

A. W. Bowen. *Progressive Men of Wyoming.* Chicago: A. W. Bowen Publishers, 1903.

Adams, Gerald M. *The Post near Cheyenne: A History of Fort D. A. Russell, 1867–1930.* Boulder, Colo.: Pruett, 1989.

Alberts, Don E. *The Battle of Glorieta: Union Victory in the West.* College Station: Texas A&M University Press, 1998.

Anderson, Eunice G. *Second Biennial Report of the State Historian of the State of Wyoming for the Period Ending September 30, 1922.* Cheyenne: State Printing Office, 1922.

Andrist, Ralph K. *The Long Death: The Last Days of the Plains Indian.* New York: Macmillan, 1964.

Athearn, Robert G. *William Tecumseh Sherman and the Settlement of the West.* Norman: University of Oklahoma Press, 1995.

Austerman, Wayne R. *Sharps Rifles and Spanish Mules: The San Antonio–El Paso Mail, 1851–1881,* College Station: Texas A&M University Press, 1985.

Ball, Durwood. *Army Regulars on the Frontier 1848–1861.* Norman: University of Oklahoma Press, 2001.

Bandel, Eugene. *Frontier Life in the Army 1854–1861.* Glendale, Calif.: Arthur H. Clark, 1932.

Bayard, Samuel. *The Life of George Dashiell Bayard, Late Captain, U. S. A., and Brigadier General of Volunteers Killed in the Battle of Fredericksburg, Dec. 1862.* New York: G. P. Putnam's Sons, 1874.

Belshaw, Maria Parsons, and George Belshaw. *Crossing the Plains to Oregon in 1853.* Fairfield, Wash.: Ye Galleon Press, 2000.

Billington, Ray Allen. *Westward Expansion: A History of the American Frontier.* New York: Macmillan Co., 1967.

Bourke, John G. *The Diaries of John Gregory Bourke,* Vol. 2. Edited by Charles M. Robinson III. Denton: University of North Texas Press, 2005.

———. *On the Border With Crook.* Lincoln: University of Nebraska Press, 1971.

Brown, D. Alexander. *The Galvanized Yankees.* Urbana: University of Illinois Press, 1963.

Brown, Larry K. *The Hog Ranches of Wyoming.* Douglas, Wyo.: High Plains Press, 1995.

Brown, Mark H. *The Plainsmen of the Yellowstone: A History of the Yellowstone Basin.* New York: Putnam's Sons, 1961.

Buecker, Thomas R. *Fort Robinson and the American West, 1874–1899.* Lincoln: Nebraska State Historical Society, 1999.

Capron, Cynthia J. *The Indian Border War of 1876: From Letters of Lieutenant Thaddeus Capron.* Reprint. January 1921. Springfield: Illinois State Historical Society.

Carrington, Frances C. *My Army Life and the Fort Phil. Kearney Massacre.* Philadelphia: J. B. Lippincott Co., 1911.

Carrington, Margaret I. *Absaraka: Land of Massacre.* Philadelphia: J. B. Lippincott & Co., 1878.

Carroll, John M., and Lawrence A. Frost, eds. *Private Theodore Ewert's Diary of the Black Hills Expedition of 1874.* Piscataway, N.J.: CRI Books, 1976.

Carson, Christopher. *Kit Carson's Autobiography.* Edited by Milo Milton Quaife. Chicago: Lakeside Press, 1935.

Chalfant, William Y. *Cheyennes and Horse Soldiers: The 1857 Expedition and the Battle of Solomon's Fork*. Norman: University of Oklahoma Press, 1990.

Collins, Catherine Weaver. *An Army Wife Comes West: Letters of Catherine Weaver Collins (1863–1864)*. Edited by Agnes Wright Spring. Denver: Denver Public Library, 1954.

Collins, John S. *Across the Plains in '64*. Omaha, Neb.: National Printing Co., 1904.

Colton, Ray C. *The Civil War in the Western Territories*. Norman: University of Oklahoma Press, 1959.

Coolidge, Richard H. *Statistical Report on the Sickness and Mortality in the Army of the United States, Compiled from the Records of the Surgeon General's Office, Embracing a Period of Sixteen Years, From January 1839 to January 1855*. Washington, D.C.: A. O. P. Nicholson, 1856.

———. *Statistical Report on the Sickness and Mortality in the Army of the United States, Compiled from the Records of the Surgeon General's Office, Embracing a Period of Sixteen Years, From January 1855 to January 1860*. Washington, D.C.: George W. Bowman, 1860.

Crawford, Lewis F. *The Exploits of Ben Arnold—Indian Fighter, Gold Miner, Cowboy, Hunter, and Army Scout*. 1926. Reprint. Norman: University of Oklahoma Press, 1999.

Crook, George. *General George Crook: His Autobiography*. Edited by Martin F. Schmitt. Norman: University of Oklahoma Press, 1960.

Cullum, George W. *Biographical Register of the Officers and Graduates of the U.S. Military Academy at West Point, N.Y. From Its Establishment, in 1802 to 1890*. Cambridge: Riverside Press, 1891.

Daily Sentinel Printing. *The Territory of Wyoming: Its History, Soil, Climate, Resources, Etc.* Laramie City, Wyo: Daily Sentinel Printing, 1874.

Dale, Edward Everett. *The Range Cattle Industry: Ranching on the Great Plains from 1865 to 1925*. Norman: University of Oklahoma Press, 1960.

David, Robert Beebe. *Finn Burnett, Frontiersman*. Glendale, Calif.: Arthur H. Clark, 1937.

Dick, Everett. *The Sod House Frontier 1854–1890*. Lincoln: University of Nebraska Press, 1954.

Dodge, Richard I. *The Black Hills Journals of Colonel Richard Irving Dodge*. Edited by Wayne R. Kime. Norman: University of Oklahoma Press, 1996.

———. *The Powder River Expedition Journals of Colonel Richard Irving Dodge*. Edited by Wayne R. Kime. Norman: University of Oklahoma Press, 1997.

Dunn, J. P. *Massacres of the Mountains: A History of the Indian Wars of the Far West 1815–1875*. 1886. Reprint. New York: Archer House, n.d.

Farmer, James E. *My Life with the Army in the West: The Memoirs of James E. Farmer 1858–1898*. Edited by Dale F. Geise. Santa Fe, N.Mex.: Stagecoach Press, 1967.

Fairfield, S. H. "The Eleventh Kansas Regiment at Platte Bridge," *Transactions of the Kansas State Historical Society.* Vol. 8, 1903–04. Topeka: State Printer, 1904.

Finerty, John F. *War Path and Bivouac or, The Conquest of the Sioux.* Chicago: M. A. Donohue & Co., 1890.

Frazer, Robert W. *Forts of the West.* Norman: University of Oklahoma Press, 1977.

Frederick, J. V. *Ben Holladay the Stagecoach King: A Chapter in the Development of Transcontinental Transportation.* Glendale, Calif.: Arthur H. Clark, 1940.

Garavaglia, Louis A., and Charles G. Worman, *Firearms of the American West: 1803–1865.* Niwot: University Press of Colorado, 1998.

Goetzmann, William H. *Army Exploration in the American West, 1803–1863.* New Haven: Yale University Press, 1959.

Goshen County, Wyoming. *Wind Pudding and Rabbit Tracks: A History of Goshen County.* 2 vols. Torrington, Wyo.: Goshen County History Committee, 1989.

Gould, Lewis L. *Wyoming: From Territory to Statehood.* Worland, Wyo.: High Plains, 1989.

Gove, Jesse A. *The Utah Expedition 1857–1858: Letters of Capt. Jesse A. Grove, 10th Inf., U. S. A., of Concord, N. H., to Mrs. Gove, and special correspondence of the New York Herald.* Concord: New Hampshire Historical Society, 1928.

Gray, John S. *Centennial Campaign.* Fort Collins, Colo.: Old Army Press, 1976.

Greene, Jerome A., comp. and ed. *Battles and Skirmishes of the Great Sioux War, 1876 - 1877: The Military View.* Norman: University of Oklahoma Press, 1993.

———. *Morning Star Dawn: The Powder River Expedition and the Northern Cheyennes, 1876.* Norman: University of Oklahoma Press, 2003.

———. *Slim Buttes, 1876: An Episode of the Great Sioux War.* Norman: University of Oklahoma Press, 1982.

———. *Yellowstone Command: Colonel Nelson A. Miles and the Great Sioux War 1876-1877.* Lincoln: University of Nebraska Press, 1991.

Grinnell, George Bird. *The Fighting Cheyennes.* Norman: University of Oklahoma Press, 1971.

Hafen, LeRoy R. *The Overland Mail 1849–1869: Promoter of Settlements. Precursor of Railroads.* Glendale, Calif.: Arthur H. Clark, 1926.

Hafen, LeRoy R., and W. J. Ghent. *Broken Hand: The Life Story of Thomas Fitzpatrick, Chief of the Mountain Men.* Denver: Old West Publishing Co., 1931.

Hafen, LeRoy R., and Ann W. Hafen. *The Utah Expedition 1857–1858.* Glendale, Calif.: Arthur H. Clark, 1958.

———, eds. *Powder River Campaigns and Sawyer's Expedition of 1865.* Vol. 12 of *Far West and Rockies Historical Series.* Glendale, Calif.: Arthur H. Clark, 1961.

Hafen, LeRoy R., and Francis Marion Young. *Fort Laramie and the Pageant of the West, 1834–1890.* Lincoln: 1938. Reprint. University of Nebraska Press, 1984.

Haines, Aubrey L. *Historic Sites Along the Oregon Trail.* Gerald, Mo.: Patrice Press, 1981.

Hassrick, Royal B. *The Sioux: Life and Customs of a Warrior Society*. Norman: University of Oklahoma Press, 1989.

Hebard, Grace Raymond, and E. A. Brininstool. *The Bozeman Trail: Historical Accounts of the Blazing of the Overland Routes into the Northwest, and the Fights with Red Cloud's Warriors*. Two vols. in one. Glendale, Calif.: Arthur H. Clark, 1960.

Hedren, Paul L. *First Scalp for Custer: The Skirmish at Warbonnet Creek, Nebraska, July 17, 1876*. Glendale, Calif.: Arthur H. Clark, 1980.

————. *Fort Laramie in 1876: Chronicle of a Frontier Post at War*. Lincoln: University of Nebraska Press, 1988.

————, ed. *The Great Sioux War 1876–1877*. Helena: Montana Historical Society Press, 1991.

Holliday, George H. *On the Plains in '65*. Washington, D.C.: n. p., 1883.

Hunt, Aurora. *Major General James Henry Carleton 1814–1873: Western Frontier Dragoon*. Glendale, Calif.: Arthur H. Clark, 1958.

Hunton, John. *John Hunton's Diary 1873–'75*. Edited by L. G. Flannery. Lingle, Wyo.: Guide-Review, 1956.

————. *John Hunton's Diary 1876–'77*. Edited by L. G. Flannery. Lingle, Wyo.: Guide-Review, 1958.

————. *John Hunton's Diary 1878–'79*. Edited by L. G. Flannery. Lingle, Wyo.: Guide-Review, 1960.

————. *John Hunton's Diary 1880–'81–'82*. Edited by L. G. Flannery. Lingle, Wyo.: Guide-Review, 1963.

————. *John Hunton's Diary 1883–'84*. Edited by L. G. Flannery. Lingle, Wyo.: Guide-Review, 1964.

————. "Pioneer Days at Bordeaux," *Second Biennial Report of the State Historian of the State of Wyoming for the Period Ending September 30, 1922*. Edited by Eunice G. Anderson. Sheridan, Wyo.: Mills Co., 1922.

Hutton, Paul A. *Phil Sheridan and His Army*. Lincoln: University of Nebraska Press, 1986.

Hyde, George E. *Life of George Bent, Written from His Letters*. Edited by Savoie Lottinville. Norman: University of Oklahoma Press, 1968.

————. *Red Cloud's Folk: A History of the Oglala Sioux Indians*. Norman: University of Oklahoma Press, 1987.

————. *A Sioux Chronicle*. Norman: University of Oklahoma Press, 1993.

————. *Spotted Tail's Folk: A History of the Brule Sioux*. Norman: University of Oklahoma Press, 1961.

Jackson, W. Turrentine. *Wagon Roads West: A Study of Federal Wagon Road Surveys and Construction in the Trans-Mississippi West 1846–1869*. New Haven: Yale University Press, 1965.

Jensen, Richard E., ed., with intro. *The Indian Interviews of Eli S. Ricker, 1903–1919.* Vol. 1 of *Voices of the American West.* Lincoln: University of Nebraska Press, 2005.

Johnson, Dorothy M. *The Bloody Bozeman: The Perilous Trail to Montana's Gold.* Missoula, Mont.: Mountain Press, 1983.

Jones, Robert Huhn. *Guarding the Overland Trails: The Eleventh Ohio Cavalry in the Civil War.* Spokane, Wash.: Arthur H. Clark, 2005.

Jording, Mike. *A Few Interested Residents: Wyoming Historical Markers and Monuments.* Newcastle, Wyo.: Mike Jording, 1992.

Josephy, Alvin M., Jr. *The Civil War in the American West.* New York: Random House, Inc., 1991.

Kansas State Historical Society. *Fifteenth Biennial Report of the Board of Directors of the Kansas State Historical Society for the Biennial Period July 1, 1904, to June 30, 1906.* Topeka: State Printing Office, 1907.

Kelly, Fanny. *Narrative of My Captivity Among the Sioux Indians.* Cincinnati: Wilstach, Baldwin & Co., 1871.

King, Charles. *Laramie or, The Queen of Bedlam. A Story of the Sioux War of 1876.* 1889. Reprint. Fort Laramie, Wyo.: Fort Laramie Historical Association, 1986.

Lang, Theodore F. *Loyal West Virginia from 1861 to 1865.* Baltimore: Deutsch Publishing Co., 1895.

Larson, T. A. *History of Wyoming.* 2 vols. Lincoln: University of Nebraska Press, 1978.

Lavender, David. *Fort Laramie and the Changing Frontier.* Washington, D.C.: National Park Service, 1983.

Liddic, Bruce R., and Paul Harbaugh, eds. *Custer and Company: Walter Camp's Notes on the Custer Fight.* Lincoln: University of Nebraska Press, 1995.

Lindmier, Tom. *Drybone: A History of Fort Fetterman, Wyoming.* Glendo, Wyo.: High Plains Press, 2002.

Lowe, James A. *The Bridger Trail: A Viable Alternative Route to the Gold Fields of Montana Territory in 1864.* Glendale, Calif.: Arthur H. Clark, 1999.

Lowe, Percival G. *Five Years A Dragoon ('49 to '54) and Other Adventures on the Great Plains.* Norman: University of Oklahoma Press, 1965.

Mackintosh, Barry. *The Historic Sites Survey and National Landmarks Program: A History,* Washington, D.C.: National Park Service, 1985.

Madsen, Brigham D. *Glory Hunter: A Biography of Patrick Edward Connor.* Salt Lake City: University of Utah Press, 1990.

Majors, Alexander. *Seventy Years on the Frontier.* 1893. Reprint. Columbus, Ohio: Long's College Book Co., 1950.

Martin, George W., ed. *Transactions of the Kansas State Historical Society, 1903–1904.* Topeka: George A. Clark, 1904.

Mattes, Merrill J. *Capt. C. L. Easton's Report: Fort Laramie to Fort Leavenworth Via Republican River in 1849.* Topeka: Kansas State Historical Society, 1953.

———. *The Great Platte River Road: The Covered Wagon Mainline via Fort Kearny to Fort Laramie.* Lincoln: Nebraska Historical Society, 1969.

———. *Indians, Infants, and Infantry: Andrew and Elizabeth Burt on the Frontier.* Denver: Old West, 1960.

McChristian, Douglas C. *An Army of Marksmen: The Development of U. S. Army Marksmanship During the Nineteenth Century.* Fort Collins, Colo.: Old Army Press, 1981.

McClintock, John S. *Pioneer Days in the Black Hills.* Edited by Edward L. Senn. Norman: University of Oklahoma Press, 2000.

McDermott, John D. *Frontier Crossroads: The History of Fort Caspar and the Upper Platte Crossing.* Casper, Wyo.: City of Casper, 1997.

McDermott, John D., and R. Eli Paul. "Grattan's Last Stand: How a Brash Lieutenant, Drunken Interpreter, Mormon Cow, and a Thousand Lakota Warriors Started the First Sioux War." Typescript copy, 2004.

McDermott, John D., and James Sheire. "1874 Cavalry Barracks, Fort Laramie National Historic Site: Historic Structures Report/Historic Data Section." Washington, D.C.: National Park Service, 1970.

McGinnis, Anthony. *Counting Coup and Cutting Horses.* Evergreen, Colo.: Cordillera Press, 1990.

Meeker, Ezra. *Ventures and Adventures of Ezra Meeker: Sixty Years of Frontier Life.* Seattle: Rainier Printing Co., 1909.

Mumey, Nolie. *Wyoming Bullwhacker: Episodes in the Life of James Milton Sherral.* Denver: Range Press, 1976.

Monnett, John H. *Tell Them We Are Going Home: The Odyssey of the Northern Cheyennes.* Norman: University of Oklahoma Press, 2001.

Mothershead, Harmon Rose. *The Swan Land and Cattle Company, Ltd.* Norman: University of Oklahoma Press, 1971.

Murray, Robert A. *The Bozeman Trail: Highway of History.* Boulder, Colo.: Pruett, 1988.

———, comp. *Fort Laramie: Visions of a Grand Old Post.* Fort Collins, Colo.: Old Army Press, 1974.

Murtaugh, William J. *Keeping Time: The History and Theory of Preservation in America.* New York: John Wiley and Sons, 1997.

Nadeau, Remi. *Fort Laramie and the Sioux.* Lincoln: University of Nebraska Press, 1982.

Nevin, David. *The Expressmen,* The Old West Series. New York: Time-Life Books, 1976.

Nye, Wilbur Sturtevant. *Plains Indian Raiders: The Final Phases of Warfare from the Arkansas to the Red River.* Norman: University of Oklahoma Press, 1987.

Oliva, Leo E., *Fort Hays: Keeping Peace on the Plains.* Topeka: Kansas State Historical Society, 1980.

Olson, James C. *Red Cloud and the Sioux Problem.* Lincoln: University of Nebraska Press, 1965.

Orton, Richard H., comp. *Records of California Men in the War of the Rebellion, 1861 to 1867.* Sacramento: State Printing Office, 1890.

Ostrander, Alson B. *An Army Boy of the Sixties: A Story of the Plains.* Yonkers-on-Hudson, N.Y.: World Book Co., 1924.

Paul, R. Eli. *Blue Water Creek and the First Sioux War 1854–1856.* Norman: University of Oklahoma Press, 2004.

———, ed. *The Nebraska Indian Wars Reader, 1865–1877.* Lincoln: Nebraska Historical Society Press, 1998.

Red Cloud. *Autobiography of Red Cloud: War Leader of the Oglalas.* Edited by R. Eli Paul. Helena: Montana Historical Society Press, 1997.

Reid, Whitelaw. *Ohio in the War: Her Statesmen, Generals, and Soldiers.* 2 vols. Cincinnati: Robert Clarke Co., 1895.

Reigel, Robert Edgar. *The Story of the Western Railroads from 1852 through the Reign of the Giants.* Lincoln: University of Nebraska Press, 1963.

Robertson, John, comp. *Michigan in the War.* Lansing: Mich.: W. S. George & Co., 1882.

Robinson, Charles M. III. *General Crook and the Western Frontier.* Norman: University of Oklahoma Press, 2001.

Rodenbough, Theophilus F. *The Army of the United States 1789–1896.* New York: Argonaut Press, 1966.

———. *From Everglade to Canyon with the Second United States Cavalry.* 1875. Reprint, Norman: University of Oklahoma Press, 2000.

Rollinson, John K. *Wyoming Cattle Trails.* Caldwell, Ida.: Caxton Printers, 1948.

Root, Frank A., and William E. Connelley. *The Overland Stage to California.* 1901. Reprint, Columbus, Ohio: Long's College Book Co., 1950.

Sandoz, Mari. *Crazy Horse: The Strange Man of the Oglalas.* Lincoln: University of Nebraska Press, 1992.

Settle, Raymond W., ed. *The March of the Mounted Riflemen: First United States Military Expedition to Travel the Full Length of the Oregon Trail from Fort Leavenworth to Fort Vancouver May to October, 1849.* 1940. Reprint, Lincoln: University of Nebraska Press, 1989.

Schubert, Frank N. *Buffalo Soldiers, Braves, and Brass: The Story of Fort Robinson, Nebraska.* Shippensburg, Penn.: White Mane, 1993.

Scott, William Berryman. *Some Memories of a Palaeontologist.* Princeton, N.J.: Princeton University Press, 1939.

Smith, Sherry L. *Sagebrush Soldier: Private William Earl Smith's View of the Sioux War of 1876.* Norman: University of Oklahoma Press, 1989.

Spring, Agnes Wright. *The Cheyenne and Black Hills Stage and Express Routes.* Glendale, Calif.: Arthur H. Clark, 1949.

Stallard, Patricia Y. *Glittering Misery: Dependents of the Indian-Fighting Army.* Norman: University of Oklahoma Press, 1992.

Stansbury, Howard. *Exploration and Survey of the Valley of the Great Salt Lake of Utah, Including a Reconnaissance of a New Route Through the Rocky Mountains.* Philadelphia: Lippincott, Grambo, and Co., 1852.

State of Iowa. *Roster and Record of Iowa Soldiers in the War of the Rebellion Together With Historical Sketches of Volunteer Organizations 1861–1866.* Vol. 4, 1st–9th Regiments, Cavalry. Des Moines: State Printing Office, 1910.

Steffen, Randy. *The Horse Soldier 1776–1943,* Vol. 2, *The Revolution, the War of 1812, the Early Frontier, 1776–1850.* Norman: University of Oklahoma Press, 1977.

Sunder, John E. *The Fur Trade on the Upper Missouri, 1840–1865.* Norman: University of Oklahoma Press, 1965.

Tate, Michael L. *The Frontier Army in the Settlement of the West.* Norman: University of Oklahoma Press, 1999.

Thian, Raphael P. *Notes Illustrating the Military Geography of the United States 1813–1880.* 1881. Reprint, Austin: University of Texas Press, 1979.

Thompson, Jerry. *Henry Hopkins Sibley: Confederate General of the West.* Natchitoches, La.: Northwestern State University Press, 1987.

Thrapp, Dan L. *Encyclopedia of Frontier Biography.* Glendale, Calif.: Arthur H. Clark, 1988.

Todd, Frederick P. *American Military Equipage, 1851–1872,* Vol. 1. Providence, R.I.: Company of Military Historians, 1974.

Triggs, J. H. *History of Cheyenne and Northern Wyoming Embracing the Gold Fields of the Black Hills, Powder River and Big Horn Countries.* Omaha, Neb.: Herald Steam Book and Job Printing House, 1876.

Unrau, William E., ed. *Tending the Talking Wire: A Buck Soldier's View of Indian Country 1863–1866.* Salt Lake City: University of Utah Press, 1990.

Unruh, John D. Jr. *The Plains Across: The Overland Emigrants and the Trans-Mississippi West, 1840–60.* Urbana: University of Illinois Press, 1993.

Utley, Robert M. *Frontier Regulars: The United States Army and the Indian 1866–1891.* New York: Macmillan, 1973.

———. *Frontiersmen in Blue: The United States Army and the Indian 1848–1865.* New York: Macmillan, 1967.

———. *The Indian Frontier of the American West 1846–1890.* Albuquerque: University of New Mexico Press, 1986.

———. *The Last Days of the Sioux Nation.* New Haven: Yale University Press, 1963.

Vaughn, J. W. *Indian Fights: New Facts on Seven Encounters.* Norman: University of Oklahoma Press, 1966.

———. *The Reynolds Campaign on Powder River.* Norman: University of Oklahoma Press, 1961.

Walker, George M. "Eleventh Kansas Cavalry, 1865, and Battle of Platte Bridge," *Kansas Historical Collections.* Vol. 14, 1915–18. Topeka: State Printer, 1918.

Walker, Henry Pickering. *The Wagonmasters: High Plains Freighting from the Earliest Days of the Santa Fe Trail to 1880.* Norman: University of Oklahoma Press, 1986.

Ware, Eugene F. *The Indian War of 1864.* New York: St. Martin's Press, 1960.

Watkins, Albert, ed. *Publications of the Nebraska State Historical Society.* Lincoln: Nebraska State Historical Society, 1922.

West, Elliott. *The Contested Plains: Indians, Goldseekers, and the Rush to Colorado.* Lawrence: University Press of Kansas, 1998.

Wheeler, J. B. *The Elements of Field Fortifications for the Use of the Cadets of the United States Military Academy at West Point, N. Y.* New York: D. Van Nostrand, 1882.

White, David A., ed. *News of the Plains and Rockies 1803–1865.* Spokane, Wash.: Arthur H. Clark, 1998–99.

White, Richard. *It's Your Misfortune and None of My Own: A New History of the American West.* Norman: University of Oklahoma Press, 1993.

Woodworth, James. *Diary of James Woodworth across the Plains to California in 1853.* Eugene, Ore.: Lane County Historical Society, 1972.

Wooster, Robert. *The Military and United States Indian Policy 1865–1903.* Lincoln: University of Nebraska Press, 1988.

Young, Harry. *Hard Knocks: A Life Story of the Vanishing West.* Chicago: Laird & Lee, Inc., 1915.

Young, Otis E. *The West of Philip St. George Cooke 1809–1895.* Glendale, Calif.: Arthur H. Clark, 1955.

ARTICLES

Adams, Donald K., ed. "The Journal of Ada A. Vogdes, 1868–71." *Montana* 13 (July 1963): 2–17.

Alder, Lydia D. "The Massacre at Fort Laramie." *Improvement Era* 12 (June 1909): 636–38.

Anderson, Grant K. "Samuel D. Hinman and the Opening of the Black Hills." *Nebraska History* 60 (winter 1979): 520–42.

Anderson, Harry H. "The Controversial Sioux Amendment to the Fort Laramie Treaty of 1851," *Nebraska History* 37 (September 1956): 201–20.

———. "Harney v. Twiss; Nebraska Territory, 1856," *The Westerners, Chicago Brand Book* 20, no. 1 (1963): 1–3, 7–8.

Bray, Kingsley M. "Teton Sioux Population History, 1655–1881," *Nebraska History* 75 (summer 1994): 165–88.

Carroll, Murray L. "The Wyoming Sojourn of the Utah Expedition 1857–1858," *Annals of Wyoming* 72 (winter 2000): 6–24.

Clough, Wilson O. "Mini-Aku, Daughter of Spotted Tail," *Annals of Wyoming* 39 (October 1967): 187–216.

Danker, Donald F. "The North Brothers and the Pawnee Scouts," *Nebraska History* 42 (September 1961): 161–79.

"The 1850 Overland Diary of Dr. Warren Hough," *Annals of Wyoming* 46 (fall 1974): 207–16.

Flanagan, Vincent J. "Gouveneur Kemble Warren, Explorer of the Nebraska Territory," *Nebraska History* 51 (summer 1970):171–98.

"Fort Laramie," *Annals of Wyoming* 9 (January 1933): 752–59.

Gray, John S. "The Salt Lake Hockaday Mail: Part 1," *Annals of Wyoming* 56 (fall 1984): 12–19.

———. "The Salt Lake Hockaday Mail: Part II," *Annals of Wyoming* 57 (spring 1985): 2–12.

Hammer, Kenneth M. "Freighters and Railroads: The Growth of the Black Hills Freight and Stage Lines and the Role of the Railroads," *Journal of the West* 20 (April 1981): 21–30.

Hedren, Paul L. "Captain King's Centennial Year Look at Fort Laramie, Wyoming," *Annals of Wyoming* 48 (spring 1976): 103–108.

———, ed. "Eben Swift's Army Service on the Plains, 1876–1879," *Annals of Wyoming* 50 (spring 1978): 141–55.

———. "Garrisoning the Black Hills Road: The United States Army's Camps on Sage Creek and Mouth of Red Canyon, 1876–1877," *South Dakota History* 37 (spring 2007): 1–45.

Heib, David L., ed. "An 1850 Gold Rush Letter From Fort Laramie By A. C. Sponsler, a Thayer County Pioneer," *Nebraska History* 32 (June 1951): 130–39.

———. "We Live at Fort Laramie: Interviews With Old Timers," *Denver Westerners Roundup* 34, no. 4: 9–21.

Henderson, Paul. "The Story of Mud Springs," *Nebraska History* 32 (June 1951): 108–39.

Hill, Burton S. "The Great Indian Treaty Council of 1851," *Nebraska History* 47 (March 1966): 85–110.

———. "Thomas S. Twiss, Indian Agent," *Great Plains Journal* 6 (spring 1967): 85–96.

Hull, Myra E., ed. "Soldiering on the High Plains: The Diary of Lewis Byram Hull 1864–1866," *Kansas Historical Quarterly* 7 (February 1938): 3–53.

Hunton, John. "Pioneer Days of Bordeaux," *Second Biennial Report of the State Historian of the State of Wyoming* (1922): 94–99.

———."Reminiscences," *Annals of Wyoming* 6 (January 1930): 262–71.

Johnson, Laura Winthrop. "Eight Hundred Miles in an Ambulance," *Lippincott's Magazine* 15 (June 1875): 693–99.

Jones, Hoyle. "Seth E. Ward," *Annals of Wyoming* 5 (July 1927): 5–18.

Larson, Alfred. "The Winter of 1886–87 in Wyoming," *Annals of Wyoming* 14 (January 1942): 5–17.

"Letter of Thomas S. Twiss, Indian Agent at Deer Creek, U.S. Indian Agency on the Upper Platte," *Annals of Wyoming* 17 (July 1945): 148–52.

Mattes, Merrill J. "The Crusade to Save Fort Laramie," *Annals of Wyoming* 50 (Spring 1978): 6–57.

———. "A History of Old Fort Mitchell," *Nebraska History* 24 (April-June 1943): 71–82.

———. "Potholes in the Great Platte River Road," *Annals of Wyoming* 65 (summer/fall 1993): 6–14.

McCann, Lloyd E. "The Grattan Massacre," *Nebraska History* 37 (March 1956): 1–25.

McChristian, Douglas C. "The Bug Juice War," *Annals of Wyoming* 49 (fall 1977):253–61.

———. "Fort Laramie—After the Army: Part I, The Auction," *Annals of Wyoming* 73 (summer 2001): 12–23.

———. "Fort Laramie—After the Army: Part II, The Community," *Annals of Wyoming* 73 (autumn 2001): 20–40.

———. "Fort Laramie—After the Army: Part III, "Preservation," *Annals of Wyoming* 74 (autumn 2002): 14–31.

McDermott, John D. "No Small Potatoes: Problems of Food and Health at Fort Laramie, 1849–1859," *Nebraska History* 79 (winter 1998): 162–70.

———. "We Had a Terribly Hard Time Letting Them Go: The Battles of Mud Springs and Rush Creek, February 1865," *Nebraska History* 77 (summer 1996): 78–88.

Mellinger, Phillip J. "Frontier Camp to Small Town: A Study of Community Development," *Annals of Wyoming* 43 (fall 1971): 259–69.

Moris, Charles W., ed. "Joseph Warren Arnold's Journal of his Trip to and from Montana, 1864–1866," *Nebraska History* 55 (winter 1974): 463–52.

Munkres, Robert L. "The Plains Indian Threat On the Oregon Trail Before 1860," *Annals of Wyoming* 40 (October 1968): 193–221.

Murphy, William. "The Forgotten Battalion," *Annals of Wyoming* 7 (October 1930): 383–401.

Murray, Robert A. "The John 'Portugee' Phillips Legends, A Study in Wyoming Folklore," *Annals of Wyoming* 40 (April 1968): 41–56.

Nel, Johanna. "A Territory is Founded: Political, Social, Economic, and Educational Conditions in Wyoming 1850–1890," *Annals of Wyoming* 61 (fall 1989): 2–12.

Owens, Patricia Ann. "The Overland Mail in Wyoming," *Annals of Wyoming* 61 (fall 1989): 13–19.

Pennock, Isaac. "Diary of Jake Pennock," *Annals of Wyoming*, 23 (July 1951): 4–29.

Regan, James. "Military Landmarks," *The United Service* 2 (August 1880): 146–62.

Riter, Maria Inez Corlett. "Teaching School at Old Fort Laramie," *Annals of Wyoming* 51 (fall 1979): 24–25.

"Scientists' Search for Gold, 1875: Walter P. Jenny and Henry Newton," *South Dakota History* 4 (fall 1974): 404–38.

Smith, Job. "An Experience of the Plains," *Improvement Era* (August 1908): 755–58

Studley, Hiram W. "Letter Describing a March to Utah in 1859," *Annals of Iowa* 13 (April 1923): 611–18.

Trenholm, Virginia Cole. "The Bordeaux Story," *Annals of Wyoming* 26 (July 1954): 118–27.

Unthank, O. B. "The Danger Days of 1867–1874," *Nebraska History* 7 (1924): 27–29.

Vaughn, J. W. "The Fort Laramie Hog Ranches," *TheWesterners, New York Posse Brand Book*. 13, no. 2 (1966): 39–41.

Whiteley, Lee. "The Trappers Trail: The Road to Fort Laramie's Back Door," *Overland Journal* 16 (winter 1998-99): 2–16.

NEWSPAPERS

Army & Navy Journal
Cheyenne Daily Leader
Chicago Daily Tribune
Denver Rocky Mountain News
Fort Laramie Scout
Guernsey (Wyo.) *Gazette*
Lander (Wyo.) *Wind River Mountaineer*
Leavenworth (Kans.) *Daily Conservative*
Lingle (Wyo.) *Guide-Review*
Omaha Weekly Herald
Oskaloosa (Iowa) *Independent*
Salt Lake City Daily Union Vedette
Scottsbluff (Neb.) *Star-Herald*
St. Louis Republican
Torrington (Wyo.) *Telegram*
Virginia City Montana Post
Washington, D.C. National Tribune
Winners of the West

INDEX